YOUR
SECOND
LIFE

Books by
Gay Gaer Luce
YOUR SECOND LIFE

BODY TIME

BIOLOGICAL RHYTHMS IN PSYCHIATRY AND MEDICINE

(with Dr. Julius Segal)

SLEEP

INSOMNIA: *The Guide for the Troubled Sleeper*

YOUR SECOND LIFE

VITALITY
AND GROWTH IN MATURITY
AND LATER YEARS
FROM THE EXPERIENCES
OF THE SAGE PROGRAM

GAY GAER LUCE

A Merloyd Lawrence Book

DELACORTE PRESS/SEYMOUR LAWRENCE

To Fay,
and to all of us who have joined together in love and
curiosity, in foolishness, wisdom, and hope, to create this
process we call SAGE.

A MERLOYD LAWRENCE BOOK
Published by
Delacorte Press/Seymour Lawrence
1 Dag Hammarskjold Plaza
New York, N.Y. 10017

Drawings by Patrick Maloney

ACKNOWLEDGMENTS

Excerpt from SILENT MUSIC: *The Science of Meditation,
Consciousness, Healing, and Intimacy* by William Johnston:
Used by permission of Harper & Row, Publishers, Inc.
Excerpt from MEDITATION IN ACTION by Chogyam Trungpa:
Published by Watkins (London) and Shambhala (Boulder, Colorado).
Used by permission.
Quotes on pages 242–244 from GESTURE OF BALANCE by Tarthang Tulku:
© 1976. Used with permission of Dharma Publishing.
Diagrams from THE MASSAGE BOOK by George Downing and Anne Kent
Rush: Copyright © 1972 by George Downing and Anne Kent Rush.
Reprinted by permission of Random House, Inc., and Bookworks.

Manufactured in the United States of America
First printing

Designed by Oksana Kushnir

LIBRARY OF CONGRESS CATALOGING IN PUBLICATION DATA
Luce, Gay Gaer.
    Your second life.

    "A Merloyd Lawrence book."
    Bibliography: p.
    Includes index.
    1. Aged—Psychology. 2. Aged—Mental health.
3. Self-actualization (Psychology) 4. Exercise for the
aged. 5. Sage. I. Title. II. Title : Sage program.
BF724.8.L82   155.67   79-3950
ISBN 0-440-09864-5

ACKNOWLEDGMENTS

I would like to express my love and appreciation to all of you who have taken part, directly and indirectly, in my life and in this book as I was writing it. Hal Bailen, Eugenia and Don Gerrard, and Paul and Fay Gaer, you have managed to live with me somehow. Thank you.

Because I used to be a writer, I expected writing this book to be easy, and it was especially difficult. On a screen in the back of my head was an image of all of you at SAGE as I tried to write your story without misrepresenting you, insulting you, hurting your feelings, or omitting what you would have considered important. As I contemplated the variety of attitudes and programs that evolved at SAGE in the first four years, I felt doomed to inevitable failure. Eugenia listened patiently to all these doubts and got me to suspend judgment long enough for the story to unfold as I saw it. Don Gerrard lovingly coaxed me into writing an outline and some stream-of-consciousness material, with which he connected me and Sam Lawrence. I was then committed by contract to Delacorte Press/Seymour Lawrence, and by promise to SAGE and NIMH, but I was still unable to write. My brother, Paul Gaer, sat me down and talked me through the introduction, which got me started. Margaret Bomar kept me going with enthusiasm and moral support as she gave me back typescript. Then came the transformation of a morass into a readable book. It took shape out of the special editorial genius of Merloyd Lawrence, who structured and pruned. I am grateful, Merloyd, for your patience and precision, and surely I must be speaking for every reader. During the final stages of rewriting I was appreciative for the help of Robert Shelby and comments by Wendy Brewer, Adelaide Kendall, Claire Soskin, Charlotte Knight, David Cunningham, Toni Montez, and Ken Dychtwald, and for the super-swift typing of Jackie Wilson. For extraordinary help with the illustrations I am grateful to Patrick Maloney, Katherine Dudley, Paul Gaer, and Mildred Glacken, as well as to those who posed for them: Herbert Archibald, Berthe Schumann, Vivian Steeves, and Edith Goodwin. Thank you all.

There are a great many of you, perhaps a hundred, whom I would like to thank in different ways. Rinpoche Tarthang Tulku, you and the Nyingma community have been an abiding source of inspiration and learning. There would be no book without you who helped to found SAGE: Eugenia Gerrard, Carol Spencer, Susan Garfield, Goodwin Watson, Ken Dychtwald, Richard Fauman, Virginia Goldstein, Erik Peper, and the intrepid first core group: Helen Ansley, Frances Burch, Anne and Clyde Johnson, Alice Kalish, Eleanor Karbach, Margaret and David LePage, Mac MacDonald, Herb Pillars, May Schwarz, Vivian Steeves, and Coetta Wilson. The fullness and inspiration of that starting year was enhanced by the special sessions of Jack Schwarz, Jean Porter, Bob Treadwell, Alissa Goldring, Robert Spencer, Larry Sheridan, Ed and Linda Avak, Stanley Keleman, Frank Wildman, Richard Moss, Jean Houston, Harold Wise, Gail Worth, Patricia Westerbeke, Don Westerbeke, Bernie Rappaport, Robert Monroe, Arif Rechtschaffen, Ruth Young, Naomi

Emerling, Stephan Sheaver, and Helen Palmer. You helped us to expand our personal vision.

In 1975, a year after we began, SAGE became known in the community and we were asked by Marci Adamski of the Oakland Library Project Outreach Program to extend our program into institutions for the elderly. This initiated a new branch of SAGE, the Institutional Program. Richard Fauman's documentaries elicited requests around the country for workshops and presentations. SAGE then needed an office, and the first one was Alice Kalish's back bedroom. SAGE also needed extensive funding. We are indebted to Drs. Julius Segal and Howard Davis of the National Institute of Mental Health. They encouraged and enabled us to apply for a three-year, $500,000 Demonstration and Evaluation grant, which NIMH awarded SAGE for the years 1976–1979. Applying for a grant would have been impossible without the expertise of Dr. Lee Otis and the Institute for Research in Social Behavior. IRSB has nursed SAGE into maturity and administered our NIMH grant. We have appreciated you and your skillful means. We have also appreciated the beginnings of administrative order brought us by Wilma Jordan and Beth Bexton. We are indebted to a number of individuals and foundations for survival in penniless times. More recently these have sustained the institutional program, the evolution of NAHG, and parts of our program not covered by our NIMH grant. I would like to thank those of you who prefer to remain anonymous and the San Francisco Foundation, the L. J. and Mary C. Skaggs Foundation, the Luke B. Hancock Foundation, the Levinson Foundation, Lore's Fund, the Institute of Noetic Sciences, the Carheart Foundation, and the National Institute of Mental Health.

SAGE in 1979 is a large organization quite unlike its initial group. Amazingly it survived its growth from a small emotional family into a large yet participative organization. Its success owes a lot to friends who gave generously of their consultation and advice on finances, goals, and organizational development, with special thanks to Hugh Mac-

Lean, John Levy, John O'Neil, and John Wilson. SAGE has received enormous gifts of talent, skill, and time from hundreds of people too numerous to identify and credit. I feel sad about that, and it would have been endlessly complicated to try to include every name, checking with each person whose name should have been included, and sorting out those who prefer to remain unmentioned. A book totally devoid of names seems ghostlike, so I compromised by omitting almost all names and second-guessing where I did include them.

Because I have been writing out of my own experience, I have emphasized the founding of SAGE. By alluding so often to Ken, Eugenia, and myself I may give the impression that we are the superstars of the organization. That would be very misleading. Initially we played dominant roles in shaping SAGE. In fact our dominance served to suppress the talents and leadership of many staff members who are now running the organization and creating its new programs. In January 1978 Eugenia retired, and by spring Ken and I were no longer on the Executive Committee that made our ongoing decisions and ran the organization. The institutional staff was composed of: Aron Gilmartin,* Dorothy Ennis,* Stafford Buckley, Gene Kunitomi, Sarah Newbern. The core-group staff was composed of: David Cunningham, Frieda Agron,* Herb Archibald,* Ardella Browder,* Mildred Glacken,* Virginia Goldstein, Toni Montez, Bill Love,* Gay Luce, Worden MacDonald,* Wan Ho Choa Lee,* Mudita Nisker, Claire Soskin,* and Vivian Steeves.* The Administrative Staff was composed of: Wendy Brewer, Adelaide Kendall, Alice Kalish,* Sandra L. Rider, Marion Janson, and David Cunningham, and Mudita Nisker directed the training of interns in the programs. Kenneth Dychtwald ran national development and the National Association of Humanistic Gerontology. (Former core-group participants are identified by an asterisk.)

Prompted by their needs for interdependence and the continuation of their own development, core-group graduates began forming a substantial community. Frances Burch, Eleanor Karbach, Herb Pillars, and Vivian Steeves brought leadership from the first core group. The second core group had been the spearhead of the community following the death of one of its members. Claire Soskin, Herb Archibald, Rose Eden, Dorothy Ennis, Elizabeth Grant, Steve Sherry, and Frieda Agron were important in shaping it. The community represents the next stage of exploration and deepening for all of SAGE. Meanwhile the process is being tried out, varied, and recreated in many other regions by professionals who have trained at SAGE. Phyllis Phelps, Dorothy Saxe, Geri Meyer, Deanne Davidson, Barbara Raines, Jeanette Segal, Charlene Gay, Jean Range, and many others, we are gaining clarity and enthusiasm from your inventive work. Quite a few participants in core groups are now teaching at SAGE and elsewhere in their communities. Some are accomplishing what we could not do in the program. Berthe Schumann, for example, maintained a meditation group on the *Course in Miracles*, which received mixed-to-scant attention when it was tried in a core group. Members of Groups III and IV met for an entire year in an experiment in communication skills, which has had ramifications for the community and all of SAGE. They included Frank and Barbara Boydstun, Ardella Browder, Minnou Cannon, Helen Cooper, Bill Love, Sylvia Simon, Fanya Carter, Wan Ho Choa Lee, Lois Fitzgerald, Mildred Glacken, Tillie Helman, Margaret Holabird, Charlotte Knight, Mildred Rimov, Clara Robbin, Ruth Van Pelt, and Audrey Waterman. We missed Ernest Weiss, Rachel Perkins, and Rose Dellamonica. Thank you all for being willing to experiment.

By the time this book has been in print long enough for you to have a copy, there will be a hundred more people creating the next chapter of SAGE. I would like to thank the many of you whom I do not know, and you who have not yet joined us, and the many of you who may use our history and impetus to invent your own way of improving the quality of experience and consciousness in later age.

CONTENTS

INTRODUCTION: WHAT IS SAGE?

In January, 1974, a group of twelve adventuresome older people (aged sixty-three to seventy-seven) met together with four younger people to explore the myths and realities of the aging process. The group called itself SAGE, an acronym for Senior Actualization and Growth Explorations. This first experimental program continued for over two years. By word of mouth many new people came to us, people who hoped to become reexcited about life—like falling in love again. Their experiences with us opened them up to their own sense of aliveness, of unforeseen possibilities for their lives and new styles of being. The discoveries made in SAGE were so startling that similar programs began across the country and in other parts of the world.

What we and the first few SAGE groups discovered about the possibilities and excitements of old age provides the contents of the first section of this book. The second section explains specific skills and exercises. The epilogue was written for people who may wish to start groups and

who may want to know more about SAGE as an organization.

HOW SAGE BEGAN

In 1971 I was a disillusioned writer. I felt discouraged that
my books on sleep and biological rhythms contained so
little that was of any practical use to readers. I began to
explore hypnosis, yoga, and methods that might help people improve their own health and well-being. Naturally as I
experienced these methods I wished I had been taught to
use them when I was a child. They would have changed
my life. It occurred to me that I could try teaching children
these things that would have made my own life freer, less
neurotic, and more pleasurable. I decided to experiment
with a program for children that included:

How to relax. I had been "high-strung" and restless,
so tense that I did not know what it meant to be otherwise.

Self-hypnosis. Had I known how to deal with pain, I
wouldn't have needed elaborate gyrations to avoid it
and would have spent less of my time anticipating, in
dread, the dentist's office.

How to avoid involuntary hypnosis. I remembered
that I went into a peculiar state of paralysis when
angry adults yelled or even talked to me. I behaved in
a trancelike, obedient way and deeply absorbed the
nasty things they told me about myself.

How to deal with feelings of fear, anger, and love.
Most of my energy went toward holding down my
feelings and avoiding the threatening feelings of my
peers.

How to focus. I never learned how to study or to
keep my attention from wandering. It took twice as
much effort to learn.

How my body works. As a child I was terrified of

my own body, which was a mystery. I had no idea
how my feelings affected my body nor that I could actually control and use my body as my instrument.

How to recall dreams and incorporate them into
daily life.

While I was beginning to develop the skills I needed for
this program for children, my mother came to visit me in
New York. As we spent time together I realized these were
skills she could use, too. For instance she was having a
hard time falling asleep. I thought that if she could learn to
relax at will she could fall asleep. She practiced with the
help of a biofeedback instrument. A band of electrodes on
her forehead sent signals into an amplifier speaker that
clicked rapidly whenever she tensed her forehead muscle
and clicked less when she relaxed. Using this feedback she
found it amazingly easy to visualize a spiral vortex through
which she would travel out into sleep. That excited her interest. Next she learned some yoga breathing exercises,
and she amazed me by holding her breath to a count of one
hundred. The control she developed over her own system
became apparent a month or so later when she was involved in a head-on automobile collision in which she remained calm and cool and practiced her breathing.

She had been driving about forty miles per hour down a
one-way street when an eighteen-year-old in diabetic
shock, who was fleeing the police, came from the other direction. He had already hit several other cars. He came at
her at about thirty-five miles per hour. They collided at a
total of ninety miles per hour, completely wrecking both
cars. Yet she was totally calm when the ambulance arrived
and, despite her age and vulnerability from a previous accident, she left the hospital before the eighteen-year old.
She was now convinced of the power of her mind and
ready for more new experience.

Dr. William Soskin, a friend and an unorthodox psychologist, introduced her to a special music procedure in which

she laid down comfortably and relaxed into a trancelike state and listened to classical and other music through earphones. Through this process she began to have an affirmative visionary experience. At the age of seventy-one it was the opening of a door she had not looked through since childhood.

My mother is a rare woman, a fine artist, and an intellectual with great curiosity. I wondered whether her new adventures and the changes I was seeing were purely signs of her own unusual character or whether some of these same experiences would have an effect on other older people.

At that time centers of gerontology did not contain much information about transcendent experience in older people, about their special abilities, or about preparation for death. The literature was mainly concerned with the limitations of age, decline of abilities, and loss of strength and energy. Most institutions I read about were, at best, caretaking places where the weak and unwanted were stored. After a brief library research I decided to remain an ignoramus, since I could not quite believe that growing old was so joyless. There were too many remarkable older people: Joseph Campbell, Frank Lloyd Wright, Bertrand Russell, Picasso, Pablo Casals, Georgia O'Keefe, Buckminster Fuller, Maggie Kuhn, Margaret Mead—or people on the streets who were full of vitality and spicy wisdom.

What did it take to grow old like them? What indeed does it take to grow?

In early childhood one is expected to grow. A child is offered challenges. Children are held, hugged, nurtured, and made comfortable in their being, knowing their worth through a deep tactile contact with others. We usually undervalue the importance of affection and contact in learning, and touching virtually stops in early adulthood. By contrast with adults a child is in constant motion, and nobody is surprised if he makes odd sounds for hours or odd faces in the mirror, plays roles, talks to imaginary playmates, stands on his head, leaps and rolls and chortles, or whirls just to feel dizzy and fall. Nobody is surprised, for he is growing. He doesn't have to be self-conscious—we all know that free play is how a child grows.

Wouldn't we all grow at any age in a similar situation? But the stereotypes of our culture say:

Old people should be dignified and circumspect.

Old dogs can't learn new tricks.

Old people are closed-minded, set in their ways, slow, senile.

Old people are ugly.

There is no future for old people. Why teach them?

Old people don't want to use or touch their bodies.

Old people like to sit still and be quiet.

I didn't believe these propositions, nor did my friends. We decided to experiment. If we created something like the situation in which children grow, wouldn't we all grow?

WHO WE WERE: 1974

After a year of discouraging library research I gave up, hoping that somebody else would point the way. I enrolled in a summerlong program with a learned Tibetan lama, Rinpoche Tarthang Tulku, and was introduced to extraordinary psychological practices over a thousand years old. In that same program were two women who wanted to try these methods with older people: Carol Spencer and Susan Garfield.

Carol had studied the problems of aging for her doctoral dissertation in psychology, but she was less interested in pathology than meditation, Tai Chi, and the possibilities of spiritual development.

Susan, a documentary filmmaker and a lucid perfectionist, was also attracted by the possibilities of service and spiritual development.

The project didn't really begin until I met Eugenia Gerrard at a dinner just before Christmas, in 1973. Her mother was dying of a mysterious degenerative disease, was prematurely aged, and was in a nursing home, and Eugenia was profoundly interested in aging. An intense person, physically tiny and beautiful, she spoke with a Texas accent and formidable strength. She had trained in breathing, dance therapy, and later, family therapy, but she worked mainly out of her own feelings, sharing her love and her problems as she taught people the methods that had been helpful in her own life.

Kenneth Dychtwald arrived several months after we began, lean, young, bristling with energy, fresh from four years of apprenticeship in group-leading, yoga, and body therapies at Esalen. He brought charisma and brilliance and an eagerness to change the negative image that he, himself, had had about aging.

Since I was basically shy, I had fashioned my early life as a loner–lecturer–intellectual writer about coming trends in health. Until 1973, when I spent eight months in a self-development program called SAT, I'd never been in an ongoing therapeutic group. Biofeedback gave me my first experience working with people. Erik Peper and I had experimented with biofeedback as a way of training people to heal themselves of illnesses like colitis and hypertension. Even though I lacked group experience, my inspiration was fired by Rinpoche. Some of the ancient Buddhist practices had a surface resemblance to bioenergetics, Reichian therapy, or other mind-body therapies, but their purpose was to lay a path for wholeness in a well-defined spiritual sense. These exercises and visualizations had blown my own world wide open, and so, although my experience with them was skimpy, they were my tools, along with Western relaxation methods.

After we began, many people with other skills began to volunteer their help. They heard by the grapevine that we were having a good time working with people our parents' age, and they were drawn by our premises, which seemed very "far out" back in 1974.

STARTING PREMISES

There is a purpose to old age: a future to be fulfilled. Rinpoche has said, "The first part of life is for learning, the second for service, and the last is time for oneself." It is a time to discover inner richness, for self-development and spiritual growth. It is also a time of transition and preparation for dying, which is at least as important as preparation for a career or family. Out of this inner growth come our sages, healers, prophets, and models for the generations to follow.

People need special conditions for deep growth: affirmation, challenge, guidance, stimulation, encouragement, support, deep emotional nourishment, and permission to be unselfconscious—to be themselves. These conditions are as necessary for older people as for children.

Growth and well-being are enhanced by increasing pleasurable experience. Rather than dwelling on problems and negative feelings, older people need to experience magnificent alternative ways of being, new facets of themselves, new ways of exploring and controlling their minds and bodies , so that old problems recede and dissolve.

Each person is unique and will unfold in his or her own way. A smorgasbord of techniques should be available so that each person can choose the ones that suit him or her the best.

Nobody can be compared with anyone else. Each person's odyssey of development will be different, and so each person must be listened to carefully and supported through his or her particular needs and quirks, until the person finds his or her best way of unfolding.

Older people may develop faster than young people in certain respects. Older people already have an experienced wisdom that young people need to read in books. They also have less investment in ego, since they are no longer creating a career or raising a family, and this may give them the freedom to adopt new attitudes and life-styles.

Many of the ailments of age are reversible. Many chronic symptoms are the result of long-term reactions to stress, along with generally poor diet and sedentary life. After learning relaxation methods to "unstress," many symptoms diminish, and a person can regain vitality.

Our thoughts and attitudes create our feelings and shape our bodies and lives. Although we shape much of what we experience in life, we do not discover this source of control and creativity until we are well along in life and have learned millions of beliefs and habits that are not even conscious—such as the way we sit down in a chair or respond when somebody uses language we don't like. The fact that we are unconscious of the way we sit down, or the way we form preferences, does not mean that we have no underlying attitudes. Growth is the process of making these hidden components of ourselves conscious.

Old age can be a time of emancipation from the inhibitions and habits learned in childhood. From our early family life all of us absorbed social amenities such as being nice or putting up with boring situations or stern moral judgments on the "other" half of the world. This can be a time of emancipation from these constricting social customs and views.

Old age can be a time of truth. All things are transitory— human relationships, nations, the stock market, and life itself. Even the sun and stars are in transition. To grow old is to enter a major transition: The closer we come to death the closer we come to reality and truth. Usually we are forbidden to talk about this, although *it is the human condition*. The more openly we can share this transition, the more we can accept the greater reality that is our lives.

We began with these propositions and asked ourselves how we could construct a program that would counter the negatives, avoidances, and lies we learned to live with, such as the pretense that life is unending and death will never happen. We realized that we were trying to create a paradox: reality, together with maximum pleasure.

THE PLACE

Until the right house appeared on the market, the plan remained a private fantasy. It took almost a year to find a house with a sufficiently large living room, an older house built of redwood, set among trees by a stream in Berkeley. After a couple of months of painting and furnishing I expected a group would materialize instantly. I posted notices around town announcing a free exploratory program for people over sixty. Then I waited. Not one inquiry. Soon after that I met Eugenia. She was compiling a directory of services for the elderly and she asked a colleague at the League of Women Voters if there were twelve older people crazy enough to experiment with their lives. That was Christmas, 1973. By January 14, 1974, a group was ready to start.

THE PARTICIPANTS

It had been an overcast but dry January in Berkeley, and the weather was chilly. We had turned the heat up and raked the leaves from the winding brick path outside. Eugenia, Carol, and I waited for the first members like teenagers waiting for that first glimpse of a blind date.

A forlorn figure, plaid cap pulled down over his eyes, limped down the path with his cane. He was shy and depressed, and he said he was so old that his memory no longer allowed him to recall names and he could no longer participate in church social groups. We found out later he was only sixty-seven and that it was a particularly bad day for him. He also told us that his sleep was terrible, and he suffered from intense tension headaches. Born in a small Western town, he had bummed on the railroads during the Depression, had done ranching and gardening, and had worked for the telephone company.

Soon a small woman bundled up in a red coat arrived

and inspected the place. She asked a hundred questions about our training, credentials, and what techniques we were using. She was the fomenter of the program, a bristling, pert, incisive woman, certain of her rights and her opinions, competent, but feeling at the time that her life was over, and that she was useless. She was seventy-four. Her husband and lifelong companion was dying of cancer. What was left? By age seventy-six, two years later, she was in another city leading groups of her own and doing some writing.

These two firstcomers were active people by temperament. They had been politically active all their lives—on opposite sides of the fence—and they fought violently. The others were different, some of them mellower, others more private, but altogether a "gutsy" group.

One woman in her mid-sixties had experienced more of the "growth" movement than we. A beautiful and inward person she had grown weary of being the only older person in each of these workshops.

There was also a tall, slender black woman who really caused us to wonder about the genetics of aging. She had a quality of wonderment and youth that made us doubt she could be in her sixties. She didn't even have lines in her face. Although she had suffered bouts with cancer, she was looking forward to going back to school in journalism and poetry.

Another was a woman of seventy-four who said she was deeply depressed and lonely and considered her marriage responsible. She was shy and had never been in a group before. After eight months in the group she felt confident enough to get a divorce and rejoin a sister in Florida.

A sensuous, attractive man with painful arthritis had been a union leader, a fighter, all his life. His tension was so great that he would talk in an ordinary conversation with fists clenched. Relaxation exercises and breathing were a beginning of comfort for him and the group itself, and they eased his acceptance of retirement. After a few months he began to take some of the massages and relaxation methods home to his wife, a counselor, who was so impressed with his change that she asked to join.

One woman in her early seventies had been withdrawn and shy all her life, never expressing her feelings. For the first five months she said virtually nothing, but sat with a Mona Lisa smile in the group. Suddenly, at one point, she found herself in an outburst—saying things, expressing herself, as she had never allowed herself in adulthood. Not too many months later she had emerged as an outspoken leader within the group.

A wry, handsome, retired phone-company executive was the oldest member of this group (seventy-seven). Although he complained of stiffness and heart disease, he was athletic and very active. He was shy and only after he had been in the group for a while did we discover that he had become an artist, a poet, and a real master of ceramics since his retirement.

One of the last to arrive was a stunning woman, whose radiance suggested that she had come to teach us, not the other way around. At our initial biofeedback session Carol and I looked at each other as we started: We felt silly placing electrodes on her forehead. Her aura was strong, and she bore an inner serenity to which we doubted that we could add anything. Only much later did we discover that the group contributed to her composure as she did to ours.

Each member was unique and memorable. One had been a bohemian who lived in a common-law marriage for forty-six years in the days when that was very unusual. Others had been in politics and unions, had been accountants, secretaries, and bookkeepers. One woman had to drop out because she was too busy running a foster home. They were not leisurely people, as we had imagined. They were busy either with families or in the community.

Their ages ranged from sixty-three to seventy-seven.

HEALTH OF PARTICIPANTS

We had asked each participant to fill out an extensive medical- and family-history questionnaire and to get a physician's permission to join.

They and their physicians considered them healthy. This is what is considered healthy over age sixty in our country: Three of the eight women had had radical mastectomies— breast removal because of cancer. One had had a colostomy—removal of the lower bowel and rectum due to cancer. One man had undergone a total hip replacement two months before. Another two had serious hypertension. A later member had Parkinson's disease. There were widespread complaints of arthritis, headaches, insomnia, migraine, and indigestion.

Despite all these problems the group was reasonably free of drugs. Only three people took tranquilizers, sedatives, or pain killers on a regular basis.

SCHEDULE

We held one group meeting each week for as long as people would tolerate it, usually three to four hours, generally from 1:00 to 4:30 P.M. We found that we gained a great deal of momentum from having a long session and sometimes extended it to a whole day, with relaxation exercises for rest. On another day each week we held an individual session with each participant. This might be an hour of biofeedback, relaxation exercises, breathing, specially tailored yoga asanas, interpersonal exercises, counseling, or perhaps just listening and comforting. The individual sessions were intended to answer the person's particular needs at the time.

CHARGE

There was no fee for the first group. Subsequent groups asked each member to contribute ten dollars or fifteen dollars a month if it presented no hardship. We would have been limited to wealthy people had we expected to support our work by fees. We knew we would have to seek foundation support and other means of income.

THE CONTRACT WITH PARTICIPANTS

Each participant had to agree to commit him- or herself to two sessions a week, for at least six months. Each person also promised to spend an hour a day on home exercises. After all, if they were going to reverse habits and symptoms that had built up over sixty years of daily tension, they were not likely to succeed unless they repeatedly did the exercises.

After the physical examination by their doctors they had signed a form stating that they would be responsible for their own safety and health throughout the program. We were not insured when we started, and we took the attitude that older people are not babies and are able to take care of themselves.

INDIVIDUAL SESSIONS

Our first individual sessions began with relaxation. We used a simple method of letting people know whether they were relaxing or not. It was usually a biofeedback instrument known as an electromyograph (EMG), which looked like a portable radio and consisted basically of an amplifier and sound maker. The person in training would lie down or sit with three electrodes placed on the forehead—these were flat discs of conductive material that would transmit muscle tension to the amplifier. The number of clicks the person heard through earphones reflected the amount of tension. Usually, because people tend to tense their foreheads, we put the electrodes on the forehead to start. They would then close their eyes and think relaxing thoughts or follow their breath mentally. Soon the clicks would thin out. As they relaxed they would hear fewer and fewer, and the meter on the instrument would show the degree of relaxation.

Even one or two sessions with this instrument provided dramatic insight for people who had not seen the connection between their thoughts, feelings, and bodies. One man was shy and anxious when he first arrived. His father had been a stern unapproachable minister, and it seemed as though the small boy in him was always ready to be rebuffed. He wondered whether he could do anything with the biofeedback. Then he began to listen to the clicks. Soon he yelled, "Hey! I can change the clicks with my thoughts! When I lie here and see the sheep pouring over the Montana hills it goes click—click—click. But when I started worrying about where I parked my car, the damn thing began clicking like mad, like static on the radio."

Recognition of this connection between thoughts and muscle tension, of the mind's influence on the body, was a major step in self-transformation.

Soon it was possible for him to breathe and relax the tension headaches away. At this point his physician was able to decrease his doses of Valium, and within two months he was not taking it at all. By then it was clear that his poor memory was not due to age: The poor memory had been due, it seemed, to a side effect of Valium and to anxiety. With returned memory he began to participate easily in groups, since he was a natural raconteur and country wit. Two and a half years later this same person was becoming well known in the community as a counselor and teacher, a speaker on radio and television programs, and a writer with a biography in print.

How it happened was a path of hard work. It did not take place overnight—nor was it typical—because nobody in the process was like anyone else.

After several weeks these one-to-one sessions were completely individualized. Many people found breathing exercises profoundly releasing. One person needed self-hypnosis for pain, another person needed autogenic training for hypertension symptoms, another needed special exercises for limbering, and another needed permission to cry and a shoulder to cry on, someone who would listen. Others needed instruction in meditation or yoga.

RESPONSE FROM OUTSIDE

Our program as yet had no name, yet within three weeks the phone began ringing as people with talent offered to help. I remember going into the kitchen one sunny afternoon after a group session. There was a large-boned "yogi" with a pigtail, sitting crosslegged in a chair. "Whom did you come to see?" I asked curtly.

He replied, "I came to offer my services."

How suspicious I was! I was not used to people openhandedly offering their talents. The "yogi," Bob Treadwell, simply and humbly made himself available, with his training in Shiatsu, a Japanese form of massage, and in Tai Chi, and in chanting. For many months he was an integral part of the group.

We had been in session about five weeks when a darkbearded graduate student from the University of California appeared at the door and announced that he wanted to videotape our sessions. Still suspicious and brusque I asked to see what he could do. We borrowed a portable video camera and bought some half-inch tape. Richard Fauman's beauty of presence and his artistry with the camera ultimately meant that he was part of nearly every session with that first group for a year. Despite worn-out and outdated equipment he managed to produce two exquisite documentaries and a training film. One of these tapes received an award in an international competition and became the vehicle by which many thousands of people learned about SAGE.

As word spread that something interesting was happening in our living room, a stream of trained professionals offered special sessions in bioenergetics, Alexander method,

acupuncture, breathing, psychic development, Sufi dancing, nutrition, and massage. Many of them were well
known, and a few of them stayed. Virginia Goldstein and
David Cunningham brought the methods of art therapy.
Sarah Newbern began to share her psychic insights. A tight-
knit group of about seven began to form, and we began ar-
ticulating our philosophy.

OUR AIMS: HOLISM AND HEALTH

We knew that we had to enjoy the program as much as the
older participants if it was going to work, so we planned to
continue only methods that helped, tickled, or excited us.
It was not going to be a program *for them*. It was for us, *all*.
We decided to teach in teams, since we knew enough to
make one good teacher if you put us all together. That way
we could learn from each other and each spend part of the
time being a participant.

Only mavericks would undertake such a program. Here
we were with full-time unpaid jobs, no insurance, lots of
expenses, and we spent our time with old people. Even our
families thought we were a little crazy.

Mavericks tend to disagree with each other. But we were
agreed in our quest for a quality we called *holism:* We
wanted to deal with whole people, body-mind-spirit, and
not give exercises for the ankles or eyes, or for revitalizing
the memory. Holism is not a collection of techniques
passed out by experts, it is an attitude and a sharing. "It is
a passionate way of looking at people, not in their sepa-
rateness but in their fullness," Ken Dychtwald explained.
"Holistic health is a recognition that we aren't parts of who
we are—not just a leg, arm, a thought, or an arthritic
joint—not who we used to be or who we might be: We are
all those things."

Having agreed that our aim was holistic we began planning a program for health. Often we battled over what
health meant. We knew it was not simply a given quality

that was taken away by age: It had to be part of a process of living. Health is freedom—from pain, from disability, from emotional hang-ups and mental confusion. Our culture teaches us many ways to be unhealthy; we get the message from the junk-food sellers and the violent programs on TV. We are taught, in first grade, to stop feeling who we are ("You can stand in the closet if you're going to cry"), and to give up our lives for good grades, reputation, and later, money. Many of us have lived like speed demons, living up to other peoples' expectations, and ideas about life.

Out of ignorance about the basics of health we abuse and neglect ourselves for fifty or sixty years and then react with indignation, surprise, or grief when we find ourselves with intractable ailments, aches, stiffness, or arthritis. Life is movement. City life is mostly sedentary. Look at the child, restless, ever in motion, always growing, grasping, tumbling upside down, expressing his feelings freely and exploring himself. Then he goes to school, where in many places he must sit as motionless as he can for eight hours a day. After school comes work. What we do for relaxation is beer and television. Golf only on Sundays. Watch movies, watch baseball. We learn a pattern of ever greater closing up, quieting down. The less we move the less we feel the need to move. Breathing less deeply in armchairs. Moving fewer muscles, less strongly. Strength diminishing with diminished movement. Limberness diminishing with diminished movement. Ideas, feelings, playfulness also diminish with diminished expression. We become quiet, polite, unexpressive.

The years themselves do not diminish anybody. It is the way we have learned to live them, giving up a little of ourselves at each step—whether to survive on a job, please a spouse, or keep peace in the family, whether from exhaustion or pure laziness.

Yet perhaps the state of the physical body is not the only sign of health. What about the great Hindu saint Ramana

Maharshi or Suzuki Roshi, a Zen Buddhist teacher and great leader? Both of these teachers died of cancer. Yet, as they pointed out, the cancer was unimportant to them. It was not overwhelming. They did not spend their days immersed in pain; it was a mere speck on their consciousness. Perhaps health is a way of seeing or experiencing things. Perhaps a highly developed mind allows a person to endure the same physical problems that overwhelm the ordinary person, but without being crippled or submerged. If such freedom of consciousness were a key to health, how could we begin to work toward that goal and share it with the older people?

OUR METHODS

As we started SAGE, we wanted to offer the methods that had helped us personally to counteract our lopsided way of living. Relaxation and breathing helped people to undo knots of lifelong tension, in a context of group intimacy and support, where people could begin to be frank and open and secure with each other. We gradually built up a repertoire of physical exercises, yoga, and Tai Chi, along with meditative exercises and chanting, all of which helped us tone sagging muscles and increase limberness and balance—in mind and body.

During our first months together we enjoyed many group games. We lay on the floor and listened to music through our feet, our sense of smell, taste, our chests, our pelvises. We learned to "see," "taste," and "smell" sound. We shared life lines of our lives, through drawing and photographs. We told our dreams to the group, in such a way that each person could experience each dream as a guided fantasy. We did movements, mirroring each other. We massaged each other's feet, shoulders, and necks, faces, hands, whole bodies. We learned to lie down and get up without straining. We made a chorus of strange grunts, groans, sighs, and murmurs. We learned how to use our intuitions and develop psychic abilities. We learned to chant, breathe in unison, meditate, and attempted to experience what it would be like to float free of our bodies.

Generally we did not talk a lot, but we experienced exercises and then shared what we had felt. These conversations allowed everyone in the group to realize that whatever he or she experienced was "right": There was an enormous range of possibilities. In every group we taught a breathing method, known as *roll breathing*. Its purpose is deep relaxation—physical, emotional, and mental. One woman found herself sobbing, relieving herself of past griefs; while another fell asleep, and yet another said she felt nothing at all, and was terribly bored. We learned there was no "right" way to feel: Each person would get what he or she was ready for at that moment.

Sometimes we would do something very simple—gently massaging around our eyes and then opening them slowly to see passively, receiving each other, with a thrill of fresh vision—seeing someone's face as if for the first time.

Then, as if we were indeed in childhood, we began making faces at each other, in a contest to see who could make the funniest, ugliest, most improbable face. Herb became a rhinoceros. Each one was more outrageous than the last. We laughed until we hurt, and then we went on to another game.

Play is dynamic. It lets us be who we are—so long as we are not shy, self-conscious, and holding back. We began to play in our SAGE groups after we had relaxed and had grown close enough to drop our self-consciousness. Even at that we weren't always ready for what came next.

One psychiatrist in a group complained, "I don't like all this messing around—making noise." A sophisticated woman said, "I can see making music, but this is just chaos!" after we had played with instruments. We would cavort around the living room, touching our elbows to the knees of others, bumping hips, touching noses to elbows. Afterward everyone looked flushed and cheerful. Still somebody would complain, "I want to learn real exercise, not just do this unstructured messing around. I don't learn anything from this."

But they would do it, nonetheless. And they looked happier afterward than they did after a formal lesson in Tai Chi.

Play was a way of opening doors.

Many of the favorite exercises of SAGE members are given in Part Two of this book, along with some of the other methods that people have found useful and creative in their lives, and some exercises that may stimulate the imaginations of professionals and others who would like to start a group. Needless to say it is not possible to put all of SAGE into a book, for there are many exchanges between people and group experiences that are too subtle to bear much impact in written form.

MAKING A NAME FOR OURSELVES

During our first year and a half costs ran about $15,000. This included rent, furnishings, equipment, telephone, office supplies, and tapes. Some of this was supplied by contract from the National Institute of Mental Health for a video-tape documentary. Our survival the first year was largely thanks to one member of the first group who gracefully, and almost anonymously, supported our work, as well as to small contributions from all the participants. Nobody was paid. We all had full-time volunteer jobs for the first two years.

In the summer of 1975 we decided to apply to the Alameda County Mental Health Association for a grant. We then realized that a group without a name would be discounted. One dark night when everyone was especially weary, we met to select a name. We thought of hundreds. There was a consensus on none. After a while we were too tired to care, and we wanted the name by morning. The name SAGE had been a file heading when the project was still a fantasy in my head under the title: Rediscovering the Mysteries. Nobody loved it, but it wasn't objectionable.

The name grew on us. SAGE fit our self-image. We didn't come across too many other SAGEs in the world, just one trucking company and a mind-development group in San Jose. We filled in the acronym with the words: Senior Actualization and Growth Explorations. A pompous mouthful, still it described what we were trying to do and we thought it would sound legitimate to agencies. Several participants gagged over it.

One asked, "What in God's name does 'actualization' mean?"

"The full realization of all your potential. . . ."

"What do you mean growth? I think I'm full-grown now—I hope so."

We worried about it for two weeks. Other things captured our attention and time went by. At first many people seemed to ask what SAGE meant. Later people simply accepted it, as we did. We were finally an entity: We called ourselves SAGE.

That was how we began, with one "core group" and a handful of staff. (We called them "core" groups because we felt that the older people in these groups and our work together was the core of our program.) By 1978 SAGE was nationally known, largely through its video-taped documentaries, presentations, and workshops, and through a few articles. There were twenty-five people on the staff. There were eight core groups and a training program for professionals. A large program was being conducted in nursing homes and other institutions. At least two dozen groups in other cities and states had begun, inspired by SAGE, along with a new network of active groups joined together in the National Association for Humanistic Gerontology.

Part
1 ❧ DISCOVERIES

1 ❧ LONGEVITY

Our culture idolizes the young and creates a bogeyman of age. Hardly anyone likes to think about growing old. This is ironic since the alternative is to die young. Is old age necessarily so terrible? Look at what life is like for older people in other cultures. If you were an elderly Yaghan, living most primitively in the fierce country of Tierra del Fuego, you could expect to be lovingly cared for by your children and never left alone. If you were an Arandan, hunting in the Australian forests, you would be most respected when you became a "gray-head," and you would become gifted with magical powers when you reached your most decrepit. As an Eskimo, on the other hand, you might be put out to die in the snow, or buried alive in one African tribe. Each culture deals differently with age. In ancient China and in parts of Asia today an old and infirm member of the family would be exempted from worldly duties and freed to speculate on the mysteries of life in this universe, taking on the role of philosopher. In many cultures, supposedly more primitive than our own, it is the aged, the gray head, the ancient, who presides in the *kiva*, or ceremonial chamber, and explores awareness of being in a spiritual sense, an experience that is sometimes mystical. It is precisely the kind of experience that Western young people have sought through drugs, and through esoteric disciplines. If the older people of our own culture had a tradition of self-development, and devoted their time and attention to such exploration, they would become the teachers of millions of high school and college people who have few alternatives now but to follow religious men of other cultures.

It seems odd that old age should be so generally unrewarding in a society as wealthy as ours. Many groups on earth have had less to offer the elderly than we. Where food is short, older people are cared for in a meager way, sometimes abandoned or even killed. But, in most societies, the older people take on the role of the bridge between the mundane and the supernatural. They are the shamen, the healers, medicine men and women, sorcerers, priests. The Navajo Indians, for instance, would not begin to train a medicine man until he had raised a family and passed middle age, indicating what kind of person he was. Contrast this with our training men to be doctors by age twenty-six. In some societies the duties of the elderly begin around eighty. In the United States eighty is considered beyond the pale. Nonetheless we are very interested in longevity and fuss over anyone who lives beyond one hundred.

In our country the average life expectancy for a man is sixty-seven and for a woman seventy-five, according to *The United Nations Yearbook of Demography*, 1972. A man could add from one to almost five years to his life expectancy by living in Canada, England, Japan, Sweden, France, Denmark, or the Netherlands. According to these data women might shorten their lifespan in most European countries, or gain just a year or so in Denmark, Sweden, or the Netherlands. It may surprise you to know that while life expectancy is said to have risen by twenty years since the turn of the century, that only represents a reduction in infant and childhood mortality. For those already sixty-five it has increased only three years. It is said that we could add ten years to the average lifespan if we did not succumb to cardiovascular and renal disease.

The leading causes of death among elderly people in the United States are: heart disease and strokes, cancer, flu and pneumonia, and accidents. Ruth Weg has written a revealing chapter called "Changing Physiology of Aging: Normal and Pathological" in J. Birren and D. Woodruff, eds., *Aging* (New York: D. Van Nostrand, 1975). It shows not only what we die of, but tells the correlations between the diseases of "aging" and how we live:

1. Arteriosclerosis
   Atherosclerosis
   Coronary disease
   Cerebral accidents
   (stroke)
   Hypertension

   High fat, high carbohydrate diets; sedentary life-style; tension; cigarette smoking.

2. Chronic pulmonary disease

   Cigarette smoking; air pollution.

3. Obesity

   High caloric intake; lack of exercise.

4. Osteoporosis

   Inadequate calcium and protein intake (probably also lack of exercise and poor diet for lifelong endocrine function).

5. Periodontal disease

   Malnutrition and poor tooth care.

6. Senility

   Malnutrition and social isolation.

7. Sexual dysfunction

   Low-level health from above factors; ignorance; social stereotypic attitudes.

It is clear that our life expectancy, and the quality of our later years, is diminished by the kinds of stresses we live with: the high calorie, fat-rich diet we eat, along with a sedentary life-style, environmental pollution, and habits such as smoking. We are the richest nation, and the most overfed people in the world, yet we suffer malnutrition from eating processed foods that are leached of their nutritive value and from choosing foods that do not give us the balance of minerals, vitamins, fiber, protein, and other nourishment that we need for health. Additives, particularly sugar, hasten our decline and may soon make the United States the diabetes capital of the world. As a nation we encourage competition and high performance, in which profit matters more than people. This creates a stressful pattern of life that is directly related to our consumption of coffee, alcohol, and cigarettes, and to the chronic diseases that impair our old age and eventually kill us.

We also reduce our life expectancy with planned obsolescence: Just as automobiles are manufactured to be abandoned at a certain age, human beings are expected to retire. There is no economic role, and no cultural imperative to give older people a sense of their importance to generations that follow. It is taken for granted that older people should produce less and consume less. A man like Pablo Picasso, the painter, defied tradition by creating prodigiously into his nineties, including fathering a child.

None of us can look at this distorted picture without wondering how we can extend our health, and our lives— now! To begin with it may be helpful to look at some of the factors that seem to go along with a very long, healthy life.

There are several groups of people in the world who live longer than we do. Among them it is common to see an eighty-year old doing heavy farming. Food is sparse, and while life is vigorous, the older people have more privileges and more to say about how things are run than they do among us. Some scientists have been skeptical about these longevity pockets in the world, while others have gone to study them. Their findings break some of our myths about the conditions for a happy, vigorous old age. And the truth may not be entirely welcome, for it is not a soft life.

Among the 819 people living in 1971 in the village of Vilcamamba, 4,500 feet high in the Ecuadorian Andes, nine were over one hundred. The odds of finding one person over one hundred among 819 people in the United States are extremely low. Another long-lived group are the Hunza, inhabitants of a small independent state in an arid valley among the towering peaks of the Karakoram Mountains that divide Pakistan from China. The Hunza live on vegetables they grow from irrigation canal water, and they go foodless for part of each winter. Their robust health is maintained on what we would consider a reducing diet, averaging 1,923 calories a day.

The two above groups are homogeneous. This might imply that it takes special genes to live so long. However in a corner of Soviet Georgia on the Black Sea is a group of Russians, Jews, Armenians, and Turks living together in a region known as Abkhasia. They are not genetically singular, yet Russian medical teams indicate that they live to a very ripe old age with very few of the debilities and limitations we accept for ourselves as older people in the United States.

Here are a few facts about their physical health and way of life, from a book by Sula Benet, *Abkhasians, the Long Living People of the Caucasus* (New York: Holt, Rhinehart and Winston, 1974). In 1972 a team of Soviet physicians examined 3,000 people who were over eighty years old. Of those 1,260 were in excellent health. Excellent vision was found in 2,370, and excellent hearing in 2,640. There are no comparable figures for the United States, but they would be almost reversed. For example the overwhelming majority of people over ninety were in fine mental health, by contrast with our people in whom arteriosclerosis is responsible for so many mental and physical disabilities among individuals in their sixties and seventies. In Abkhasia tests of protein and fat metabolism showed almost no arteriosclerotic changes. A sixteen-year study of 127 Abkhasians over age one hundred showed that their blood pressure remained 110/60 to 140/90. Moreover the elderly in this Georgian community readily recovered from bone breaks or diseases. In the United States if an elderly person recovers very slowly—and indeed many doctors have a pessimistic view of healing among the elderly—we say, "What do you expect at that age?" The Abkhasians do not consider sickness inevitable at any age.

Of course the quality of their society and their lives is very different from ours. They have no retirement and consider work vital. The work is largely agricultural, and the load decreases about age eighty to ninety. Men might stop going up into the mountains with spring herds and care for farm animals instead. Women stop working in the fields and do housework—serving food to a family of forty people.

They always work at their own pace, evenly, stopping to rest, never pushing, never competing, never having a deadline. They are seldom sedentary: They say it is bad for health to sit.

Their diet is unchanging throughout life: It is very spare, consisting of milk, vegetables, raw fruits, wine, nuts, no sugar, and almost no meat or fish. Food is never twice cooked or stored. Leftovers are thrown away. Nor is food cooked with spices or salt. They eat breakfasts of fresh salad, onion, radish, and pickled cucumbers rich in vitamin C.

Eating, like everything else in their lives, is done with moderation. They never eat rapidly, nor tell bad news or create tension at a meal.

Their mores are strict and dominated by elaborate kinship rules among the huge families. No emotionalism is permitted. Elders are respected highly, and children receive privileges according to the rules, not by the whim of parents. Children are regulated by community rules, never confused nor spared the details of adult life. Within the peer group competition is useless. The older generation allow children to choose their careers and lives without intrusion, probably reducing resentment at parents as well as sibling rivalry.

Physical activity at high altitudes requires a person to breathe well and have an unclogged heart and circulatory system. These people maintain a healthy sexual interest well into old age. Or in the words of one newly married man of 106, who pretended he was only 97, "A man's a man until after about 100, you know."

Late marriages are common and many women still menstruate at age fifty-five. Growing up in this society, on the other hand, would not be much fun. Privileges arrive only with age, and life there is ascetic and spare.

We can see some of the factors that may be important in Abkhasian longevity. We, Americans, could not duplicate the childhood, social stability, work conditions, or physical environment of these Georgians. They do not even have a word for "old" in their vocabulary. Instead they say "long lived." The best we can do is to create new life-styles here and rejuvenate bodies that have aged rapidly out of neglect. We *can* change our diets and use a gradual program of physical exercise. We *can* remove some of our stressful habits and the attitudes that produce stress. We *can* improve the quality of our lives, as well as extending them.

One thing we might ask ourselves is why we want a long life. In some ways the American of seventy must have experienced more than the Abkhasian of 125 who has lived an unchanging, predictable life. If longevity is reflected in how much we perceive and experience, the average American who has moved around, traveled, or who has vicariously experienced many world events on radio, television, and in books and movies may be more like a 400-year old. The American may lack some deep satisfaction in life known by a person in a more primitive society, but the range of information would be vastly greater.

Time is, after all, the result of a state of mind. It is not a fixed measure. Anybody who has nearly drowned will tell you that it is possible to compress a lifetime into a few minutes, maybe even seconds. It is also possible to expand a few minutes so that they seem to fill hours of clock time, as meditators sometimes say.

Most of us would like to be able to experience hours—yet have them occur in just a few minutes. This is easily possible by means of exercises that demonstrate how to relax profoundly, focus your mind, and experience expanded time. Here is such an exercise.

Read it through to the end before starting it. You may want to practice getting physically comfortable and going through the stages of the exercise, setting a timer, and stretching and moving your body before you actually try the exercise.

Lengthen Your Life by Concentration

This exercise is exceedingly powerful with a group, but it can be equally effective done alone. If you have a tape recorder you can record the instructions leaving a free time interval of three minutes. You can play the taped instruction, or you can memorize the instructions and say them to yourself.

1. Once you are ready to experience hours in a few minutes, start by taking the phone off the hook or putting it under pillows. Be sure you won't be interrupted by phones, visitors, or animals.

2. Note the time as you start. Place your tape recorder, and an egg timer or alarm clock, beside you, within convenient reach.

3. It is best to do this lying down. Loosen all clothing and take off your shoes. Remove jewelry, watches, eyeglasses. Be sure you are neither too cold nor too warm.

4. Begin to concentrate on the feeling of the contact points between your body and the floor. Lie on a firm

surface; it does not have to be hard. Have your spine straight: You may put your head on a small pillow and place a pillow under your knees. Do not lie with your head thrown back nor lifted up.

5. While you're lying there, put all your attention in the back of your head and slowly move attention down your body, moving your attention to your shoulders, back, buttocks, arms, fingers, and all the way down to your heels. Feel what kind of an imprint your body makes on the surface you are lying on.

6. Now imagine that you have just been dipped in black ink and are lying on a piece of white paper. What parts of your body make an impression and what parts don't touch at all? The parts that don't touch may be a little bit tense. See if you can relax them more.

7. Now, bring all your attention to your heels. Feel their weight, how heavy they are, how relaxed. Move your attention to your calves. Feel their weight and relaxation. Now feel your thighs, buttocks, and just feel how heavy they are, the weight on the floor, and the surface that you are lying on. Feel your back and shoulders. Feel how relaxed and heavy they are. Next do the same with your arms, back, shoulders, neck, and back of your head.

8. Repeat this two more times, feeling your body relax from your heels up to your head and back down to your heels. Relax but do not fall asleep!

9. When you have done this three times, begin to allow a wave of relaxation to come up your body. At this point you may feel heavy or floating. Imagine that you are floating in very warm air or water. Allow your jaw to relax, letting your mouth fall open, your cheeks, eyelids, eyes (your eyes are closed), forehead, the place between your eyebrows which is the place of serenity. Now allow a wave of warmth and relaxation to come up from your heels all the way over your body.

With every exhalation allow yourself to relax more. Follow your breathing so that you inhale, feeling the warmth of the relaxation coming up your body, and as you exhale you feel more warmth and even more relaxed. Do not fall asleep, however.

10. Imagine that you are floating on your back in warm, shallow water like a heavy barge, and you float into a lagoon, where it is sunny and beautiful. The lagoon is very shallow and the water is warm. If you cannot swim and fear water, float on a magic carpet, or lie in the grass in the sun. The sun is shining on you gently. You imagine that you arise and walk into a lovely meadow near the water's edge; a meadow where you can hear the birds singing, the insects humming, see the distant trees. You can feel the grass around you, with the scent of flowers penetrating your senses. The fragrance is blowing in the wind. Pick a lovely spot and lie there very relaxed.

11. Now begin to allow your mind to relax just as you did your body. Each time you have a thought just let it float by gently like a cloud in the sky. If you think to yourself, "This exercise bores me," allow that thought just to float by without doing anything about it.

12. Give yourself exactly three minutes of clock time. (If you are alone you may have to open your eyes for a second to turn over an egg timer, or a cooking timer, or set an alarm clock.) Then sink back into your relaxation. After you have done this, enter your imaginary meadow, a beautiful, private place. Begin to explore it. See whether it reminds you of some place you actually visited when you were a child. Examine the details. See where you are.

Your experience may seem to occupy a whole day, or perhaps an hour or two. The actual exploration should have been given exactly three minutes of clock time.

13. When the time is up, slowly take a deep breath, clench your fists a little, wiggle your toes, and move your body just a little.

14. Take another deep breath and stretch your arms out over your head.

15. Slowly open your eyes and look around the room. Sit up extremely slowly, taking several deep breaths.

16. Does the room look different? How long did that experience feel? Sometimes people will not believe they have been exploring only three minutes.

At one workshop a vehement white-haired lady said to me, "I simply don't believe you! I know I couldn't have gone through all that in three minutes. An hour maybe. It felt like a week. I had a whole vacation. I feel like I've been on a week's vacation in the mountains. I'm totally rested." Most people have this kind of experience, although a few remain conscious of clock time and say so.

This exercise is just one of a number of ways that time compression can be achieved. It can be done in an ordinary situation with the eyes open, simply by awareness. For example one could set a clock on the table and allow forty-five minutes, saying, "This forty-five minutes will have to give me two hours." You may find that you already do this, or that you can invent ways that suit your life.

As you begin to experiment with your perception of time, you may also begin to ask yourself questions about value—the meaningfulness of each time span. How much of the time do you feel alive and good?

Where does your time go: Watch the clock one whole morning. Watch what you do with each four minutes. How much of each four minutes can you remember? You will learn exactly how you are spending this valuable time. What parts of each day do you remember? What parts do you not remember? Where did the forgotten times vanish to? When does time move "fast," and when does it seem "slow"? Which are the four-minute periods that are most meaningful? Once you have noticed which time intervals bring you most satisfaction you may enjoy more of them in your life.

As SAGE participants have discussed the issues that most concern them, very few have focused on longevity. How the remaining time is spent is paramount to most people. As one eighty-four-year-old woman once said, "The fact that I am so old is my tragedy. But I am not about to commit suicide—I want to live differently."

"I'm afraid of lingering illness—I would hate to be dependent."

"I never told anyone my fear before. I just don't want to be dependent. I told my brother I want him to put something in my orange juice without my knowing it if I'm going to be an invalid."

"I'm afraid of senility."

"I'm beginning to be afraid of traveling and doing things on my own. It makes me furious. I don't know where it comes from because I was always very independent."

"I am afraid of poverty—that I won't be able to cover my expenses if I live a long time."

"I'm afraid of being alone. I look around at the group here, and I realize that will probably happen to me. I don't want to be alone and ill—and yet I don't want to give up my house. . . ."

"I don't want to stagnate—to become boring, and irritating . . . the kind of person my grandchildren will avoid. One of my friends has been an invalid with cancer, and she has become so suspicious and irritable that I hate going to see her. . . ."

"I find my life is less meaningful now that I'm retired . . . my time seems empty . . . this is why I came to SAGE to find some other more positive ways of spending my time."

2 ❦ CHANGING ATTITUDES AND THOUGHTS WILL CHANGE YOUR LIFE

My education was probably a lot like yours. It was focused on reading, arithmetic, and manipulating the world, and did not instruct me how to understand my feelings, communicate with others, or change my attitudes.

Formal education is not concerned with health, except in a perfunctory way.

The word "health" literally comes from the root word "holy," which means the same as "whole." There can be no health that is partial, that encompasses only our bodies or feelings, or spirit. Moreover there is no way we can avoid being whole, for our slightest thought affects our feelings, our cell chemistry, our musculature—and has a subtle influence on all the people around us. Health is linked to our attitudes—even our attitudes about our own physical health. For instance after open-heart surgery people have run the Boston Marathon, a twenty-six-mile race, while others consider themselves invalids. It is not the medical label that counts. When Ramana Maharshi was dying of cancer, the disease was only a speck on the horizon of his consciousness, but most of us are filled with dread, fear of pain, and self-pity at the very thought of cancer. We have been taught to expect suffering, and the atmosphere of most medical clinics and hospitals encourages helplessness in a sick person (as if he or she were a victim), and anxiety and negativity in everyone around the sickroom. Our culture also encourages us to expect to be passive victims, unwanted, and suffering as we grow older. We can experience our lives that way—or we can change our attitudes.

We cannot wipe out poverty, illness, and social injustice—but each of us can change from inside. We can learn new and different reactions. Let's take an extreme example: The threat of a terminal illness can become an opportunity instead of just a terrible fate. A retired businessman I know was informed that he would shortly die of cancer. That was 1975. He went to Dr. O. Carl Simonton, who taught him how to meditate on healing. It meant being very honest with himself, and it was not easy—but he did it. In 1977 he looked back with gratitude on his illness. "That was the real beginning of my life. I never really knew who I was until I began meditating. My marriage is better than ever . . . I am happier." Others who would have considered themselves invalids after heart attacks or heart surgery have taken the challenge and used the Pritikin diet and exercise programs to become healthier than they ever were before. (See *Live Longer Now*, by J. Leonard, J. Hofer, and N. Pritikin, [New York: Grosset & Dunlap, 1974].)

Health depends upon our attitude toward life.

Ultimately optimum health springs from the expanded awareness of spiritual development: This enables us to free ourselves of neuroses, to be less attached to the beliefs and attitudes we learned as children, and to free ourselves of the mental traps we automatically live with as part of our culture.

If the prospect of changing your attitudes is an unfamiliar solution to the "negative" aspects of life—perhaps an analogy will help. Each of us looks out upon the world through a window of intricate stained glass, our mind. Its patterns and colors are created by our upbringing, our location in the world, language, education, genetic heritage, habits, and character. As we go through life, we accumulate more overlays of color: opinions based on experience, feelings, likes and dislikes, ways of doing things. We become very attached to our opinions and our experience—although they are only one set of ideas, amongst billions. The light from "outside" must come through our stained glass, which tends to get thicker and sometimes murky as we accumulate layers. Whatever we offer to the "outside world," we give out through this facade of stained glass, too. This is our filter. You and I cannot experience reality the same way, because our stained glass filters are different. You might try to persuade me to see less purple, but talking won't change my vision.

For instance I was brought up in a family that valued privacy, and I learned to shut the bathroom door, never speak about money, and not to express feelings readily. You may have grown up in a more open family, and you would like to chat while you are in the bathroom and let me know exactly why you are furious at the janitor. From my reality I think you are being coarse. From yours, you think I am cold. We cannot persuade each other to see differently. Both of us experience and act through our filters. The best we can do may be to relinquish some of the habits and feelings that keep out the incoming light. As I have grown older I am not embarrassed to leave the bathroom door open, or discuss my finances with friends. I am still learning to express feelings more openly. I use these examples because they are basic. There is no aspect of our lives that we don't see through many filters.

Your Stained-Glass Window

The following game may give you a rich and magnificent stained-glass window design, indicating how you see the world. It will be composed of your own idiosyncrasies. It is very rewarding to do this with other people, even in a small group. First, however, you need to spend some time alone, thinking about your experiences in life and writing notes.

1. Get six sheets of paper.

2. Write the following topic headings. Put one on top of each sheet:

> Love and Friendship
> Money
> Work
> Family
> Religion
> Health

3. Fold the paper in half, the long way. You now have divided it into two columns. On the left-hand side write the heading: Past. On the right: Present. The notes you write on the left-hand side will refer to your childhood, to the feelings and beliefs in the family in which you were raised. On the right-hand side of the page you will write about your present feelings and beliefs.

4. Write the following headings on the left-hand margin, leaving space between each one to write a few lines. You can always use more paper if you run over. The headings:

> Likes
> Dislikes
> Fears
> Desires and Expectations
> Opinions and Beliefs

5. Sit down with the Love and Friendship page, for example, and begin to think about some of your attitudes. For example when we did this together, one SAGE woman said, "In my family a girl had to be loveable, because then she would get married: Love

was her only way to get a meal ticket." Another said, "I like to be loved—I want to be loved as I am. I dislike people who control or limit or manipulate me because they say they love me." Under the heading Fears one woman wrote, "I'm afraid of being alone." Under Opinions and Beliefs one member of the group said, "Lend money and lose a friend." As we shared our feelings and exchanged, we discovered that other people remembered things we had forgotten. "I'm appalled at what I've discovered about myself," said one man. "I want my friends to come to me, to help me, be nice to me, but I don't want to extend myself to them." He blushed. One by one the other members of the group all admitted they had the same pattern. "I like friends and lovers who don't make demands," said one.

Write down everything you can think of in the present, and whatever you remember about your parents' or foster parents' opinions and feelings. Sometimes you will notice that you still have feelings or opinions that you learned in childhood.

As we discussed our families' feelings and beliefs at SAGE, many of us realized that our mothers and fathers had opposite ideas. "My mother thought friends got in the way of housework. My father wanted lots of people around, especially if they had prestige." "In my family I learned to beware of Jews and blacks—I don't feel that way today." "My family thought friends take advantage of you. The only safe love is within the family. Today I feel that the opposite is true. Only my family loves to manipulate me."

As you can see, this could be a way of finding out about your feelings, your beliefs, and those of your friends. I discovered that I had spent most of my life believing that if I had the "right" relationship, it would transform me and make my life perfect. I also discovered that I wanted my beloved to read my mind so that I never had to say what I wanted. It was amazing to see the secret beliefs that dominated so much of my life.

Write out each sheet at leisure, as fully as you can, for both your present and your past.

6. If you are doing this exercise with a group, or another person, share your writings and see if there is anything you want to add.

7. Look over each statement. Would you tell that to members of your family? Did your parents share their feelings aloud, or were they assumed, tacit? Would you be embarrassed if a friend knew your feeling or belief? If so mark it with an asterisk for privacy. Would you tell your feeling or belief to others? Evaluate the extent to which every statement is private. At the bottom of each topic, write an estimate of the percentage of your writing you would consider private and the percentage of your family beliefs that were private.

8. Count the statements: Judge how many you consider negative and how many you consider positive.

9. Find some crayons, magic-marker pens, colored inks, paints, or tissue paper in various colors.

10. Draw a simple flower design.

11. The inner petals represent your childhood home, and the feelings and beliefs you acquired there. The outer petals represent the present. Let warm colors (red, orange, yellow) represent positive statements. Let cold colors (blue, green, purple) represent negative. You can indicate intensity by the strength of the color. Each petal represents one major subject from the sheets you have written.

12. Color in the petals from your written sheets. You may want to add shapes and create new color codes, too. Since this does not begin to cover the multitudinous dimensions of your life, you may want to add petals and internal shadings. For each aspect of

each topic that you fill in, ask yourself how much of it is private. Cover the private area with soft gray. All privacy areas should be colored twice—first in a hot or cold color, with gray on top.

Take your time with this. You may even want to do this over the course of several weeks. When you feel you have done enough, look at the wonderful colored pattern that emerges. Hold it up to a lamp or a window. Look at the colors. Ask yourself: what is the most obvious thing you can do to let more light come through?

You may want to disregard these categories altogether and ask yourself about foods you like or don't like. You might look at your clothing: Are you fastidious, sloppy, how do you dress? Do you like to see people kissing? Do you like to be kissed? Were your parents demonstrative? Did you express anger at home? How? Do you allow friends to know about your finances? Do you have strong beliefs about handling money?

Whatever you do, be as detailed as you can and as honest. The aim is self-discovery. It is only an exercise for seeing your perceptions as they color your view of the world.

Perceptions are not forever. All of us change. If we decide that we want to change, deliberately, the best way to start is by experiencing more pleasure. That may sound odd, or even immoral. Actually it is the opposite of immoral, since we're more nurturing and generous when we, ourselves, feel relaxed and nourished. It is easier to give out of a sense of fullness. Many of us have become so confused by a Puritan ethic that we think it is selfish to give ourselves real pleasure. Like many of you I grew up thinking that it took some pain, and certainly effort, to be virtuous. This is a habitual filter on our view. We forget the effortlessness of real loving. Remember how a child turns to you with dazzling affection and quite as suddenly turns away to do something else. Children constantly explore things that bring them pleasure.

They are not embarrassed to show deep unabashed pleasure in their bodies, their faces. We adults often feel embarrassed by pleasure and spend precious energy dissembling. Pleasure is still a source of healing, of satisfaction, and a way of expanding. It should fill us like the air we breathe, if most of us weren't taught to avoid it. Bad. Wrong. Sensual and sexual pleasure were discouraged among children. Babies are still punished for sucking their thumbs, fondling their genitals, or happily feeling their bodies. This is a destructive message, implying there's something wrong with their bodies and with feeling good about themselves.

Most people would not endure the sorrows and hardships of life without pleasure, yet the sources of permitted pleasure vary from one family to another, and one culture to another. In our country we think pleasure comes from things outside ourselves, from movies, television, entertainment, food, other people, people who are sex objects, from sports, and from possessions. If we feel depressed we can always buy something, or turn on the television. We also think our bodies must be healed by doctors, and we forget that doctors cannot heal, that only nature heals. We think we need to be comforted by someone else, or that we can be massaged only by someone else. Worst of all we think we can only be loved by someone else, and we forget that we cannot be in a position to love someone else unless we first love ourselves. Because we have been taught that pleasure lies outside, we are falsely dependent on externals. We relinquish what is actually our own source of inner strength, our independence, self-sufficiency and flexibility.

Many of us covet flexibility as a most desirable attribute of youth, and we would regain a lot of flexibility if we could learn how to give ourselves deep pleasure. The process of becoming our own best companions, and most pleasurable comforters, is almost magic.

Watch how this happens as you try the following exercise. However to do the exercise with effect you need to do it wholeheartedly, with all your attention. Take an hour so that you set aside plenty of time. Make sure that you won't be disturbed. Sit in a comfortable place and loosen your clothing and take off glasses and any constricting jewelry. The reason for this is that anything tight causes a slight tension, a miniscule distraction from your wholehearted concentration.

Our Thoughts Create Our Feelings

Lean back very comfortably and take some deep breaths until you feel your body relax and your mind relinquish its business.

1. Try to recall the most wonderful love of your life. Recreate it. Visualize how your beloved looked, moved, talked, felt. Recall how tremendously "in love" you were. Recall the moments of bliss, pain, anxiety, and magnificent openness it gave your life. Your feelings came about because of something you saw in another person—but it was *your feeling*. Now feel that love, long after the relationship is over. Open your eyes, look around the room with that feeling. Go and do some ordinary thing—holding that feeling, that tenderness. Look at your own hand with that joy and tenderness.

2. Close your eyes again. Recall your most impor-

tant love in great detail. Who was that person? What does he or she make you feel today? Where did that love go? Where is that love now? Maybe you think it died, or it was caused by some external force that took you by surprise, by ambush, and held you prisoner for a while, then let you go. But look again. Maybe something was triggered within you, releasing your own blissful feelings, so that you could experience the bliss and love around you that you once knew as a baby.

Look for some memory of that feeling within you. It is still there, permeating your body. Then slowly, very slowly, open your eyes and gaze around the room with that same feeling. Hold the feeling as long as you can. Does the room look different to you when you have that feeling?

If you practice this exercise daily for three weeks, you can begin to maintain this feeling in your everyday life. You can summon the feeling wherever you are, without needing to go through the long relaxation exercise. Notice how you react to other people and how they relate to you when you have this joyful feeling. It is not selfish and smug to spend time summoning joy for yourself because you also spread feelings of relaxation and contentment around you. As you remember your feeling of joy, and gaze around, see how the feeling changes your perception.

All of us have been deeply in love, and imagined that the joy and luminosity came from some magical outer force or from the other person. Eventually something happened, and the love seemed less intense. We looked at the same person with different eyes. And the world seemed ordinary again. What changed? Of course the change was in us. Romantic love is so highly regarded in our culture, and so confused with mating; we are taught to wait for certain very specific circumstances before we may be totally spontaneous and open to another human being. We say we fell in love. Usually this person meets certain unspoken inner demands, treats us the way our grandmother or beloved father used to, or makes us feel tall and powerful, or protected and secure. We have a set of very complex inner demands, or expectations—and when the world meets those demands we may feel joy or bliss. If a situation or person fits the complex set of expectations that control our experience (even though we don't articulate them), we feel bliss. Most of the time we close ourselves to bliss because our fussy inner expectations don't get satisfied. When we are disappointed in our expectations we often grow tense and closed and blame the world for failing us. And when we grow tense, we seem to suffer more. Our problems look worse. The only antidote is a feeling of openness and joy.

Practice this pleasure exercise often, inventing variations that suit you. As you become comfortable with the exercise, you may begin to notice how you control the filters through which you see the world; you can make it rosy or gray. Don't be discouraged if you don't glow with joy the first few times—most of us feel inwardly embarrassed when we are told to feel pleasure. Don't be discouraged if the results aren't dramatic: It takes many repetitions before you notice the change. At first it may even seem as if these exercises do not, in any way, help you with your real problems, yet ultimately they cannot avoid helping you.

Anyone who lives accumulates problems, but their effect upon your life depends upon how you deal with them. If a neighbor plays his radio so loudly that it annoys you, do you tell him that it is bothering you? And can you tell him pleasantly, so that he isn't insulted? Or do you sit and brood over the interruption? Do you allow yourself to become angry before you do anything about it? Most of our troubles are solvable. The problem is not usually outside—it is in you, and how you react, how you deal with the outside. You may be stressed by long lines at the supermarket:

You probably have a choice to go at hours when the lines are short. You may hate traffic: Again you can try to schedule yourself to avoid it. You may have health problems. You feel an unusual sensation in your stomach. You can make an appointment for a medical examination right away, or you can worry about it, wondering whether you have cancer or a hernia. You may have made all your expenditures, expecting a check that is too late. Instead of sitting about and fretting you can tell your creditors and review your finances so that you have more leeway in the future.

As these things happen we all have gut feelings. Our bodies express tightness, headaches, eyestrain, indigestion, insomnia—unless we allow ourselves to feel precisely whatever comes up. Usually we are most upset by unresolved feelings. If I look around in the present, I see that it is a sunny day, in a quiet, plant-filled room, and I am sitting in a green dress at a green typewriter. It has no overtones of any emotion: just greenness and light. I am pressing the keys of the typewriter. But in the back of my mind there are faint images, images of what troubles me. I feel a pull. Some part of my attention is not here at the present moment, on the ball of the typewriter as it moves under my fingers. I can, with a little effort, slice that deviating attention off—and suddenly there is nothing else. I am here. It almost seems that the light level has gone up. I am aware of the features of the typewriter, and the vibrations in my body from typing, the way my spine rests and the way I sit.

It is easier to experience the present when it is pleasant than when it is painful. At SAGE we often argued about the best way to accomplish our goal of greater health— whether we should create new and pleasurable experiences or analyze problems in the manner of therapy. We did both. We began to see that people who had a sense of immediate satisfaction were able to relax their vision of things. We played games, silly games. A woman in her mid-seventies began to lose her self-consciousness during games. One bright autumn afternoon we went around the room, each of us singing a line or two from a song that we particularly liked. Shyly she confessed that she had always been afraid to sing in a group, yet wanted to. We began to coax and beg her to sing to us. After long coaxing she began in a timid voice, singing a favorite Gilbert and Sullivan song. As she sang, with the encouragement of everyone there, she began sounding stronger. When she finished she was glowing. It may not seem like much to people who easily perform in groups, but those of us who are shy will understand why she was almost in tears as she finished. "I never thought I could do that. You young people don't know how hard this is. I've spent seventy-four years creating an identity, and now you're helping me to undo it."

Everyone agreed that it was hard. And everyone agreed that the small triumphs were worth it. It was more exciting to live. The old mold no longer held each of us so strongly. It didn't matter where we started from, so long as we started to allow the possibility of new feelings and attitudes.

Starting was very difficult for some people. "How can I spend time on my own pleasure when there is such suffering in my family?" "I'm an angry person. If I stopped being angry I'd have to stop being a shop leader." "I believe there are more worthwhile things to do than lolling around in imaginary scenes." If someone were to tell me to change I would resist, think up reasons why I should stay as I am. But in a SAGE group nobody was telling anyone to change. We were simply in an atmosphere that permitted it. I could see others beginning to sing in front of the group, or show tears when they felt them—and I also wanted to share in their feeling of triumph, of having overcome an inner barrier, having changed a personality trait that they thought was "permanent."

Most of us have lived out some variation of our cultural message, a message that is not designed to improve our health or well-being. Here are a few of the premises that act as filters of our perception of reality, colored bits in our stained-glass window. At SAGE most of us agreed that this was our training:

- Virtue means giving up what you want and making efforts to do what someone else considers virtuous.
- To be unselfish, considerate—a good person—one must overlook one's own needs, substituting the needs of others.
- It is important to be nice, to be pleasant, even if it means hiding one's real feelings and honest thoughts.
- There are higher things to heed than our bodies. For instance it is more important to sit still and study than to run around and exercise as one's body may desire.
- A valuable person is one who produces something, like this book, or money, or who performs, is a good cook, or a good carpenter.
- Whatever one produces is more valuable if it costs a lot of effort. "It was really a lot of work." It is not so valuable if it was easy.
- Whatever costs a lot must be better than things that cost little.
- As schoolchildren we received our basic training in self-abnegation and suffering. At the very time when our physical growth made us want to move, we were taught to sit still in school, going to the bathroom at the teacher's whim, not the behest of our bodies. We were taught to remain silent, obedient, and swallow what authorities had to say rather than learning to think. We were distinctly taught not to hear the feelings we had, or the needs of our bodies, as if we were disembodied little intellects.
- Success is important and you need to sacrifice some emotions and spend less time on friendship and family, less time relaxing.
- It is important to go after what you want—to grasp and collect things.

- It is bad to show or admit feelings of sadness, gratitude, fear, or vulnerability. Your weakness will be your downfall. If bad feelings occur in your body, go to a doctor.
- If you are physically sick, people will help you, but if you have unhappy feelings, people will look down on you.
- You are the only one who has such inner doubts, self-condemnations. You are the worst person, and you had better keep secret what you are really like.
- It is not your fault: Whatever happens, you are the victim. You are the victim of your diseases.

Ironically our culture gives us messages to nurture weakness in ourselves, to cultivate illness and misery. We have an elaborate legal system that encourages people to play the victim. Yet we all know that we prefer being around people who are happy, self-reliant, and harmonious. Human beings are not innately miserable. We have learned how to place more and more filters between ourselves and others. As a result many people do feel worse as they grow older and dare not share their inner selves. This means we are isolated. "We have believed in a utilitarian social structure, and we are no longer useful," explained one retired executive at SAGE. "But you can stop any time you want. You are still alive."

In this moment we are alive. You are reading this page at this moment, somewhere indoors or outdoors. You are in a lighted place. You are sitting, or lying, or standing. You are breathing as you read. You are a radiant being.

We do not have to hang on to our suffering. We may have been programmed and have programmed ourselves, beginning with our unremembered responses to our parents. But we are also more than our program, for we can change it, as we discovered again at SAGE. As we increased our pleasure and sensitivity we loosened the hold on our old ways of being.

3 ❧ RELAXATION AND OPTIMUM HEALTH

To be well is not simply to get by from day to day without painful symptoms. It is also a state of consciousness, of joy in living, of vitality—a sense of integration of body, mind, and spirit, a sense of integration with the people and world around one. At SAGE, and in this book, we focus on the many dimensions of health: We know, for instance, that nutrition and proper weight are important. We know that we must exercise our bodies or lose limberness and vitality. We also know that we need love and close communication with others. We need ways of reducing stress and of reacting differently to stress. One of the biggest sources of stress comes from our lack of appreciation of ourselves, so we need to love ourselves to become healthy. Each of us knows that deep within lies a core that is dimensionless, deep, eternal, and creative, and which we can touch if we are quiet and relaxed enough to listen.

The skill of relaxing at will is basic to optimum health. If you can relax at will you can move from the crowded basement of events and thoughts to a spacious high floor from which you can observe your life and have time to respond sensitively, with choice. From a state of relaxation the other dimensions of health are easier to obtain. But what is relaxation?

Most of us have been brought up to think of relaxation as a state of collapse. Some think it is sleep, oblivion, not being conscious. Others think of it as flaccidity, a total limpness of the body. Quite a few people describe themselves as most relaxed during the pleasant exhaustion after a good game of tennis or other vigorous physical activity. Some feel relaxed after drinking, when in a state of torpor. Quite a few people say they relax by watching television or reading a good murder mystery. Many people say they are relaxed after orgasm. It is rare to hear anyone say they are relaxed while carrying out their day-to-day activities, for the usual image of relaxation is one of a supine body, a sunbather on the beach, or someone sprawled out on a carpet or bed.

Almost everyone would agree that relaxation means the absence of muscular tension. We look at the softness, the flexibility of babies or housecats and see continued relaxation. Pick up a normal cat and his or her body is soft and pliable, conforming to your arms. Babies, too, seem to be relaxed, although alert, and subject to tension only in brief bursts such as during anger, pain, hunger, before trying a new motion, or after a spanking. The infant and, presumably, the cat are relaxed throughout most of their day. They are not in a state of collapse. Far from it. Both are exploratory, interested, curious.

There is another visible attribute in both babies and cats that is essential to relaxation. They do not hold back their feelings. When a baby is upset, the crying is loud and clear. When a cat feels threatened by your gesture, you may get scratched in a flash. Anger, fear, hunger, loneliness, merry feelings, and ecstasy are all expressed without censorship. A cat wanting to be touched, or a young child, is suddenly on your lap. A burst of affection and the arms around your neck say it, or the cat rubs against you and purrs. The negative feelings are shamelessly open, sullenness, pouting, rage, or sorrow.

This, too, is relaxation. Much of the tension we feel comes from the gradually learned withholding of emotional expression. Emotional openness is relaxed. Emotional censure requires that we hold back tears, anger, that we clench our jaws, keep our chests compressed, that we never show fear, and hold our tensed arms silent when they would otherwise beat something in rage.

Relaxation has many aspects. It is not just a matter of tensing and relaxing muscles.

It is a matter of relaxing the whole body.

It is also a matter of relaxing emotions.

Beyond that it is not possible to relax fully with an unquiet mind. Your mind affects your body chemistry, musculature, and glands, your every cell. So if you sit down to relax but you are conducting a long conversation in your head, your mind cannot be quiet, and somewhere it is continuing tension in your body.

If you don't believe that your mind can instantly produce such physical changes, try the following exercise. Read it through and then do it.

Close your eyes and imagine a nice ripe lemon. Pick it up and feel the oiliness of the skin. Now take a knife and cut it in half. See how juicy it is. Imagine a glass. Squeeze a few drops into the glass. Now bring the glass to your lips and taste it.

What happens in your mouth?

◇ ◇ ◇

Well that was just a thought; 90 percent of the people who think of a lemon immediately notice that they have more saliva in their mouths, that their mouths pucker a little. A mere thought causes the saliva glands to secrete more. This is the power of the mind to affect the body. Whether we are conscious or not, every thought we have affects our bodies. To relax this incessant barrage on the body from the mind, we need to know how to quiet our minds so that we are not thinking unnecessarily. Relaxation is a state in which we are mentally quiescent, not busily chattering to ourselves. To attain this state people have used many kinds of exercises, many of them known as meditation. These are exercises for reducing the internal chattering and allowing us to focus upon a single thought—such as a mantra.

There is still another dimension to relaxation that is deep and important. It may surprise you. Think about it. In order to relax deeply and release feelings and thoughts, you need trust in the universe! If you can't trust the universe, you will always have the impulse to control it. We cannot relax if we are worrying about whether it will rain tomorrow, or whether we are aging too fast, or when we will die, or how rapidly we can recover from an operation. If we are trying to run the universe, we will never be able to relax. If we need to control everything, including other people, we are unconsciously distrustful of the universe. We don't trust "God" to have created each person uniquely for his own purpose, and nature according to a reliable structure, or life and death in an acceptable way. You don't need to believe in God to have faith in the universe: It is a kind of certitude that needs no church, and no images. It is a certain knowledge in the "rightness" of things as they are, even though you or I may not understand them. At times we may feel as Job did, that there are many injustices, but we are small human beings and cannot judge the whole, since we cannot even see it. Without acceptance of the rightness of the universe, you must try to control your own fate—you can never relax.

The deep, unarticulated beliefs that lie beneath our behavior and our feelings are the foundations of relaxation or tension.

There are many relaxation exercises in Part Two of this book. Actually, I consider most of what we do at SAGE to be a form of relaxation: physical, emotional, mental, and spiritual. We are relaxing many kinds of barriers. As we do this, our lives and our bodies change, we have more peace of mind and more pleasure in living.

How relaxed are you? The following short list of questions will allow you to observe your own patterns and take stock of your tensions.

1. What are your three most important beliefs?

2. What are your three immediate goals—and what obstacles do you face in achieving them?

3. Are you happy? What evidence would you give another person to demonstrate your happiness?

4. Do you hurry? When the phone rings, or the doorbell sounds, do you rush? Do you find yourself mentally pressured when you have an appointment?

5. How do you feel about loud noises? Do you move to a quiet place? Is your place quiet?

6. How do you breathe? Listen to the sound of your breath, or feel the movements—is it slow and deep, or shallow and rapid?

7. How flexible is your body? Can you move your head and neck so that you can see behind you? Can you bend over? Do you feel limber?

8. Do you express your feelings? When you feel sad do you allow yourself to cry? When you are angry can you say so openly?

9. Can you assert yourself, stand up for your rights? Or do you let people walk all over you? For instance a doctor treats you in a way you don't like. Do you say so, or do you hold back politely and smolder?

10. Are there situations in your life that repeatedly stress you? What have you done to remove yourself or change them?

11. Do you have a space of your own where you can be alone when you want to?

12. Can you sit quietly and listen to music, or look at an object without thinking of a hundred other things?

13. Can you fall asleep easily?

14. Do you know what things raise your spirits and what things depress you? Do you know what things give you energy and what drains you?

15. Are you easily irritable?

16. Do you take time out to become absorbed in something you enjoy—a hobby, crafts, art, walking in the country, bird watching, gardening?

17. Do you get some physical exercise each day or every other day?

18. Do you have chronic symptoms of any kind?

If you can answer the first three questions, you are on the way. As an index of tension this is crude, but you can get some idea about yourself. If you honestly answer 4 "no," you probably do not hurry yourself unnecessarily. Noise is a stressor, and the body responds by shooting out adrenalin and muscle tensions, which return to normal more slowly as a person grows older. Try to live in a quiet place. Number 6 is your own index, and if your breathing is very shallow it is probably a sign of prolonged tension, and perhaps lack of exercise.

If you are flexible, and you express your feelings openly, you are apt to be relaxed. This includes asserting yourself. You needn't be impolite, you simply need to be honest and to assert your needs. The tenth question is not easy for most of us: Sometimes we have chosen a life situation that is most difficult. It may even be killing us, but we won't give it up—such as a job with a boss who treats us badly, or a marriage with someone who won't respect our needs. Often we feel we would be judged morally wrong if we made the choice to put our own needs and health first. Of course other people do the judging—remember they don't have to live in your skin. Only *you* can judge what is best for you. If you can answer "yes" to 11 through 14, that is a sign that you know how to relax. Irritability is usually a response to stress, and a tense person is far more irritable than someone who is relaxed. The more that things "get to you" and irritate you, the better sign you have that your tension level is high. Your tension level will diminish if you do daily exercise and relaxation procedures. Finally most chronic symptoms are the residues of prolonged tension in response to stress. If they are severe, you have a gauge on the extent to which you have reacted to stress and lived with tension in body, mind, feeling, and spirit.

We start accumulating tension in school. Sitting still for many hours a day is not the best thing for children, but that is the first lesson of school. In crowded public schools children must learn to control their bladders and evacuation until a teacher permits them to use the toilet. That degree of control is also a stress. Children are taught to hide their feelings. That is a stress. After years of controlling feelings a person may not feel them any more. It may seem as if the feelings have died. As we learn to deaden ourselves, not to cry, not to laugh too much, not to express feelings that the people around us don't want to hear, we also learn to use the logical, language-oriented side of our brain to control and pull in our natural selves. We gain something, for we are socially acceptable. We lose something, our own feelings—and we create diseases.

Symptoms are the body's way of telling us that there is too much stress. Each of us have particular target organs that immediately respond to stress. It might be stomach and gas, or the heart and angina, or clogged arteries. It might take the form of asthma, or hiccups, skin irritations, or blurred vision. Many common symptoms are due to stress if they recur again and again: headache, tics, blurry vision, dizziness, fatigue, cough, wheezing, backache, muscle spasms, itching, palpitations, sweating, rapid heart rate, impotence, pelvic pain, stomach ache, diarrhea, frequent urination, dermatitis, hyperventilation, irregular heart rhythm, high blood pressure, delayed menstruation, and vaginal discharge.

This list comes from a book, *Feeling Fine*, by Dr. Arthur Ulene, who lists them as the most common reactions of his own patients. Do you have any of these complaints? Simply recognizing them and paying attention is the start of changing them.

It is becoming clear to medical doctors that the diseases of old age in our country are only indirectly related to age. They represent repeated stress reactions to chronic tension. Of course the longer tension has continued the more likely there will be severe symptoms.

It is important to realize that it is our reaction to stress that accumulates and becomes disease: It is not the stress itself.

We actually need some stress and challenge in life, and our bodies contain the natural mechanisms for dealing with it. If somebody says, "I'm going to hit you!" you get ready. Your muscles brace, you breathe a little faster; you are ready to fight or run. Supposing you are really frightened: Your hands and feet get cold as the blood vessels contract and blood goes into the core of your body. Your adrenal glands have put out hormones that release energy from all your cells. By the activation of your sympathetic nervous system your blood pressure goes up, your heart rate increases, you breathe faster, and your muscles have a quicker flow of nourishing blood. Your chemistry is changed. Your gut reacts and gets ready to evacuate. A brilliant physiologist, Dr. Hans Selye, studied this response to stress which he called a general adaptation syndrome. He saw that there were three stages. The first was an alarm reaction. The entire body is mobilized. After this comes a resistance stage, in which the mobilization of the body has raised your resistance and energy way above its normal levels. Now if the stress isn't quickly over, but continues for some time, this heightened resistance will be followed by a period of exhaustion. In other words there is only so much energy to use for adapting to stress. After a while your energy is depleted.

Our bodies seem to have been designed to meet brief challenges. They are designed to discharge a huge energy that is mobilized—to permit us to kill the dragon, or run from the tiger, to put out the fire, to make love, or flee. What happens to that energy when we do none of the above? Our tissues are still in a state of alarm. Our blood pressure still rises.

Actually our bodies go through the same changes whenever we are challenged, but we may not notice it because we have been taught to hold back anger, fright, and tears. We may be driving and somebody honks at us suddenly; we are startled but cannot do anything about it. We even feel that surge of adrenalin, which is part of what we call feeling startled. Or perhaps somebody does something that makes me angry, but I have learned to hide anger, and so I don't say anything. I am very polite, but my body is building up the fast pulse and high blood pressure anyway. It lasts a long time. Later I feel fatigued and downcast. I have to take a driving test and feel afraid I may fail. There is no way to cry and talk about my fear: I simply tense my chest and hold my jaws stiff—stiff upper lip—and go through with the test in a state of nervousness and distraction, upset by my own withheld feelings. Afterward I am very tired.

Think of the amount of difficulty we cause ourselves before an ordeal such as surgery! I can remember having no opportunity to tell my doctor I was angry at him for failing to diagnose my polyp earlier. Nor to speak out and cry about the fear of not surviving. There were many feelings: Each feeling that was not discharged was associated with a tension of the muscles. Muscle tension invariably changes our chemistry. So I actually went into surgery in the worst possible way, without experiencing, perhaps even recognizing, my feelings and holding them in with my precious energy. Is that a familiar predicament in your life and the experience of your friends?

As a child I found it frustrating, even enraging, to stifle my feelings, but by adulthood I sometimes do not even feel the feelings anymore. The cost of this suppression of feeling is enormous. It takes energy to prevent feeling from coming out.

You can demonstrate how much energy it takes to hold back feelings by this simple exercise:

Hold your hand out in front of you while you read the next page: hold your fist *tightly clenched.*

At first you may find it painful to hold your fist tightly clenched but after a while you will notice that it no longer feels so intense. Hold it tight as you read on.

This holding is what we learned in school as children. After a lifetime we can see the results in the posture and texture of our bodies. Look at someone stooped over as if the weight of the world sat on his back and shoulders. Look at someone whose shoulders are pulled in, chest flattened with the tears and frustration that were never expressed. Look at people with set jaws, tightly clenched. Look at people who push out their chests, and chins, defiantly. Others you see have the look of small children collapsed in the chest, and stomach forward, with exaggeratedly curved backs. There is no reason why our bodies shouldn't be as straight in later life as in childhood. There's the catch. If you look at children you see that they begin to adopt the characteristic posture of their parents at an early age, three and four, the *lordosis* (curved spine), the jutting chin, the pinched-in shoulders. That posture expresses an attitude. It also feels "right" to the person, because it is the only posture he or she has known. Over the years, if our habits remain the same, the posture becomes ingrained and our bodies are shaped more and more rigidly.

Undoing the tension of a lifetime, at any age, happens slowly, with patience. Relaxation is not an alcoholic collapse. It is not easy. It is a gradual healer. Being relaxed does not mean being "spaced out." It is more like the relaxed walk of an alert cat, or a child ecstatically feeling the sun on his body. Because you are not merely physical, your relaxation is not merely physical. However you may want to begin by relaxing muscles and focusing on your body. You can do some of the relaxation exercises in Part Two of this book and discover how different the world feels when you are no longer tense.

The tension in your body comes from holding back emotions, not expressing anger or fear, not asserting yourself when you have needs. It comes from your mind, always busy thinking, trying to find something, making lists, remembering, planning. It comes from some deeper anxiety, perhaps, that makes you think you need to control everything in your life, the weather, other people, and the way your body reacts.

How is your fist? Did you keep it clenched tightly? Release it now. Relax your hand. Do you feel some warmth in your hand? Did you feel some fatigue from holding your fist? Or did you cheat and let your fist relax early? If you held it tight you will now sense how much energy it drained. This is energy that we usually waste. We spend an enormous amount of precious energy holding our bodies tense in an unconscious way. We don't realize that we are tired from holding our bodies tensely. We are accustomed to being tense. It is familiar. We no longer feel it because tense muscles send a chorus of messages to the brain, like heavy static. Relaxed muscles send fewer nerve messages.

What would you do if you had more energy?

Most of us do not associate relaxation with increased energy, yet you can tell from this one example that relaxation releases the energy used in tension. This may explain certain extraordinary people, who seem to need very little sleep, yet who work prodigiously. I know several people like that. One, a psychiatrist who runs a large practice and a research laboratory, enjoys all the hubbub of his twenty-hour day. He has time to read, to meet with friends, and to travel, for he sleeps only about three hours. Another man, a Western spiritual teacher, sleeps about two hours a night and eats very little, yet he has as much energy and vitality at fifty as a young child. Among people who practice meditation and who are satisfied and pleased with their daily lives, you will find many who sleep less and need less rest than they used to. However you will also find that these people pace themselves. They do not move with undue hurry. They rest when they are tired. They spend their energy carefully only on things that matter to them. You can release extra energy for yourself as you begin to practice the different aspects of relaxation in this chapter and in Part Two of this book.

You will notice throughout this book that relaxation exercises precede most exercises in imagery, fantasy, visualization, massage, and even exercise. The instructions will become familiar. They are repeated because they are important.

Before you start a relaxation exercise, always take the phone off the hook, and arrange that you will not be interrupted, even by animals. Make sure your room is a comfortable temperature: If it is chilly, put on a sweater or cover yourself with a light blanket. Loosen clothing and take off any jewelry, watch, earrings, or glasses. You may never notice that these are distracting, yet your nervous system will react to any stimulation—such as a constricting watchband.

When you are ready, allow yourself plenty of time for

each exercise. The following exercises are meant to be done sitting or lying down. The great advantage of sitting is that you will not fall asleep. The aim is to *stay awake, not to fall asleep!*

Often during guided fantasies at SAGE there would be the purr of a couple of people snoring. We would gently awaken them by touching their feet. The skill of relaxing deeply can only be acquired if you stay awake.

After the exercise take time to feel any changes that have occurred. Don't just get up and resume your schedule. You need about a minute for reentry.

Relaxation Exercise

1. Lean back in your chair and sigh deeply. Feel your feet on the floor and your back against the chair, your buttocks on the seat. Feel the pull of gravity. With each breath you take, pay attention to the exhalation—with each exhalation let yourself sink more deeply into the chair. Allow yourself to feel relaxed and heavy. Let your arms and legs become heavier and more relaxed. Do this for ten minutes but do not go to sleep.

◇ ◇ ◇

In 1974, when we first tried this at SAGE, one woman said that it frightened her.

"Can you describe what frightened you?"

"I felt as if my body was melting. I couldn't find the boundaries. After a while I felt huge like a balloon. I thought something terrible was happening to my stomach and feet, but when I raised my head they looked normal."

Odd as it may sound, these unfamiliar feelings are a good sign of relaxation. Each person feels it differently. Another person in that group said,

"I don't like this relaxation at all. I feel as if I'm falling. I have to catch myself. Then I tense up."

His feeling of falling was a common one. He was truly letting his tension go. It did not mean that he was having a stroke, as he worried. He was really relaxing his body and mind.

If you have unusual feelings, you can be pretty certain they are the feelings of relaxation. The reason that they are strange is that you are rarely so relaxed when you are awake.

2. Sitting comfortably begin to imagine that every time you exhale you are bringing a cloud of warm air through your body. As you exhale, particularly draw the warm air down through your arms and hands. You might imagine the summer sun on your body, or sitting in a warm bath. Now concentrate upon your hands. Feel them becoming warmer and warmer.

"I had the most ridiculous sensation when I did that."

"What was it?"

"I felt as if my whole body was getting huge, and it filled up with a delectable orange color. I started even to smell something like oranges. Is it possible to have smell images?"

"Yes."

"Well I smelled oranges, and all kinds of fruit. Then I smelled a soap my mother must have used when I was a baby. It was a kind of smell that made me feel very secure and warm inside. . . ."

One person may have smell memories. As people warmed their arms and hands repeatedly at SAGE there was an enormous diversity of reactions. Most people began to enjoy it. "I like the sense of power. I can heat up my body. I've been a chilly person all my life and now I know I can sit down and all I have to do is think about taking a warm shower, and I'm warm all over."

Some people found it easy. Others said it was very hard for them. Some had deep childhood memories, others saw colors, smelled smells, or said it was quite mundane. "I just imagine I plug myself into the wall like a heater and I light up."

3. Concentrate your attention on your hands. After taking a few deep breaths to settle down, begin exhaling warmth down your arms into your hands. See how much you can feel your palms, your fingers, the back of your hands. See if you begin to feel a little prickling. If so, pay attention until the prickling grows stronger and spreads throughout your hands. (You may want to focus on only one hand: Pick the hand in which you feel the most sensation.) See if you feel some swelling. Let your hands swell up as large as they can. See if you feel some pulsing or throbbing. Allow that feeling to become very strong. Now see if your hands are warmer. Allow them to become very warm.

Warming the hands has been used to help people thwart the symptoms of migraine headache. One woman at SAGE was truly ecstatic the first time she warmed her hands, relaxed, and felt her incipient attack dissolving.

"I feel really hopeful for the first time in fifteen years," she said. "I've had these symptoms almost every day. Now I really believe there is something I can do about them without taking a lot of drugs."

Another woman said, "I feel almost tremulous about this, because I have had such trouble with my hands. I have been troubled with terrible pain in the cold—and it doesn't even have to be very chilly out, about fifty degrees. I went out for the first time—yesterday—I forgot my gloves, and wondered shall I go back and get them. Then I thought, well, I'll make them prickle instead. It worked. I was so tickled I wanted to tell all my friends."

"Warming the hands," said one man, "is so relaxing I can go to sleep."

As you can see, there is always a range of reactions. For every person who loves an exercise, there is one or maybe two who hate it. Moreover an exercise will change each time you do it. Don't judge the effects until you have practiced the exercises at least four times. Many relaxation exercises build upon one another. As you become more deeply relaxed you will notice different sensations. As you practice you will feel the effects more rapidly.

A typical response from someone with a lot of persistence was this comment from a man who had been skeptical at the start.

"It used to take me fifteen minutes, and I mean it was a struggle to feel any difference in my hand temperature. Now I can warm them up in ten seconds. The best thing about it is that the concentration, or whatever, makes me drop all my worries. When I do, my arthritis doesn't hurt so much."

4. Sit down and make yourself very comfortable. Begin as you did in the first exercise, by feeling yourself get heavier and more relaxed as you exhale each breath. It is almost like settling down more with each exhaled breath. When your arms and legs feel heavy and relaxed, allow them also to feel warm. You can exhale, feeling more warmth in your hands and feet, and say to yourself, "I feel relaxed and calm."

Now you are going to go on a journey to a special place of your own. Imagine that it is your favorite time of year, and you are in a spot that you specially loved and have remembered. Take some time to let a scene come to you—wildflowers blowing on a hill in the mountains, trees in a garden, fragrant with flowers— the rolling mists of early morning at a lagoon, or the pounding of the surf at the shore. As you begin to see a scene you love, enter it, and walk around. It is your place. It is a place of quiet and peace, and of pleasure where no one will disturb you. Spend some time enjoying this place and examining details.

When you are ready to leave, make fists with your hands, stretch, and take a deep breath. Open your eyes slowly. Take a minute to see how you feel before you get up.

After doing this exercise one SAGE participant sat in her chair looking astounded and mute for several minutes. "I didn't know I could do that!" she said. "I could swear I was in Zurich on a vacation—everything was so clear. I can't believe I just imagined that. I feel as if I were gone a month."

We always hoped that someone would feel the power of images so that all the rest of the group could see how deeply such an exercise might reach. Some people reacted just the opposite. One woman said, "I found that boring. I can't do these things at home. My husband thinks I'm crazy." Another member of the group said, "I want to talk about more important things than how my foot feels." But others were beginning to say they had more energy than they expected, and some people were noticing a diminishing of symptoms as they did their relaxation work at home. As we all did the exercises, we began to feel more whole. We are also giving up some of the commentary that our proud, righteous minds would make about every experience, labeling and judging. That mental voice was growing more silent. It stopped nagging so much.

In many ways the process of relaxing may seem undramatic and very slow. It is. Simple things are important. You can allow your stomach to extend and take deep breaths instead of holding it in with tight clothing. You can take time to notice your surroundings. You can take space for your own needs and begin to assert yourself, if this isn't already your habit. It is very important for you to be straightforward about your needs. In the beginning you may ask yourself, "Is this really me?" It may feel unfamiliar. It will be unfamiliar, for the familiar state for most of us is tension. The early stages of relaxing are the most difficult. This is the time when you need to set aside twenty minutes a day for feeling yourself and relaxing. You need to begin to know what you are feeling deep inside. Feelings are your natural survival apparatus. They are essential to your well-being—even though you may not always be feeling happy. Feeling unhappy is part of adult life, too. However it is time to give yourself permission to be human—to express feeling and not be ashamed.

Make a pledge to yourself—for revitalizing your life—that you will give yourself permission to feel without judging your feelings. You will not be ashamed of your feelings. They are true. They are what you feel. They are your guide in life. They are the inner voices that tell you what you need to do—for yourself. They were given to you as a gift of nature, to enable you to survive.

Maybe at first you will think that your feelings are often negative. As you begin to watch yourself relaxing, as you begin to express yourself from moment to moment, you will begin to discover that feelings change. They are not always negative. They shift. Chinese medical theory says that the suppression of any emotion is the cause of disease and that no emotion takes precedence over another. As you watch your emotions change you may find that they are not so important. No one of them lasts forever. You may even notice that you can change your feelings.

Because crying, and sadness, are so strictly disciplined in childhood—especially for men—this is an important expression to begin cultivating. Dr. Wolfgang Luthe, a Montreal psychiatrist famous for translating *Autogenic Training and Therapy* by Johannes Schultz into English, and for his own research on this form of self-healing and psychosomatic disease, has commented that crying is an important release of the nervous system. Ideally each of us should cry for a few minutes every day, to release tensions that otherwise accumulate in the brain. Far from being ashamed of it, we should do exercises to provoke crying if we are unable to let tears come naturally.

At the start, however, you must be patient with yourself. Treat yourself as a lovable small child. If you feel like crying, allow the tears to come out, remembering they are a releasing mechanism of the nervous system. By holding them back you prevent your own nervous system from getting rid of tensions; instead they accumulate. This damages the eyes. Anyone who has fought tears knows how tensions mount. Holding back crying means that you hold your breath, you tighten your neck, you tighten your jaw muscles, you compress your chest. The next time you feel like crying—but don't dare—feel your body. Feel what you must do to hold on.

As one woman of 74 commented at SAGE:

"We've been schooled to view crying as something to avoid, and I know in my particular case I couldn't shed a tear in front of my husband, and I've been living with him for fifty-four years."

Not to be able to cry is to be deprived of an important step toward total relaxation. This is not a joke. Men as well as women need this release. At SAGE we have used the following exercise to help people learn to cry in private.

Crying Technique

Make certain you will not be interrupted by phones or people. Sit comfortably.

Now place your hand on your upper chest, over the collarbone. Begin to breathe only as deeply as your hand, no deeper. Breathe rapidly and make a sound. Listen to the feeling in your voice as you pant and begin to make the sound of a baby crying. Listen to it. Allow yourself to feel its sadness. Allow yourself to make the sound of sobbing. Think of the things that are causing you sadness and grief. Allow yourself to make the sounds that go with those griefs. As you do this, give yourself permission to be human. You should have no trouble releasing. Stay with the exercise if it is difficult at first. Do this if you feel the beginning of a headache in the temples. This is often a sign that you have been controlling crying and have accumulated such tension and eye pain that your head aches. If you feel a little tension at the temples, take time out, and do your crying exercise. When you can work up enough self-pity to sob for a few minutes, you will release that tension. You will feel as others have: "What a relief!" That relief is relaxation.

◇ ◇ ◇

One afternoon we tried crying in our group. Most of the members had a difficult time. I had led classes before where it took only one person's sobs to release everyone in the group. One woman began crying. Later she said, "I was unaware of how much I had stored up for so long. I think I cry more because I try so hard to hold it back." She went home and practiced. Two weeks later she said, "I can cry all right. Now I'm so good at it I haven't been able to read lately because my eyes are so swollen from crying. I thought I would feel better immediately, but I feel tired." It took her about five weeks of crying often, and feeling hopeless and weary, before she began to feel what a load she had left behind. Most people do not do that. Some people may cry a little, and they find it easier to cry when they feel sad or hurt, thereby resolving the feelings at the moment they occur. Still any process may take some patience. We have practiced daily since childhood to achieve our tension and self-control! We cannot undo it all in an hour. It is safer, and healthier, to go through a slow process, not to try to change in an hour or two of exercises.

As you read this, are you aware of the way you are sitting? How does your spine feel? Are you aware of the different parts of your body? Can you feel the air around your skin? Can you feel your seat on the chair, your feet on the floor? Can you sense your heart beating? Is there a taste in your mouth? What is the color of the light on the page?

Our bodies are the vehicles for great pleasure, yet we are taught to restrict our awareness and mainly notice our bodies when we feel discomfort. Sometimes noticing makes us anxious because we have learned to associate almost any unfamiliar sensation with a symptom of illness. Do not be surprised if you have this reaction as you begin to pay attention.

Quite a few people become anxious when they begin relaxing deeply. First of all relaxation allows you to feel much more, especially in body locations that have been tense. As you relax, you may begin to feel energy moving in your fingers and legs, bubbling in your stomach after eating, pulsating in your hands. Feeling a lot means sensitivity, not sickness. At first you may also feel symptoms more. However if you will remain calm and listen to your sensations, you will be rewarded by discovering that there is a rich seething of life going on under your skin. You will begin to smell smells, to see and hear more acutely. Just realize that it may not be easy to feel again once you are out of the habit. You will not be the first person to feel anxiety when you first hear your heart beating loudly, or sense a tingling up your arms and legs or around your face. Usually people are waking up—not sick—when they feel these subtle sensations. All of us need to learn to feel again, and it takes as much learning as learning to swim, or ride a bicycle.

As a gift to yourself, toward greater feeling of vitality, give yourself a half an hour a day to do one of the relaxation exercises in this chapter or in the second section. Suspend your judgment, for nothing changes instantly. See if relaxation brings a new quality of pleasure and energy into your life.

4 ⌘ "LET ME SEE HOW YOU BREATHE AND I WILL TELL YOU HOW YOU LIVE"

One day a lanky retired actor looked around the sunny room at all of the SAGE people and remarked, "I noticed that my baby grandson breathes with his whole body. His diaphragm moves. But when I look around the room at us, I see that we are just breathing in the chest."

"I get dizzy if I breathe deeply," responded one woman.

"I never noticed how I breathe," commented another.

Anyone who has been sedentary for twenty or thirty years will not breathe very deeply. If you suddenly start taking deep breaths it is possible to feel dizzy. This doesn't mean that it isn't good for you. It means that your brain mechanism for air intake is set too low. Like a thermostat this mechanism regulates the balance of oxygen and carbon dioxide. The balance depends upon how much air you breathe. If you breathe shallowly, on the whole, you have to breathe more rapidly. When you start breathing deeply again, this mechanism takes a little time to readjust. This is why you get dizzy. However, as you practice, your brain resets its regulator: Now you begin to breathe deeply and less often. Soon your deeper breathing becomes involuntary.

"If you did nothing but practice some breathing exercises and become aware of your breathing, you would radically change your life," Eugenia said to the group. Each new group of people doubts that, and many resist the exercises with vehemence. One elegant woman in her early seventies complained about her fatigue and lack of spunk and energy. "I hate these breathing exercises," she would comment, yet by the spring of that year she was bragging about her energy and the long, long hikes she would take. Another woman, venturesome and worldly, felt equally skeptical about long laps of breathing at home each day. "I can't see that this is doing anything for me," she complained. "I know I am used to the business world where you do something to accomplish something."

"Keep doing it," Eugenia retorted.

"It's so boring," she said. But in six months she was telling the group, "You know, I'm not sure what has happened to me. I used to be hardly able to drag myself out of bed. Now I have so much energy that my body moves faster than my head.

"I got up the other day, and I found myself in San Francisco—almost before I decided to go. I was up and out. I never really believed that breathing would do this for me. Actually I've been trying to give up smoking. When I feel a yen for a cigarette, I take a couple of deep breaths and the need goes away. I do the same when I'm tempted to eat snacks. I breathe until the hunger just vanishes. Then—to make my testimonial complete—I use it if I can't seem to wake up, fast breathing. If I can't seem to fall asleep, I use about fifteen to thirty breaths in bed and it puts me right to sleep."

What is the magic of the human body that makes it possible to obtain both energy and rest out of the same breathing exercise?

Every time you inhale a miracle begins. First the membranes of your nose filter the air and kill harmful bacteria, while warming the air to body temperature. The cleansed, warmed air goes down your windpipe, or trachea, which divides into branches, tubular structures called bronchioles. These then lead into millions and millions of tiny air sacs that compose the lungs. The lungs are like sponges. They contain so many air sacs that if they were spread out flat it is estimated they would cover 14,000 square feet. The lungs not only send oxygen to every cell in the body, but they also regulate hormones. The lungs, heart and blood, and muscles work together to bring oxygen to every part of the body, from the brain to the toes. The most important muscle is known as the diaphragm. It resembles an elastic sheet, between the chest and abdomen. When it expands downward, it makes room for the lungs to elongate. The chest expands, the belly expands, and air rushes in. When the diaphragm muscle relaxes, the chest contracts, compressing the lungs, and the air is expelled. This rhythm brings oxygenated air into the tiny sacs of the lungs where there is blood, impure blood. A form of energy exchange occurs as the blood takes up oxygen into its red cells and releases carbonic acid and other wastes to be exhaled. The hemoglobin molecule in blood is similar in many ways to the chlorophyll molecule in plants. Chlorophyll absorbs energy from light and carbon dioxide and oxygen is released. Hemoglobin absorbs oxygen, both of them forming the link between the solar system and life.

The blood that leaves the lungs is rich and red. It is carried to the left auricle of the heart, where a contraction forces it into the left ventricle, where the contraction (or beat) forces it out through the arteries into the capillaries of every part of the body. The blood relinquishes its nourishment by a form of energy exchange. Now the used up blood returns by the veins. It is bluish in color and full of wastes. The impure blood enters the right auricle of the heart. When this chamber becomes full, the heart muscle contracts, forcing the blood into the right ventricle which sends it into the millions of hairlike blood vessels of the lungs. There it will be cleansed and filled with oxygen.

The heart pumps some 700 gallons of blood each day. How hard it works and how much oxygen reaches our body tissues and brain depends upon our breathing. Our brain responds to the amount of carbon dioxide in our blood to adjust the rate of breathing.

How we breathe affects our heart and our feelings. Many of us breathe only with the middle and upper portions of our lungs. Thus we are ineffective at squeezing out the toxic wastes, and yet we have to squeeze out the wastes for new air to come in. The base of the lungs, however, may remain stagnant, holding stagnant air. When people feel that they cannot inhale deeply, they often don't exhale fully. They try to add fresh air without removing the stagnant air from the bottom portion of their lungs. The result is fast, shallow breathing, which is usually associated with feelings of anxiety, or discomfort.

Long, slow, deep exhalations allow the stagnant air to be removed and fresh air to enter in. When breathing becomes deeper and slower, the heart does not have to beat so fast. Heart rate may drop from seventy-two beats a minute to fifty or forty. The heart is no longer having to work so hard. During a breathing exercise, as the breathing becomes slower and deeper, the blood pressure drops, the body relaxes, and the nervous system becomes calm. Deep breathing thus takes a burden off the heart and nervous system.

Oxygen is the essence of life for our tissues. Without a continuous supply of fresh oxygen tissues age and degenerate. Digestion is hindered. Elimination becomes difficult. The brain requires three times as much oxygen as any other organ. Without it our thinking process becomes slower. We "space out." We fatigue and cannot remember things. This makes us anxious and tense. Without oxygen brain cells quickly die.

Shallow breathing cannot give you an optimum sense of

being alive, of calm, happiness, or well-being, because it burdens your heart and deprives your brain. Deeper, slower breathing brings about a miracle of change in the body, and a change in feeling.

Many members of SAGE have heard this information impassively. Usually somebody says, "Prove it!"

Get to Know Your Breathing Rhythm

Probably all your life you have taken your breath for granted. You probably don't know how it sounds unless it disturbs you. You may have learned special breathing exercises for yoga, or underwater swimming, but how is your ordinary, normal breathing?

Begin by getting comfortably seated in a chair, without tight clothing, and sit as straight as you can. Now just close your eyes and breathe. Decide which part of the breath you like best: Is it inhalation or exhalation? How do you feel in the moment just after you have inhaled, just before exhalation? How do you feel when you have exhaled all the breath out and haven't yet inhaled? Spend ten minutes just watching how you normally breathe.

Ask a friend to do this, or a group of friends. Then compare your experiences. You will discover that people have many different feelings about the parts of the breathing rhythm.

I personally love the exhalation, for I feel like a child, free and relaxed, swinging up into space. But the pause before I inhale again may worry me if it lasts too long. Then comes a rush of air into my lungs. Instead of relaxing me being filled up with air makes me feel stuffed, and the slight pause before exhaling is a pause that I tend to rush. I can't wait to relax again.

I am always amazed to hear people say that exhalation makes them uncomfortable: That they love the feeling of inhaling, or the pause just after inhaling, when they feel full and secure.

All of us are different. And these differences speak about very distinct life patterns, patterns of feeling. We are probably alike in one way. Most of us have grown up controlling our feelings with our breathing. Certainly I own up to stifling feeling such as anger, grief, and fear by keeping myself from breathing, holding my breath, swallowing my feelings. I can remember the time when I realized I knew how to stop my feelings: I was eight, seated between my parents at what must have been my first movie, *A Tale of Two Cities*. Toward the end was a scene of a beheading. I was terrified. My father and mother acted as if there were nothing to be scared of. I looked at the clock over the theater door because I could not bear to see the screen, and I held my breath, and clenched my fists. I knew then that I had a way of not crying and acting "like a baby."

Dr. Bruno Hans Geba, an Austrian-born physiologist and psychologist, would point out that this was the beginning of a subtle chain of behaviors by which I would stifle my own feelings and do what somebody else told me I should do, not what I felt like. If you are afraid of feeling, hold your breath.

"Breathing is a natural human function," he has written in *Breathe Away Your Tension* (New York: Random House/Bookworks, 1973). "You cannot overbreathe yourself." "You cannot hurt yourself breathing."

Nonetheless many people say that breathing makes them feel lightheaded or peculiar. It is unfamiliar, like deep relaxation. "Where do these sensations and emotions come from?" asks Dr. Geba.

"Well the moment you breathe deeply, more energy becomes available in your body. Where there is energy flow, there is motion. You can experience this motion in many different ways: as sensations like tingling, numbness, or vibration, or as emotions such as sadness, joy, or anger, and finally as actual body movements that go with these emotions, like crying, laughing, or striking out. So, therefore, if you are afraid to feel, one of the most effective ways to keep yourself from feeling is to control your breathing."

In fact many of us control deep emotions by breathing shallowly. Each pattern of breathing has an emotional tone. You can become acquainted with the various kinds of breathing by a simple exercise. Eugenia often introduced a group to the experience of deep breathing by giving them this procedure for comparing the different patterns that we evolve unconsciously in the course of our lives.

Discovering How Breathing Patterns Affect Your Feelings

1. Sit comfortably. Loosen any tight clothing. Feel your feet firmly planted on the floor. Now put one hand flat on your collar bone, near your throat. Close your eyes and breathe only into that part of the lung cavity: don't breathe into your chest or stomach. Take time for ten to fifteen breaths.

How does this make you feel? Take a moment or two to register your feelings before you stop.

If you feel a little anxious or panicky, remember that the feeling will not last. Sometimes people gasp, or feel as if they had been running. Sometimes people feel upset or harried after doing this. Register your own feeling and then go on to the next exploration.

2. Put your hand on your chest. Close your eyes and breathe into your upper chest only. Do not breathe into your diaphragm or stomach. This is not a deep breath. You should move only the part of your chest that your hand rests upon. Do ten to fifteen breaths.

Once again you may have found that you had to breathe rapidly to get enough air. Some people feel that this is a familiar feeling, the way they breathe when they are stifling tears or feeling anxious. If you feel anxious or upset, once again it will not last. Register your own feelings. Then go on to the next pattern.

3. Put one hand on your diaphragm, just under your chest. Put the other hand on your chest. Now breathe into the diaphragm. Move that hand, but do not move the hand on your chest. If it seems difficult at first, be patient. You used to know how to do this when you were very young. Take ten to fifteen breaths. Close your eyes and register your feelings. Many people say that this feels "better," that it is a more satisfying breath. How do you feel?

4. Now place your hand below your belly button. You might want to locate your navel. Place your hand about three finger widths below your navel. This time see if you can draw air way down into your lower abdomen, so that your hand moves up when you inhale, but your chest and diaphragm do not move. Your chest will only move at the very end of the breath. This means that your lungs extend fully and fill completely with air.

Sometimes this is easier to accomplish lying down.

If you try several positions, but still find it difficult to breathe into your lower abdomen, you are not alone. Be patient and keep trying. Try to develop five to ten long, slow, abdominal breaths.

Sometimes an image helps. You might imagine that you have nostrils in the middle of your lower back, and that you can breathe directly from this "nose" on your back into your stomach. If that doesn't work, you might imagine that you are filling a long balloon inside your stomach: You have to inhale into the bottom to first fill the end of the balloon.

Deep abdominal breathing may be the most important exercise you do.

◇ ◇ ◇

When you look back at the different experiences you have had in these patterns of breathing, you can sense which mode brings in the most air. Surely if you breathe just into your collarbone, you are drawing air only into the uppermost part of your lungs. That is all you get. It is not much. You have to gasp. The upper lobes are the smallest part of the lungs, yet many people breathe this way. Some people retract their abdomen, raise their shoulders and collarbones, and breathe shallowly. This is very common among people who wear girdles and tight clothing. A great many people with respiratory illnesses have been breathing this way all their lives.

Breathing exercises need to be practiced. If you simply read these exercises and try them once, they will do you little good. Pick one and do it daily for several weeks.

The following exercise is probably the most important for starting, since you cannot do other breathing exercises until you learn how to breathe into your abdomen.

Deep Abdominal Breathing

This exercise is best done in comfort and leisure. Be sure that you will not be interrupted. Take the phone off the hook. Lie on a firm surface, preferably a carpet or mat or folded blanket on the floor. Try to lie so that your back is straight: You will need to bend your knees and prop pillows under them so that your lower back touches the floor. You may need a pillow under your head so that your head is not thrown back.

When you have found a comfortable position, place your hand on your lower abdomen—about an inch and a half below the navel. Take long breaths as if you were blowing up a long balloon. Every breath is bringing oxygen to all your cells, and by transformation, turning the food you eat into body warmth, the energy to think, feel, and move.

Pay attention to the way each breath comes through

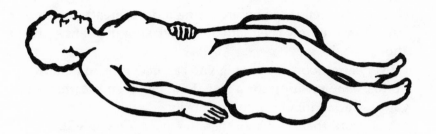

the nose and down your windpipe. Feel it filling your belly. Feel your lungs stretching and filling. Feel the rise of the incoming breath, then a momentary pause. Feel the ebbing wave of the breath leaving your body. As you exhale, try to make sure you let all the air out. Pay attention to the air leaving your body and moving out beyond your face. Focus on the momentary hiatus when you have exhaled and the breath is out. You may feel a special kind of relaxation just then. Let yourself fall gently into that relaxed feeling. Then start over and watch the breath coming in.

How much you get out of this exercise depends upon paying close attention to your breathing. If other thoughts intrude, that is all right. Let them go by. Turn your attention back to your breathing and how it feels.

As you lie in bed each morning, you can draw your knees up and plant your feet on the mattress. Take ten deep breaths into your lower abdomen, paying attention to each breath. As you do this you will begin to become acquainted with your own pattern of breathing deeply.

If you become irritated during the day, or angry, or frustrated, you can short-circuit these negative feelings and tensions simply by taking eight deep breaths and putting your attention on the breaths as you did in your exercise. Nobody can tell that you are doing a deep breathing exercise. They can only see that you are relaxing in a tense situation.

Every afternoon or evening you can take time to lie down in this same position for a rest. Take ten deep breaths into your lower abdomen, into your belly.

Not more than two months after we started SAGE, one man came in with the surprised and pleasant expression of a man who's gotten kissed when he least expected it. He said he had been doing his ten breaths into the belly before getting up in the morning, and during long waits at the pharmacy, the check-out counter at the co-op, and red stop lights. But he hadn't noticed the change in himself until one morning he and his wife went to breakfast. They were talking, and he didn't notice what he ordered—excepting that when the breakfasts were set before them he had a large order of extra toast by mistake. "Ordinarily I'd have blown my stack and chewed out the poor son of a gun behind the counter. But I just looked at it, took three deep breaths, and I had to laugh. My wife couldn't believe it. She said, 'I don't know what you're doing, but I know you better go on doing it.' That was a dramatic indication that the SAGE process, and the breathing, were changing me from an irritable old cuss into a calm, civilized somebody."

Ancient Chinese doctors considered that breathing was energy from heaven. So it is. Literally. Each time you inhale a breath you imbibe oxygen that comes from the interaction of the sun—a star—with plants on earth. Sunlight is essential for the action of green plants, which generate oxygen into the air. So, as you breathe, you inhale oxygen to all your cells, taking direct energy from the planetary system beyond earth. You might see how it feels to have that image in the back of your mind as you practice deep abdominal breathing. You are breathing air in from the universe and breathing back out into space. Some people have said that this expands their sense of space. Others say it relaxes them and makes them feel deeply connected with those distant points of light that shimmer in the night sky. One lawyer with severe hypertension found himself doing this rather than just watching his breath. "I can go so far out that I drop everything on my mind during a single breath, before I come back. It's relaxing—maybe because I feel that each breath takes me way out into space for an eternity."

If you have practiced abdominal breathing, and you can do it with some ease, you are ready to learn a procedure SAGE people have used as one of the important keys to self-discovery and growth. We call it "roll breathing." When I started to write this book, I went around to the members of the first two groups to find out what exercises they still practiced after their formal training period was over. Hardly anyone omitted the roll breathing.

"I'd rather go without dinner," laughed one woman.

"I do the roll breaths in the bathtub when I want to relax."

"I do the roll breathing to go to sleep," said another. "I try for ten breath cycles, but usually I'm sleeping before I'm through. I also do it to reduce pain and when I just want total refreshment—like when I've been out visiting and I'm tired."

One man thought for a moment. "I do at least ten cycles to relax myself before I do exercises. Then I do exercises gently, not forcing. Sometimes when I'm working around the house, fixing something, I may turn my wrist or ankle, and if I relax myself then by breathing, I don't have so much arthritis pain."

These statements are mostly practical. However in the long run, sleeping better, gaining much energy, and reducing pain may seem like side effects of a much deeper process. If you practice no other exercise in this book, you might consider choosing this one to learn carefully and practice daily.

Roll breathing, as we did it in SAGE groups, became a

healing process. It was taught to us by Eugenia, who had worked for two years with Dr. Bruno Geba. He had evolved the process out of his understanding of gestalt, Reichian therapy, and of autogenic training. Actually people have practiced a similar method for several thousand years in yoga breathing.

Breathing is a reintroduction to emotions and feeling parts of the body that you excluded from your consciousness as a young child. Contact is the first step in healing. However our bodies store all the history of our experience, and so we may experience memories and stored feelings as we make contact with our muscles. Sometimes people find themselves apprehensive and anxious. If this happens to you, don't fight it. Allow yourself to be apprehensive for a little while. Fighting and suppressing take energy which will conflict with the energy in you that is attempting to express anxiety or apprehension. A conflict of energies, like a political conflict, produces a block. You no longer feel the original impulse of apprehension, but your energy is not flowing. So instead you may feel depression, neck pains, tension, stomach aches, or insomnia. . . .

Similarly if you feel your lip quivering and feel sad, let yourself weep. Geba suggests, if you are scared, that you hold your breath after each inhalation to a count of six. Inhale, count to six, holding—then exhale. If you are stubborn, and do not run from your feeling, your anxiety will begin to seem less frightening. If you stop the exercise, the anxiety will remain with you and have the power to prevent you from going farther. Whatever you feel is what you need to give yourself permission to express. You may feel silliness, or euphoria.

Roll Breathing

Once you have decided to do the roll breathing, take your phone off the hook and make certain that you will not be interrupted for at least an hour. It is particularly important to be comfortable, to put your jewelry, contact lenses, glasses, and shoes aside. Wear loose clothing. A loose robe or pajamas are excellent.

Lie on a firm surface—a mat, carpet, folded blanket—on the floor or, if necessary, on your bed. Your back should be straight. Place a pillow under your head so that you are comfortable, and two or even three pillows under your knees. Take time to arrange yourself physically so that the small of your back touches the surface you lie on and you feel very comfortable. The comfort of a long session needs a straight spine. Your head should not be tilted forward nor thrown back. Feel your hips on the surface. Eugenia usually advised people, "Do not change your breathing. Just observe it at first. I usually ask people to put their hands at their sides—if that is comfortable—and place their hands with the palms up. That is a receptive position. However if you're not comfortable that way, forget about it."

When you have relaxed and begun to sense the rhythm of your natural breathing, place one hand on your chest and the other hand way down on your lower abdomen, just above the pelvis.

1. Take ten slow breaths into your abdomen, moving only the hand that rests on your belly. If you always find that you move the hand on your chest as well, you need to practice breathing into your abdomen some more.

As you develop your breathing, you may want to try breathing in through your nose and out through your mouth. Some people with blocked nasal passages find that it helps to start breathing in through the mouth. If you find this necessary, you may want to keep a glass of water handy in case your mouth and throat become dry. Since it is disruptive to get up in the middle of a breathing session, have water and throat-moistening lozenges beside you, if you tend to need them. Often the process of breathing will clear the nasal passages.

2. With one hand resting on your chest, and the other on your lower abdomen, take one long breath into the abdomen. When it is full, add air and fill your chest. As you do this, you will first lift the hand on your abdomen and then the hand on your chest. It should be a kind of rolling motion, as if the abdomen were a rising wave, followed by a rising wave in your chest.

Practice this until it becomes easy and natural. At first you may be like the rest of us and try expanding your stomach by muscular force. Your stomach will move out, but it will be hard. Similarly if you force your chest out, it too will feel muscular. And the movement will be jerky.

When you get tired stop.

Then practice again, letting the air go way down into your belly, like filling a balloon, and then let the air fill your chest. After you can feel the roll you can let your arms rest beside you comfortably.

After 10 roll breaths (belly and chest) you should stop. Breathe normally and lie there with your eyes closed. See what you feel happening in your body. It may seem very subtle or infinitesimal. Pay attention to it: whether it is a slight tingling on the bridge of your nose, your hands pulsing, your feet tingling, a slight feeling of chill. The energy is moving. If you lie still and pay attention to it, you will feel it travel from one place to another.

◇ ◇ ◇

Practice the rolling breaths so that you feel at ease with them. "It took me every day for three weeks," said one woman, who used this method to get rid of migraine symptoms. "It wasn't very dramatic at first." I remember the first three times I did this, I was cold and fearful. I covered up with blankets and lay watching my own nameless fear. After a while I warmed up and the fright melted away. The next time I did it, I began to feel tense in my shoulders and neck, and feel sore spots that hadn't been there at first. As Eugenia pointed out, 'Those are places where your energy is blocked. You can relieve them by giving them a little massage. Then lie back and see what it feels like.'

"I began to feel warmth, and streams of energy, like tiny particles racing through my shoulders and down my arms and torso. Soon I felt excited and energetic."

If you feel taut or tense in your muscles after breathing, massage any spot that you can reach. If you cannot reach, use a back scratcher or bath brush. Sometimes the old sore spots will vanish, but new ones will take their place. Again be kind to yourself and give them a brief massage.

You may feel a kind of buzzing sensation, or vibration. That is good. Pay attention to it. Watch it move. You may have muscle twitches, itching, shivering, numbness, cold hands, or tightness. These sensations are all the result of new energy you brought into your body by inhaling deeply. Energy produces activity, and this may be an experience of physical sensation, or one of sadness, joy, anger, or fear. Whatever happens is what your own nervous system needs at that moment. It is a release of blocked energy. Only your nervous system knows what should be released first. Nobody, not your spouse or the world's greatest therapist or guru, could know your body better than it knows itself. Your nervous system will release tension in its own way, and according to its own order and your particular needs. Your nervous system is always right! Therefore, be assured, whatever happens is appropriate and good.

Breathing increases energy and therefore feeling. The alternative is to stop feeling. To be anesthetized. Sometimes the feelings are unfamiliar. You may not understand what is happening to you when you first start roll breathing. Try to repeat to yourself that it is your brain's way of releasing pent-up blocked energy. However if you get too anxious and uncomfortable, roll over onto your stomach. You will feel more protected.

You might say to yourself that anxiety is a feeling your body needed to release, and so even though it is uncomfortable it is a healthy sign.

When we first began to do this roll breathing at SAGE, we had no idea what to expect. One woman, under considerable stress, breathed only twenty cycles when her face turned green. She began to sob angrily. "I hate breathing. It makes me too sad." When a person cries I like to hold him or her, and sometimes I find myself crying, too. Then both of us feel better and can talk. Three months later the same woman was saying, "I use this breathing for energy when I'm in a lull. I do about fifteen breaths and then I feel just fine. Sometimes I use it to relax, to put myself to sleep." That year the amazing differences in reactions were an indication to us that every person experiences a complicated progression of unpredictable changes.

Now that you are becoming familiar with this way of exploring yourself, you will want to become more systematic and gain more energy. Now you can lie with your hands at your sides, not touching your body. When you inhale into the abdomen, then into the chest, and exhale, you have completed one cycle. Ten of these breaths would make ten cycles.

IMPORTANT: BUILD UP YOUR ROUTINE SLOWLY.

It will do you no good to do thirty roll breaths and get dizzy and scare yourself with hyperventilation. Begin with a cycle of ten breaths. Then lie still watching your sensations and feelings. Each day you can work up to more cycles. Eventually you will be able to do roll breathing for thirty minutes or an hour.

When twenty cycles are easy, begin to alternate. Do ten cycles of roll breaths in a slow, easy fashion. Then do ten cycles of deep but quick breaths. This may take a little effort. Finally do another ten cycles of long slow roll breaths. Now lie with your eyes closed, breathing normally and feeling.

◇ ◇ ◇

FOR BEST EFFECT YOU SHOULD PRACTICE EVERY DAY.

As one SAGE woman put it, "The effects depend upon how much I get into it, whether I'm distracted or not. If I really get into it, I feel enveloped in my own breath. . . . It is pleasurable. Sometimes I'm aware of where I feel tight. Last night I was aware I was tight in my shoulders. The floor was cold. I began to get a sense of security in the sensation of being enveloped in my own breath. . . ."

"Eugenia told me I had to practice daily for God knows how long," recalled one man. "After fourteen days nothing happened. Then I found I got energy all day from it. . . ."

Repeatedly SAGE members said that daily practice was important in maintaining the effects of the process. One woman said, "I had my migraine under control, the symptoms which used to be there almost daily were rare and mild, so I stopped doing my exercises on a trip to Los Angeles. And the migraine began to come back. I realized that it was up to me. I had to do the relaxation and breathing to prevent the symptoms. When I stopped and went back to my old habits, the symptoms came back."

It does not seem so demanding—to practice for an hour and remove symptoms that have been plaguing you for fifteen years. Still each person at SAGE seemed to have gone through the same stages: practicing daily for several months, dropping it, finding old tensions and pains re-

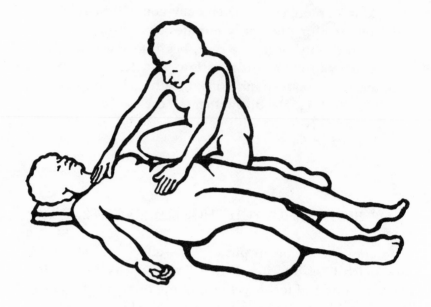

turning, then resuming practice. It often helped to work with a partner. In fact that was the way we usually began.

If you can work with a friend, or relative—taking turns doing the breathing and the guiding—you will find that this adds depth and a new dimension to the breathing.

Working with a Partner

Pick a partner you can feel at ease with. Someone who shares your sense of adventure and exploration.

Set aside the time and space: It will take two hours for both partners to have a session. You need to make certain you will be free of interruptions. Get comfortable. The breather should be in the lying posture with pillows supporting the legs under the knees. The guide should also be comfortable, sitting close beside the breather.

1. Sit comfortably or kneel beside your partner. You should be able to place one hand on your partner's

chest and the other hand on his or her abdomen—yet remain relaxed and comfortable.

2. Making contact. You may or may not know your partner at first, and so you want to sense him or her. It helps to breathe as your partner does. If you watch him or her breathing, and imitate the breath, you will begin to feel as your partner feels. Listen to the breath. See if the roll breathing comes in jerks. If so your partner may be trying to control inhalation. If the exhalation sounds jerky, he or she may be trying to control it. If your partner continues this way, you might suggest breathing through the mouth if it is easier.

Contact is very personal, and some people are afraid of it. Be sensitive to that. You might begin by saying aloud, "I'm going to place my hand on your hand. Is that all right?" Then do it. Ask yourself what *you* would like. Start with the hand contact. See if your partner's hand is cold or warm. Can you feel the rhythm of your partner's breath in the hand? Go very slowly. When you think your partner is ready to feel your hand on his or her arm, say aloud, "I'm going to place my hand on your arm so that you will know I am here as you breathe."

Your partner should keep his or her eyes closed for the most part.

3. *Listen and deepen the contact.* Now ask your partner to take some deep breaths, deep as if filling a balloon. Listen to the breaths, where they catch. Imitate them, yourself. See if you can get into a rhythm with your partner. When your partner has begun to breathe smoothly into the lower abdomen, so that the bellow rises with inhalation, you can let him or her rest for a minute or so.

Judge whether your partner is ready to feel your hand on his or her abdomen. Tell him or her what you are about to do. "I'm going to place my hand on your belly—your lower abdomen. It will help you breathe to feel my hand."

Now ask, "Breathe into my hand!"

Two things may happen: a person may force his or her abdomen against your hand as if there were a lot of muscles contracting against your hand. This isn't what you want. If your partner starts doing that, ask him or her to slow down and say that it doesn't make any difference how big the belly gets. What's important is that the belly be relaxed. This feels very different. Once you've done it for a while, you'll know the difference. You should have your hand down on the person's abdomen, just an inch above the pelvic bone. Next you want to put your hand on your partner's chest and you want him or her to breathe first into the belly, and then up into the chest. Tell your partner, "I'm going to put my hand on your chest, and I want you to breathe into my hand on your abdomen, and *then* into my hand on your chest." Be very patient. Don't tell your partner he or she is doing it right when he or she is not. Encourage your partner if he or she is. After you have been doing this a while it will seem perfectly natural to you; you'll feel more comfortable.

(Clearly the more you have practiced, the better you will become at guiding. In fact you will begin to discover many things that are not included here.)

4. *Pacing.* Now begin to pace your partner by asking him or her to follow your instructions.

"I'm going to ask you to breathe into my hand on your belly, and now into my hand on your chest, and now out. And into my hand on your belly, and into your chest, and out. . . ." Keep in mind your partner's normal pacing. Watch the rolling, wavelike motion of the body and listen to the breath so that you know it is not forced and tense.

Now guide your partner in ten long, slow, rolling

breaths. Watch closely for any changes of skin color or signs of tension or fatigue. If you see these, allow your partner to stop and breathe normally, paying attention to sensation. Then resume. Never push or force your partner beyond what he or she is willing to do. After ten cycles of roll breathes at a slow pace, ask your partner to take ten short, rapid, deep breaths. Your guidance will make it easier, but never press your own rhythm on your partner. After ten cycles of short breaths, take your partner through ten long cycles again. That is a total of thirty cycles.

5. *Be assuring.* After this cycle of thirty breaths you will want to ask your partner to stop and breathe normally.

"Feel your entire body, and when you feel like it, tell me what you feel. I will just sit here. Are there any spots that feel tense?" Your partner may feel tingling, or sore, or emotional. Help him or her by assuring that this is fine, and that any feeling that comes up is the right one.

During the next cycle of long breaths you can massage, gently but firmly, any spot that felt sore and that your partner wants massaged.

Sometimes people say, "I'm not feeling anything." They may mean that it is subtle, small. They don't count tingling hands. Ask them if they don't feel some tingling, or warmth in the arms or legs or face. Often the breathing energy brings up emotions that have been held down: People feel like crying. Reassure your partner that any feeling is important. "Let it happen, and stay with it." Don't avoid your partner's feeling. Your role is to offer your partner reassurance. You are there to listen, not to advise. You are there to offer Kleenex if needed, to encourage your partner to go on, to hold his or her hand.

Whatever happens is important, a part of a healing process. Don't force, and don't try to talk away or in any way stop your partner's feelings—even if they are uncomfortable for you.

◇ ◇ ◇

One woman in her mid-seventies used to complain loudly, "I hate breathing. It makes me cry. I've cried every day for a week."

"How do you feel after you finish crying?"

"Tired."

"And later?"

"Oh later I go out and do my shopping and I have a lot of pep." After several weeks of crying the breathing made her feel relaxed and energetic.

Do not judge a session or yourself. Try to be as open and reassuring as you can. You play the role of guide and anchor. It is wonderful to do the roll breathing with a partner for this reason: someone to hold onto. I prefer to hold a person who is crying, perhaps to cry with him or her myself. Do only what feels comfortable to you, and throughout the session keep tuned to your partner's breathing rhythm by imitating it yourself.

Sessions done with partners are often deep and powerful to an extent that is harder to achieve alone. Perhaps this happens because of the reassurance, but SAGE people had powerful experiences both together and alone.

Surely you cannot predict what will happen. At SAGE we experience every kind of emotional release we could imagine.

One woman, who had just recovered from a serious cancer operation, lay for a long time after breathing with a blissful, serene smile on her face, tears streaming out of her eyes. "I was carried back to childhood," she said. "It was so vivid. I remembered staying with my uncle, and my father, and a little dog I used to love. They promised me they would take me hunting; it was a hunting dog. I heard the ringing of church bells, and the quietness of Sunday. It brought tears of joy to my eyes." After this experience she began to do this quite often by herself.

Another woman who was working on breathing by herself felt it was the catharsis of a long period of pain, the lifting of a huge burden of unexpressed grief. "I breathed for a while, and then I went into the bathroom and looked in the mirror. I was horrified at who was looking back. I thought of all those who had loved me, and I had to laugh at what they had seen and yet loved me nonetheless. Then I went back into the living room and breathed again and began to weep. I wept excessively for two hours. I wept away a score of sorrows. One year I lost six people. My brother died, and it was so heavy it put me into the hospital. After this I found I could use the breathing any time I wanted to wipe out these pressures and sorrows. I now feel as if I am starting a new life."

One man had an experience that rocked the house with laughter. He was working with Eugenia, and we could hear him begin to laugh from the other room. He arched his back and flung his arms around her. Hollering with laughter, "Hey, I love you!" He could feel the energy surging up his spine and spinning out through his limbs, causing him to move jerkily, like a marionette. It was an unforgettable hour. After that he was never quite the same. He was a more lively, sexier, more gregarious man. He moved as if he liked his body, and of course everyone began to respond to his verve and pleasure in himself.

As you work with roll breathing the experiences change. There is no telling what you will find. It is like a gold mine, a hidden autobiography.

At SAGE we have asked people to do roll breathing once a week with a partner, and then every day at home by themselves. It is important to become familiar with the process, to feel at ease with it. Becoming easy with roll breathing is becoming at ease with oneself, and with the realities of one's very human nature.

We are emotional beings. Emotions are neither good nor

bad; they are merely emotions. In order to be human you must give yourself permission to feel and to express. Some people become tight, taut, and controlling of their feelings—but we are born humans with feelings. We could have been born snakes, or dogs, or chickens. We could have been earthworms or trout. But we were born human, and it would be a shame to waste our passage here on this earth by forbidding our own greater nature, by trying to repress, control, or avoid who we are. Who we are is the step to who we can become.

Roll breathing, if you do no other exercise, and if you do it consistently, can be a major step toward a new life. As you practice it you will find that your lungs and brain adjust to greater amounts of air. You may breathe thirty cycles and then wait. Again you may breathe thirty cycles and wait. As you get better at it, you may need to breathe longer cycles of forty or fifty breaths, and take the air in a little faster, in order to receive any benefit.

During the first months of breathing and relaxation, the first group members exclaimed with joy about the aches, pains, and other symptoms that were diminishing. Then came a time when each member felt so healthy that he or she would think the daily practice was unnecessary. After stopping for a while the symptoms always came back. People could not undo their tension rapidly after a lifetime. They needed to do deliberate relaxation exercises each day. "It's miraculous almost," said one woman. "My lower back is now well. It was so bad from age sixty-five to seventy-four, I wore a heavy girdle. Now I don't. I haven't had it on this year."

After a year and a half away from frequent SAGE meetings the members of the first group were still practicing—and each person had developed a daily routine. The roll breathing is a staple exercise—like bread. It works for relaxation, whether shallow or deep. Relaxation is essential before you move your body or your mind. You cannot safely and beneficially do any physical exercise without first getting deeply relaxed.

One group member looked back on her two and a half years doing breathing and working with SAGE. She said that its biggest benefit was ultimate self-reliance. "I don't have a rigid routine anymore: I listen to my feelings, the way my body feels. I know that I am responsible for how I feel, and that I have the capability for changing how I feel. I feel responsible for myself now, and for my body. I am finally autonomous."

If you learn that you can change your own physical feelings, rid yourself of symptoms, change your feelings so that you feel more optimistic about life, and expand your own awareness, you have taken control of a great deal in living that most people believe depends on others— parents, doctors, or priests. "I am now amazed, at how much I can do for myself."

IF YOU ONLY HAVE TIME FOR ONE EXERCISE OUT OF THIS ENTIRE BOOK—UNLESS YOU ARE PHYSICALLY AND EMOTIONALLY RELAXED—TRY THE ROLL BREATHING. It will open all kinds of doors for you.

Breathing for Specific Healing.

Your breathing is as potent as muscle relaxants and pain killers. Once you have learned to breathe into the abdomen and can use this to relax yourself, you can begin to direct the attention of your breath. It is best to do this lying down, in your most relaxed position, but it can be done sitting, too.

Close your eyes.

Now feel just below the navel—you can place your hand there if you don't feel it. Just let your body settle and feel that place below the navel. Take a deep breath and let it out. Now find a relaxed breathing rhythm and breathe into that place.

When you have taken about twenty breaths: Imagine that there is a funnel, an opening in the top of your head, and as you breathe, the air comes down this funnel through your torso and into your belly.

When you breathe out, your exhaled breath goes through the legs, arms and hands, and then your chest, and out the top of your head.

Now open your hands and feel the breath flowing into your hands.

Become aware of the sensations in your hands. Are they cold? Are they warm? Are they prickling or pulsating? Now imagine breathing into your hands.

Now imagine that the air you inhale is a beautiful color. With your eyes closed you may see the color permeating your body as you breathe in. Sense that color coming into your hands.

Now focus on your body and see if you feel any sore or tight spots. If you can have such a spot—and can reach it—place your hand on it. Now just breathe into your belly. Relax and focus your attention on the spot where your hand is. Begin to sense the color and the feeling in your hand. Let a word come into your mind.

Now breathe directly into the spot that feels sore—even if you cannot reach it with your hand. Breathe the color into it. And do this several times. If your mind wanders, that is all right. Just gently bring yourself back: Breathe the color into the spot that feels sore.

Most people are very skeptical about an exercise like this, especially the first time. It takes some practice to become aware of the color and to be able to focus one's breath on a sore place.

"I don't believe in this stuff," said one woman. "I absolutely don't, but I had such a kink in my neck. I could see this nodule, and I couldn't turn my head. So I did what you told me. I wasn't sure I was breathing right. I put my hands up there and they were icy cold. And when you said to think about a word, I thought a word 'gone.' And it's gone! That pain was something fierce and it's gone!"

A woman said later, "I see people running to the doctors, or reaching for a pill every time they have a pain—and I realize how much I have changed. I used to be that way. And it didn't even help me. Now I breathe."

5 ❧ SELF-IMAGES

It is interesting that so few people expect fun after age sixty. Visitors sometimes came to a SAGE session and gawked. They were astonished to find old people who danced, moved with grace, embraced with affection, were limber and, above all, who laughed and laughed. Why is it we are supposed to become decrepit and grouchy and stiff when we get old? Why couldn't we become sensual, graceful, and gracious instead?

At SAGE and throughout the country it is happening. It is happening through exercise, through contact of people within each group, through relaxation, movement, and largely through a change in attitude.

One SAGE member was reminiscing about an afternoon that showed us how little playfulness is expected of older people. "About sixteen of us were stretched out on the floor of the large living room in two rows—eight pairs of bare feet meeting eight other pairs of bare feet in the center. What for? Why "to communicate" using our feet, of course. Doesn't everybody do that? Well right in the middle of our exercise the doorbell rang. A delivery man. His eyes swept over that room full of wall-to-wall people, mostly gray-haired, feet in the air, pushing, kicking, caressing, tickling. I tell you, the look on his face was something I'll treasure forever: shock, amazement, the temptation to run. We all burst out laughing: a room full of senior citizens with feet in the air, laughing our heads off. The delivery man was clearly appalled and surprised to see a bunch of nice old people wriggling around on the floor in such an undignified way. When they all looked at him and burst out laughing, he must have been certain he was in a "nut house."

I cannot read what was in the delivery man's mind, but I do know that in my thirties I had very stringent expectations of adulthood—dignity and sobriety. I thought it was belittling for adults to go in for "nursery school games," and I held onto my self-consciousness like armor. I'm often surprised at my own attitudes and don't realize I have negative expectations until one pops out. At SAGE we spent quite a lot of time asking ourselves what we expected in old age. What did our participants think about being old? This is what some of them said:

"When I arrived at the first meeting and found myself faced with a group of old women (98 percent women) and men, my feeling was, 'What am I doing among all these old people? I don't belong here—not yet—not ever.' I almost defected, but came back out of curiosity. Becoming more involved helped me overcome one more prejudice: I realized that old people were essentially people with varied dimensions. . . ."

"Being put in the category of an older person was a very negative experience. I was used to being with younger people and this was difficult."

"There were twenty-three of us—only three men. I hate being around a lot of older women. That's what makes me hate being an old woman."

When my mother was seventy-five she told me, "I never

thought of myself as growing old. In fact I never think of myself as old until I look in a mirror, or feel an ailment . . . then I'm surprised. . . ."

A good-looking psychiatrist in a core group commented, "I look in the mirror and see frown marks and wrinkles. My hair is gradually turning from gray to white. It isn't as if I dislike what I see. I just wouldn't mind looking in the mirror and finding my reflection the way it was when I was forty, or thirty, or twenty. . . ."

"Now, if I look in the mirror and see any signs of age it's very disturbing."

"I haven't accepted it, either. I hate it. My body and my mind and the work I can do do not match what I see in the mirror."

"I cannot separate my feelings from my resentment at having extra burdens placed upon me . . . the responsibility of a handicapped husband who is ten years older than me. . . ."

As we began to share our attitudes about age, we also wondered where our attitudes would show up physically. "Where do you feel these things in your body?" Eugenia would ask.

One spicy woman felt age in her shoulders, as if she had been carrying the world there. Another said she felt it was very difficult to breathe, and that her respiratory illness represented her age. One person felt it in his diaphragm, another in her stomach. I feel it in my eyes, farsighted and unfocused.

Where do you feel age in your body?

Close your eyes and feel the places.

As we talked about our feelings toward aging, we also discovered how we limited ourselves. "The other day I was thinking of scrubbing my kitchen floor. But the brainwashing about being older was in me so strongly that I didn't. It *wasn't* that I *couldn't* scrub it. It was just that I accepted a false limitation. . . ."

"It's like thinking I should retire just because I'm sixty-eight. Why my father didn't retire from being a dentist until he was eighty-three, and that was because he wanted to. . . ."

"There are places I don't go because I feel they don't want old people around. But I don't really know that that's so. I just have that in my mind."

"I'm sixty-eight now, and two years ago I had pretty much given up hoping that there would ever be a man in my life again. Then last year I had the most wonderful relationship I have ever had. It's over now, and I wonder . . ."

"I've definitely given up on men. I wish I could hope for something to happen . . . but I don't."

"I've even stopped hoping I would make new friends. I'm eighty-three. Until I came here I didn't think people liked me or would talk to me, because I was older."

"I don't think I've tried to make friends, really, in the last few years. I always heard people say that it's harder to make new friends when you are older, so I think I stopped trying."

"I know I don't hope for much with younger people any more," said another. "I know I won't have the energy to keep up."

"I can outdo most younger people," said a woman of seventy-three. "I used to think I couldn't. But around here I work a longer day and I don't get as tired as they do. They're always complaining."

Self-imposed Limitations

Write a list. Make it as comprehensive as you can. Include: the kinds of clothes and foods you buy or don't buy because you think you shouldn't; places you avoid because you feel unwanted or unsafe; situations that you could actually handle, but which you avoid on the basis of being too old—such as scrubbing a floor, painting a wall, sitting in the sun without sunglasses, climbing hills or stairs, starting a new career, enrolling in college or high school, learning to knit, buying a pet, traveling alone. Think of things you *think* you can't do. Inspect your reasons: See if they are rationalizations. Perhaps age is not the real limitation.

◇ ◇ ◇

On one of our introspective afternoons Eugenia said, "I read where the oldest person in the world just died, at 167. I'd like you to think that you could live to be 167."

Living to 167

Try it yourself. You can always refuse the gift. But you might accept it provisionally. What would make that next hundred years truly wonderful for you? Remember, if you have another hundred years to live you are quite young now, even if you are eighty. And there are people such as the Akbhasians who do live to 130 and even into their 150s. For them 60 is not even middle-aged by our standards. Try thinking about this.

◇ ◇ ◇

When Eugenia asked this question, members of the SAGE group said:
"I suddenly got very relaxed."
"I suddenly felt very young."
"I felt burdened with so much time. I didn't know what I'd do with it."
"God—I'll be in project SAGE for 80 years!"
Everywhere we pry, we find hidden attitudes about aging. One woman in her early seventies had gone through the death of her husband when she first came to SAGE,

and after she recovered and felt more sprightly all her friends remarked on how young she looked.

"Why is young so good?" she would snap. "Whenever anyone wants to say anything complimentary to me, they say, 'Oh, you look young,' or 'You seem so young.' I wish they would say something else." Her indignation revealed her sense that she had almost fallen into our national trap, the acceptance that to be young is to be wanted, approved, admired, cherished, to be considered beautiful and strong; but to be old is none of that.

How many times do we compliment someone by saying they look younger? How often do we remark sadly of someone, "He has certainly aged!"

Often we equate with youth an appearance that really means health and relaxation. Lack of wrinkles suggest relaxed, unstressed faces, with limber movements and good cheer. A combination of factors produces wrinkles, sagging muscles, depression, and white hair. Some are genetic. You will notice that many Asians have unlined faces and dark hair into advanced age. Fair-skinned people may accumulate more visible blemishes, but many of these American wrinkles come from overexposure to the sun and from tension in response to stress and from poor diet. Some of the visible aspects of age come from sagging muscles due to lack of exercise. A bent-over posture and dragging walk also reflect response to stress. Our muscles reflect disease and unhappiness. Excepting for some genetic determinants of skin and hair most of the visible attributes of age are due to ways of living and feeling—not to age.

On one of our many explorations of hidden attitudes at SAGE we massaged each other's hands. We looked carefully at the hands we were massaging and felt them. Afterward we talked about what we had discovered. One woman said, "My partner's hands seemed so young. They weren't discolored or marked, and they felt strong."

Once again we experienced the hidden attitude: Unmarked, strong hands belong to the young, not the old.

Because this is so prevalent, and so insidious, Eugenia asked us to do another exercise.

Old Hands

You can do it with a friend. Massage the hands of a friend your own age. Afterward *look your partner in the eye* and let him or her know that you are paying a compliment when you say, "I notice that your hands are old because they are veined . . . or . . ."

That was one of the most exciting exercises we tried because each of us felt a little scared at the beginning. We were about to say something forbidden, the opposite of what most of us had learned. We were about to say something that was not socially acceptable, or habitual. Because it seemed a little threatening at the start the discoveries were particularly important to us.

This is what people said:

"I knew my partner's hands were old because I found somebody very graceful in them, and bordering on fragile."

"I got the feeling of somebody who had worked a lot and who is very happy about it."

"I felt all that strength and experience."

"Would you trade all that strength and experience you've acquired in aging to be young again?"

The group answered loudly, "NO!"

"I think," remarked a woman in her mid-seventies, "in our culture, where age does not have any positive connotation, it's only in the last several years I feel a little more comfortable with it. What helped me was to be in a women's consciousness-raising group that I started for women over fifty. We kept supporting each other by saying that it is good to be fifty or older. That took a lot of the charge out of the feeling of being ashamed of being older. I remember I asked a good friend of mine her brother's age and she responded angrily, 'We don't ask those questions in my family!' I said, 'I remember how I felt a few years ago. I felt that same way about questions about my age, but I don't feel that way any more.' Still I am constantly trying to work with my feelings about age because I'm constantly caught up in feelings that are negative."

We all get caught up in those feelings because they surround us. They are part of our culture. Our biggest weapon for overcoming them is to bring them out in the open and look at them. This is especially hard when we have learned to feel ashamed and not to talk about such things. We found at SAGE that it is easier to talk in the context of a structured exercise.

Forbidden Remarks

Write down the ten things you would not say to another person regarding his age. ("I think you look older than your age. I think you dress like an old woman. Your memory is failing. You seem rigid.") Ask a friend to do the same thing and share your lists with each other.

◇ ◇ ◇

At SAGE the responses to this sharing varied. Eugenia recalled trying on an old blouse that her husband especially liked, but the sleeves no longer fit because her arms had grown heavier with age. Her husband noticed, implying that her arms should have been the same at forty as they were at twenty-nine.

A beautiful and elegant member of the group responded that she had just made herself a new pair of slacks and was trying them on for her husband. Her husband said, "Your tummy sticks out." She said, "I got so angry. At my age, without a girdle, my tummy *can* stick out! I found myself very angry that he should be expecting me to look the way I did when I was thirty-seven or thirty-eight years old."

"Oh, men! My husband and brother-in-law both come out with the same thing. In their mind's eye we still look the same as when they first met us, and that's the way we're supposed to stay."

"I know, this country is so youth oriented you can't grow old gracefully, even if you want to. I looked in the mirror about a week or two ago and noticed that my eyelashes are gone. There are only tiny little ones left. It gave me a start. Not that it's so important, but my eyes have always been my best feature."

As the discussion continued we discovered that we were victimizing ourselves and setting a negative example for our children. Some of us were asking the same kinds of questions at forty as others asked at sixty or seventy. Were our skins too wrinkled to be attractive any more? Were our hands old and veined? Would our tummies stick out too far? Would we still have sex appeal and be desirable in another year? Men and women both wondered whether anyone would consider them attractive. Would anyone want to be close to us?

Look what was happening! We were a bunch of relatively healthy and happy people in a sunny living room, worrying about our wrinkles and our appeal. At that very moment we were living our lives. We realized that we were struggling for the right to be ourselves. What a ridiculous struggle! How can we be anything *but* ourselves? Still we spend most of our lives trying to be something else, trying to be younger, prettier, stronger, more agreeable, more reliable, fitting someone else's idea of who we are. We victimized ourselves and blamed our age.

"I think we have to be very careful not to suffer from self-inflicted wounds. I find young people very delightful, for example. But I don't find them looking down at me. I'll get smiles from young girls sometimes, and I know it's on account of my gray hair. But I wouldn't misinterpret that. I wouldn't go out of my way to say someone is looking at me as a doddering old fool, because it isn't true."

One eighty-year-old woman said, "It's also important to me that you young people are willing to spend time with us. It's a feeling that we're not discarded. That we're contributing to your understanding, and we have some value to you. . . ."

"Yes. I like being with young people and not having them feel, 'You're just an old lady and don't understand us.' "

In the course of the discussion it turned out that several people found their attitudes changing because of their opportunity to discuss them. Working together had revealed new images, a more positive picture of aging and the possibilities for us as we grew older. A psychiatrist remarked that SAGE was following a trend in modern psychology, of turning inward, and using it to help improve human interactions.

"Well it's changed my self-image. I have more energy and openness to things."

"I see the humor in situations more: I'm looser."

"As the oldest one here I'm surprised that the body gets included in everything. It's been difficult for me. I never thought much about my body or my feelings before."

The process of group discussion, of sharing, at SAGE is a process of ever-greater directness and frankness. Gradually each group began to reveal all the little attitudes about aging that we had hidden before. Without sharing them and airing them out we might go on pretending that they didn't exist in our minds, or that hidden attitudes weren't influencing our actions and our lives. Once we began to learn that other people in the group shared our worst shames and fears, it took the power out of those habitual attitudes. Whenever a SAGE group would meet it would reveal almost every possible feeling, background, fantasy, and thought that you might find on earth. At some time in each of our lives we have been murderers at heart, panderers, prostitutes, furies, bribers, molesters, gunmen, and cowboys. We have all entertained many "wicked" thoughts as well as multitudes of "good" ones. We are all human. And so within each group we simply have to forgive and accept the fact that humans have a negative as well as a positive side to their personalities.

Having lived a long life makes the acceptance and forgiveness possible. We may have hidden our thoughts. We may have repressed our feelings. But they have tinted our being.

When a group begins to accept this broad human frailty, then it is easier to express feelings and to talk to each other frankly.

As you comb through your own attitudes about aging, look at your roles and postures: shyness, motherliness, gruff okayness. How often do you count yourself out of life situations on account of your age? One elegant woman of seventy-three was so shy and reticent in her group that she never could accept a favor. If someone wanted to drive her to a meeting, she would find it hard to accept. She gave favors easily, but could not receive. "There are so many demanding old people who are disliked by younger people for that," she said. "I don't want to be like that." But, in fact, her inability to accept a favor was not really based on age, although she said, "I don't think enough of myself. That is I have self-esteem but some sort of inferiority complex, too. The world is so youth-oriented these days." As she later began to see, age was merely accentuating a problem that has been with her all her life.

Do you do that? Do you refuse situations—because of your age—when you have been shy about them all your life? Can you receive as well as give?

As you have grown older have you become more like what you always were? Sometimes your perspective is clarified by visualizing who you were. We did this at SAGE in the form of guided fantasy.

Who Were You?

1. Make time: an hour when you will not be interrupted. Get very comfortable, lying down with no tight clothes.

2. Tape-record the following narrative; adapting it to yourself. Or ask a friend or relative to read it to you slowly.

3. NARRATIVE: "Take a few deep breaths, relaxing as you exhale. Exhale all your worries, concerns, thoughts.

"Now, I'd like you to go back in time to when you were fifty years old. Who were the people in your life then? If you were working, what kinds of things were you doing? See yourself clearly. See your arms, legs, body, and face. Ask yourself: How do I feel about that picture?

"Go back another fifteen years, to the time when you were thirty-five. Who were the people you lived with? What was life like for you then? What did you look like? How did you feel? Get a picture of yourself at that age.

"If your pictures go out of focus, pay attention to your breathing. Breathing deeply will keep you centered.

"Now go back to age twenty-five. What was your life like then, and what were your daily activities? Who were the important people in your life? How did your life feel to you?

"Now go back to graduation from high school. Can you see your school building? Teachers? Classmates? What was life like for you then?

"Now see if you can go way back. Can you remember what it was like to be very small, age two, three, four? See if you can recall being smaller than your parents. Can you see them as they were when you were a tiny child? What did you feel like at that age? What did it feel like to be small and helpless?"

4. When you have seen and felt these images, begin to take a deep breath and stretch, and as you stretch take all of yourself in, from earliest childhood to the present moment.

When we first did this fantasy together, one SAGE lady laughed until tears came into her eyes. She had been married twice, and each time was very difficult. "I was seeing how I used to make myself over to please my husband. Sometimes I imagine I want to be twenty or thirty again, but when I look at the pictures I realize I wouldn't go through that again for anything."

"I haven't changed. I am aghast how little I've changed. I was a stubborn baby. I'm just that stubborn now."

"I wish I could have told myself how things would go. I might not have been so frightened and so worried all the time."

Many people wished they could have told their young selves something that would have made the process of growing up less harsh, less insecure and frightening. With that suggestion we developed another fantasy in which people could give their young selves some solace. It was a powerful experience. If you would like to experience it for yourself, once again you may want to ask a friend to read you the narrative, or you can tape-record it and listen.

Advice for Your Child-Self

Make sure you will not be interrupted by phones or people for an hour. Make yourself very comfortable, lying down.

1. Focus on your breathing. Allow your jaw to relax, your mouth to fall open, and breathe deeply. Close your eyes.

2. Begin a slow, easy breathing pattern. Inhale to a count of four. Hold. Then exhale slowly. To a count of eight. Let the breath come in. Do this a number of times.

3. NARRATIVE: "As you exhale, let all your tension leave. Let your concerns and thoughts go out with your breath. As you relax deeply, begin imagining a house that you lived in when you were around twelve years old. See yourself walking toward the front door. Go inside the house and walk around. Now open the door and walk outside. There is a path through a garden. Walk down the path and head toward your favorite tree. As you approach your favorite tree, your mature self will see your twelve-year-old self walking toward you. You see yourself at age twelve. Your twelve-year-old self can see you as you are now. As your child-self comes toward you, what help can you offer? Is there any advice you could give? What would you have said to your twelve-year-old self if you had met him or her on the path? Could you say something that would have made adolescence and youth easier, or more pleasurable?

"Speak to your twelve-year-old self. (Allow plenty of silent time for this.)

"Slowly say good-bye, and turn around. Walk toward the house, and go inside. As you enter the house, begin to let go of the past, becoming aware of yourself as you are now."

4. Begin to wiggle your toes and fingers. Move your feet and your hands. Move your legs and become aware of your surroundings. Slowly open your eyes in the present.

◇ ◇ ◇

As we did this on a chilly afternoon in 1977, we returned from the sounds of our childhood to the sounds of the hotel we were working in, and the clatter of the nearby restaurant. Most of us had been far away. One woman was sobbing quietly. Another sat up, wiping her eyes.

"If only I could have told myself that I was all right—not to have been so scared and ashamed, not to think everyone in the world was better than me."

"I was so timid," said a man, "so afraid of being rejected. If I could have seen myself now I wouldn't have believed it. It would have given me heart to do better."

"I would have said to myself, 'You don't have to be perfect.' In my family we kids had to be perfect. We had to do everything right."

"I saw myself when I was nine years old. I had just read a fifteenth-century novel, a romance in which a message was scratched on glass. So I took my mother's diamond ring and scratched my name on the window, thinking she'd be pleased. But all she could do was rant about how expensive it would be to replace the glass and how it ruined the value of the house. I wanted to say, 'Oh, I'm good all the time; can't I do *anything* bad?' "

As one member of the group described reliving the death of his father, we all realized that it would have meant a lot to our young selves to have seen ourselves fifty or sixty years later. It would have been reassuring. We also realized that we were still suffering from events that had traumatized us when we were nine, ten, twelve. We were not living wholly in the present, for we were gripped by the past, those painful yet dear anchors of our identity. They hurt, and they told us who we were. Why did we go over and over the most painful events? Why did we hold them so dear? The discussion began to make us ask some questions about our identities, about who we were at that moment.

We did an exercise that many SAGE groups have found fulfilling. This exercise requires only a few sheets of paper, a pen or pencil, and time to contemplate.

Who Am I?

Make certain that you will not be interrupted. Have paper and pen at hand. At the top of the page write "WHO AM I?"

Take as long a time as you wish to answer. When you have finished, write the question again.

Do this *ten* times. You may find that you need to take several days or even a couple of weeks to finish answering ten times: "WHO AM I?"

When you have answered the question ten times to your own satisfaction, write the date at the top of each sheet and put your answers away in a drawer or notebook for six months. In another six months you may want to repeat the exercise.

When SAGE members answered the questions again after six months, many of them found that they had changed and were answering differently than at first. The question "WHO AM I?" is a simple one at first sight, but it turns out to become more involved and complex as you think about it.

The answer to this question is a reflection of all your thoughts, hopes, fears, the material image of your history, your family, your reactions to living, loves and hates, your special ruts and difficulties, and your weaknesses and strengths. Many of these facets of yourself are subtle and inward. Some are hard to perceive. But many of your qualities, of who you are, can be seen by anybody looking freely at you. That person can see not only what you want to show, what you would like to be, but all those other aspects of yourself that you hide. They are written in the expression of your eyes and mouth, the lines on your face, in the way you carry yourself, your walk, your way of breathing. Your innermost secrets actually show in your posture and bodily ailments. A person does not need to be psychic to look at you and tell you about yourself after a few glances.

After all we do not come fully formed into this world, with only some genetic tendencies. You may have inherited fine, dry skin and straight brown hair, but you didn't inherit the way you grit your teeth or hunch your shoulders.

The formative years of childhood do not create us: We also create ourselves. We play an important part in the drama of self-formation. The events, and our reactions to them, slowly become part of our build, our walk, our habits, our thoughts, our structure. For instance if you hold your breath under tension as a child and continually restrict your breathing so as not to cry or explode, you may find that you become susceptible to bronchitis, colds, pneumonia, and respiratory illnesses. You may be controlling your breathing to hold onto feelings of grief or anger at adolescence, but the chances are that you are not aware of this habit as it persists into early adulthood. At forty-five or fifty-five you suddenly discover that your respiratory volume is not very good. You cannot inhale and exhale as much air as you should. Moreover you notice that your shoulders hunch forward as if protecting your chest. You were not born that way. You didn't inherit hunched shoulders genetically—even if your parents had the same posture. You may have copied them. In any event you slowly, imperceptibly, produced them.

If you had a hard time expressing anger or grief as a child, it is likely that you will have a hard time expressing these emotions as an adult.

The fact that the habit of withholding feeling should show in your body is an example of our wholeness, of the fact that feelings and body are part of the same whole. Ken Dychtwald expressed it well. "It is a manifestation of the unity of body, mind, and spirit. Our feelings and our flesh and our memories and dreams are somehow stuck together, fit together. When I'm working with a person's body, it's clear to me that I'm not just working with a physical structure that has limbs and moves a certain way. I'm working with a body that *is* the person. The body is the creation of this person, the expression of this person. The body has to be seen as a whole, because that is how it is created."

To some people this is a frightening concept, for it means that whatever we think and feel is visible. It shows materially in our bodies. Our negative attitudes and habits imbued themselves in our flesh. On the other hand if we are the creators of our bodies, we can change them. We can change our habits, thoughts, feelings, and as this happens our bodies also change. For instance supposing we began to move more, walk, bend, and become less sedentary. Our breathing would change. Our muscles would develop tone. We would develop more endurance and feel more integrated and lively. Our sense of physical well-being would manifest itself visibly, and we would seem more pert and cheerful, as well. Others would respond more positively to us, and we, in turn, would have a better self-image.

Books describing this very process have been written in recent years, and several on this topic by Stanley Keleman, Bruno Geba, and Kenneth Dychtwald are listed in the bibliography.

6 ❦ SELF-IMAGE AND MASSAGE

Self-images change from deep inside rather than from reason, intellect, or will. Self-images change slowly, as we begin to feel differently in our bodies, to breathe differently, and smell and taste differently, see differently, and especially to feel our feelings. Perhaps our bodies always remember the basic nourishment we received from our parents when we were infants, being held and touched. These were our earliest communications of love and validity, and we never stop needing them. In other parts of the world adults continue to touch and reassure each other in ways that most Americans don't. In Italy, France, India, and other countries grown men or grown women may walk with their arms around each other, innocently and fondly. They embrace without embarrassment, stroke each other, and show a certain aliveness and contentment in their faces.

At SAGE we began to find out how powerful and how positive it was to touch each other. We began very gradually and tentatively, since many of the people in groups felt like this:

"I never like people to touch me unless they are members of my family. I never did until I came here. Now I am less embarrassed—I even enjoy being hugged. . . ."

"I hate people putting their hands all over me. . . ."

"In my family it was considered bad taste."

"In my family it just wasn't done. And you didn't touch yourself. That was considered dirty."

Many of us have somehow absorbed the message that our bodies were bad and we should neither explore nor enjoy them. This meant we had never learned even the most rudimentary ways of massaging away aches and pains for ourselves. We hadn't touched our own bodies enough to have a tactile map of our muscles and bones. This prohibition was a key to a negative self-image for many people. As we talked about the possibility of massage, members of the group frankly expressed their feelings:

"I don't want to take off my clothes. My body isn't pretty any more."

"It's one thing when you are young. But later on . . . besides I've had a mastectomy."

"I'm too fat. I've always been overweight. . . ."

"My legs are skinny."

As we went around the room everyone felt ashamed. Could we learn to accept wrinkles, baggy skin, scars from operations, fat hips and tummies, gnarled toes? Was it true that older bodies were ugly? What would it be like to see each other without clothes? We all seemed to fear going naked. By age fourteen I undressed in a clothes closet at boarding school because I thought it was wrong for my roommates to see my naked body. If other people found as many faults with my body as I did, they would rather not look at it. In any room full of good-looking people, most people probably think that their bodies are not acceptable.

Massage implied that people might see your body. It implied getting touched.

"I've never been massaged at all. I'm seventy-four and I

never was sick or anything, so nobody ever massaged me. . . ."

"Somehow I feel all right about *giving* massage, but I *don't* like to *receive* it."

"The only people who ever gave me a massage were men—lovers."

"I always thought of massage as the kind of thing you did before you made love. It seemed too personal, too involved with sex. . . ."

"I never liked my body, and so I never undressed in front of anyone, not even my husband . . . and I'm seventy-six."

"I'm thirty-two and I feel a lot like you do. I'm self-conscious about my flaws . . . my breasts are too big. . . ."

We all had feelings of apprehension, fear, and excitement—as if we were about to break through an important taboo and discover something. As the year progressed, a visiting massage teacher would arrive on Wednesday mornings when no other activities were scheduled. She would set up a table in front of the fireplace. One by one each member of the first group overcame their objections. At their own pace they came to be massaged and began to enjoy the stretched-out, relaxed feeling. As we started to work on one another we discovered to our astonishment that *everyone* had a lovely body. Nobody walked around naked in my family home, so I hadn't seen older bodies— ever. I was as surprised as anyone. People with older bodies were *not* ugly! Many of them had baby skin. Their bodies felt good. Women who had lost breasts simply had transparent skin, flatness, and sometimes a scar. It was not the unimaginable mutilation we expected. The same thing was true of a colostomy. It was all exaggerated in our minds. Moreover as people relaxed and enjoyed their massage, they became lovelier, pinker, and wrinkles vanished. Lines of tension eased away. They began to look really vital and beautiful.

They would get up after a massage refreshed and look at themselves in the mirror with sparkling eyes, pleased. In a subsequent core group we began our massage sessions with six tables in a single room. We started out in robes and towels, intending to begin with shoulder massage. Soon the coverings seemed unnecessary. It didn't seem important to hide our bodies from each other. Perhaps we no longer cared how we looked, because we *felt* so differently about ourselves. From then on the group was never the same—it was warmer, more candid, happier.

"I feel like we have let down barriers," one woman summed it up. "We trust each other. That lets me be more relaxed."

If you would like to change your self-image, and also ease away aches and pains, start with the appearance and feeling of your own body. Before you begin any physical movement, you need to prepare your mind and feelings. The following exercises were extremely helpful at SAGE.

What Is a Human Body?

Set aside a morning or afternoon without interruptions. Take the phone off the hook. Make sure you are in a warm room. You may want to use a bathroom. Wear a robe that opens easily, and be certain that you have enough light.

1. Stand in front of a long mirror, naked. You are a person from outer space. You have never seen a human body before. You don't know what it is for. Move your hand. You have never seen a hand move before. You don't know what *causes* it to move. You may move your arm and head and attempt to see what causes it to move. If you touch the skin it becomes pink. What remarkable thing is happening beneath your skin? What happened behind your eyes? Where does the moisture come from in your mouth? Examine this strange, miraculous form as if you had never seen one in your life.

When you have seen the strange miracle—that a creature from outer space would see if it watched you—then take a break. Get a piece of blank paper and a pen or pencil.

2. Now close your eyes and breathe deeply for a few moments. Take off your robe and look in the mirror. Draw yourself as you see yourself. Don't expect to be Rembrandt. It doesn't matter whether you can "draw" or not. Just note down some of what you see. Do you see big hips and small shoulders? A big stomach and tiny hips? Are the legs thin or heavy? Are they straight or bowed? Is the chest caved in or thrust out? Do you stick your neck out and carry your chin forward? Do you hunch your back? Do you walk leaning back as if retreating?

What does your face show? What do the wrinkles show: merriness, kindliness, laughter, grimaces of tension, anxiety, worry, tenderness? Your wrinkles tell a story of feelings, of muscle movements, tensions and relaxations. What is the story they tell you?

Look at your feet: What kind of feet are they? Are they sturdy, and do they carry you well? Are they slender? Are the toes short or long? How is your arch—high or flat-footed?

What do your hands say? Have they worked hard? Are they strong, gentle, fragile, tender, heavy, child-like, delicate . . . ?

What does your pelvic area say? Are you sexual or asexual? Are you tilted forward or back? Is this part of your body as well-developed as your arms? your chest?

If you looked at yourself from the waist up, and from the waist down, would you see a great difference in the top and bottom of you? Is one part heavier or better developed?

Look at yourself for ten minutes and then write some notes to yourself about what you saw.

◇ ◇ ◇

This is what some SAGE members saw in themselves:

"I saw a lean and hairy old man—shoulders a little small, but not bad looking. Strong arms. I have done a lot of work with those arms and hands. I looked at myself and realized I'm not such a dismal old guy. . . ."

"I couldn't stop thinking about how I *should* look, I mean, I don't want that big stomach. My skin is nice."

"I thought I wasn't going to be able to stand looking at myself in the mirror. I put it off and put it off. I just didn't want to see myself. I don't know where I got the idea I was deformed or something. I looked, and I said to myself, 'That's me.' I was surprised. I didn't look awful. A little too much lard on the thighs. . . ."

When we asked people what mood they felt before they looked in the mirror, some of them said they had been quite relaxed, others fearful, anxious, or resentful. As you did this exercise, what you saw was reflected in the mirror, but *how you saw it* depended upon your mood, your thoughts, and your subtle inner feelings. Anyone who looks at you sees you through their own feelings, prejudices, and conditioning. You also look at yourself that way. We all perceive through eyes of judgment or flattery, happiness or anger—distortion lenses that often are adjusted to negative feelings. The reason for seeing through negative feelings very often is that we are generally in a state of some tension. This also changes our bodies. Tension means that our muscles are slightly contracted, our bodies pulled in, our faces more lined and taut.

You would look different if you were exceedingly relaxed. Try it.

One way to relax yourself before you look at yourself in the mirror is by a kind of massage that you can give yourself. First, however, you will need to tune your hands.

We are encased in a physical body and skin, but our energies extend way beyond our skins. Most people can feel a layer of warmth around the skin, a thermal layer. We know that other energies are radiating from our bodies as well. If you put your hand near the aerial of your radio or television, the sound and picture become stronger. Bioelectric fields surround us on earth, and we generate fields, too. Some people see these fields in the form of radiant auras around the body, like a giant transparent eggshell of light. Saints have been pictured with halos, radiant energies around the head. Saint or not, everyone has this kind of radiance, or aura. When a person comes close, he or she enters your field. When you move near someone, you enter that person's field. By paying attention to the sensations between the palms of your hands you can begin to learn how to feel those energy fields.

Tuning Your Hands

Sit comfortably and take several deep breaths, following the breath with your attention. After you feel deeply relaxed, begin paying attention to the feelings in your hands.

1. Rub your hands together until they are warm and tingling.

2. Move them about two inches apart and hold them parallel. Put all your attention on your palms of your hands and inner surfaces of your fingers.

3. Imagine that the air between your hands is growing thick, maybe even gelatinous.

4. Move your hand slightly—like an accordion, closer, farther. You may feel a magnetic pull between them.

5. Pay attention to what you feel: You may feel heat. It may seem that there is a density between your hands. You can stretch it by pulling your hands apart. You may begin to feel prickling, tingling.

As you practice, you will begin to feel great sensitivity in the inner surfaces of your hands, as if your skin were like radar.

6. When your hands begin to feel sensitive, hold

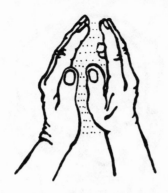

your palms over your face and close your eyes. Do your hands feel anything? Does your face feel anything? Try your shoulders, your legs, your chest.

◇ ◇ ◇

If you do not feel much of anything at first, you are normal. It takes practice. Do this exercise every day. You can do it lying in bed. You will surprise yourself by feeling very sensitively with your hands. You will find that you can feel other people without actually touching their skin.

Tune your hands this way before you start a massage. Of course you will want to be sure you are not going to be interrupted, and that your room is quiet and warm. If possible do your self-massage in a place where you can comfortably leave your upper body nude.

Self-Massage: Face, Neck, Shoulders

You will now become both the masseur and the person being massaged. Treat your body like someone you love. Tune your hands, and hold them over your face—feeling the shape of the energy from your face.

1. Close your eyes: Place two forefingers beside the bridge of your nose, on either side. Make small, firm circles down the sides of the nose. Feel for the place where your cheekbones begin. Firmly press your cheekbones, feeling the structure of your skull. Press-

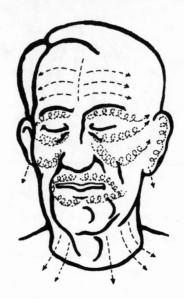

ing on the cheekbones, near the nose, will help to clear your sinuses.

2. Make firm circles along the cheek bones to the jaw muscle. To find the jaw muscle, open and close your mouth. Feel the "hinge" and firmly, slowly, massage that muscle. Let your mouth hang open.

3. Bring your forefingers under your nose and press. Now firmly and slowly begin to massage your gums through your upper lip, working toward the ears. Feel your gums with your finger. Now switch and feel the fingers with your gums.

When you have massaged your upper gums, do the lower gums the same way. Make slow firm circles, starting in the center and working toward the ears. Massaging the gums will help them stay healthy. People's gums tend to recede as they get older, and massage helps them to regain tone. Moreover people with dentures say that their dentures fit better when they do this gum massage.

4. Massage gently under the chin and around the cheeks.

5. To massage around the eyes always begin at the bridge of the nose and work toward your temples.

Never press on your eyelids. Make firm, slow circles with your fingers on the bony orbit around your eyes, starting at the bridge of your nose and working outward. Do the lower orbit, then do the upper orbit. Massage them three times. People say that this refreshes their eyes, and that they see better afterward.

6. Place your fingers or your palms together in the middle of your forehead, and pull your forehead toward your temples as if you were stretching taffy. Do this several times and it will take the tension out of your forehead.

7. Don't forget your ears. We expect to hear acutely, yet who among us does anything to help the circulation in our ears? Grab each ear at the top. Use two fingers on each ear, pulling and stretching the rim of your ears in a circular motion, moving down toward the ear lobe. Pull the ear lobe. Do this three times.

Now place the palms of your hands over your ears. Press and pull your hands away quickly. This gentle popping will stimulate the inside of your ears.

Take a deep breath and now look at yourself in the mirror. If you stopped with facial massage, your face would still begin to look more refreshed, alive, and smooth.

Self-Massage: Neck

1. Turn your head to the right, then the left, and feel how easily and how far you turn. This massage will loosen your neck and can help relieve the tension that causes headaches.

2. Take a deep breath and tune your hands.

3. Slide your hand up the back of your neck to the last vertebra. Find the place where your spine and skull connect. Feel the ridge of your skull. Right below the ridge of your skull is an indent, a hollow. It is in the very middle of the back of your neck. If you cannot

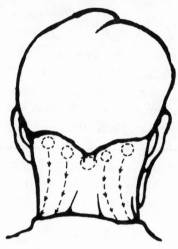

feel it, look up at the ceiling, raising your chin. Now feel for that hollow place just under your skull at the top of the back of your neck. Place two fingers there, or your thumb, whichever is more comfortable. Close your eyes and breathe.

Make *slow, firm* circles.

Do five circles the first time. Work up to ten.

As you massage, the indentation will become more relaxed and will feel deeper. Be patient. Do not expect it to happen all at once. With a little massage each day your neck will loosen up considerably.

4. Staying at the base of the skull on either side of the indentation you will feel a muscle. Place two fingers at the top of each muscle beside the indentation. Again make firm, slow circles. As you relax these two points, you will relax your whole body.

5. Move on the ridge, beside these muscles, about the width of two fingers. Again make firm circles at the base of your skull. These points may feel slightly tender. If you have a headache, massaging these points gently but firmly may help you remove the headache.

6. Bring the flat of your hands, or all of your fingers, to the back of your neck. Start at the base of your skull and firmly smooth the big muscles down

toward your shoulders. Smooth all the muscles of your neck, moving down from the head toward the shoulders. If this is an area in which you have aches or soreness, you may want to learn several different strokes. These are outlined in a readable book, *Aches and Pains: How the Older Person Can Find Relief Using Heat, Massage, and Exercise,* by Robert Bristow (New York: Pantheon, 1974). This book shows photographs of the best postures for massaging different parts of the body. The author points out that you can accomplish various goals by using your massage differently.

You can use the flat surface of the hand to slowly, gently stroke muscles. In severe pain you cannot go further than this. It helps circulation and will soothe pain as the muscles relax. The same slow, long strokes can be done with greater pressure if the muscles are more relaxed, but not if they are in spasm.

After sore or stiff muscles are relaxed, you may feel granule-like points, like grains of sand. These usually hurt. By pressing them with your fingertips in circular motion, you can disperse them and relieve the "trigger points" of your pain.

If your problem is circulation, you may want to squeeze a muscle and then gently release it, like kneading bread. This is a particularly good stroke for the following massage.

Shoulders

Sit or stand comfortably.

1. Place one arm behind your back. Run your other hand over your chest to the opposite shoulder. Squeeze the shoulder muscles. Knead them. Close your eyes and feel your hand kneading your shoulder and neck muscles. Take a deep, long breath. Another.

The reason for holding one arm behind your back is

to relax that muscle and make it more amenable to massage. If it hurts, do not do it that way.

2. Slide your hand back down your chest, and now place that active arm behind your back and massage the other shoulder with your other hand.

This is a massage that you could do before you dress in the morning or after a shower. If you do it in the spirit of providing love and stimulation and pleasure, you will bring your body alive. We have been taught to be embarrassed at the idea of giving ourselves pleasure. Yet this is what we require to be fully alive.

Try to keep your mind on your massage. As you follow your fingers with your attention, you maximize the benefit of your massage. When you are done, turn your head from side to side. See how your neck feels.

The magic of massage is not mechanical. It requires your attention to the feeling of your fingers dancing on your muscles and skin. Paying attention may take some practice. Everything we do well requires practice. Can you remember how many hours you practiced trying to stand when you were a baby? No ballet dancer practices more than a child learning to walk.

If you massage yourself mechanically it will merely improve your circulation. However if you do it with attention, and allow yourself to feel pleasure, something very different will happen. As you practice feeling pleasure, your deep, innermost self-image will begin to improve.

"I do that neck massage every day. I can turn my head more easily to see cars behind me when I'm crossing a street. I don't get so knotted up driving."

"I can remember the first time I gave someone a neck and face massage. It was a woman in my church group. She had a terrible headache. I did the back of her neck, and she said her headache was gone. I sure don't have headaches myself any more."

"I don't know why I don't massage my whole body every day. I feel so good afterward."

"After I've done it for myself for a while, then I like to do it for someone else."

At SAGE we began on ourselves, massaging our own hands, feet, legs, arms, necks, shoulders, and faces. In the second section of this book there are further instructions for massaging your own legs, feet, hands, and arms. Many people in SAGE core groups began to find that massage was a part of life that they did not want to give up. Some participants signed up for massage courses with good teachers. Others paired up and massaged each other. When they asked for a good book of instructions, there was only one on the market, *The Massage Book*, by George Downing (New York: Random House/Bookworks, 1972).

Massage has a sordid connotation for many people, unfortunately. At SAGE the process of examining our attitudes and of developing real bonds within groups allowed us to see that the existence of sleazy massage parlors shouldn't deprive us of this healthy way of relaxing.

One core group was feeling so relaxed by its eleventh meeting that its members were ready to learn whole body massage. People brought robes, bathing suits, and towels that afternoon. There were three rooms with massage tables. In one room people would work clothed. In another they would be nude. And in a third room they could do whatever combination felt good. Nobody *had* to do anything. The choices were open.

People arrived very excited, keyed up. They joked a lot, and acted nervous. One woman in her seventies had never undressed, even in front of her husband. A man in the group had never seen any woman other than his wife in the nude. Everyone felt hesitant and anxious. Before beginning massage the group sat around and discussed its fears.

"How many people have the possibility of doing something really new in their lives at this age?" asked Eugenia.

"It is really taking a risk. I don't think I'd ever do this on my own. I know I wouldn't."

"How many older people actually have the chance to begin giving and receiving massage?"

"I suppose we all have the chance: we just don't seem to do it."

"Hey, I'm really nervous about this. What is my wife going to think if I go in the room where they undress?"

The experience was unforgettable for everyone there. Afterward they sat around looking at each other, and smiling.

"Why didn't we ever discover this before?"

"I know—it's these clothes that keep us apart. I feel so much closer to you all now."

"You know, women look older with their clothes on. When they take them off they have young bodies underneath."

Everyone in the group seemed to agree. They looked better without clothes. They felt better about themselves, knowing that. And feeling better about themselves the group was suddenly much closer. There had been many barriers to closeness in their lives—fears and poor self-image, clothing, and conventionality. After the massage session they discussed how much more comfortable they were with each other and how they had repressed their sexuality. The feeling of comfort and closeness did not vanish after the session was over. The group had taken a very big risk, had overcome lifelong barriers and made a breakthrough. From then on the members began to trust each other deeply about other things in their lives, about illness, and relationships. The members had begun to overcome the sense of isolation and coldness they had complained about earlier; they were on their way to developing a real and reliable closeness with each other.

7 ❧ INTIMACY
AND SEXUALITY

How many deep, intimate relationships do you have in your life? If you can honestly answer that you have one or more, you are most fortunate and unusual.

Intimacy was almost a taboo word in my childhood. It implied a sexual relationship, but somehow even pornography was more acceptable. Sex surely did not create intimacy. Married couples lived together for many years and had sexual relations without deeply knowing each other. Intimacy was more threatening than sex, somehow, and more compelling. People were afraid of intimacy. Why?

Perhaps intimate relations, such as we have with our brothers and sisters when we are very young, provide our only opportunity to be honest and open with others. And our only honest feedback. We are truly vulnerable. Intimate relations are those in which we can reveal to someone the worst of our fantasies, the silliest of our beliefs, the inner recesses of our minds and feelings. Deep intimacy implies that we lower our defenses, reveal who we really are, and receive feedback. If this is so, intimate relationships may offer our only hope of learning about ourselves as adults.

Intimacy is a favorite topic of conversation at SAGE. In the early groups most of us looked back on our lives and felt that they had lacked deep intimacy. I was among many who could look back on a long marriage with almost no intimacy. Like others who had had this experience, I felt that it made me feel separated, isolated. As we talked about our longing to be accepted for who we were, we managed to overcome our barriers, shyness, and withdrawal. The group became intimate, and there was a new atmosphere in the room. It was not the secretive quality of sexual intimacy, but more like warmth and satisfaction. When this happened in our discussions, some people said they did feel sexual, while others described themselves as more childlike, free, secure, and playful. As time went by it became clear that all of us longed to live more of our lives in this open state with each other. These were the good times. The exciting times. They were times when we could take risks, such as venturing to massage each other.

Close contact was valued, and it was not random. At SAGE we began building contact within a group from the first meeting. As the group became more secure, more candid, and close, the participants noticed a shift in their feelings about each other and their own self-images. They also noticed changes in their relationships with family. "This is the biggest change in my life. I never used to like being close, excepting with my grandchildren, and they were small. Now I find that it relaxes me. I even asked my husband to give me a shoulder massage the other night. I never would have thought of that before."

Certain well-picked exercises brought about an immense change in mutual self-image. One of these was an exceedingly simple exercise, one that you might try with a friend, if you wish to risk deepening the relationship.

Back to Back and Face to Face

Close your eyes and take three very deep breaths. Sigh and relax.

Sit with your back against your partner's back. This is easy when you are sitting on the floor or carpet.

Feel your partner's breathing rhythm through your back.

Sense your partner's feelings by his or her breathing. You can do this by imitating your partner's breath.

Without speaking one of you lean on the other very slowly. Relax and let your head come to rest against your partner's head. Let your shoulders relax. Lean on your partner as far as your partner can bear your weight. You may be able to lean on your partner completely, totally relaxed.

Your partner should begin to straighten up very slowly, allowing you to lean, totally relaxed.

Massage each other, back to back. You may massage your partner by rolling your head against his or her neck and shoulders. Now put your hands behind your head and feel your partner's neck.

Let your partner lean on you.

Repeat the entire procedure.

When you straighten up again, and your partner has massaged your neck and head, turn and face each other.

Take off your glasses if you wear them.

Without speaking decide which of you will go first and feel the other person's face. Let the first explorer gently put hands on his or her partner's face, exploring the features. Both partners should have their eyes closed. Then switch and let the second partner explore.

When you have both gently explored each other's faces, open your eyes and tell each other how it felt.

A great buzz went up in the room after Eugenia first led this exercise. Two women who had not known each other well threw their arms around each other. "I didn't know I liked you so much. Then I felt your back rubbing against mine. It was your spine tickling me." People were astounded at the pleasure and relaxation they drew from feeling themselves back to back. They were amazed at the affection conveyed in that simple contact with another person's back. Then when they explored each other's faces, they touched each other with a fond tenderness that they hadn't felt an hour earlier.

The process of this exercise is subtle. Each step leads to the next. If you were to reverse the order and touch your partner's face first, neither of you would have had sufficient time to relax and sensitize your bodies. Without that relaxation you cannot respond openly and tenderly when another person touches your face. Whenever you do an exercise like this one, it is important to move very slowly, allowing yourself ample time to relax. Afterward it is good to breathe deeply, to sigh, and let yourself feel the full impact of the exercise. Done at a leisurely pace this exercise leaves people glowing.

You may think that you do not like being touched. One woman in our group confessed that in eighty-three years she had not liked being touched. "I was never married. I live alone. I just didn't like anyone touching me." But when the group had done some breathing and a contact exercise like this one, she said afterward, "You know, John was stroking my arm and I thought, 'I feel like purring.' I really liked that. My whole body felt as if I were being stroked. I felt so good I decided I liked being touched after all."

There is no secret to the way in which these exercises work. They give you a chance to become deeply relaxed. Then you can develop a relaxed contact, without words. A pleasurable physical contact allows you to be open. In this state you can be caring and honest at the same time. Intimacy is a state of deep, personal communication, of feedback. Without intimacy we have no way really to see ourselves, and no way to grow. As Eugenia often said, "Without that human bond and closeness there is no way to move out of my usual habits of thinking." Here is an example that she offered to the class, which is an exaggeration of what happens among older people in our society.

"I was thinking about a man I worked with who didn't want to be touched at all. He had Parkinson's and didn't like to lie down for long. He'd start shaking and that made him embarrassed. Over a period of time we worked out something, which was physical exercises to help him open his chest and voice projection, helping him get his voice again. The really demoralizing effect of the disease—the feeling of not having a good image of himself—we began to work on with mirrors so that he could look at his face and see what parts were immobile and didn't show much expression. He was really excited by the feedback. He'd gotten to a certain place where the muscles in the face just became totally rigid around the mouth. That was my observation. He began to see that it was a defense for him. That was exciting work to be doing at age sixty-seven. He said, 'God, I began to see that I've been doing this all my life, but now my face is like a mask. It's gotten so heavy.' As soon as he got in touch with this habit, he began to be able to start changing it. I think the important thing about feedback is that until a person sees what they are doing they can't change. You need to give honest feedback—and to get it.

"I'm working with three people who are eighty years old. One woman wanted me to give her a massage, and she began to talk about her body and how it used to be beautiful, and now it was flabby and ugly. My being able to see her body nude was the beginning of changes for her, because she could really talk about an experience. She could feel her body, and it still had a lot of pleasure and vitality. Still that wasn't the way she described it."

Lack of intimacy, and lack of honest feedback, allows us to become strange, weird, dotty, and "off-the-wall." Older people in our society do not get much day-to-day, honest, and nurturing feedback. Supposing your voice was weak, and you flicked your fingers to get attention when you wanted to speak, but people saw you and never asked why you were flicking your fingers. You might flick your fingers more violently, since the gesture was overlooked, and clear your throat. It could be extremely frustrating to have something important to say and have nobody listen. You might flick your fingers and clear your throat and strain.

After a while you might overhear someone passing by saying, "Oh, her, she's dotty. She just sits there making that strange face and grumbling and moving her fingers. She's crazy."

Nobody has bothered to find out what is going on. In

small ways we ignore even the people who are close to us. Perhaps it is a habit. We neither want to reveal our true selves nor ask others about the parts of themselves they keep hidden. Yet so long as we hide, as we hold barriers between ourselves and others, we are stuck. We hide from ourselves what we really know, and we hide from others. It is understandable and human to do so. Our own fears, insecurity, and sense of inadequacy or weakness hold us closed to ourselves and others. It puts us in the bind of living lives that are not quite real, of having relationships that are not quite satisfying, of always feeling neither loved enough nor free enough to be ourselves. So it is hard to face the joy and suffering of our lives. If we deny ourselves intimacy, we deny ourselves the nurturing and the help we might use to change, to open up a little bit. We might discover that whatever we have to hide is no worse than what others are hiding, that our friends and neighbors have the same feelings of shame, problems, drives, curiosities, and negative feelings.

One way to help ourselves out of the sense that we, alone, are living life out in this hidden and harsh way is to allow the delicate relaxation of exercises to bring us into contact with other people. One exercise that we have enjoyed a great deal at SAGE is an exploration of another person's face.

Exploring a Face

1. Find a partner to work with. You can sit on a couch, chairs, or the floor, but one of you must be directly behind the other. The person seated behind is the explorer.

2. Both of you should remove eyeglasses if you wear them, and earrings.

3. Sit quietly and take five deep breaths, paying attention to the breath. Close your eyes—both of you.

4. Explorer, you can reach around your partner and gently explore your partner's face with your fingertips

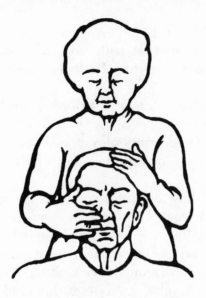

and hands. Explore as if you were blind and needed to feel the contours of your partner's face in detail, the hairline, the nose, cheeks, jaws, lips, and eyes.

5. When you have felt the contours of your partner's face in detail for about ten minutes, move back slightly and put your hands on your own face. In what ways does it feel different from the face you were just exploring? Could you recognize your own face in the dark just by feeling it with your fingers?

6. Now switch positions: Your partner moves behind you and becomes the explorer. Go through exactly the same steps from 1–5, taking ample time, and not speaking.

7. Now open your eyes, and sit face-to-face with your partner and share what this felt like to you. What kinds of things came into your mind as you were being explored? As you explored? What kinds of feelings came up?

◇ ◇ ◇

Here are a few comments from SAGE participants:

"I never realized your face was so much like mine!" exclaimed a delicate woman in her seventies to a woman in her thirties. "It was so soft, and our mouths are both small—and our bones, too. I felt like your sister. But we don't look alike."

"I never noticed your ears before. I got lost just going around your ears."

"I felt your fingerprints on my face. Your fingers are so light. It was very loving and I felt like I wanted to hug you."

"I could feel how beautiful your face is—totally different from the way I see it with my eyes open. Isn't that strange? I felt more love touching you than just seeing you."

Needless to say these exercises were extremely popular among SAGE participants, even though people usually balked at first. Another exercise of this kind allows you to speak to another person through the palms of your hands.

Listening Hands

1. Find a partner and sit comfortably facing each other. Place your palms against the palms of your partner. Close your eyes and take a deep breath.

2. Listen to your partner through the palms of your hands. You can move your palms, but don't speak. Get to know your partner through the palms. Give yourself ten minutes.

3. Open your eyes slowly, look at your partner, and share your experiences.

◇ ◇ ◇

At SAGE this innocuous-seeming exercise would draw out people who had never spoken in groups.

"I felt a sort of pulsing energy in my hands," said one woman. She was pink and her eyes looked excited. "My partner let me in. She wasn't frightened at all. I would come in very close. I felt as though I were the aggressor, and she didn't enter my space very much. That puzzled me. She and I are very different on the outside, but we feel similar on the inside."

"It was rather like a dance," said one man, stiffly.

"My partner was willing to explore and be adventuresome. I think he would be an interesting person to do things with."

"I felt I received complete trust, and what I wanted was more stroking and more love."

The palm-to-palm exercise is one version of a nonverbal contact exercise that became a favorite at SAGE. Perhaps the important aspect of such exercises is not talking. The partners do not talk until after the experience. This allows everyone to experience each other freshly, in a tactile way, and without the usual judgments.

Another variation of this exercise is done lying down, with the soles of your feet against the soles of your partner's feet. Ken Dychtwald would lead this exercise with his typical verve and playfulness, yet the experience was profound for everyone. You don't have to do these exercises seriously, reverently, or with any particular attitude excepting one of sensitivity.

Footsie

1. Find a partner and pick a place where you can lie with the soles of your feet against each other. You are going to communicate only with the soles of your feet. This is a good exercise to do with someone you don't know well. You will discover how much you can learn about another person through the soles of his or her feet.

2. You can do this without a guide or you can use these instructions as a narrative that can be read to you slowly, or played on a tape recorder. The narrative comes from one of Ken's sessions at SAGE.

3. Place your feet against your partner's feet and lie still, experiencing the feeling of your partner's feet.

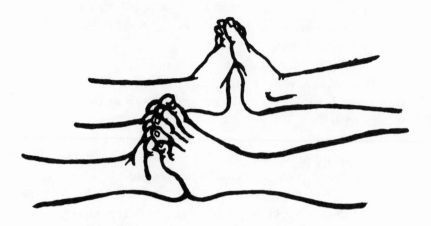

Don't do anything else. Feel the pressure of your partner's feet on your own so that there are places you are
more aware of than others.

4. Now with your feet one of you say hello. Introduce yourselves to each other. Now lie still and just
experience your feet again.

5. Now let your partner introduce, say hello, and
do something that your feet might like. "No orgasms,
though," said Ken, "you get warts from too many
orgasms."

6. Now press your feet against your partner's feet.
Be aware of your partner even though only your feet
have touched. Be aware of some new information you
have about what your partner is like, and what he or
she has to share with you.

7. Now, in some way, let your feet do something
that you think your partner's feet would like—one
person going first. In any way that's comfortable you
can move both your feet on one of his, you can press,
stroke, and share something new, and then when you
have given your partner something, stop.

8. Let your partner give you something now and
lie there, receiving it. Spend a few minutes giving and
taking whatever you'd like.

9. Now slow down. Be aware of your feet and your
partner. This time do to your partner's feet what you

would like him or her to do for yours. One partner at a time. Slow down and place your feet against each other, and be aware of your partner and the strokes or contact they seem to appreciate.

10. After a few minutes exchange.

11. Now be aware of your feet again and, with your eyes closed, and not moving, become aware of the style you use to argue or fight. How do you usually do it—by provoking, pecking, withdrawing, or getting sullen? With your eyes closed, and using your feet in your own special way, pick a fight with your partner. No sounds, just your feet. Make the fight exaggerated. Now slow down and get quieter. Make up with your partner, in your own style, by your feet.

12. Now it is your partner's turn to pick a fight and make up.

13. Now each of you do to your partner's feet what their feet told you they would like.

14. Now become totally passive. Take deep breaths. Feel your partner's feet. If you can imagine that the contact with your partner's feet gives you a kind of direct link to his or her feelings, try to get a sense of what it would be like to be him or her. Try to imagine really being the person who is your partner, mingling your perspectives, and allow yourselves to open, to become receptive to your partner. Perhaps you have learned something about his or her uniqueness, sensitivity, and needs.

15. Keeping your feet in contact, breathe in slowly and deeply and exhale fully. Take five deep, deep breaths. And now, with your feet, say good-bye to your partner.

16. Slowly withdraw your feet and lie still for a moment, feeling your feet and how much you have learned through them.

17. Sit up and share your experience.

◇ ◇ ◇

"I felt embarrassed about the contact, or shy, or self-conscious," said a younger woman in the group. Her partner said, "Oh, that's too bad. I loved it. I've always felt my feet were sensitive, and we had different ideas of what we wanted done. I felt I failed you. I didn't remember what you liked."

"I thought Mary was very loving. That was the feeling I got from her, loving as a person."

Mary asked, "How do you like the way I fought?"

"To me it was like a little cocker spaniel. To me that was the way I took it; it made me smile."

Fighting was an important topic. Most people had never shown irritation or anger in the group. Now they wanted to share how they were when they were angry.

One couple, a handsome, lanky pair who had been married for fifty-two years, were particularly pleased with the sharing.

"I didn't fight the way I usually fight," said the wife.

"How would you usually fight?"

"Straight on. I don't stop. I just go straight, pow!"

Her husband said to his partner, "Can I try something? Ask my wife how she thinks I fought you."

His wife replied, "He'd wait until you start in and then give you back what you gave."

"No, he didn't do that at all," said the husband's partner. "He just completely withdrew. I couldn't find him at all."

"Well he doesn't do that usually. He waits until I fight and then he says that same thing back to me that I say to him."

To be able to fight, even with the feet, allowed us to say things we had never said to each other before. One woman told her partner and the group how it was to feel his softer side through his feet. He was usually gruff and undemonstrative. "I felt one side—one energy—that was very strong, and one that's lucid, open, and receptive." He said, "She comes across in her feet warm, friendly, almost like youth. I felt unequal. It would have been nice to subtract a few years. I envied her a little."

"My personality came out clearly. I was concerned about my feet being so cold that they'd be uncomfortable."

"They weren't cold. You were both soft and tender, and also quite a definite person. A person who likes fun, playful."

Eugenia remarked, "This is a technique used in the Masters and Johnson sex therapy. Not with the feet but with whole bodies, the idea of one person being passive and the other being active, with no genital contact at all, just simply doing something for a long time that you like to do to another person. I was thinking that it is intimate because you learn so much: You're not looking at each other but you have so much experience. You can do it with your feet, or your hands."

A few weeks after this exercise the husband and wife who had been married fifty-two years practiced it at home together. They were glowing and excited as they talked about how much it helped them in their relationship. "We told each other things we never had said before in all these years." It was a new way of listening to each other, of suspending the old habits and being together in a different way. It broke some kind of logjam, some kind of trap that people get caught in, whether they live alone and stick with a routine, or whether they have been married a long time."

One radiant and elegant woman in her mid-seventies said, "Well I am just feeling all kinds of things I haven't felt in twenty years. It's almost shocking," she laughed. "I didn't even know you could just touch somebody's feet and feel so *much*, so much joy, and oneness—it's like making love, really. Only a year ago I'd have been embarrassed to say that. I just didn't know you could have something like orgasm from just touching somebody's feet—or you could be so *close!*"

Asian spiritual disciplines developed what are known as

Tantric methods, whereby people can combine their energies in a disciplined manner and achieve a union on a level that is religious rather than sexual. The important first step in any kind of union at all is the abandoning of one's mind, one's thoughts and observations, one's fussing.

(If you think this is not pertinent to your own mind, try sitting with your eyes closed for exactly ten minutes. Notice all your thoughts, images, fantasies, and sensations. You may discover that your mind is busier than you thought.)

Tantric yoga is a demanding discipline, in which the participants practice concentration and breathing in order to unite body and soul. Actually a first step in any kind of tuning to another person is to breathe in the same rhythm. Try sitting next to someone and adopting their breathing pattern. As you do this you will begin to have a glimmering of what they feel. Breathing together brings an understanding that no words can achieve.

As SAGE groups have enjoyed greater intimacy, through exercises and relaxation, they have come to discuss the problematic aspects of intimacy, too. For almost everyone intimacy has been neglected, because in their childhood and youth sexual relationships—whether with the opposite sex or the same sex—were considered taboo. In one group, as we sat around and talked, four out of seven women had been only in all-girl schools. Sixty years ago when they were in high school, dating as it is now was not even imaginable.

"My brother took me to dances," recalled one woman with a shy smile. "He chaperoned me wherever I went. In fact I never danced with another boy. I was lucky to have a brother, since that meant I could dance with somebody besides a girl."

Touching, holding hands, talking frankly, and even sharing fears about sex had been forbidden. "Nobody in my house would dare to mention sex," said one woman, and five others nodded. "I didn't know anything about sex; my mother gave me a book. I feel I still don't know very much compared to these younger people. I can't believe them. They seem so free."

"I wish I were going to high school *now!*" This seemed to echo what many of the women in the group seemed to feel.

"I was very shy," said one man.

Although reluctant to begin talking about it the group began to bring up many topics and possibilities that had never occurred in our discussions before. It was a group that had been together for a year and a half. The members resented feeling that sexual love was only for the young. "I went to an est sexuality seminar," said one woman in her early sixties. "It was very important for me. We had to tell a stranger things we had never said before about sex. I used words I never used before. And I met someone I had an affair with. I wish I had known those things all the years I was married. It was the best sexual relationship of my life."

There are a lot of myths about sexual inadequacy and aging, and our society perpetuates the idea that desire has been cooled by the years, that frail, older people may be in danger if they make love, that people become sexless as they age. Actually we all know that these are myths, but they are part of an entire cultural outlook. Sexuality is more than the reproductive system, hormones, and sexual intercourse. It has to do with relationship, with a capacity for involvement, intimacy, and warmth. It is a reaffirmation of the connection between oneself and another.

By talking about sexuality, openly, with people who are relaxed and feeling close, it is possible to take some veils off the cultural stereotypes. One of the things we discovered quickly was that while men may fear impotence as a sign of age, at least older men are encouraged to remain sexually vital.

"It's fine for a man of seventy to marry a woman thirty years younger. It's even okay for a woman of twenty years to marry a man old enough to be her father—that's normal.

But if an older woman goes with a younger man, it is considered awful. Older women are just left out, considered repulsive."

Another woman said, "But we agreed we had the same problem. We want a man in our life."

"That's my problem, all right! I had a man—and *he* was my problem. He didn't know how to live with another person."

In SAGE, the women are mostly between sixty-five and seventy-five—and, as in the rest of the country, they outnumber the men. Some of the members are married, but after a marriage of thirty to fifty years there is monotony, and sometimes this leads to lack of interest in sex, or to involvement with other partners. In one group most of the women thought that physiological changes were overrated as the cause of decreased interest in sex.

"I feel these exercises we are doing, like the pelvic one (see exercises in Part Two), have started feelings in me that I forgot I could have," said one.

Kinsey, in his surveys, found that women did not become less sexually aroused with age, but that actually regular sexual stimulation and activity would overcome the effects of hormone depletion or other age-related changes. He reported that women who masturbated regularly remained more sexually alive and capable of sex. Indeed Dr. Ruth Weg and other gerontologists have found that lack of sexual function really derives from other factors in general: disease, excessive eating, alcoholism, and emotional disturbance.

These studies indicate that regular sexual intercourse might be a way to maintain physical tone, since intercourse is like climbing a steep staircase, or running, and raises heart rate, blood pressure, and oxygen consumption in the same ways as strenuous exercise. The increase in some adrenal steroids may create a greater sense of well-being, especially in people with arthritis, so that contrary to being a threat to life, sexual activity may be therapeutic.

Masters and Johnson have developed a successful method to help older people with sexual complaints. They suggest that people have their sexual activity early in the day, when their energies and hormones are at their highest. They recommend masturbation to preserve potency in men, and glandular lubrication in women, as well as to stimulate general well-being. Surely it is important to maintain a balanced diet and an exercise program, as Robert Butler and Myra Lewis point out in their somewhat clinical book, *Sex after Sixty* (New York: Harper and Row, 1976). There is now an abundance of research and clinical evidence to show that sexuality is just as basic in later life (or as irrelevant) as it ever was. Some books on the subject are: *The New Sex Therapies* and *The Joy of Sex* (see bibliography). Because of the enormous change even in the last fifteen years, so that sexual habits, hang-ups, and education can be openly shared, this is a resource that most older people (and the younger people) did not have access to before. Our society's image of older people as neuter is purely a myth, but by sheer repetition it has been elevated to a fact. Many older people have accepted the myth, and professional therapists have gone along with that acceptance.

If anything the need for nurturance increases at a time of life when there are many losses. Nurturance means many things, and not necessarily sex. It does mean touching and affection. It means acceptance and intimacy. If nurturance leads to sexual love, then older people may need a new kind of sex education to understand and extend their capacities for relationships and for expressing the affection and feeling that go with being alive.

As we have talked about intimacy, about the need for closeness, for sexual expression, for deep relationships, some people in SAGE have begun to consider new lifestyles, polygamy, living in groups rather than isolation, and relationships with people of the same sex. By creating taboos against unorthodox relationships we have been keeping ourselves apart, and actually some of the worst problems of age come not from age itself, but from giving in to society's myths. Just looking at those myths and rules, just considering what you believe and how that affects your life, will be a source of new alternatives. It is surprising how new attitudes, and relaxation, can make one feel entirely different, a new person.

8 ✌ DREAMS
AND SLEEP

Our intimacy deepened as we began sharing our dreams. We had been prompted to write down our dreams by an artist who was writing a dissertation on them. At first many of us thought we did not recall our dreams. Most of the group reported dreaming little. Nonetheless we agreed to write down whatever little fragments we recalled when we woke up in the morning, and whatever mood we felt.

We began, somewhat tentatively, sharing our night chimeras, and we found that we didn't need much to obtain a clue to our inner process.

"I went out of the house and down the road. I saw a bicycle and it was broken. . . ."

That was all this man remembered on our first afternoon.

Now we began to view the fragments we remembered in the manner of the gestalt psychologist Fritz Perls. Dr. Perls offered no symbols, no theory, no interpretation. Only a point of view: Everything in your dream is you. To understand the dream you need only rephrase it as if you were the director of that inner play. Make every noun a part of yourself. In this way you can begin to see the rich meaning of even such a small fragment:

"I sent myself out of the house-part-of-myself and down the road-part-of-myself. I see a bicycle-part-of-myself, but it is a broken bicycle-part-of-myself."

The man whose dream it was began to smile broadly. "That *is* the way I feel." He had a sense of being closed in by his family, of wanting to be on the road, unrestricted, freer. But his vehicle—his body—was in need of work. Although his one-sentence fragment seemed innocuous on the surface, you can see that it expressed a deep feeling of frustration, longing, and vitality.

It does not take years of psychoanalysis to explore the messages that your dreams offer to you every night. Nor can anybody outside you understand them as well as you can. They are messages from you to yourself. It is like a letter to yourself from the part of you that is deeply buried, hidden, ignored, maybe feared. Jung, who spent most of his life analyzing deeply the dreams of his patients, found that the dreams spoke of unconscious feelings so deep and so hidden that some of them came out of the collective memory of the human race. He proclaimed that only the dreamer can fully know the meaning of the message in the dream. To accept somebody else's interpretation is to accept another person's theory about you.

Exploring Your Dreams

You can use this same process by writing down your dreams.

1. Keep a notebook and pen beside your bed, or a tape recorder. When you expect to recall dreams you are more likely to do so.

2. If you awaken, move very slowly. Let yourself lie and recall. Wait. Dreams are like movies on clouds. They evaporate if rushed or pushed.

3. When you finally remember something, however

slight, begin to write it down. The tiniest fragments are useful. If you write down how your body feels and what mood you are in you have a lot of information even if you recall no dream fragments at all.

4. Look at the fragment, the mood, and body feeling. It may contain events from yesterday and a straightforward message for you. It may, indeed, tell you something you need to do.

5. Rewrite your dream so that you put "part of myself" after every noun. In addition to the plain message dreams conceal additional information, like icebergs in the sea. Most of it is invisible at first. The gestalt method of rephrasing a dream allows you to start reaching for the hidden meanings. After all everything you dream came out of your brain. It was your private movie projection. It comes from your memory, your body, your perceptions, filtered and changed by your particular personality. For this reason when you rewrite a dream you make yourself everything in it.

It may seem very clumsy to reword dreams that way. And it may not seem impressively revealing at first. Still as you do it, you will begin to see something magical about the way your feelings and your mind work in images, how the very ordinary items of daily experience—your room, cutlery, books, clothes, food—are also experienced as part of yourself.

During our first sessions on dreams many members of the group began to offer theirs, but one dream, shared by a woman, stood out in all of our memories. It spoke for us all.

"I'm standing in a shady valley. Across the valley is a narrow path up high on the side of a mountain. The path is cut by three narrow but deep streams that become waterfalls after they cross the path. There are three lovely red wool blankets laid across the streams as bridges. Are they magically strong enough to carry me safely across or are they a trap that will let me fall to my death?"

During relaxation sessions we had used some red-and-orange, or red-and-purple mohair blankets to cover people, and they were so soft and spectacular in color that the members of the group often commented on them. With that piece of information you can begin to see the meaning of this dream.

Rephrased it said: "I have myself look across the shady-valley-part-of-myself to a narrow path-part-of-myself, on a high-part-of-myself, a side-of-a-mountain-part-of-myself. The path-part-of-myself is cut by three narrow but deep streams-parts-of-myself, that become waterfalls-parts-of-myself after they cross the path-part-of-myself. There are three lovely red wool blankets-parts-of-myself. Are those parts-of-myself magically strong enough to carry me across or are they trap-parts-of-myself that will let me fall to my death?" In gestalt form some of the meanings of this dream were clear to the whole group.

As she began talking about the light, the path, the stream, and the blankets, she became more emotional. She was unfolding many of the fears that our SAGE process brought to the surface in each of us. Was the comfort and the excitement and promise of SAGE something fragile, something that would collapse under her weight, and send her plunging to her annihilation?

Quite a few people in the group began to express similar fears. As another woman put it, "I've spent seventy-four years making my identity. Here I am and you are asking me to throw it away or abandon it—and I find I'm doing that. I'm changing. But I have to tell you it's hard!"

There wasn't anyone in the room who didn't share some of that tension and fear. To grow is to change, and in order to make room for change we have to abandon, drop, and forget some past habits, some former part of ourselves. Before each growth phase there is a small dying, and as Stanley Keleman puts it, each of us does it in our own character- istic way. Once we have allowed ourselves to stop a habit pattern, we may feel lost, at sea for a little while. We have not yet formed our new behavior and feelings, and the transition can be very frightening. It is the same transition that men face upon retiring, the transition mothers face when children leave home. In later life every loss or poten- tial loss brings about that partial dying of oneself.

What this woman asked was whether that growth part of herself, symbolized in the mohair blankets with which she had been covered and warmed during many emotional ses- sions at SAGE, would actually sustain her. Would they allow her to cross through the valley of the shadow—of her husband's death—and possibly her own? Or was that hopeful part of herself a trap, and the vision of great heights and light a false promise?

We asked that question with her. All of us are committed to some kind of inner probing, some kind of faith. As we clear out the restrictive, negative, conditioned habits of mind and feeling, we come closer to home, to something deep in our natures. Eugenia would call it "God." I would call it the reality of which our lives are such a tiny frag- ment, and which is the meaning and purpose of our lives. Still at the level of everyday sorrow and struggle we had no pat answers. The dreamer still wondered why her husband lingered on. He was dying and her feelings were mixed— sorrow, pity, impatience. Her frankness laid her open to the anger of people in the group. She did not pretend to love nursing him, nor to wish him to last longer. She was hopeful, yet she was also doubtful that anything she was doing left her any better off. Indeed was she trapping her- self into a real disaster?

There was no way to know at that time. Her husband died that summer, and she began to work with Ken, teach- ing in a home for the elderly, as well as attending SAGE. A year and a half later she had moved to another city, and was beginning to teach groups of professionals how to work with the elderly. She had become aware of herself as an energetic, free, happy woman. She even wrote an article saying that life began at seventy-six. One might say that this was a happy ending, except for the fact that life is not fixed, and there are no permanent states of being.

Transitions are usually difficult. Her decision to move was a hard one. On the night before she was to catch her plane to a new city and new life she fell and broke her hip. This accident said all that she, herself, had not said, about the difficulty of leaving. Still she had already brought herself into good physical condition, so that she healed rapidly and was able to leave in six weeks and begin driving a car again. Who knows whether that accident was necessary? A therapist could speculate that if she had really worked on her dreams, expressed more of her feelings of ambivalence, fear, and insecurity, perhaps she would not have fallen on the eve of departure. Speculating is useless. However as we went on into a further exploration of our dreams, we began to see how this information might save us from having to experience unconscious events—accidents—in waking life.

Our next step, suggested by an artist Virginia Goldstein, led us to recreate our dreams for the entire group, so that each one of us experienced the dream as if we had dreamed it ourselves. Occasionally somebody dreamed something important to all of us, and this method of sharing made us into one dreamer. The method was simple. It works whether there is one listener or twenty. It is a way of allowing another person to dream your dream.

Sharing a Dream

1. Make sure your listener or listeners are comfortable—preferably lying down with eyes closed. Use a technique for relaxing them. You might use a relaxation method from the back of this book, a breathing

method, or make one up. Your listener should be deeply relaxed but not asleep as you talk.

2. Tell your dream vividly, as if it were happening while you talk. You might enhance the vividness by closing your eyes and redreaming it as you speak.

3. When you are finished, leave a few moments for your listener(s) to react to the experience. Then ask them how they dreamed the dream and what it meant to them.

One year a man in the group told us a dream that I will always remember. If I didn't have a transcript of the session, proving that it was his dream, I might be persuaded that I had dreamed it myself. It stood out as a mythic dream, a fable of what we were all trying to do as we changed our habits and our lives. Here is the dream narrative:

"There was a field and a snake was coming toward me, fourteen to fifteen feet long. I was looking at it and something told me I couldn't move as fast as it could, so there was no use running away from it, and it kept coming toward me, and then I wondered whether or not it was poisonous. I couldn't figure that out. I looked around for some sort of weapon and the ground was bare, and I looked down and all I had on were shorts. I thought I would have to fight it and take my chances. As it got really close to me, it had yellow tentacles that came out with a small head on each one. It was coming closer to me; as it got four or five feet from me, I was braced to deal with it. I couldn't see any reason for it.

"When it got close all these tentacles came out and the snake arched its head up and looked at me. There was a little creek, so I backed to the other side of it, thinking that the snake was coming for water. It was coming in a direct line to me. As it got about five feet from me it pulled back its head and all those tentacles came out that I hadn't noticed before. It looked menacing and then I woke up.

"I sat up and I didn't want to dream about it again, and I could almost see the snake; the dream had been so vivid and in color and everything else. I didn't want to dream about it again and I couldn't put it out of my mind. I got up and walked around the house and came back. I thought about the dream quite a bit, and I tried to recall what my reactions were as the situation developed and I didn't know how to figure it out. I've never been particularly afraid of snakes."

As the members of the group straggled to a sitting position many of them looked stunned.

"You were really confronting danger," remarked one man.

"I can tell you how I experienced it. I felt as if some part of me is moving too fast. It's coming closer to my core. As it comes closer it feels menacing and I want to fight it. As it gets closer it multiplies—as if some part of myself is changing."

"That was heroic. You were about to kill a dragon."

Surely there was a heroic quality in the dream that all of us recognized. The snake, the symbol of a search for forbidden knowledge, was there for all of us, too, as we continued our work together, digging deeper into ourselves, exposing more of our true selves, and facing the changes that we were bringing about in our lives, as we admitted to ourselves what we really felt. Often we were living out lives that we only half wanted, or that contained elements we constructed earlier, out of different needs. Now we were stuck with them—unless we were willing to confront the danger and act like the dreamer and take a stand.

Often as we stopped analyzing and simply thought about the richness of our dream experience, of the incredible depth of mind, the universe underneath our superficial social feelings and behavior, we were awed. Did we really have access to the whole of human experience in our dreams? Could we experience all the basic, archetypal images—the experience of birth and death, of the hero's journey, of not only racial consciousness but the primitive, organic stages of evolution?

As we continued to share our dreams every two weeks or so, people who hardly remembered dreaming began to recount long and involved stories. Sometimes, to discover some of the hidden emotional meanings, the dreamer would act out the different parts of the dream. Once again the process was based on gestalt psychology. And it is simple.

Acting Out a Dream

1. Write down whatever you remember of your dream.

2. Imagine that you are each object in your dream. Really put yourself into feeling what it would be like to be the house, the key in the lock, the front step under your foot, and so on. Acting out each part of a dream may prove to be one of the most satisfying ways of discovering yourself. If you are sharing your dreams with someone, this process becomes a very deep process of sharing yourself.

Dream sharing in this fashion was perhaps the first experience one group had in openly showing feelings. A visiting gestalt therapist who facilitated our first session had asked for a participant who had experienced this kind of unfolding and would be willing to risk sharing his or her own feelings. Eugenia volunteered. She told a dream of dropping her pocketbook into a muddy pool and diving in with her clothes on to search for it at the bottom.

"What is it like to be the pocketbook?"

"You hold my keys and my security," Eugenia said.

Then she began to experience the pocketbook-part-of-herself, lost on the bottom of a muddy pool. Soon tears were falling down her face, and one woman rushed to hold her, protectively. Other members of the group also looked upset and angry at our guest for "making Eugenia cry." But Eugenia wiped her eyes and smiled.

"I cry very easily," she said, and she began to point out that she had not really understood the meaning of her dream until she began to act it out and feel the deeper feelings. When her feelings came to the surface, she began crying.

Many people went away from that session upset, yet two years later it stood out in their minds as a milestone. Why were they upset? "I'm just afraid of feelings. We never showed feelings in my family." Yet feelings are the electricity, the energy in our dreams. Mere images would hardly be memorable. Feelings are the energy in life. They are complete messages at each moment, but they are transitory. After that day many of us were able to express ourselves more freely, to cry if we wanted to, or express our anger within the group. Although it seemed upsetting at first the group agreed that this session gave everyone permission to express and feel strong feelings. This was the depth they had been hoping for. Older people in groups often said that though they were fatigued by confrontation, they also wanted excitement, energy, hope, and growth. People often assume that older people want to remain protected, sheltered from ever feeling anything. That assumption seems quite false if SAGE is any indication. Although people who are not accustomed to expressing emotion are shy at first, repeated practice in a secure group has changed such habits. We no longer need to be so polite, to withhold our real selves from each other. As we share our dreams we are sharing our innermost selves.

There are many ways to use your own dreams, as you will discover if you pick up one or two of the dream books from the Bibliography. This chapter has touched on dreams as a mode of deepening your understanding of yourself and sharing that with others. There are also methods for consciously directing your dreams to reveal solutions to problems, to tell you what you need to know. One entire culture, the Senoi, a tribe that lives in Malaysia, is reported to have based its society on the sharing of dreams, to have selected leaders by their dreams, and have generated an unusually peaceful way of life. This group is cited in Patricia Garfield's book, *Creative Dreaming* (see bibliography).

One winter afternoon a member of the group asked me why we dream. She knew I had written a book on sleep, and therefore I should know. The book was already ten years old, and to me it seemed a century old. I had written it from the point of view of science, observing what can be seen from the outside, certainly outside consciousness. It seemed a very limited part of the story, now. I remembered standing, excitedly, in laboratories where people slept all night with tiny electrodes on their scalps, with wires leading to a console that showed their heart rates, eye movements, and brainwaves.

In the early 1960s it had been discovered that about every ninety minutes, all night long, a person would start moving his or her eyes in sleep as if looking at something. The breathing and heart rate would change, becoming more irregular. Hormones would surge. Males would get erections. The body seemed excited. If awakened during these rapid-eye-movement periods people—even those who said they never dreamed—almost always recalled dreaming. Not that they didn't dream in between, but during these periods there were vivid dreams, often starting with mundane, short episodes early in sleep, and toward morning becoming more bizarre, colorful wild dreams. Whatever this function meant for man, it was discovered in all mammals. Monkeys seem to dream in images, periodically, all night. Presumably other animals do, too. But why?

At the time I was writing, one theory seemed to cover a

lot. It said that our brains resemble computers which are deluged with new information all day, so long as we wake. Much of this is important and needs to be stored in long-term memory. During dreams we pull out the file drawers to put in new associations. According to the memory theory, at least, this dreaming phase is necessary for all animals. In addition to helping us assimilate new material into our previous store of experience, it has to do with the functioning of the nervous system, and the body, a periodic need for an alerting, so that the vulnerable sleeping beast could be ready to defend itself.

New theories of dreaming attempt to explain what goes on at the cellular level in our brains during sleep. But no single theory could hope to cover the purpose of dreaming, which is so threaded into the purpose of life. I now look back on the simple concepts of mind-brain-and-consciousness that I had when I was writing scientifically, and I feel how inadequate they were to explain the mysterious dimensions of our inner lives and of the nature of our mind. How could we explain the dreams and visions by which "ordinary" people have educated themselves in unusual skills? How could I explain the tailor who absorbed psychiatry from a dead psychiatrist, or the person whose virtuosity on the piano came from "a spirit guide"? The objective explanations of our physiological needs to dream cannot help us in the realm where neither scientific method nor instruments work too well—the exploration of the nature of our consciousness.

In some of the disciplines of ancient India, dreams, sleep, and waking consciousness were not treated as separate. Laboratory scientists have often described delta-stage sleep as oblivious. Most of us, if awakened from this phase of sleep, would be disoriented, would not remember anything, and would say it was oblivious sleep. But we are Westerners. We use our minds as we have been taught. Nobody ever taught us to make a connection between waking consciousness and deepest sleep. Yogis know how.

In the late 1960s, Swami Rama allowed Drs. Elmer and Alyce Green to wire him up and test him at the Menninger Clinic in Topeka, Kansas. In one experiment Swami Rama quickly entered delta sleep and snored away in his chair. Alyce Green, in her soft voice, repeated innocuous statements, such as "It's raining today but it may be sunny tomorrow." Swami Rama slept for a while, then he "awakened." He said that this was for him like a state of recording. When he sat up and opened his eyes he would play back what had happened during his snores and delta brainwaves. He repeated all the sentences and remembered phones ringing in the room upstairs and footsteps of people moving. Yet he was totally rested.

There is a discipline, known sometimes as dream yoga, that can help to create a greater continuity between waking consciousness and sleeping consciousness.

Between Waking and Sleep

As you are falling asleep, maintain the image of a candle burning. See the flame. Prolong the time, and as you begin to fall asleep see the flame growing more distant. The longer you can hold onto the flame, and the more aware you become of the transition into sleep, the closer you will came to bridging that "gap" between waking consciousness and "sleep."

◇ ◇ ◇

Even if you do not have the persistence to practice this exercise every night, you will begin to understand something about the arbitrary boundaries we set on consciousness. Dreaming is vivid—perhaps more vivid than our so-called waking experience. Perhaps our dreams represent our real consciousness, while waking requires only our superficial attention.

A lot of our nightly work could be done wakefully. Jack

Schwarz, a Westerner who is a self-taught teacher, with profound powers of vision, has shared with many people his own method for cutting the psychic drudgery out of his sleep. Jack sleeps little. An hour or two a night. He does not wrestle with "unconscious" problems as most of us do in our dreaming. He clears each day as he goes. In his book, *Voluntary Control,* he outlines a method that all of us could use. I have found it extremely helpful, and it is very simple.

Nightly Review

Before you go to sleep at night, reserve half an hour or an hour to review your day. Close your eyes and get deeply relaxed. Imagine that you are watching a giant movie screen. Relive everything you did that day. Watch your actions. What did you feel? Scrutinize even trivial events or thoughts or feelings that might be harmful. Ask yourself: "Did I do any harm today? If so, how can I repair it?" You may feel that you insulted someone or hurt someone's feelings— and you can actually apologize. Other harms might seem to be hidden from others, and only you can repair them within yourself. For instance were you dishonest to yourself or others? Did you have nasty thoughts about anyone? Did you say something nice, but feel very resentful? Before you go to sleep you can rectify these negative traces in your mind just by recognizing them. You will be doing some of the work that usually occupies your sleep. Then you can go to sleep with a cleaner conscience.

You may find that your sleep changes quality if you do this nightly review. Often we awake unrested, as if we have battled all night long. It seems strange. There was nothing dramatic happening on the immediate day before. Still if we were to look over the trend of our lives we might perceive that we are in deep subterranean conflict about something, that we have feelings we do not share and gripes we don't express. If we could begin to deal with these feelings each night, consciously, we might not only feel more rested, we might need less sleep.

Many people think they need eight hours sleep, and that they will always sleep as they did when young. When they sleep less they torture themselves about it. As we shared our dreams at SAGE we also discovered that our sleep patterns changed with age. We compared notes one afternoon: It was clear that not one person over sixty slept through the night as they had when young. But what different attitudes we had! One man would lie in bed smiling at the jokes of the all-night disc jockey, relaxed and enjoying himself. A woman would get up and drink coffee and read until she got sleepy. Then in the wee hours she would go back to bed. Another woman would feel lonely and depressed because she was awake in the darkness. She didn't want to disturb her husband, and found reading in bed unsatisfying. Some people got up and walked around. Some drank hot milk. Others fidgeted. "I do my roll breathing," said one woman. "I lie in bed and do about fifteen cycles of breathing. Sometimes I relax enough to go back to sleep. Mostly I'm just relaxed and that gives me enough rest. I don't sleep more than two to four hours a night."

Many of us—myself included—were brought up to believe that we would be a wreck the next day if we didn't get our full night of sleep. A night without sleep and we panic. Our culture treats broken sleep as insomnia, an anathema, a pathology. We are told to take sleeping pills—and treat ourselves to oblivion. Even scientific theory corroborates this disease attitude: One theory holds that our brain chemistry becomes depleted as we age, thus we begin to have broken sleep. Older people who complain about loneliness or depression in nighttime awakening are

treated as if they are sick, given tranquilizers and sedatives. Unfortunately the repaired sleep is also attended by
side effects from the drugs. One man in our group told us
how he felt while taking Valium for months. He felt much
less alert and had thought he was losing his memory until
he stopped the drug. By treating our changing sleep as an
illness, and medicating ourselves in order to sleep as we
did at twenty, we may be missing the meaning of our
symptoms.

Perhaps there is a reason for being awake as we advance
in age. Our physiology may be guiding us toward greater
awareness and growth, despite the negativity of our culture. Surely it is an interesting coincidence that the early
hours of morning, when SAGE people said they were
awake, happen to be the same hours that have been selected as optimum time for meditation and inward reflection. In ashrams throughout the Orient and in the West,
too, young people are struggling out of bed at three or four
in the morning to meditate. Ironically it is the young who
are attempting to follow a spiritual path before they have
lived their lives. In many cultures in Asia, as well as
among our own American Indians, it is generally understood that a person should live out his mature family and
community life before taking up serious spiritual disciplines. Thus a person might begin at fifty, awakening
purposefully in the predawn atmosphere to meditate. This
is a time when the electric mantle of earth is more charged
with negative ions than it is later in the day. Our consciousness is also different, for we have separated ourselves by sleep from the myriad daytime activities. We are
rested. Our minds are perhaps clearer of outside distractions, and we are closer to the mysterious underlayers of
our being.

Perhaps we could rename this period of nonsleep. Instead of saying that it is insomnia, and an ailment, we
might recognize the rich possibilities in the waking portions of the night.

Once a man in the group asked me, "What was the greatest experience of your life in the last three months?"

Among my thoughts I remembered a night when I was deep in sorrow and tumult. As I lay sleeplessly in bed I was aware of a deep tranquility way beneath the tumultuous surface. I lay there, watching my feelings play themselves out, while I remained inwardly calm. This was not the kind of high point I had been taught to expect, but as I shared it I realized that there was something vital in the experience that could never come from lectures, orations, and external events.

9 ✤ VISUALIZATION AND HEALING

"I lie in bed and have the most wonderful thoughts, and I think this is when I heal myself." The woman in the hospital bed smiled. She was pink-cheeked and radiant. Looking at her nobody would have believed that she was seventy-four years old and had just had a large malignancy removed from her intestines three days earlier. She had always been an extraordinary person, and now she was teaching us something that we had been listening for at SAGE. Practicing relaxation, letting down barriers to intimacy, and specific skills of concentration and visualization could in fact give a person unusual healing power in time of crisis. This woman had not developed her abilities overnight, on the eve of surgery. She had been practicing for two years. The most important aspect of her recovery undoubtedly had to do with her beliefs.

Many of us grow up believing in a childlike way that a doctor will heal us if we get sick. We act as if our bodies were cars, and we take them to a specialist. If our liver is affected, we go to a hematologist. If the problem is emotional, we see a psychiatrist—as if our livers and minds were unconnected. In a crisis of faith we seek a minister or priest, thinking to restore our overall health and balance in this divided fashion. Deep down we know that everything in our way of being is related, the way we think, feel, move, breathe, eat, make love, sleep, talk, work, and daydream. Our illness or health involves all of these. We also know, somewhere deep inside, that we are connected to a larger reality, call it nature—of which we are an insignificant little part. It is this larger nature that heals us, not the surgery, psychological therapy, or drugs. None of them can make cells grow. None of them can infuse us with the vital energy of life.

Usually we pay no attention to our well-being until we have unpleasant symptoms. Then we want relief. We do odd things. Imagine that you treated your car the same way you are willing to treat your body. You are driving along and the voltmeter begins to show a symptom. It oscillates and buzzes erratically. Instead of stopping everything to find out the cause you paint it over and keep on driving. Everything is all right for a while, but the paint doesn't cover the irritating noise. So you stop at a gas station and have it ripped out. Most of us would not be willing to treat our cars this way, yet we are often willing to use drugs or surgery this way on ourselves. Most car owners would stop for an overhaul. Yet how many body owners would stop their lives and make a real inner search into the components of their illness? The causes of our illness are hidden within the complexities of our being. This is a somewhat different view than we expect from Western medicine.

We have grown up expecting that "medicine" can heal us by giving us the right injection, pill, or surgery. These treatments often do get rid of the immediate symptoms, so we feel better. But next week, or next month, we find we have another ailment. We don't see them as related. Few of us take responsibilities for the life-style that leads to these ailments. We only know that periodically we add a new symptom. Some become chronic. We have various logical explanations for this. We say that influenza is caused by little beings known as viruses, but this doesn't explain why some people get sick and die in an epidemic while others don't become ill at all.

For lack of better explanation we could say that the cause of illness is divine, and the healer is the same as the cause, divine. In ancient times in India, Egypt, Arabia, and Greece healing was a spiritual process. It involved a change of attitude, or mind, known as *metanoia*. People went to healing centers where they meditated and underwent severe challenges until this change of heart could happen. All of us know of people who were supposed to die, and who miraculously survived. Sometimes they articulated some elusive but powerful inner transformation. There are many curiosities like these in our medical literature. For instance there is the case of a man in his fifties who went to an Eastern hospital for removal of a stomach cancer. The doctors opened him, took one look, decided it was hopeless, and closed him up. They sent him home. But they forgot to tell him he was hopeless. He assumed he was cured, that God had given him another chance, and he began to live his life differently in gratitude. He wasn't seen again until nine years later, when he had a coronary. He had no sign of cancer.

Belief is far more potent than we like to acknowledge. We give lip service to the idea that our thoughts create us, but at heart we deny it. Otherwise we would have to examine our thoughts carefully. We would ask how they affect us and others. What happens when we think angrily, in doubt or greed, or when we make small negative judgments that pass through our heads without causing external ripples? We like to imagine these thoughts are unseen, forgotten. But they are not forgotten by our minds or our bodies. Disease and healing are related to our deepest and most unadmitted ways of thinking and believing. This is why sharing those secrets, admitting them, and seeing them, can be part of a healing process. After that they no longer have such a tight hold on us.

For many people a dramatic healing process begins when they begin to relax their inner guard against the ideas or mysteries they have resisted and can surrender to the natural sequence that is beyond the control of medical doctors or any human being. An attitude of surrender is not easy to acquire. Most of our blocks to healing probably come from inner resistance. It takes the form of tiny tensions throughout the mind and body. For example we do not allow our real feelings to show. We refuse to cry or vent real fears and anguish. This containment can cause tension at a level too subtle to be immediately observable. Nonetheless it is there. We resist giving in to anesthesia, we cannot trust the very people into whose hands we have placed ourselves. At the deepest level we resist what is, thinking there is some evil in our distress, illness, and death. We imagine that we should be in control of the overall life process. Resistance and tension act as amplifiers for pain and mental discomfort. When a person is able to give in to the ongoing process of his own life, surrendering to it and accepting whatever happens, that attitude is likely to accompany healing.

People sometimes come to that acceptance through religious inspiration. Sometimes it comes through a process of quieting and meditation. A healer is a person who can in some way expedite this acceptance and healing process. Often this is a person with abundant selfless love, whose energy may give the sick person a boost, and whose presence can instill trust, acceptance, and calm. In the early 1960s a small study indicated that surgical patients who opted to use hypnosis instead of anesthesia healed remarkably fast. The explanation seemed to show that they were unusually relaxed, trusting, and in a positive mental state due to the hypnotic suggestion, in contrast with people who were not mentally prepared and simply went into anesthesia in a state of anxiety and tension.

As you have been reading this book and doing some of

the exercises, you have been augmenting your own powers of self-healing. There are books in the bibliography that can carry you further. And you can practice some of the simple exercises in visualization that SAGE participants have found helpful.

Some of these exercises are undoubtedly ancient in origin. They must have been passed down from one shaman or family member to another for thousands of years. You are not likely to experience very dramatic results at first, but you will inevitably strengthen your ability to focus. It should become easier to sustain an internal image or point of concentration. This ability is a powerful tool. If you begin practicing while you feel well, it will become your ally in a time of crisis or pain. The following exercise is one that you can practice with others and alone.

Healing Hand

1. Make certain that you will not be interrupted for an hour. Make yourself very comfortable, either sitting or lying down, but do not lean on or lie on your hands.

2. Take five deep breaths. Follow your breath with your attention so that you feel it dividing as it enters your nostrils, going down your throat into your lungs. Feel the exhalation coming back up and out your nose or mouth. Relax deeply. Each time you exhale, allow yourself to drop outside thoughts, feelings, or concerns.

3. Become acutely aware of your right hand. Feel its skeleton. If you don't feel it, imagine it. Imagine that you inhale through the fingers of your right hand and exhale out through the fingers. Become very aware of each finger, and of the palm and back of your hand. When you feel a moving sensation in your hand go on to the next step.

4. Become aware of your left hand, inhaling and

exhaling through the hand. Be aware of the sensations in your fingers, in your palm, and the back of the hand. When you have vivid sensations go on to the next step.

5. As you take a breath, inhale through your right hand, up your right arm. Exhale down the left arm and out the left hand. Practice this until you feel a flow of sensation as you breathe and your arms begin to relax. They may feel long and heavy. Let go of any tight muscles. Let the breath warm and relax them.

6. Now feel the breath coming in your right hand and going out through your left hand as if you are making a circle through your body. Take slow, full, relaxed breaths.

7. Begin to feel your right hand as having a lot of power in it. You can imagine that the left hand is exhaling leftovers, while energy is building up in your right hand. You may feel some quivering or vibration. Feel the power building in your right hand.

8. Now notice some part of your body that doesn't feel good. Place your right hand about six inches over that spot. Continue to build the energy in your hand and transmit it to the part that feels badly. Your left hand is getting rid of wastes as you exhale through it. Discard those wastes. Do this for three minutes.

9. Stop and see whether there has been any change in the part of you that did not feel so good.

10. Continue to build energy in your right hand and let go of wastes through your left hand. You can place that energized right hand over another ailing spot on your own body, or over someone else who is ill.

11. If someone is ill or achy, try building up the energy in your right hand and placing your right hand about six inches above the place they describe as sore, tight, or tense. You can nourish them with your energy.

◇ ◇ ◇

"I feel really foolish doing this," remarked one woman after a SAGE practice session. "It feels like a lot of hocus-pocus, yet I have to admit when I put my hand over my bad knee the pain went away. I just feel stupid holding my hand over someone else as if I were a magician or something."

"When I was doing this, my hand was tingling like anything. It got really hot, and I began to feel as if something was happening. It was exciting."

"I got some sensation in my hand at first, then I lost it. I couldn't get it back. I kept thinking about my car and how I'm going to manage without it."

"When I held my hand over my partner, I began to feel as if I weren't there any more, as if I were vanishing. It was terrifying."

As we did these exercises at SAGE, there was a wide range of reactions. Everyone felt excited. Some people were anxious when they worked with partners. They would forget their own boundaries and begin to feel formless and uncentered.

If you begin to feel that your own boundaries are disappearing, stop, and concentrate on the energy within you. You need to retain your sense of your boundaries. At the same time you need to leave your own problems, thoughts, and feelings behind. This is difficult at first. You need patience. Practice focusing your energy, without a stream of thoughts and feelings, toward someone who has asked for help. You need to be able to do the same thing for yourself. It can be difficult to stop thoughts and images and sustain focus. You can practice this at night when you are lying in bed. Begin with sensitizing yourself by noticing the differences between yourself and all that surrounds you—the air, bedclothes, pillow, and mattress. You can tune your hands, as you learned in the chapter on massage. Then move your hand like a radar screen over the parts of your body. Focus on the feelings in your hand and the parts of your body under it. If you lose focus and your mind wanders, bring yourself back. Treat yourself indulgently, as you would treat a small dear child who has wandered off the garden path. Repeat this twice a day.

You will appreciate an increased ability to focus when you want to heal yourself and be of help to others. Rudolph Steiner, a great German scientist, educator, and philosopher—a man whose abilities made him feared by Hitler—suggests a very simple way to begin healing yourself. He sets out a sequence of steps in his book, *Knowledge of the Higher Worlds and Its Attainment.* The first steps are within the realm of all of us.

Learning to Focus

1. Find ten minutes of tranquility every single day. Find a quiet place where you will not be disturbed. Spend ten minutes in serene contemplation. You might look at a plant, or a tree, or out the window. As you practice you will find that you have fewer distractions, and the quality of your experience will change.

After a while, if you practice this contemplation often enough, you can begin to look at an object without any thoughts at all. You can become totally immersed in caressing it with your eyes and attention. When you can become still enough to focus this way, you will find that even a simple object such as a match stick becomes interesting, rich, and full of meaning to you.

The next step comes once you have learned how to maintain tranquility and focus for ten minutes.

2. Look at yourself in the mirror as if you are looking at a stranger. Look at yourself as a stranger would see you, a stranger who has nothing at stake and sees out of a state of deep calm.

◇ ◇ ◇

Calm and detachment are particularly helpful when you are sick or in pain. In this state you needn't drain your energy with bad feelings. Moreover as you attain an attitude of inner calm you can survey yourself and sever the essential from the inessential. I think this is much harder for me to do than most of the people I work with at SAGE. I get caught up in social forms and habits, even though I see them for what they are. The Christmas holidays are a good example. I know I don't want to spend that much time, or money, and I surely don't want to eat so much rich food. Yet by January 5 I am often "stressed out."

When I know I am under stress, irritable, or lethargic, there is one visualization that really changes the picture. It is a fantasy that popped into my mind spontaneously one day, and a number of SAGE people have found it helpful. Probably, in slightly different form, it has been used since ancient times.

Perspective from Space

1. Loosen clothing, anything tight, remove glasses, watch, jewelry, and shoes. Lie down with a pillow under your knees and your head. Pick a warm, quiet place where you can be alone, and a time when you can be uninterrupted, even by pets. This exercise calls for a very deep relaxation.

2. Sit in a comfortable armchair, or stretch out on a couch or bed, and begin relaxing by breathing deeply. Close your eyes. Breathe in through your hands and out through your toes. Breathe into your feet, your ankles, your calves. Breathe all the way up your legs into your abdomen, chest, shoulders, your back. Feel the breath suffusing your head, relaxing your face. With each exhalation relax more. Survey your entire body to see whether you are deeply relaxed. If you feel any spot of tension, breathe or imagine breathing warmth into that area until the sensation dissolves.

When your body feels so relaxed that you almost cannot feel it, go on to the next step.

3. Feel your body expanding, getting lighter and larger. Breathe in to the count of four. Hold for a count of twelve. Breathe out to a count of twenty. Each time you exhale, relax more. Exhale your crowded thoughts, tensions, worries. Inhale new energy.

4. Now with your eyes closed begin to imagine yourself sitting on a small platform about two thousand feet above your house. You cannot fall off. It will not drop. You are secure. You are about to look down at your own life through a magic telescope. It will let you see through walls. It will allow you to see a week in a few minutes.

5. As you look down from your platform, first scan the geography around your home. What is there around you? Where do you usually go? There is a whole terrain surrounding the home in which you live, the place you may work, and the places you usually go. Look down and map the usual routes you travel, the terrain in which you live most of your life. Do you usually travel the same routes, to the same

places, see the same people? Do you notice what there is in between? Do you repeat the same things over and over, or do you move around freely in your territory? What is the size of your domain? Do you always go down the same streets, look in the same stores, see the same people? Are there areas of beauty and interest nearby? Is there an invisible wall around your pattern of activity, of habit and inertia, so that you have a smaller domain than you would like?

6. Now comes the important part. Turn your telescope down on your house. Start as you get up in the morning. Watch yourself brushing your teeth, dressing; watch your thoughts. Is this what you want to think? You can speed time up or slow it down to have a close look at how you feel, move, spend your time, and how your life moves. Turn the telescope through the walls, on your own life patterns. What do you see? Spend plenty of time at this. Watch carefully. When you see yourself moving, walking, eating, see how it looks to you. Is that self enjoying what it does? Is that self paying attention? Is it eating thoughtlessly? Is it listening to its real needs, or does it confuse wants with needs?

7. Watch for habits and repetitions. Watch for emotions that come up again and again. Whenever you see a repeated emotion that is negative, watch a longer time span. Do you repeat some behavior that incurs a negative feeling?

8. Are there patterns of outgoingness and withdrawal? Do you have rhythms of restlessness, sleepiness?

9. What about people? Are your relationships unchanging? Are there things you could share with your friends and family that would change your relationships? Could you take some risks? Could you become more intimate? Are there people who could enrich your life whom you do not go out to see? Whom could you phone? Whom could you write?

◇ ◇ ◇

The first time I did this exercise myself, I was left gasping with astonishment. I saw myself like a small rat in a maze, repeating the very patterns that I knew I didn't like. Nobody was forcing me to run the same track over and over: I did it like a robot. At that time I lived in New York City in a fascinating region, but I restricted my activity to a few blocks and the people I saw were not the people I *selected,* but those whom I happened to meet on the way to the subway or by answering invitations. I saw that I did this in my relationships, too, consuming my time habitually, not out of conscious choice. I had constructed a kind of prison for myself, which had the outside appearance of being a very exciting and free life. The prison was in my mind. Not only did I constrict my movements outside my apartment. I always went through certain ritualistic motions at home. I was conservative—to save housework, I told myself. I folded my clothes neatly. I never ran in, shed clothes, kicked my shoes across the floor, and flung myself on the bed. I never thought of using my guest room as an art room, but neatly used my materials in the kitchen, carefully clearing up after each time. I did my duties, first: my work, then social calls, and finally if there was anything left, what *I* wanted.

What was important in this life? That small figure in the apartment was sitting at a typewriter, shopping, and traveling to Washington. It was staying neat, putting money in the bank, being nice to dates, mothering people, and walking the dog. Ten years later it is not possible to reconstitute precisely the details of the vision. I felt myself exploding with the insight. Was that *really* my life? How could I have trapped myself to such an extent? It seemed simple to get out of the habits, when I saw them from the perspective of looking at my life in its surroundings, and not from within. From the vantage point of space I saw what inner freedom would have meant, what possibilities lay right within my path, even inside my own living quarters. As I looked down, I saw myself as a stranger might, observing the apartment, the city and all, I asked: "Why doesn't she get up from her typewriter and run in the park? Why doesn't she train that dog not to bother her?"

Almost six years later I listened to a member of SAGE talking about his revelations from the exercise. He had seen that his attempts to retire from his union, and from the life of a union leader, had been ineffective. His few pleasures still came from his association and activities with those men.

He saw that he had potential friendships with other men and there were many enjoyable things to do in the world. He saw new activities that he could share with his wife. What had held him in the bondage of his habits? Why did he leave home so seldom? Why did he not see people he liked for lunch? Why be so isolated? His view from above showed him that his life was not a trap. There were rich possibilities all around. All he needed to do was to remember and lift the phone. Instead of puttering around the house or garden he could venture into the opportunities that lay all around him. He wasn't trapped by old age—it was his mind set.

The path out of an ingrown life and mind set often takes an unpredictable route. First you see the situation. Then you expose yourself to new possibilities. At SAGE a number of participants have experienced a kind of unfolding, discovering unused talents and real creativity. One man who had been diffident and depressed took a professional massage course and began to work with young people at a crisis counseling center, later in a rest home for the aged. He was out of his old routine, his rut. As a person who had once been physically active, but suffered from a disability, he understood the women in wheel chairs in the rest home in a way that was unique. He invented games nobody else could have thought of. He'd come in with a basket of bright-colored wool balls. The women in that rest home hadn't caught a ball for thirty or fifty years. He would stand in the middle of the room and toss a yarn ball:

"Hey, Bessie, catch this!" She would laugh and toss it back. She hadn't caught a ball since she could remember. Soon these light and colorful balls of yarn were flying around the room. People laughed. He had liberated the residents of the rest home from their feeling of stagnation.

Quite a number of SAGE participants found themselves getting out of ruts simply by sharing their new feelings and knowledge with others. They began teaching friends, or working with staff in nursing homes, running core groups, taking over the administration of the organization. They created a community of their own, so that they could meet and continue learning new exercises, meditations. They could continue to provide moral support and stimulation for each other. They began talking about seeing their lives in a new perspective.

As you try visualizing your own life in perspective, you may not see it as vividly as a movie. You may not even "see" it. You may have some feeling or image in the back of your mind, or you may "know" something. Do not worry, you will see it in a way that is right for you. Many people think they cannot visualize and can never learn how to do it. Still if you asked them, most of these people could imagine being in their bedroom and walking over to the bed and turning down the covers. In an earlier chapter you probably discovered how powerful visual images can be, by imagining that you tasted some lemon juice and noticing that you secreted more saliva. That, too, is visualizing.

Eugenia devised an ingenious way of sharpening our ability to visualize. We had been attempting to meditate on people who were not in the group one day, and several members said they couldn't get any image. Eugenia said, "Everyone in the group look at another person. Then close your eyes and see that person in your mind's eye."

The Camera

You can do this with a friend or with your own image in the mirror. Relax first. Close your eyes and

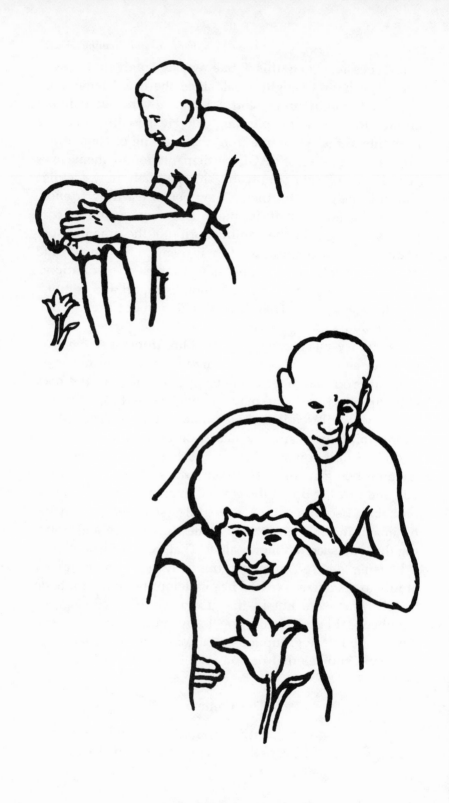

breathe deeply. Then open your eyes and look at your friend or yourself, briefly, as if you were a camera taking a picture. With your eyes closed remember what you saw. Don't struggle. If the image fades, open your eyes and take another picture. Do this at least ten times and see if the image lasts longer. You can practice this many times a day, with objects, views, and people. A friend can lead you around to an object with your eyes closed. Then let your eyes open like a camera shutter.

◇ ◇ ◇

Visualization is a mental skill that requires practice. Remember how long it took to learn arithmetic? The only way for most of us to acquire mental skills is to practice, and we are better equipped to do it as adults than we were as children.

One afternoon we all practiced slowly looking around our SAGE group at each person. Two years later I can still remember roughly where each person sat and what some of them were wearing. There was a special quality to the memory. For that span of two minutes the group became eternal. Eugenia asked us to keep our eyes closed while she called out the name of each person in the group. "Try to see in as much detail as possible," she said.

"I just see the eyes."

"I see colors—not really images. I can remember the colors you are wearing."

"I see stick people."

"I could see everyone in the group, but not myself."

As we practiced, week after week, we began to remember more. Eventually we could go home and lie in bed at night remembering visually every person in the group. It became a kind of camaraderie, for each of us had the group within us at all times. We learned that it was easier to visualize others than ourselves, so we began looking in the mirror.

Mirror Exercise

1. Take some long, slow, abdominal breaths with your eyes closed, until you are pleasantly relaxed. Stand or sit in front of a mirror. Close your eyes for a count of ten. Open your eyes softly and take in your reflection without thinking, judging, or intention.

2. Look for a minute or two and close your eyes. When you lose the image, open your eyes again, and look in the mirror. Repeat this ten or twenty times.

This exercise may seem difficult at first. We have so many judgments about the way we look and how we would like to look. As we see ourselves we also have thoughts, and our subterranean thoughts and feelings keep us from just seeing and experiencing the image. After practicing this exercise a number of times you will be able to see your face. You will be able to see it in your mind's eye. And you will be able to look at yourself impartially, as a stranger might. Sometimes it can be a profound meeting.

One member of the group did, indeed, see some fundamental truth about herself in the mirror. "I had done quite a bit of deep breathing," she said. "Then I went into the bathroom and I looked at myself in the mirror. And I was horrified at what I saw looking back at me. And I thought that if the people who loved me had forgiven all this, there must be some good in it after all. I looked for a long time into my eyes, and then I began to weep. I wept excessively, or exceedingly, for almost two hours—wept away a score of griefs—until I began to feel as if I were starting my life all over again, new."

Another member of the group, a woman who had been extremely ill earlier in the year, said, "I realized that all these years I never saw myself. I never wanted to look. It was like seeing somebody I knew very well but I never saw before."

One way of using your powers to visualize is to maintain contact with people, in your mind. For instance we decided to visualize each other at night when we woke and see whether this influenced our dreams, and whether any members of the group felt the contact. It was winter. One member of the core group was ill. We kept in mind where each person had sat in the group on the day we did our visualization of the whole group.

At night for the next two weeks we kept the group in mind. When we woke, we would immediately go around the group in our mind's eye. Sometimes one person would stand out, sometimes another. It was a comforting experience. In the middle of the darkness the group was present, companionably. We knew the others were thinking of us. At our next meeting we wondered whether we had influenced each other's dreams. Several people in the group had been dreaming of each other, and yet we couldn't find any direct evidence that we had been making a big impact on each other's dreams.

The visualization had accomplished two important things, however. It had given us a way to feel together when we were apart, and it encouraged us to practice, until we realized that we could, indeed, visualize.

At this point we decided to concentrate on the one group member who was ill. We had no thought of any occult power of healing. We knew that there was psychological comfort for her in knowing we were all with her. She had been ill frequently during the year. She had said that she had pain from a hernia. Clearly it bothered her more than she admitted. She was reluctant to talk about it in the group and unfortunately we did not press her. She was a beautiful and independent person with a highly resonant sense of humor and adventure. If we asked about her health she was likely to engross us in the beauty of a visiting blue jay on her window sill. What happened to her is worth describing, for it probably happens often to people in their seventies.

She had had some internal bleeding, and initial tests were inconclusive. Then she began to have pain. It was assumed to be caused by her hernia. She was privately alarmed, but she kept it to herself. Her doctors did not push her to come into the hospital for further tests—incredible as that may seem. Nor did she press them. This went on for months. Had she been a younger person it seems unlikely that the doctors would have allowed her to go on so long without a better diagnosis. Only when the symptoms became really severe did she go back for testing. She was told to come in for surgery at once. By this time there was a sizeable tumor in the intestines that had not been detected before. One must presume it had been there for eight months, since tumors grow very slowly in people of seventy-five.

Only a few days before her operation she told us briefly what had happened. Then we realized that self-healing and taking responsibility for one's own health could be double-edged. Somehow the group had persuaded her that she should and could heal herself, and she had been practicing visualization all year. Moreover we did not create sufficient trust or encouragement for her to say her real feelings, to entrust us with what she must have considered a negative burden. She had been so enrapt with the positive atmosphere and direction of SAGE that she had suppressed an entire part of herself, as we were to see in the next two days. In spite of her courageous outlook and cheer she clearly had feelings of fear and anger. Two members of the group became "family" and insisted on staying with her in the hospital up until the time she went under anesthesia, and from the moment she came to until she felt better. At first she needed to vent her feelings and let down her social guard. She was furious to find out that she had cancer when she had been treated casually for hernia, yet she had been afraid to find out, suspecting something was deeply wrong.

At the last minute she felt defenseless and frightened of the surgery and its aftermath. Recently a friend of hers had died of cancer. She wondered whether she would survive. When her feelings were drawn out she was able to cry, to talk, and clear her mind. By the time she was preparing for the anesthesia her mind was still, and she was focused on healing.

As she began to come out of the anesthesia sheer physical pain hit her and she complained loudly, "Can't you get me something to kill the pain? Can't you see I'm an old lady and I can't stand this!" For twenty-four hours she bitched and complained loudly. Nobody had ever seen this side of her personality.

We began to wonder whether we had unwittingly driven her into hiding herself with our strong statements about positive attitudes. We had never intended to drive negative feelings underground, yet we had forgotten how hard it is to shake off the training to be *nice*. One woman was straightforward and bitchy in the group, and some participants would get uncomfortable and edgy when she insisted on her opinions or complained of her life. Women even more than men had learned to deny any negative feelings in order to be nice. They would deny their anger even to the point of feeling suicidal. All of us had colluded, and no matter what we said about being open and uncensored, we, too, had been hesitant to be bitchy in the group. We had talked about our anger. We had expressed sorrow, fear, and grief. But we had not come out in the group completely straight. It is worth belaboring this point because there is energy and power in the negative expression. Our negativity is real. It will not vanish just because we hide it. Its effects won't vanish. Even the subtle negative thoughts infest our bodies, and the people around us. Only by bringing them out into the light and examining our actions can we see what we do.

192 • *Your Second Life*

In this case if she had complained about her pains early in the year, the group might have urged her to get a diagnosis. She could have had an early warning that the symptoms were serious, and if she needed support to face the diagnosis, the group would have been around her.

Selfishness has a survival value. Less energy is wasted in pretending nicety or false emotions. It is interesting to hear about the survival of cancer patients in treatment with Dr. O. Carl Simonton and his wife Stephanie in Fort Worth, Texas. The Simontons are well known for their use of visualization and meditation techniques, along with ordinary medicine. In looking at those who survived and those who didn't among their patients, they discovered that the survivors were not the nice, polite, uncomplaining people, but the complainers, the selfish, assertive, "unlikable" people, who were simply themselves.

In this instance the emergence of a negative streak in a very radiant person was instructive to us. After the first day the stress of terrible pain abated, and she rested. She began to act again as we had always known her. She was visualizing a deep magenta, one which seemed to her a healing color, and letting it spread through her body, especially onto the painful incision. It hovered there like a mist of color. She could feel that it was healing. During much of the day she listened to tapes that allowed her to go into a light trance. As she described it later, she hovered over her body rather than feeling submerged within it.

Her visualization was simple. She would relax, inhale a healing color, see it pervade her body, and help the wounded area. When she exhaled, she exhaled any toxins in her system, any wastes, and visualized the healing color as muddier, or fainter, or a different color. (See *Seeing with the Mind's Eye*, Samuels and Samuels [New York: Random House/Bookworks, 1975] and *The Well Body Book*, Samuels and Bennett [New York: Random House/Bookworks, 1973].)

Sometimes, as she did this, a group member would sit

with her, holding one hand about twelve inches over the incision, while focusing energy at her. She said that it felt very warm.

She spent most of her waking time in a visualization, or meditative state, and doing foot movements and exercises given her by her doctor. Visitors were limited. The surgeon had been surprised at the size of the tumor, and was expecting a slow recovery. After the first three days, however, he saw that something astonishing was taking place. She began feeling stronger, looking pink, getting restless. She wanted to walk around, despite the intravenous tubes. She was doing exercises in bed and visualizing healing much of the time. Only four days after surgery she was comforting another woman on the floor who also had cancer. Soon after her doctors were asking her to talk to another patient before surgery.

Mexican and European hospitals often have space in each patient's room or ward for family to stay and nurture the sick. This is uncommon in the efficient American hospital. We seem to have made no provision for feelings, for fear, anxiety, strangeness, and anger, and their role in tension and disease, except now in a few progressive children's and maternity hospitals. It seems as though we expect the ill and wounded to heal without love and relaxation. When a SAGE member insisted upon staying with her, it ran against all hospital conventions. Doctors and nurses objected vehemently, but finally they gave in and placed a sleeping cot in her room. As the first few days unfolded, staff people began peeking into the room to see what was going on. A nurse who had learned psychic healing understood. Others were curious. They could see that it was doing no harm. Perhaps the attention, the affection, and the meditations were actually helping. Attracted by this woman's grace and strong personality one nurse insistently requested her as a patient. She was dumbfounded by her progress. Throughout their duty time nurses would stop by to ask what she was doing, what tapes she listened to, and what process she did mentally. They never expected to see a woman in her mid-seventies snap back so rapidly from so serious a malignancy.

The color returned to her cheeks, and the brilliance to her eyes in four days. However it was too fast. She had been comforting people on the ward and entertaining family and friends. One day as she walked around she got chest pains. There was adhesion and fear of an embolism. Once again she lay flat on her back. This time she was asked not to move at all. Lying still was a reminder of her fragility. A week later, when she went home, she began to accept that the recuperation process would take a lot of energy and that she would have to cut back on her activity for some time.

By the time another woman in the group needed similar surgery, there was a precedent at SAGE, and the community was actively behind her. One person lent her tapes from Dr. Simonton. Several others met with her four days before her operation. All of them had used visualization methods themselves, to get through illness or surgery. They began by helping her release her tensions. She had not admitted how angry she was at her doctors because they had diagnosed her as having diverticulitis and only later had found it was cancer.

"I didn't realize how furious I've been." Not only had her doctors failed to diagnose her pain, but she felt they treated her in a humiliating way. The radiation therapist was gruff and brushed her aside like a child when she asked to see the X rays. Again when she inquired about nutrition, she was ignored. But she did not blow up and tell her doctors how angry she was. She had simply kept it inside—smoldering.

What would you do? Many of us have had these feelings, but we learned to respect doctors and not to assert ourselves. Hospitals and medical centers expect compliance and cooperation. Yet if you are the patient, your life is at stake. Perhaps you are exhausted or frightened. You need a positive state of mind to heal. It is a time when you need an ally, an advocate. SAGE people are beginning to do this for each other. In this instance the SAGE team probed and questioned relentlessly. They felt there was still some strong feeling not expressed.

"What are you most worried about that you're not saying?"

Silence.

"In your shoes I'd be worried about not surviving."

"I did finish my will," she admitted. Then she began wondering aloud whether she would survive, whether she should go through the family picture albums one last time.

If you cannot unburden yourself of fears and misery, meditation methods will not have much power. For most of us it is a matter of pride not to behave like a child, not to vent and scream, cry, and complain. But once you have really let it go you can relax more fully. Only after the fury and the fears had been shared did SAGE people begin to use visualization.

A member of the staff suggested, "Imagine a large strongbox—of any size or description that you like—with a lid that closes and locks. Now picture yourself putting all your anxiety, worries, and anger, and all your concerns about your family and other things in that box. Lock the lid securely. Leave all those things for when you come back to them."

When she had finished, he led her in an exercise for relaxing deeply. Because she had been practicing at SAGE this was easy and went fast.

"Now that you are deeply relaxed, see yourself as I see you. You are recovering rapidly. You are becoming vibrant and healthy. I see you coming back from the hospital and telling us in the community about your experience."

Up until the last moment, when she was rolled into the operating theater, SAGE people worked with her. They asked the nurses to give them some time alone so that she could be mentally prepared. "We're from a group called SAGE, and we think we can help her relax and heal better by using meditation."

"We know about that here," the nurse said. "In fact two years ago there was another woman up here who did that. We all remember her."

A few days later, back in her room, she was emerging from the worst discomfort. She continued visualizing. She was an artist and had a unique way of seeing. She often evoked scenes from her youth, mountain peaks with cool breezes coming off the snow, fields of pale pink-gray flowers in the wind. Her doctor was surprised at her quick recovery. Because he himself probably didn't understand the importance of mental expectation, he had loaded her down with his own worries. He said there were many things that could go wrong with someone as old as she was.

Doctors' attitudes can be a real problem for you, especially if you are older. Very often there is an unspoken attitude that is negative—that you will recover slowly, or that you will have complications. You need to help yourself not to be negatively influenced. You can.

You can be assertive and open. If you think your doctor's attitudes are negative, say so. Draw him or her out. Find out whether or not you want to entrust yourself to this person.

If you are preparing for surgery or hospitalization try to find someone who can give you emotional support during the experience. Your meditation and visualizations will be more effective with this kind of back-up. Most of us need at least one reliable advocate when we have undergone a trauma, especially if we are in a hospital.

Preparing for Healing

1. Find friends or relatives who can share your attitudes, and let them know how you feel and what you have learned. Do this now, while you are well. If you are doing exercises from this book or others, share them.

2. Choose an ally, who is willing to let you release your feelings and who will help you.

3. Ask your ally to help you assert your needs with the hospital staff.

4. Ask this close friend to stay with you to give you moral support, massage if that is appropriate, and to run errands. If you really want someone to stay with you overnight, arrange it. If you really insist a hospital will sometimes put a cot in your room.

5. Ask your ally to guide you in your healing visualizations and meditations, and to sit with you and share them.

6. You may want to ask your ally to protect you from other friends and family in the first days after surgery or recovery.

◇ ◇ ◇

After severe illness or surgery a patient usually does not have the energy to respond to family emotions, to chit-chat, or distractions. Often when we visit a sick person we drain them. We are worried about the person, caught up in our feelings, sometimes we act out of habit, condoling, moaning, fussing ineffectually. Or, because nobody visiting a hospital or a sickroom is without some anxiety, we try to amuse the patient, lighten his or her spirits with jokes, books, gossip, presents, news—all with the best intentions. Even so the impact on the sick person can be draining. In early stages of recovery the patient can be helped by your own calm and peace. If need be, stop in the lobby and breathe for a while until you feel relaxed and centered. Then you can sit, perhaps touching lightly, giving the patient energy, and putting your energy into calm. You might help the patient do a simple self-healing exercise. Here is one that is effective. Of course it is more effective when practiced first in health. Many SAGE people have said they couldn't have been so effective in healing themselves if they hadn't practiced relaxation and meditation for months beforehand.

Breathing Through the Skin

1. Find time when you will not be interrupted. Sit comfortably or lie down with a pillow under your knees. Be sure that you are not wearing anything tight.

2. Close your eyes and breathe deeply. As you exhale, let all your worries, thoughts, concerns, and previous feelings float away.

3. Imagine yourself—your entire body.

4. As you inhale, see or feel your entire body fill with radiant light. As you exhale feel or see all the toxins leaving your body through your breath and through the pores of your skin.

5. Breathe in, bringing radiant light through the pores of your skin and feeling your body fill with light. See your exhalation carry any wastes out.

Continue this for ten minutes.

◇ ◇ ◇

It is particularly effective if you and your ally have both practiced the same visualization, for when you are in pain it is helpful to have someone guide you in the visualization. When in a crisis we often forget to use the very methods we've learned, unless someone else is there who can do them with us.

You might wonder, why spend so much effort on mental healing? Eventually we all die. Why prepare for surgery or illness years in advance?

Of course we cannot undo the path of nature. All we can do is improve the quality of our experience. Most of us have grown up learning that sickness is woe, and a hospital experience is stressful. The culture we live in conspires to make it that way. But we still have some control over our experience, for we can alter our minds. By focusing on a color instead of on pain we can transform some of that energy into positive feeling. By stopping our habits of anxiety when we visit someone in a hospital we can remain centered, make real contact, and leave without having exhausted them. Pain and sickness are not enjoyable, but with some effort, they are much less terrible than we expect.

One dark evening in March a SAGE staff member had a miscarriage and went to the emergency room for a dilation and curettage. Her husband and friend acted as advocates. One doctor on duty scared her into thinking she might bleed to death if she didn't have an immediate operation. There were a few minutes of panic. Her husband said, "Wait a minute. I want to consult another doctor." At first he encountered resistance everywhere. He was going against rules. After a few phone calls he found a doctor who was willing to explain the operation and do it without any drugs. "It's very simple," he said, "takes about twelve minutes. I use a vacuum."

After a few minutes of discussion he agreed to do the operation with the husband and friend present. They asked the nurses to turn off the bright lights in the operating room until the doctor arrived. The friend and husband positioned themselves on either side of the operating table. Each took her hand, and they began long slow breathing. When the doctor was ready the lights were turned up, and he began to say at each step what he would do. "Breathe in and hold it, and breathe out." The woman's face remained completely relaxed. She had no sedatives, no anesthesia. When the doctor was finished, everyone looked at each other with pleasure. No one was tired. There had been no stress. The nurse and the aide felt elated. In ten minutes the patient was ready to go out to dinner. Contrast this with the ordeal that many people make of a dilation and curettage. Or appendectomy. Or almost everything. We do have options, but we do need each other to put them into action.

10 ❧ DYING

For several days people called the SAGE office to ask for Joe. He was one of our central staff members, a healthy person who had been jogging for ten years, who meditated, and was an inspiration for many of us. We weren't overly concerned about his absence until he didn't appear for a meeting. All day his associates sat on their anxiety. Then anxiety turned to alarm. After checking the hospitals one gutsy person called the morgue. He had been found dead near the track where he ran six miles a day. He had a blissful smile on his face.

Our shock was profound. He was one of us. He was only fifty-seven. We depended on him. We fought with him. We loved and admired him. A deep spiritual seeker who had been exploring his feelings about death in order to help dying people; he had been preparing for two years. He was ready. We were not. Once again we were confronted by the preciousness of our time together and, as Ken put it, the fragile, "paper-thin" quality of our lives. We lived under an illusion of control. But we did not control death or the larger purposes of which we feel a part.

His family flew in from many parts of the country. They wanted the service to be held at SAGE. This, they said, was his spiritual family and the home he had been seeking during his earlier life. We knew that he had left his home in the East, after retiring, to come to SAGE, but we had no idea that it meant fulfillment to him. A retired Unitarian minister and SAGE staff member, Aaron Gilmartin, led an unforgettable service in a large meeting room at the hotel where we had our offices. Concentric semicircles of chairs had been arranged for about one hundred people around a large table with a bowl of flowers and a few of Joe's favorite objects, such as a large shell and a picture of Christ. What Gil managed to do in this service was at once subtle and very powerful.

We began standing, holding hands, and feeling our feelings for Joe. Gil took the most central of all our exercises at SAGE, breathing, something we had all done together hundreds of times. He instructed us to begin paying attention to our breathing. We could feel the pulsing of our hearts, the rhythm of breath that each of us in that room shared. We were alive. Joe, who had led similar breathing so many times with us, was no longer breathing. This unspoken distinction between life and death was a statement. The breathing released our feelings. Some of us wept.

Our farewell to Joe Garst and celebration of his life with us had some of the qualities of our work together and expressed what SAGE is about. Standing and touching, as we had so often at SAGE, we sang some of Joe's favorite songs, led by his stepson. Mudita Nisker, the psychologist and dancer with whom Joe led a core group, guided us all in a meditation for speeding his spirit into the light. It allowed our love for him to empower him and us. Gil had spent hours with his family and had culled a biography of his early life, his career, and lifelong spiritual quest that finally brought him to SAGE. It was full of unfamiliar facts, about a time when we hadn't known him. As members of his family spoke, we knew him and our role in his life better. They offered memories of this gentle yet passionate man and read from his favorite books. Then members of SAGE began remembering him aloud; sometimes they recalled fights or funny situations, and everyone laughed. It was a solemn service, without a eulogy. We simply talked and shared our feelings as we felt inclined. Gil read to us a moving letter that Ken wrote to Joe.

One woman came up to a member of Joe's family afterward and said, "Boy, Joe and I never got along. We fought like cats and dogs." This service did not force anyone to pretend that things were perfect. One woman said that she and Joe had finished their business and she was ready for the relationship to be over. There was no right or wrong thing to say. No reason to feel self-conscious. Men and women both felt free to weep, openly. Afterward many of us had lunch together with Joe's family. We had a real sense of communion, having shared our feelings very fully. This is not so common today as it was when communities were smaller and families larger. This was the kind of service I would like, and would want to experience at times of loss. It gave us support and intimacy and pulled our SAGE community together in a way that was strengthening.

What some of us wanted was to see Joe's body. Many staff members and those of his family who had not already seen him went to the mortuary. Members of the SAGE community differed about the custom of viewing a body. Eugenia felt it was essential. Many of the community thought it barbaric. "I don't want my body to be seen after I die," said one woman. "I don't like what they do to you in the mortuary."

It was true that Joe's beatific death smile had been changed into an unfamiliar grimace. However without seeing his body I could not have believed that he was really dead. He had been an important person to me, the sharer of a vision, and a moral support since the start of SAGE. I was not ready to let him go. Seeing him I had to acknowledge that he was dead, and that I was alive. I had never seen my father's body after he died, and there had been no shared mourning, no expression of feelings at the service. For years I was haunted by the unfinished relationship, by the sense that he was simply on a long trip and would one day return. Barbaric or not I felt it was important for me to see the body, as Eugenia did. She said, "I remember going to the hospital after my mother died. I had to see the body. I looked her over. It was her body, but it wasn't her. I had that same feeling I had when my daughter was born and I examined her toes and her fingers, and all of her. It was awe at what life was. By acknowledging that my mother was really dead I was affirming life, too. I was alive."

Eugenia had nudged and prodded us into removing the veils of taboo and exploring our feelings about death and dying. We spent hours at SAGE, in core groups and workshops, learning how to grieve, how to allow and support mourning, how to acknowledge loss, to face dying and death. So many of us were sheltered from the basic facts of life. We were born in hospitals, to die in hospitals, and had been prevented from seeing, touching, smelling, and absorbing the fundamental conditions of life. What we were doing together at SAGE was no more than countering that deadening avoidance we had lived with in our culture. The service we held for Joe, the openness of our feelings and support for one another could not have happened excepting as the culmination of several years of continual work together. We had to use each crisis and death as a time to learn about our own feelings and beliefs. We would never have pursued our feelings with such intensity and persistence except for Eugenia. She and I started SAGE partly out of our needs to deal with dying. My father had recently died, and her mother was dying.

Eugenia's mother had progressively receded into helplessness. She lay in bed, unable to care for herself, speak, or understand. She was not old. She suffered from a mysterious brain disease. Eugenia, despite all the difficulties of transporting her and caring for someone in this state, brought her from Texas to California. She wanted to be near her before she died. It was an extremely stressful time for her, visiting her mother, touching her, talking to her, hoping, and losing hope. Not many weeks before she died, she was taken to the hospital in critical condition in need of oxygen. There she momentarily regained her ability to recognize the family and to speak. Then she relapsed and died. "I wouldn't have missed that chance to be with her as she was dying, not for anything. Life is so fleeting. I valued the chance to make real contact with her."

Eugenia's experience freed and inspired many people who might have passed up the opportunity to be with a dying parent or friend, who might have found it inconvenient to travel a long way, or who were uncertain about interrupting their lives with a long dying process. As she pointed out, this transition can never be repeated. "I had learned everything from my mother, how to walk and talk, how to dress, to become a woman, how to live. This was my one chance to learn from her how to die. Death tells us to treasure the time we have because we never know when it will end, and we cannot control the time we will die. To run away from dying, or dying people, is to avoid acknowledging how precious life is. That time and that person can never be brought back."

Expressing grief or fear is hard for many of us. We are well trained at keeping down our deepest feelings, even when we know it is time to release them. We learned how true this is at SAGE. We had spent hours every week exploring our feelings and making it possible to share feelings without self-consciousness. We cultivated our closeness and kept repeating to one another that it was okay to be human. It took us several years before we could experience together the kind of community we felt in our service for Joe, and the freedom we had to be ourselves. It had taken several years of consciously creating intimacy and deliberately confronting the topic of death and of dying.

A year earlier a member of a core group had died, a woman in her seventies whom we had grown to love. The SAGE staff and core group members were not yet a community then. This woman was the first core-group member to die. We all knew that somebody would inevitably die, and that we were spending a great deal of time and conscious effort coming to know and love each other, only to lose each other one day. When it happened we were not yet ready to share our feelings as a whole group.

Initially some of us younger staff members reacted more strongly than her friends in the group. We seemed to be overreacting. As we sat in our afternoon group, to which she would never return, we mourned her. Many group members were cool, offhand. They said they no longer allowed themselves to feel too strongly. They had lost too many people. Grief took too much out of them. That seems to be what we tell ourselves: that we will save energy if we do not express grief. Yet that afternoon the tension and fatigue in the room suggested that the unexpressed feelings were still strong and present.

On the spur of the moment Eugenia invented an exercise to unseal those feelings. It is an exercise you can adapt for yourself. "Close your eyes," she instructed us, "and see Rose in your mind's eye. When you have an image of her, find out what part of yourself she represents."

"I see a young girl, just emerging."

"I see someone dependent and clinging."

"I see a power and artistic talent just starting."

"I see my trapped self."

"An immensely caring woman."

We placed an empty chair in our circle for her. Now Eugenia asked one of the men to leave the circle and sit elsewhere in the room.

"Now let's do the same thing with Herb."

The group began to express its feelings about him, what he represented in each person. An empty chair was left for him.

"Now remove Gay."

As each person left the group it became small. Suddenly people began to weep. They were losing parts of themselves with each person who left the group: at some point it had become too drastic to deny any longer.

That was an important session for us, not only because we discovered what parts of ourselves we lost in the loss of each other, but we saw a way of bringing these feelings to the surface. We would never have expressed how much we cared for each other. How much it meant to have each other present. Often we took each other for granted. We acted calm about an illness and stoical about a death. We let our feelings remain dormant. Perhaps this is the importance of uninhibited mourning, for it allows us to recognize our own deep feelings.

Most of the time instead of using an exercise to bring our feelings to the surface we do the opposite. Rather than permit ourselves to face the full meaning of a threat or loss at the time it happens, we repress the feeling, stay numb. That means we don't admit the full meaning of the people we care about, either to ourselves or to them. These unspent feelings seem to stay with us in strange ways. For instance there were people at SAGE who were still mourning people who had died twenty or sixty years ago. They had not been able to deal with the feelings at the time, and they were still unable to shake the traumatic effects. Once feelings are released, you usually feel energy. Emotion is, indeed, the motion of a feeling expressed, carried outward. If the motion of our feelings is stopped, we use our energy in holding them back. At SAGE what we could do was to share with each other precisely these feelings we were forbidden to express in our families and which were usually cultural taboos. The taboo subjects turned out to be things we felt we couldn't cope with.

Sex and death are two topics of conversation during which nobody's mind wanders. People don't sit and pick their nails or play with their clothing and look out the window. Nobody can be neutral or uninvolved. If they play cool, they are trying not to feel their feelings. Ultimately we cannot escape them: Our bodies know our feelings. Our dreams know our real feelings. The deep recesses of our minds are crammed with them. They are part of us. No way we can escape. Our best alternative is to bring them to the surface and use them.

If our feelings of loss are hidden and our fears about dying are suppressed, we may not be able to act upon the things that have real meaning to us because we will not yet know ourselves. We have all seen the extent to which the topic of death and of dying has, until recently, been taboo in our society, something to be feared and avoided. The avoidance has even extended to the elderly and to dying people. At the very time in their lives when people may need help and support the most, we avoid confronting the real needs. How many elderly people in institutions live polite, apathetic, isolated lives—already counted off? Sometimes they are dismissed as senile, which is another way of saying that nobody wants to find out what they are actually experiencing. Perhaps they are in transition, finishing up with unfinished feelings and life events. Certainly when Eugenia and Mac, a former core-group member, worked together for three years in a rest home, they discovered that people who were supposed to be senile were leading intense inner lives. One black woman who had been brutalized when young was sitting on unexpressed rage. Another woman who was supposedly "spaced-out" was communing with her dead husband in preparation for dying.

Not only were dying people avoided. In many institutions deaths became disappearances. A roommate died in the middle of the night and the body was taken away silently. No word was said by the staff, no feelings expressed. Is it any wonder that so many people sit and stare out the window, or at television, or at the wall? The most important transition, ending life, was overlooked and nobody was encouraged to feel or speak about it. What is left? By overlooking people who are old, who are dying, by overlooking death, we diminish the value of life.

We all have strong feelings about dying, ourselves, and about the deaths of people we love, but how many of us talk about them, share with others our fascinations and fears? It would change our lives and our relations with one another if we could admit our feelings.

When Ken began working in an institution, he spoke about it in a way that seemed important. "When I went to the group the first time I remember asking one of the women how old she was and she said, 'I'm ninety-one and I'm going to die on my birthday when I'm ninety-two.' I didn't say it, but my first reaction was, 'Oh, no you won't, you'll live forever!' Whenever people in that place would get into telling their children or grandchildren about how they thought they were going to die, the family would say, 'Oh, Gram, you won't die.' Which is ridiculous. If somebody is in the hospital, sick, you never say, 'You might die.' You say, 'You'll be well. Everything will work out.' "

That is what my father said on the night before he died. One of the few things I regret is my part in allowing him to die in isolation. None of us could bear to acknowledge that he was dying, and we kept wishing he would get better, acting cheerful, talking about his future. Although he knew we loved him, we would not allow him to talk about dying, and by maintaining a polite lie we deprived him of real contact. Despite his dazed look he was a man who knew where he was. He was in a hospital dying, and his family was acting as if he weren't, and all were suffering underneath. Had we all been honest, we would have shared those last weeks and had a feeling of real closure and closeness.

Surely we could not fool him about our real feelings. Nothing can be kept secret. Feelings, however hidden, are vibrations of energy that broadcast themselves into the world and people around us at all times. Our most private thoughts are known by those around us, even if they are not conscious. Thus if we love someone, they know it without our words. If we are angry, or dislike someone, the person knows that, too. We may not be aware of our own feelings, but we transmit them.

Grief is an inevitable part of life, unavoidable, yet many of us have been taught to hold back our feelings and not to admit their intensity, as if we could avoid pain by not expressing it. By doing that we also prevent ourselves from experiencing some important release, a letting go that is the essence of vitality and rebirth.

Time for Grief

You may want to think about this for yourself. Take a few minutes, if there is some death that has gone unfinished in your life, somebody who died, or who's dying, find someone to whom you can really tell what that feels like for you.

Eugenia told a group of trainees, "Going through my mother's death made me think a lot about the process of dying. It's an issue I raise with everyone I work with. When someone dies in the nursing home I bring the subject up. Somehow recognizing it and talking about it changes it for everyone. One of the common responses is, 'Oh, I don't know. I don't have any feelings about it.' Then we'd talk a little more and the person would say, 'I can't afford to have any feeling. It happens too often.' I feel like giving people an opportunity to express some of their feelings. I'm working with a woman who's eighty. She had to have an operation two weeks ago and she said, 'Well, I've got everything ready. I burned all my husband's records. He was a doctor. I have everything labeled about who it's to go to.'

"I was giving her a massage and I was down at her feet. I said, 'So you're ready to go?' There was a long pause, as if I wasn't supposed to ask that. She said, 'Is anybody ever ready?' "

That is probably the statement that most people make. Who among us is ready? What does it take to be ready? One way of exploring that question for ourselves in SAGE groups was to find out what we felt remained unfinished in our lives. The exercise that we have done so effectively at SAGE is extremely simple, and you can do it for yourself by taking pen and paper, and a little time for reflection.

Are You Ready to Die?

1. Sit comfortably, with paper and pen nearby.

2. Take some time to relax with your eyes closed.

3. If you died tomorrow, what would you leave undone? Write out all the things you can think of. It may be: Who would take care of my cat? What about my unpaid bills? What about my sick daughter? Or you may have other concerns: My ex-wife and I are still angry. It doesn't feel finished. I don't want to die until I regain my faith in God. I don't have faith in anything. I'm not ready. It may be an unfinished communication: "I never told my son I love him—and why I have no money to leave." "I know my daughter is just waiting to be rid of me—but I've never said it."

4. When you imagine dying, what are some of the things you worry about? At SAGE people most commonly said they did not want to be a burden on someone else. They did not want to suffer, to become helpless or senile, and particularly did not want to burden somebody. Some people feared pain. Others feared losing control of their lives. What are your concerns?

5. Write your obituary. You may write an epitaph, too, but your obituary should be a long article about who you were and what you did with your life. Do

you think the writer would call you a good person or bad, someone who helped others or didn't? What kinds of idiosyncracies, tastes, adventures, family, or profession will the writer describe? What kind of character and personality was this person who was you?

6. See if there is someone in your life with whom you can share these things.

◇ ◇ ◇

Dying and growth have much in common. Eugenia and I learned a great deal about this seeming paradox as we worked with Stanley Keleman, a unique therapist-philosopher. He had focused intently on body energies as a key to life satisfaction. At one point early in his career he called himself a chiropractor, and at another he became a bioenergeticist. But basically he worked and taught out of direct observation, and a deep, almost mystical appreciation of his own nature. Stanley was concerned with dying because it was typical of the movement of living which he saw as a succession of transitory stages. As he pointed out, at each stage a person would have to let go of some old behavior in order to make way for a new one. This began with life itself, in the womb, and took a characteristic form throughout a person's life. An infant, for example, must let go of his mother's breast to become weaned and independent. The child must let go of being a protected baby at home and enter the social world by going to school. Whether it is letting go of mother's hand, whether it is ending bachelorhood to be married, having a first baby, or saying good-bye to a dying parent—or dying oneself—the process is similar. And each of us will do it in our own characteristic way.

"Letting go is the willingness to experience unconditionally, but that may be possible only when someone dies," Stanley wrote in his book, *Living Your Dying*. It means relinquishing the habits and feelings, the behaviors that kept you "feeling like yourself." It means letting go of your identity in one stage in order to proceed to another phase of your life. Unless you did end your pattern of behavior—such as going to a job for fifty years—you would be stuck there for life. On the other hand when you retire you risk a sense of being disoriented, uncertain, in transition for a period of time until you start a new pattern. The way you typically end phases in your life, the way you let go, Stanley told us, is the way you will die.

When we talk about readiness to die, most of us act as if dying were not a part of our lives. Stanley Keleman often asked people whether they wanted to die slowly or rapidly. If you look at your style of living, he said, you know how you will probably die.

How do you want to die? Do you want to be conscious and aware? Do you want to be snuffed out quickly? Close your eyes and see yourself dying.

Eugenia asked this question during a day-long SAGE group on dying. Ten of us were there and our answers were all different.

"I want to die alone, quietly."

"I'm going to die in my sleep."

"I'm going to die suddenly. I'll never know what happened."

"I'm going to die with my family around me. I'll tell them what I'm seeing."

"I want to die by myself, slowly, but not so I'd be a burden on anyone."

"I want to die in a garden in the late afternoon in the sunlight. I want to be held by someone I love and trust."

"I want to be held by someone, but I don't want them interrupting me and asking a lot of questions."

Several people said they didn't care exactly how they died, just so they didn't suffer from a lingering, burdensome illness.

Watching Yourself Die

1. Take some deep breaths. Relax completely. Close your eyes.

2. As if you were watching a movie, watch the scenario of the way you want to die. Where are you? Who do you want to have with you? What are you doing?

Sometimes a bizarre scene will pop into mind. Just watch it. It does not mean that things will happen that way. It only means that this is what you see right now.

As we did this exercise in a group one day, tears were streaming down the face of one man. He was not feeling sad. He had seen himself in a meadow, with his wife and one of his sons, and he had never known how much they loved him. Another man said he had left his body in half sleep. I saw myself, ancient, skinny, in a wheelchair in an Asian orphanage, being pushed toward an open window and launched like a missile. It was comfortable to talk about such images at SAGE and speculate without being considered morbid or unnatural.

Still, for many of us, these exercises were only a preamble to self-discovery. We had managed to repress our deepest fears so successfully that we could manage imaginary situations and deal with them intellectually. Eugenia gave us a chance to probe our feelings more deeply, giving us an exposure to intense ways of experiencing ourselves. These sessions were powerful and sometimes evoked life-changing insights among the SAGE participants and larger groups attending SAGE workshops.

Eugenia trained many people who worked in such institutions as convalescent hospitals or nursing homes. They were nurses and social workers and other professionals. To them she said, "One thing I feel very strongly is that you can't deal with other people who are dying until you have dealt with your own feelings about dying—that is your own dying."

The following exercises will help you get in touch with your own feelings about dying. They were adapted for SAGE from Stanley Keleman's book, *Living Your Dying*. They are good exercises to do with somebody you trust. If there is no one to share them with, write down your observations about yourself.

Endings and Transition

1. Make sure that you will not be interrupted for at least an hour. Remove constricting clothing, jewelry, contact lenses, or glasses. Sit comfortably in a chair and close your eyes.

2. You are going to take a trip backward in time, to the first days you ever left your family to go to school. Try to remember as much as you can. You will need to begin reliving that experience. Try to remember the first day of school—or one of the first days you were in school. Stand up. Keep your eyes closed, and imagine you are entering that class as a small child. Get an image of the room and the day. You are tiny. How did you make that turning point? How did you handle it? You may not think you remember, but feel your body. Express what you were feeling with your body, or let it express to you. Were you fearful, hanging onto your mother or sibling? Were you crying? Were you angry or defiant? Were you brave? Did you get sick? Were you excited? Were you eager? Rebellious? Cooperative? Sneaky?

This was a major turning point in your life. It was your entrance into society, the entrance of society into your infant world. You were suddenly subject to an authority other than your family. How did you handle it? Did you just swallow your feelings and comply? Did you resist? What did you feel and what did you do?

This was the same authority as the doctor who says, "I'm not going to release you. You are going to stay here in the hospital." How did you handle that authority situation when you were young? How do you handle it now?

3. Write down your observations or share them with your partner. If you can do this exercise with a group you will begin to discover how many different possible responses there are. Each of us selects a pattern and lives with it, conceiving that way of reacting to be the only alternative. But in truth people handle turning points in their lives very differently. Some are crushed by change; others are challenged, excited, and grow.

4. Take a break of fifteen or twenty minutes.

5. Relax, breathe deeply, and close your eyes. Go back in time.

6. Remember your very first sexual experience and how you handled it. You might have been six, or twelve, or sixteen—it doesn't matter. You may have lived on a farm and seen animals copulating or birthing, or you may have been playing with friends and showing each other your genitals. You may have read something or masturbated. Simply try to recall that first experience and feel in your body how you handled it. How did you handle the excitement? Did you try to stamp it out? Did you stop the excitement? Did you go with it? Were you ashamed, proud, fearful, feeling pleasure, pain, satisfaction, or frustration? Try to reexperience your body position during that first experience. What muscles tightened? Did you become forward and open? Did you become shy or adventuresome, aggressive or passive? Did you hold back,

repress your feelings, and pretend they weren't there?

It doesn't matter what your pattern was. Just see whether you can recognize your pattern. Now see how this pattern influenced your subsequent sex life.

Early sexual encounters are turning points. From the safe world of being neutral, we emerge as sexual beings. There are many social prescriptions laid upon us. How we react to these is relevant to how we are going to die. Think about that pattern and write down your feelings and observations, unless you can share them directly with a partner or group.

7. Think about how you end things. How do you end relationships? How do you wind up a phase of your life? Think of important endings in your past. It might be the end of school for you and the beginning of work life. It might be the end of single life, the beginning of marriage. How did you feel as you were deciding to get married, and just after you did? What happened to you after the birth of your first child? How did you say good-bye to someone close who left your life? How did you make a move, a change of jobs, a decision to retire? Were you sudden or gradual? Did you resist the change until you had no choice? Did you express your feelings or deny them? Did you become emotional? Did you withdraw or share your feelings? See if you usually ended things in pretty much the same way, whether it was a broken love affair, a marriage, a friendship, or a move to a new place. How did you feel about entering adolescence, about taking on the responsibility of parenthood, about menopause? All of these are transitions, turning points that imply the ending of one phase of life and beginning of another.

◇ ◇ ◇

If you can see your pattern of endings, it offers you the possibility of changing if you want to. You will die your death as you are carrying out your life. If you make changes violently, you are likely to die that way. If you are explosive, you may be the kind of person who has a coronary. If you withdraw, you may die slowly, in small steps.

Most of us live our lives out of touch with our own brevity. If we remembered that we are going to die, at each instant, we might spend our time on earth differently. We might forego some of the boring repetitions, the trivia, the negative postures, the focus on material things. We might take more risks in order to discover what does satisfy us in living. For the most part we do not remember that we will die. As Carlos Castaneda wrote in *Tales of Power*, we forget that death looks over our left shoulder. We may say the words. But we really live our lives removed from death, sugar-coated, pretending life won't end, focusing elsewhere.

Children and adolescents talk about their fear of dying. They ask frank questions about dead animals or relatives, and they often wonder what it would feel like to be dead. How often do you talk about it with your peers? Children ask what is on the other side. Is it terrifying? Will it hurt? Will anyone be there with me? Will I be able to fly? Will I see and hear? Will I come back as another baby? Will I remember? Are there ghosts?

When was the last time you asked these questions of anyone your own age?

It is too bad that we have all been given dogmatic answers in childhood, as if anyone really knew. "There is nothing after death." "There is an afterlife like this one in heaven." "There is reincarnation." "There is Hell." "There is life with beings in other planets, and other forms." And so on. Dogmatic answers quickly stifle curiosity and our willingness to venture and find out. If someone in authority says to us at an early age, "All experience ends with death," then there is nothing to expect or discover. We may take years to discover that there is something else, another way to life that we can unfold for ourselves. The same is true of dying. We can only understand how we feel about dying by trying to die a little bit. We must experience, without censoring, some foretaste of our own death.

Stanley Keleman's half-breath exercise offers an ingenious and profound way to uncover some of your deep feelings about dying. You can do this exercise alone, but it is best done with someone else. The range of possible ways to react can be experienced by doing this with a group of people. We adapted the exercise for groups at SAGE.

A Taste of Death

1. Pick as a partner some friend or family or group member that you would like to die with. In this exercise you will get in touch with real feelings about dying, fear, panic, excitement, letting go, the adventure of the unknown.

2. Sit comfortably.

3. Take a deep, long breath and exhale fully.

4. Close your eyes.

5. Take a deep, long breath, counting the seconds, and exhale.

6. Take a breath that gives you half as much air as you had last time, and exhale fully.

7. Cut the last breath in half.

8. Take in *half* as much air as you did last time, and exhale.

9. Each breath should be half the last one, until you are down to no air at all. Pay close attention to your body feelings. Don't avoid them. Don't cheat! Really continue cutting your breath until you are out of oxygen. Then wait as long as you can, watching your feelings.

10. When you absolutely have to take a new breath, do so, watching your feelings carefully.

11. Share what you experienced: Write it down if you are alone.

◇ ◇ ◇

Some people get too frightened to do this exercise correctly. Some avoid their feelings.

"I felt very aware that this was an exercise. I couldn't play-act my way into dying."

"I find this foolish and ineffective."

Some people are startled by what they discover about themselves.

"I felt a palpitation in my gut that reminded me of crying deeply."

"I felt total panic."

"I was gasping. I felt I wanted to hang onto something. I was terrified. For a moment I thought I was really dying."

"I felt fear, at first. I got really cold. Then I felt like I went through a big wave. I gave up. I was floating. I suddenly felt wonderful. Images came into my mind. I became almost ecstatic!"

"I got to a point where I no longer cared. I felt deeply relaxed. It felt pleasant."

"I felt like I was floating above my body, out of it, and I could have kept on going."

This exercise is graphic, and to the point. Only the knowledge of how we act will allow us to change, if we want to.

As we die we are forced to let go of life. It is the process of letting go that most of us may fear in dying. Surely we cannot vanish from this enormous universe. There is nowhere else to go. But we must change form. We cannot hold these molecules and these atoms together in the same form forever. Even the sun, the stars, and the galaxies change. Is it the change of form we fear?

If you had the choice of looking toward death as an adventure, a challenge, a pleasurable experience, instead of a fearful one, what would you prefer? That is hardly a question. Most of us don't realize that there are many possible ways to experience a life transition, in particular dying. In the early 1970s a young psychologist, Dr. Charles Garfield, worked in the University of California Hospital studying attitudes. Some of the people he saw were dying, while others were healthy.

He questioned them closely as to their feelings about death and dying. In brief his survey indicated that certain kinds of "mental" experience seemed to lead people toward a more positive feeling about dying. They had less fear and generally more positive attitudes. The experiences they had had might be called transcendent or spiritual. Some of those interviewed had had these peak experiences after taking psychedelic drugs such as LSD. Others had them during meditation. Both the meditators and the psychedelic drug takers showed less fear of death than most other people.

What was the nature of the experience that changed their view of dying? It is an experience that we have heard about all our lives. It is in the Bible. Saint Theresa of Avila, one of the great Christian saints, along with many Christian mystics and many followers of other religions, have described an ecstatic feeling of unity with all the universe. Abraham Maslow in *The Farther Reaches of Human Nature*, William James in *Varieties of Religious Experience*, Swami Yogananda in his *Autobiography of a Yogi*, Richard Bucke and others in *Cosmic Consciousness*, and countless more have described a sudden total perception of reality, of its intense beauty, feelings of being dissolved as a separate entity, of being absorbed, accepted, lifted up into the entire world, into feelings of intense love, seeing matter dissolve into light, seeing all things become intertwined, in a diffused yet intense glory. The experience involves going beyond the usual confines of the little self, the little personality one must wear for a while, and becoming boundaryless, beginning to see beyond the boundaries, to feel part of the sea, stars, and all beings. Often within this experience people mention that a sense of timelessness is important, that they no longer experienced their lives as the small, short events in which they had just been immersed. Instead they knew that they were part of an endless process. Always taking new form. Death was simply the ending that had to take place before the next form could be shaped. This is not new. Probably no person alive has not had some kind of peak experience, often in childhood, or at the last moments of dying. These experiences bring the message that life is not limited to what we ordinarily experience. Existence is not limited to what we know about, nor to the infinitesimal time span of a human life.

The implications of this experience have been succinctly stated by William Johnston in *Silent Music: The Science of Meditation, Consciousness, Healing, and Intimacy* (New York: Harper & Row, 1974).

Psychological discoveries about ecstasy at death dovetail with modern theological studies about the aging process. These speak of a double curve in the graph of human life: the downward curve of physical disintegration as the vital forces diminish, and the upward curve of spiritual energies as the core of the personality is liberated. Not, again, that this happens in every case; but ideally speaking it should happen if all goes well. From the earliest times the Hindus have had the same intuition and they have divided human life into four stages in the course of which the personality is increasingly spiritualized. . . . And then there is Jung, with his thesis that beginning with the middle period of life (thirty-five to forty-five in the West of his day) a person should become increasingly contemplative.

All these theories point to one central idea: that the life of man is (or, more correctly, ought to be) a process of spiritualization which reaches its climax with death. If this is so, what happens abruptly in ecstasy and sudden death may happen gradually in the aging process. There is the same inflow of spirit, the same expansion of consciousness; but the very slowness of the process makes integration easier. In either case, death is the door to the ultimate ecstasy (call it resurrection or nirvana or what you will), and in the lives of the mystics we find foretastes or adumbrations of this final beatifying ecstasy.

If we pay attention, we may live a double life. On the one hand we are immersed in family cares, petty problems, material things. But some part of us extends beyond this conditioned reality, some part of us that feels free, undifferentiated, spacious, light, interwoven with what is around us. These are feelings of deep assurance. They cannot be obtained by expecting them, for there is no way to coerce feeling, cosmic or otherwise. However the route used by most of the peoples of the earth since life began here has been a process now known as meditation.

11 ❧ MEDITATION AND MEDITATIVE EXERCISES

Most of us have grown up thinking that meaning lay in something we did, either in relationships with people or some accomplishment. As Eugenia put it one day:

"What would it mean to challenge the idea of our society that our time is meaningful only if you give something to someone else? Perhaps the last part of life, instead of being a time when you give something to someone else, is a time when you give to yourself. I work in a rest home where people can't get out to give anything to anybody else. They run up against meaninglessness, even though they may have given a lot at one time in their lives. Now they are helpless, and in our society that is the same as being meaningless—or is it? What would happen if I could look forward to the last part of my life as a time that I really went inward and did a lot of work on myself. Supposing that were the meaning in it for me and I geared my life that way, knowing in advance that I would have that time to myself. That is what a lot of Asian people think, and I realize that it makes sense to me."

One SAGE woman said, "People think there's something wrong with you if you do that. I feel that there is some kind of inward trend as you get older, but we older people are made to feel that unless we're outward we better find out what's wrong with us. Maybe it's my milieu. Many people who have reached retirement age are tired and want to stop working, but what is going to be the meaning of life for them?"

As one woman remarked, "I apply this to myself because I see that I usually use other people as mirrors. I'm always going around trying to get feedback as to how they see me. That's just the way I've been programmed. I had a kind of insight that I didn't have to look outside for some sort of mirror to tell me who and what I am. Deep inside, I know. The more I get in touch with it the less it matters what people see."

Somewhere, somehow, we all have an inkling that the lives we lead, the languages we happen to speak, the foods, homes, relationships we happen to hold, are not the only ones, are not sacred, are not some absolute reality of experience. They are just a lens through which we have seen a tiny portion of what life can be like on this earth. We, highly individuated, differentiated people, suffer from isolation. Our tribal brothers do not even know what that is. They do not know what it is to have separate desires or relationships that are not decreed by the tribe. They have no separate property or children. If we human species can see the reality of life so differently on this earth, what a small perception must we have of reality as a whole! Here we are on this insignificant bit of a blue planet, in the midst of a tiny solar system, in a huge galaxy, which is but a quantum, a mere teardrop of lights in the vastness of the sea of galaxies.

That immensity is where we come from. As Lawrence LeShan often said to students who were frightened of their meditative experiences, "Out of this universe we cannot fall." There is nowhere to go: We are here for eternity. But just as we changed from child to adult, we are surely going to change form, and keep changing.

We all know in our bones that this immensity is our parent. But how can we contemplate such things when we are busy making an income or raising children? It seems quite right that great philosophers and teachers and religious leaders tend to mature at the end of their lives. It should be a time that we could all look forward to, a kind of promise. We have an intuition of something very great when we are children, but we have too little experience and skill then to find what we seek.

Then we spend our years acquiring external skills and maintaining a material existence. Then what? SAGE people have commented:

"I think it's very sad that housewives who have brought up families and gone through crises, or businesspeople who reach retirement, don't feel they have any self-worth. We haven't been taught to think that we're beautiful and all of a sudden we come to these golden years and we have no faith in ourselves or courage to enjoy them."

"The people who are admired are those who are seventy-five and still doing what they have done all their lives— busy and active people."

"It's true, I've been feeling guilty about not shouldering responsibility for Christmas and Thanksgiving. Maybe it's an intuitive way of saying that after fifty-five years of that, it's *enough!*"

We asked ourselves why we couldn't slow down. Most of us felt some fear that if we stopped doing the ritual things of our lives, we would retrogress. Was it fear of dying in some way? Or a fear of beginning a second life?

There were many possible reasons why we haven't pursued our inner life with the same regard we gave externals. In part we need to quiet that external turmoil before there can be an inner life. After a full year together practicing relaxation, group contemplation, and other processes like guided visualization, the first group of SAGE participants began asking seriously about meditation. They asked for lectures, books, and instructions. And they often thought we were falsely humble or coy when we evaded such questions as "What is meditation?"

Meditation is a truly vast subject, and this chapter contains only a few introductory exercises that we used at SAGE to prepare for meditation, along with excerpts from a text on the subject.

We are extremely fortunate to be living now. Books on meditation abound. We can learn procedures and philosophy from all over the world. This was not so easy until the 1960s. Of course much of the preindustrial world has always used some kind of meditative practice in living. Usually it is a slow and undramatic process. Nonetheless the focused mind can unleash energies that exist dormant within the body in a way that may be analogous to the atomic power released by fission of the atom. An unprepared person might find this overwhelming. Partly for such reasons these disciplines were usually kept secret or esoteric and reserved for the spiritual initiate under the guidance of a teacher. But many of these exercises are available from books now. There is no harm in reading about them and they are interesting, as you may find by reading some of the books in the bibliography. A particularly helpful overview can be found in Daniel Goleman's, *The Varieties of Meditative Experience* (New York: E. P. Dutton, 1977). There is also no gain in endlessly reading *about* an inner process. Most of us have difficulty attaining the degree of focus and discipline that the most introductory exercises demand. Only by practice can we have this focus.

If you have been practicing a relaxation exercise from this book or others, you have been laying a foundation for the inner quiet that you need. At SAGE we considered relaxation of body, feeling, and mind an essential part of our weekly sessions and our daily homework. Frequently we did an ordinary exercise with an attitude that was meditative. For instance we walked very slowly across the room, concentrating on each movement.

Eventually this became a walking meditation. This is very satisfying, as you can read in *An Experiment in Mindfulness* by E. H. Shattuck (New York: Samuel Weiser, 1972), who describes this form in one Burmese monastery. To do this is to restore your appreciation of the miracle that you take for granted every time you walk. Our appreciation is probably greatest when we are toddlers and have been working for hours to stand upright, and we then take a few steps. Most of us do not remember how many hours a day we worked and what effort it took to get out of our crawling posture and place our vulnerable selves upright—an important part of our psychological development. Even as young children we quickly forgot that balance and vulnerability were important to us. We no longer felt what we were doing as we shifted our weight from foot to foot. Until we suffer from some physical impediment, we take walking quite for granted.

Walking Meditation

1. You can do this alone, but it has additional power when a group is walking. You need about forty minutes, free of all distractions.

2. You need a level space. If you are walking inside a room, move furniture and small rugs so that you have the longest possible walk, uncluttered. If you are in a group, find a lawn or a room that is twenty to forty feet long. You need to spread out and walk in silence.

3. Begin (in a group you will all begin at once, standing in lines so that each person can walk the full distance) by standing in place. Take a few deep breaths with eyes closed. Then open your eyes and softly focus on the ground three or four feet ahead of you.

4. Standing in place, begin shifting your weight from foot to foot. Just feel your shifting balance. Feel

your feet on the ground. (This is best done barefoot or in stocking feet.)

5. Feel your center of gravity. You may imagine that you have a heavy lead ball inside your abdomen just above your genitals. It is the center of your balance and power.

6. Looking ahead on the ground about three to four feet begin to take a step. Do it as slowly as you can manage. You want to walk as slowly as if the air around you were thick honey, as slowly as you possibly can. If you lose your balance going slowly, walk at the speed you can manage and practice balance exercises from Part Two until you can walk slowly with ease.

7. As you begin to walk very slowly, pay attention to the way you are breathing. Pay attention to each tiny motion, to the feeling of your heels and toes on the ground, your ankles. Feel your calves and thigh muscles as you move. Feel your hips, the joints. You will become aware of the way your pelvis tilts, your spine moves, and the position of your head and shoulders. Feel your arms. When you walk every part of you is in motion. See if you can perceive by paying attention.

8. Periodically return to your breathing. Are you breathing relaxedly? If your mind wanders from the tiny motions of your slow walking, gently bring it back. If you do this correctly, it may take you a half an hour to walk across a large room.

9. The longer you walk in silence, paying attention to each movement, the quieter you will feel when you finish.

◇ ◇ ◇

We first did this one afternoon in a living room that was only about twenty-four feet long. There were twelve of us.

We took ten minutes to cross the room. Some of the SAGE people felt tired when we finished.

"I didn't realize my balance was so bad. I found that very hard, going slow, you know. I kept feeling as if I were going to fall over." Several people said that they needed to work on regaining their balance.

"I found it very peaceful. I was surprised. My, I felt so serene when we were done. I didn't know how long we had been going."

Later this woman said, "I walk about two miles a day. Now I do it with a different attitude, more like a meditation. It's very relaxing."

The effect of a large group moving together in slow motion can be exceedingly time-stopping. It can slow down your sense of the outside world. I remember being introduced to this exercise in a church courtyard with about ninety students in a group called Seekers After Truth. As we walked on the grass, the vision of someone's heel lifting infinitesimally slowly off the ground and the toe following gave me the impression that time had almost stopped and we were all coming into a new dimension. Although this can be difficult at first, SAGE people have used this exercise well. Their initial difficulties in slow walking inspired them to practice other exercises for leg strength and balance.

It is important to practice this exercise in a relaxed state, and this becomes easier after you have done it a couple of times. Let your eyes be soft, your mouth hang open. If your eyes get tired it means you have not been relaxing them. As you become relaxed and sensitive, you will feel body sensations: These are normal, but usually *you* are too noisy to hear them.

"I became aware of internal sensations, the beat of my heart, the coursing of my blood, the way my bones hang together," said one SAGE man.

"I got into a kind of boundless state. It was sensuous."

"My mind started wandering. I was thinking of the time

and wondering about some company coming tonight. I got feeling guilty about what I was thinking, but I couldn't seem to stop."

Guilt and trying too hard seem to be problems for most of us. We have grown up learning that what we achieve is attained by effort. Yet in meditative exercises we cannot achieve anything by effort and trying.

When you try, you may be trying to become something you aren't, to accomplish something outside of yourself. All our lives most of us look for satisfaction and pleasure outside of ourselves. We think that movies, books, entertainments, events, or other people ought to provide our pleasure. We think we must create something, or achieve something in order to be satisfied. Yet all of us have had the experience of being in a virtual paradise, perhaps on a holiday or a vacation, and finding that we didn't enjoy it, and we couldn't be present. Once I had that experience standing on a pier in an exquisite bay with seals cavorting all around me. I became very depressed. I thought I should be happy or that I could force myself to be happy if I just made the right effort.

Effort destroys. When you are tense and want to sleep, relaxation eludes you. You may need to bring some feelings to the surface and express them. You can do this by being very nice to yourself. Treat yourself like someone you are deeply in love with, someone very precious to you. If thoughts intrude, admit gently what you are thinking. Then you can draw your attention back to what you began to do. Don't get involved in your thoughts. Just feel your body. Feel your muscles, especially the muscles around your eyes. Feel them relaxing. Sense the pleasantness of that feeling. Don't pay too much attention to whether thoughts flit by or not.

Feeling satisfaction and quietude in ourselves takes practice. Perhaps you have already begun, sitting in some pleasant place, contemplating. As you do this repeatedly, your mind will stop its chatter and memory, its interruption of your tranquility. If you don't believe that it is your own mind that prevents you from feeling tranquility, try the following exercise just once.

Counting Thoughts and Feelings

1. Make certain you will not be interrupted for twenty minutes by people, pets, or phones.
2. Sit in a quiet place. Put a timer or alarm clock in the room, set for fifteen minutes.
3. Sit comfortably with your eyes closed and relax as you would during contemplation.
4. Every time you have a thought, feel a sensation such as a body feeling, or hear an outside sound, experience an image or fantasy (count the experience). Count every thought, feeling, sensation, and image that you experience for fifteen minutes.

The first time I did this I spent what I considered a quiet hour, relatively devoid of thoughts and chatter, yet I had counted 1,060 items. It is not so impressive to hear about another person's experience as it is to watch your own mind's activity. Without watching the monkey that is your mind, you have no idea what animal you are about to train.

One afternoon in 1974 a remarkable yogi named Bob Treadwell began to chant during a period when the SAGE members were lying on the floor to rest from exercise. He chanted, "Om Mani Padme Hum." It is a famous mantra of compassion, recited and chanted by Buddhists all over the world. Slowly, without moving, the group members began to join the chant. They chanted softly for half an hour. Everyone was moved, although nobody had known the meaning of the Sanskrit words. (Whole books have been written on the meaning of the mantra, and you can read about it in Lama Govinda's books, cited in the bibliography.)

As people sat up following the quiet chant, a lovely woman passed out camellias from her garden. Each person sat and simply looked at the flower. There was silence. Many people said later that they felt an unusual peace and beauty. They made detailed and expansive comments about the flower they had been contemplating. Some people were already meditating. This was the kind of experience we had hoped to generate repeatedly for each group, until the members were ready to sit in silence and were relaxed enough to remain still, and focused enough to follow an instruction, and motivated enough to practice at home. Meditation is an experience, not a concept, and it grows with practice. It is a way of being, a way of experiencing. If we had begun our work together by describing meditation, we would have established concepts that would ultimately be obstacles to experience. Keep that in mind as you read about meditation in this book and others, for you can never read what your experience will be and will do for you.

Contemplation

1. Set aside fifteen minutes without interruption, and select something you would like to contemplate. It can be a vase, a piece of jewelry, a piece of bark from a tree, a flower, leaf, or stone.

2. Sit comfortably with the object in your hand or nearby. Close your eyes and take five deep breaths, following your breath with your attention.

3. Open your eyes. Caress the object with your vision. Allow it to fill your vision, and your entire attention. If you have thoughts, bring your attention back to the object. Gently silence yourself and again caress the object with your eyes.

4. Spend at least ten to fifteen minutes, twice a day. If you repeat this exercise twice a day for two weeks,

you will find that a new and lovely silence allows you to focus openly on your object of contemplation. This is a good way to encourage your mind to "one pointedness," which is an important skill.

You will discover, if you do this exercise repeatedly, that there is a richness in common objects, in fragments of natural objects, and in your communication with them that you may never have suspected. Some people seem to do this without being taught, but most of us need to practice.

This is another way to prepare for meditation. Initially when SAGE participants asked for definitions of meditation, we described sitting quietly, relaxing the body, quieting the mind as much as possible, and remaining aware. It was a process in which deep body and mental relaxation could allow the usual thoughts to fade away. Then they might be replaced by a concentration on a visualization. This might be some external symbol, or some internal function such as sensing and counting one's own breath.

When we said that meditation was a quieting, nobody seemed to be satisfied. Mere quieting hardly explained why meditation had such a powerful grip on millions of people. We encouraged people to look at their own experience and to observe that one of the important aspects of meditation was a turning inward and understanding the self. It entails a real look at one's own nature, one's character, the kinds of images and projections that one's mind persistently conjures up. At first this activity of the mind is an obstacle. It prevents us from becoming quiet and focused. And we do not yet know how to watch it without becoming involved. Those are not just thoughts, they are *our* thoughts. Those images and memories are not just any images: They are *our* life. After a while we can suspend our attachment to them and watch them as if we were visitors to the mind of a stranger.

The first step is removing ourselves from the chatter. We

are always conversing with ourselves, distracting ourselves with plans, with prospects, anticipating what we will say or do or how we will feel. And if we are not busy anticipating the future, we are immersed in the past, in memories, longings, and retrospects. This prevents us from being immersed in the richness of what is happening right *now*. What is happening as I write this sentence and you read it? You cannot read it if your mind is elsewhere. Yet you cannot force your mind to stop its commotion. You must patiently *allow* it to stop. The more stern discipline and effort you use to stamp out your inner chatter, the more your mind will keep churning over. You may wonder, as many SAGE people did, how you can ever begin to experience inner quiet.

Quieting the Mind

You can begin by taking an assigned time each day—whether it is ten minutes or half an hour—and just sit without interruption.

1. Sit comfortably and loosen or remove any tight jewelry, glasses or clothing.

2. Take a few deep breaths with your eyes closed and your attention on your breathing.

3. Sit and watch whatever is behind your closed eyelids. If it seems like "nothing," watch the nothing. Your mind will grow more silent if you are kind to yourself. You cannot force it. So if your attention wanders, and you start to go off into a fantasy or thought, bring your attention back to watching what is behind your eyelids.

This simple discipline will slowly build your tolerance and ability. As you practice, however, you must stay with your moment to moment experience. It is important not to get stuck in feelings or sensations or grasping something in particular. The beginnings of a deep experience and knowledge are already in you. They exist as you live your life.

Meditation does not mean only sitting still with your eyes closed. It is an attitude. You carry it with you and use it. Rudolph Steiner suggested paying close attention to plants and children and young animals.

Look at all things growing and flourishing, and also pay close attention to dead leaves withering, fading, and dying. You can observe these things around you simultaneously. Feel them, but do not judge one better than another.

You can do the same with sounds. Listen to sounds without identifying them—a car engine, a bird, an airplane noise. Just hear the sounds around with detachment and without labels.

See if you can do the same thing when you listen to people. Listen silently, with your inner self, without comment or judgment. If someone expresses an opinion with which you disagree or that makes you feel uncomfortable, don't stir. Practice listening with quietness.

Look at yourself with the same dispassion. When you look at yourself do not ignore your thoughts. They are as important in your being as tables and chairs are in your house or apartment.

You may want to look at the way you use your energy. How much energy do you expend in casual conversation? Talking takes energy, like anything else. How much of your energy do you spend in responding, being vexed, angry, fearful, emotional, or contentious? For example do you need to be right when you are in a debate? If you begin observing yourself, you are beginning an attitude of meditation.

The fruits of meditation and the power of a clear vision can be observed in the unusual accomplishment of some of the gurus from other countries who came to the United

States without much money, following, or knowledge of the culture and language, and who developed important communities. My contact has been with Rinpoche Tarthang Tulku, who left Tibet as a young refugee after the Chinese invasion and carried out many of the sacred texts of his Nyingma culture. He began teaching and publishing these texts in India. In the early 1970s he came to California, where he began teaching a few students. The students raised money and bought and reconstructed an old fraternity house in Berkeley which became their residence and monastery. From the gift of an old printing press they began what is now a flourishing publishing company, Dharma Press. Some of the students learned the Tibetan language and began to teach and translate texts that had never been published. Others learned business or construction. They took responsibility for every aspect of their lives. In 1973 they borrowed enough money to make a down payment on another broken-down fraternity house near the University of California campus, which they transformed into the beautiful Nyingma Institute. Then they began building a country community. Their aesthetic and strong community owes itself to a great tradition and to attitudes that can be found in Rinpoche's book, *Gesture of Balance* (see bibliography).

According to Rinpoche meditation offers a way by which we can see our conditioning and see how it imprisons us; and we can then begin to decondition ourselves from our long-held, lifelong social attitudes.

> Our habit patterns are very hard to break, and even when we try, obstacles seem to appear—our desires and attachments push us to repeat the same destructive patterns. Our emotional needs habituate us not only to material things, but very subtly to our self-identity. We do not want to lose our sense of control over ourselves, our environment, or even other people. But until we let go of our attachments to personality

and self-image, it is difficult even to see these life patterns, let alone to change them.

We can observe our life patterns carefully and come to accept how even the most subtle graspings and negativities cause us to suffer. As our understanding and awareness grow, we see the importance of working through our emotions, attachments, and negativities, and we also see that the ultimate solution comes from within. Then when we truly wake up to our painful condition, we can begin to change our innermost attitudes, and some real progress can be made. Although often it is difficult even to recognize what is healthy or wholesome because our environment and daily experience are so artificial, when we finally decide to act in a healthy and balanced manner, our lives naturally fall into this new pattern. We do not even need to leave our homes and families to affect these changes—for the changes are within us.

Deconditioning lifelong mental attitudes and habits is not an easy process. At some level there is really no difference between prayer, meditation, invocation, and the kind of contemplative state in which some people naturally find themselves and in which they are able to come to a greater reality in their experience. But for most people self-recognition is a hard process. Most of us would like to throw away, avoid, or neglect the negative aspects of ourselves, as though they were not part of the whole. Certainly in the Buddhist tradition these aspects of our emotional garbage are important to use and to experience fully, to witness and transcend.

Long repressed feelings and intensities can occur during meditation, and ideally you can handle them like unwieldy thoughts, seeing them, experiencing them, but not lingering on them. Many people are not sufficiently aware and controlled for this detached observation of the painful parts of the self. Some people find that a therapist or guide can be helpful in this process of self-recognition. After you have achieved some quiet, you may begin to be aware of the way your mind works, aware of the way thoughts form, the way sensory images are interpreted. At SAGE we practiced various uses of the mind-body such as seeing sound instead of listening to it, or going beyond sound "to the other side." These are various ways of moving beyond one's usual conditioning. The visualization techniques described in Chapter 9, especially Perspective from Space, are particularly helpful.

DEVOTION

> . . . Broadly speaking the basic character of meditation takes one or two forms. The first stems from the teachings which are concerned with the discovery of the nature of existence; the second concerns communication with the external or universal concept of God.

So writes another Tibetan teacher, Rinpoche Chogyam Trungpa, in his book, *Meditation in Action* (see the bibliography).

Wherever there is the concept of an external, "higher" being, there is also an internal personality known as "I," or the ego. This often means you feel yourself to be inferior and are trying to contact something higher, greater. Such meditation practice becomes a way of developing communication with a higher being. It is based on devotion. This is basically an inward or introverted meditation practice and is as well known in the Hindu teachings as Bhakti. Emphasis is placed on an inward state of *samadhi* or total immersion of one's focus, so that there is no awareness of one's own senses—only of God. One finds a similar technique in the orthodox teachings of Christianity, where the prayer of the heart is used, and concentration on the heart is emphasized, as a means of identifying one's self with a god. This necessitates purifying one's self. The basic belief is that one is separate from God, but there is still a link, so one is also part of God. By using the emotions and devotional practices that are aimed at making contact with God or gods or some particular saint, a unity is experienced. Devotional practices often include the recitation of mantras, or prayers.

ACTIVE MEDITATION

The other principal form of meditation is almost entirely opposite in its approach, though finally it might lead to the same results. There is no belief in a higher and lower. The idea of different levels, or of being in an underdeveloped state does not arise. One does not feel inferior and what one is trying to achieve is not something higher than one's self. Therefore this practice of meditation does not require an inward concentration on the heart. There is no centralizing concept at all. Even such practices as concentrating on the psychic centers are approached differently. Although certain teachings of Buddhism mention it, the practices are not based on the development of an inward center. This basic form of meditation is concerned with trying to see what is "the discovery of the nature of existence," in Chogyam Trungpa's words, there are many variations on this form of meditation. They are generally based on techniques for opening one's self. The achievement of this kind of meditation is not, therefore, the result of some long-term arduous practice to attain a higher state. Nor does it necessitate falling into any kind of inner trance state. It is what one might call working meditation or extrovert meditation, where skillful means and wisdom must be combined like the two wings of a bird. There is no question of trying to retreat from the world. Without the world, meditation would be almost impossible to practice. The individual and the external world are not separate but merely coexist together. Therefore the concept of trying to communicate and trying to become one with some higher being does not arise.

In this kind of meditation practice the concept of *nowness* plays a very important part. In fact, it is of the essence.

> One has to become aware of the present moment through such means as concentrating on the breathing, a practice which has been developed in the Buddhist tradition. This is based on developing the knowledge of nowness, for each respiration is unique, it is an expression of now.

Chogyam Trungpa's words on the melting away of the ego are very beautiful, and speak to the separation process that we begin in early infancy and maintain later through life.

> We try to segregate ourselves from the external and this creates a kind of gigantic bubble in us which consists of nothing but air and water or, in this case, fear and the reflection of the external thing. So this huge bubble prevents any fresh air from coming in, and that is "I"—the Ego. So in that sense there is the existence of the Ego, but it is in fact illusory. . . . That is why the concept of Egolessness is not really a question of whether there is a Self or not, or, for that matter, whether there is the existence of God or not; it is rather the taking away of that concept of the bubble. Having done so, one doesn't have to deliberately destroy the Ego or deliberately condemn God. And when that barrier is removed one can expand and swim through straight away. But this can only be achieved through the practice of meditation, which must be approached in a very practical and simple way. Then the mystical experience of joy or grace or whatever it might be can be found in every object. That is what one tries to achieve through vipassana, or "insight" meditation practice. Once we have established a basic

pattern of discipline and we have developed a regular way of dealing with the situation, whether it is breathing or walking or what-have-you, then at some stage the technique gradually dies out. Reality gradually expands so that we do not have to use the technique at all. And in this case one does not have to concentrate inward, but one can expand outward more and more. And the more one expands the closer one gets to the realization of centerless existence.

"If in meditation I lose that which I so desperately struggle to maintain, why meditate?" The first benefit of meditation is that all of life becomes more vivid and enjoyable. It takes on the magnificent hue of some vacations or of special moments in childhood, times in which you proceeded from instant to instant, enjoying the present, and were not constantly distracted inwardly or pestered by thoughts of what you should have said or what you should do tomorrow, or will you buy the bread first and the eggs second—that laundry list of things that distracts our attention from experience. Another reason is that meditation may eventually bring you into contact with a larger reality. We are, after all, small creatures gifted with a consciousness that we hardly put to very full use. Much of our consciousness is educated to verbalize, articulate. But the experiential part of our consciousness is the only part that can actually know greater realities. There is a limit to the number of techniques we can learn, books we can read, or traveling we can do. But there is almost no limit to what the mind can encompass and experience directly. This means liberation from the smallness of living only on a mundane level, in local reality, living up to social expectations, of what my family wants, or what pleases my neighbor. Being human we have a thirst for knowledge larger than we learned in school, a knowledge that imbues life with depthless, infinite meaning. To invest ourselves in inner development means liberating ourselves from a drudging, material view of life, a view that life is as we see it on the surface. To break out of the bubble of ego that divides us from the rest of reality is to enter a kind of consciousness in which we can exist and experience all things. Living becomes awesomely alive, and dying takes on a new dimension.

UNFOLDING MEDITATION

Among the many books on meditation I have found no statements more penetrating than the simple advice given us by Tarthang Tulku in *Gesture of Balance*. Instead of offering more meditative exercises or advice on how to meditate, I would like to quote from this immensely helpful book.

> Almost all spiritual disciplines practice some form of meditation. Ordinarily, meditation is viewed as a form of thinking used in combination with words, images, or concepts. But meditation is not thinking *about* something.
>
> Traditionally beginning meditation involves certain practices, such as intense concentration, the visualization of various images, or the chanting of mantras. Teachers emphasize different practices depending on the needs of the student. For instance a teacher may tell one student to go alone to a quiet place and be completely silent for half an hour or forty-five minutes, and he may tell another to go to the mountains or ocean and chant very loudly. Someone else may be instructed to gaze at the sky and just be open. Others may be given devotional or ritual practices.
>
> Generally, however, our practice should be whatever calms and relaxes us, whatever works best for the development of stillness and concentration. Meditation helps us to be calm and happy, to enjoy life, to be cheerful, and to deal effectively with both our physical and mental problems. . . .

So simply, how do you meditate? First of all, the body must be very still, very quiet. Physically relax your muscles and let go of all your tension. Then sit in a comfortable position and stay completely still, not moving at all. Breathe very softly and gently . . . inhale and exhale slowly and smoothly. As much as you can, completely relax so that your entire nervous system becomes calm. Then quiet your mind; still your thoughts through inner silence. There are various ways to do this, but as too many instructions may be distracting, just very naturally relax your body, breath, and mind. The body becomes still, the breath balanced, and the mind and senses very peaceful. At this time you deeply feel and enjoy your senses coming alive. You can see that meditation is not a difficult task or something foreign or imported—it is a part of your nature.

There is no need to try to accomplish some goal, since trying itself becomes an obstacle to relaxation. Pushing yourself too hard, or attempting to follow a rigid set of instructions, may cause problems—for when you exert too much effort, you can find yourself caught between getting something and not getting it, making internal reports to yourself while trying to be silent. When you try to conceptually experience the "perfect meditation," you may end up creating endless internal conflicts or inner dialogues. . . .

When you are just learning to meditate, it is best to experience yourself totally, without rejecting or excluding any part of yourself. All of your thoughts and feelings can be a part of your meditation—you can taste each one, then gradually move on. In this way, you can begin to discover the various subtle layers and states of the mind. The mind simply observes its own natural process; every thought, desire, and motivation is a natural aid to this basic type of meditation. . . .

When memories or discomforts arise, you may feel a little uneasy, but this feeling will pass if you do not mentally hold on to any thought in particular. Just remain very loose and quiet and do not think "about" meditation. Simply accept yourself. You are not trying to *learn* meditation; you *are* the meditation. Your entire body, breath, thoughts, senses, and awareness— your total being—are all parts of the meditation. You do not have to worry about losing it. Your entire energy-field is a part of the meditation, so you do not need to follow any specific instructions or worry about achieving a particular experience. . . .

As we experience this deeper level of meditation, we find that the nature of mind *is* meditation. And this, itself, is actually the enlightened experience. This experience is free from everything, and yet at the same time, it manifests all and everything. This, itself, is liberation.

Part 2 ❧ EXERCISES AND TECHNIQUES

12 ❧ STRESS AND RELAXATION

Relaxation and tension, opening and closing, are basic rhythms of being alive. An alternation is healthy, but sometimes we react tensely without relaxing, and stress—or reaction to stress—seems to dominate. Whenever life has been a prolonged struggle, people's faces have been lined with tension, their bodies bent and distorted, so that they eventually fit the stereotype of old age, bent over, shoulders hunched, and head thrust forward. This is not the aging process, but reaction to a lifetime of stress.

The antidote to tension is relaxation, which was a developed art for ten centuries before the concept of stress was invented. Deep relaxation is the prerequisite for meditation, for self-healing, for inner change. It is the basis for the ancient Hindu discipline of communion that we call yoga, as well as for the martial arts and many religious practices. Nonetheless in our experience at SAGE some of the most effective relaxation exercises have been modern. One form in particular, known as progressive relaxation and evolved by a physiologist-physician, Edmund Jacobson in the 1920s, will be described later in this chapter.

Many of the illnesses found in city populations are probably reactions to stress, ailments called diabetes, colitis, and hypertension. What is stress, in fact? Dr. Hans Selye, a physiologist known for his work on stress, defines it as a nonspecific response of the body to any demand. Stress is a condition of both physical and psychological arousal. In his book, *The Stress of Life,* Dr. Selye says something worth repeating:

> Among all my autopsies (and I have performed quite a few) I have never seen a man who died of old age. In fact I don't think that anyone has ever died of old age, yet. To permit this would be the ideal accomplishment of medical research. . . . To die of old age would mean that all the organs of the body would be worn out proportionately, merely by having been used for too long. This is never the case. We invariably die because one vital part has worn out too early in proportion to the rest of the body. Life, the biological changes that hold our bodies together, is only as strong as its weakest vital link. When this breaks—no matter which vital link it be—our parts can no longer be held together as a single living being. . . .
>
> Stress is essentially the rate of all the wear and tear caused by life. And stress is not necessarily bad for people. It is actually important because without our adaptation to stress we would not even survive. But unequal stresses placed on various parts of the body *are* the corrosion that cause one part to wear out before another and unnecessarily shorten the life span.

Stress reactions go on in the body whether we know it consciously or not. When you are startled, there is a rise in heart rate and blood pressure, changes in the distribution of blood, away from the stomach and the skin and into the brain and the muscles. There is a release of energy-producing compounds, such as blood sugar and fatty acids in the blood. The adrenal glands work very fast, releasing adrenalin to speed up this energy release. Some of the metabolic changes occur slowly and last for days, or even weeks, until there is a gradual restoration of the body to the prestress condition.

When a person is stressed there is an enormous chemical change, whose effect is to break down carbohydrates, fats, and proteins in the body to provide energy for the muscles, and also to slow down the body's synthetic processes. The construction of new cells in the body, its repair work, is inhibited by stress. This "emergency production" of a stress reaction is the primitive reaction of the lower parts of the brain which have readied us for fight or for flight throughout the centuries. The muscles and the whole system are getting ready to fight the enemy or to flee. But what happens in modern society when a worker gets stressed by his boss, for example? Can he scream, fight, or run away? Can he release all the energy that has been sent into the body? Indeed not! We are so well trained to control our emotional expression that many of us have learned not even to *feel* these stress responses within us, excepting perhaps as a vague twinge in the stomach. An enraged or frightened person is likely to be unaware that all this has happened within him or her, excepting that at the end of the day, he or she has a headache and perhaps at the end of a number of years hypertension or arthritis.

As you are reading about the consequences of stress, you may be feeling a little tension. Here is a brief and unobtrusive exercise that can help you read the rest of this chapter with a more relaxed feeling.

Sighing

People often sigh with relief, sometimes with impatience or sadness, or with boredom. The sigh itself releases tension and allows the person to take in oxygen. Sighing is letting go. It will make you feel better. It performs an important service for your body by relaxing and energizing you at once.

Try to forget your inhibitions and make a loud noise when you sigh. Take a deep breath. Hold it for a couple of seconds. Now sigh until all of the air is out of your lungs. Make a loud groaning, sighing, moaning, bellowing sound come out. Do it again: take an even deeper breath. Practice sighing. Five good sighs contain more energy and relaxation than a bucket of pills. When you finish sighing you may feel like yawning a little. You will be ready to go on reading.

◇ ◇ ◇

Drs. Friedman and Rosenman have written a very readable book called *Type A Behavior and Your Heart* (New York: Alfred Knopf, 1974), which shows how certain personality traits, competitive drive, ambition, and impatience can lead to heart disease. It is a book whose ideas apply to many Americans, whether or not they are coronary patients or Type A personalities, for many of these traits are built into our culture. We live in a society that rewards the Type A personality by giving him a better job or more money. Nonetheless a person with this kind of personality can change.

The advice given by Drs. Friedman and Rosenman to reduce the toll taken by excessive ambition and time pressure is particularly relevant as people get older. They suggest that any Type A person should try to diminish his or her destructive sense of urgency by greater self-knowledge, by really appraising who he or she is, and they offer some questions to begin with: Do you have a sense of humor? Are you flexible? How many of your activities have to do with your concern for art, literature, music, philosophy, history, science, and the wonders of the natural world around you? They suggest that you really evaluate free-floating hostilities and not allow yourself to rationalize. Try to estimate how easily you can receive loyalty and affection, and also, the amount of absolute courage you have. If you detect big areas of fear, do not overlook them, explore them. How honest have you been in your life? How often and under what circumstances have you cheated or lied and borne false witness against your neighbor? Painful as they may be, all those questions are essential in trying to change. You must not be afraid to ask them repeatedly until you have found answers.

In essence you have to return to your real self, the self that was masked by social demands, before you can revive your real personality, the personality that you had as a child and that underlies all social achievement.

One of the most difficult changes for a successful person, especially the Type A person, is retirement. Whether or not a person has retired, the same evaluation and renewal of an earlier personality is essential. Many of the suggestions in Drs. Friedman and Rosenman's book for rehabilitating a Type A personality are exactly what any person must do on retirement: a reevaluation of one's self, of one's life goals, and what things are meaningful. The retired person needs to establish patterns for using leisure, use of lonely spaces of time to enhance and broaden one's character, rather than to allow past habit to limit one further.

Clearly our illnesses come partly out of the way we have lived, and so it should be possible to reverse symptoms by changing our habits. This has been the message we have found in SAGE, where people in their seventies began to straighten their posture or to lose symptoms such as headaches, lower back pain, and depression. Relaxation exercises were an important aid to change.

Dr. Edmund Jacobson's method of progressive relaxation was designed to teach patients how to cope with stress. Jacobson worked in Chicago, almost unknown for years to a world now keen on his work. He wanted to teach people how to recognize subtle levels of tension, and then how to attain profound relaxation. His method is the basis for many other Western relaxation methods, such as the La-maze breathing method for natural childbirth, relaxation for hypnosis, and behavior therapy. Jacobson found that a person who learned to tense and relax a particular muscle got the feeling of relinquishing tension, and could then begin to recognize tension anywhere in the body and eventually learn to let that tension go. His method has been used to treat ulcers, tension headaches, hypertension, and many other psychosomatic ailments.

Progressive Relaxation

Posture. Lie flat on your back—unless you cannot—on a bed or the floor with your legs spread a little so that they are not touching each other. There should be a pillow under your head and probably also under your knees so that your spine is straight. As usual you need to be sure that you are not wearing any tight clothing, shoes, eyeglasses, jewelry, hairpins—nothing constricting or distracting. Take a minute with your eyes closed to go through your body and make sure you are as relaxed as you can be to start. Move around until your body is comfortable. You might feel a wave of relaxation spreading up your body from your heels and legs, over your hips, stom-ach, abdomen, your chest and back, arms, shoulders, neck and face. This is simply preparation.

Relaxation means not doing anything. You cannot make an effort, or worry, or try. Paradoxically if you try, you will automatically make yourself tense. You need rather to *allow* yourself to relax. Most important is to allow your mind to let go of all the lists and con-versations it may have. Let it be empty.

1. *Left forearm.* Lie with your arm relaxed and at rest beside you, palm down. Bend your left hand backward from the wrist. Keep the rest of the arm at

rest. Place all your attention on faint sensations in the upper forearm. Hold the hand up for a minute or two, and then let it drop. Focus attention on the upper forearm. See what the change of sensation feels like. This is relaxation. Repeat three times.

Feel heaviness and warmth in your entire body.

This is enough for the first time.

2. *Extensor muscles of the forearm.* Go through the same preparation as you did the first time. Begin by bending your left hand back, as you did the first time, and feeling tension sensations in your forearm. Do this three times.

Now turn your arm over and bend your hand forward, from the wrist. While bending the hand forward pay attention to tension sensations in the lower forearm. Hold the wrist forward for two to three minutes, then relax it. Do this three times.

Now relax your entire body and see whether you feel a difference between the left arm and the right arm. Really compare the way they feel.

Now repeat with the right hand, bending the hand back three times and forward three times.

Now lie quietly and compare both arms.

Ordinarily, as Dr. Jacobson and other clinicians used this method, they proceeded very slowly and thoroughly, week after week, adding only one new muscle group at each session. Only the person doing the exercise can know how thoroughly he or she is relaxing. It is terribly important not to deceive yourself at this juncture. Perhaps you need to spend four or five sessions just bending your wrists and feeling your arms. Perhaps you can do almost the entire body at once.

3. *Upper arm: biceps.* Begin as you did the first time, relaxing. Bend your wrists as before. Then begin by bending your arm at the elbow, letting the wrist hang limply. Hold the arm until you begin to feel a sensa-

tion in the upper arm. Then let the arm fall. The arm should plop down, or else it is not relaxed. Do this three times. Now compare your right and left arms. When you have taken time to feel the subtle differences, do the entire exercise with the right wrist and right arm.

4. *Extensor muscles of the upper arm.* As before begin with your preparation, getting relaxed and comfortable, but make certain that you have three or four books beside your bed or mat, so that you can use them in the exercise.

Bend the left hand back and let go. Bend the left hand and wrist forward and let go. Bend the left arm at the elbow, holding, until the sensation of tension registers. Then let go.

Now place four or five books under your left wrist. Press your wrist down on the books until you feel tension in your upper left arm. Let go. Do this three times.

Now remove the books, relaxing your entire body, and feel the difference between your right and left arms.

Now go through the entire process three times for your right arm.

Relax and feel the difference between your arms and your legs, your shoulders, your neck, your facial muscles.

People who wish to continue the entire Jacobson process can easily follow the instruction in his book, *You Must Relax* (New York: McGraw-Hill, 1962). At SAGE we have used the method less thoroughly and have used other methods to feel tension and relaxation in the entire body.

Entire Body Relaxation

1. Prepare yourself, lying down, by removing tight clothing and jewelry and getting very comfortable. You will want to pay attention to each body part as you tense and relax it. One fluttery, nervous woman I knew in college used to say that she made her husband very jittery, as she did this in bed at night. "He used to ask me why I was wiggling and convulsing that way. I'd say it put me to sleep, but he never understood how. I'd wiggle my toes, then my feet, then my knees. By the time I got to my hips I'd be yawning."

2. Lie still and clench your toes, bending them back, and hold. Now release them.

In this exercise do both sides of the body at once.

Bend your toes and your instep. Hold. Release.

Tighten your toes and your instep, and bend your foot back at the ankle. Hold. Release.

Now tighten your toes, instep, ankles, and your calf muscles. Hold for as long as you can. Release.

Tighten your feet, ankles, calves, and thighs. Hold as long as you can. Release.

Tighten your feet, your leg muscles, and your buttocks. Hold as long as you can. Release.

Tighten your feet, your leg muscles, your buttocks, and your lower back. Hold. Release.

Tighten your feet, your leg muscles, your buttocks, your lower back, and your stomach muscles. Hold as long as you can. Release.

Tighten your feet, legs, buttocks, lower back, and stomach and take a deep breath and hold it. Hold as long as you can. Release.

Tighten your feet, legs, buttocks, lower back, stomach, and chest muscles and make fists. Hold. Release.

Tighten your feet, ankles, calves, thighs, buttocks, lower back, stomach, chest, shoulders, and fists and arms. Hold. Release.

Tighten your feet, legs, buttocks, lower back, stomach, chest, shoulders, fists, arms, and neck. Hold. Release.

Tighten your feet, legs, lower back, and buttocks, your stomach, your arms, chest, back, shoulders, and neck, and this time clench your jaw. Hold. Release.

Tighten your feet, legs, lower back, buttocks, stomach, arms, fists, back, shoulders, neck, and jaw, and frown hard. Hold. Release.

Finally tighten your feet, legs, buttocks, lower back, stomach, chest, fists, arms, shoulders, back, neck, jaw, and frown and squinch your eyes tightly shut. Hold yourself very tight, feeling the intensity of the tightness. Then let go.

3. Follow the sensations that travel around your body. Feel your body become warmer, heavier, expanded, tingling, however it feels. Let your mind follow the sensations.

4. Feel how heavy your feet are, your legs, and but-tocks and back. Feel the relaxation and weight in your chest, in your abdomen. Feel the weight of your back and shoulders and arms. Feel your face and your neck and shoulders. As you move your attention over your face, feel your muscles melting, your eyes floating re-laxed. Let your jaw hang open. As you take a deep breath into your abdomen, feel a wave of relaxation coming all the way up your body.

5. Feel the air coming into your lungs and bringing energy. As you lie very relaxed you can exhale out into the universe. Feel the air around you, the sounds that touch you. You may feel like some great receiver, or flower, tender and relaxed, feeling the vibrations of the world around you.

Now that you have read this section, you may want to try using it. There are several ways to go about this. You may want to ask a friend or relative to read it to you while you do the exercise. You might also read it to a tape recorder, at the correct pace for you. Then you can play back your own voice and let it be your guide. Some people find all of this unnecessary and can simply read the exercise and do it. After a few rep-etitions it becomes exceedingly easy. The exercise can be used to fall asleep, or for other purposes such as preparing for fantasy or visualization exercises.

Before doing this exercise remember one rule: Pay close attention to every sensation you feel. Do not do anything—not even relaxation—unless it feels all right to you. Do not tense beyond your capacity. You want to feel a very slight strain, but *not* pain! Only you know how you feel from inside. Only you can deter-mine how you should be doing these exercises so that they are beneficial and not harmful.

If you have any problems—symptoms such as arthritis or other symptoms that make you feel the ex-ercise should be varied or is wrong for you—do not harm yourself. Either change the exercise or don't do it until it feels right.

Most of us have been so accustomed to letting other people, especially the authorities—doctors—tell us about ourselves, our bodies, that we have forgotten that we are the final authorities. Only we can be responsible for our bodies. Only we can tell, really, how we feel from the inside. This is the main rule of SAGE. It is the reason that people do not hurt themselves. It is the rule for all of the exercises in Part Two of this book.

This exercise can be used for a quick rest, a pick-up during a busy day. It takes only ten minutes, yet it combines several potent principles of relaxation. It allows gravity to straighten the body, while your concentration and breathing energize your body. Some SAGE members have claimed that it was the most important short exercise they knew.

It comes from the work of F. Alexander, an Australian actor whose own speech problems led him to analyze his body and the way his tensions and habits distorted his posture. Out of years of painstaking self-observation he devised a therapeutic method by which people could begin to sense postural tensions and correct them.

Each flaw in posture, such as sticking your chin out, or collapsing your chest, or arching your back, represents a state of feeling. As children we learned to control feelings, as we were hauled kicking and crying to have an injection, or to school, and we tightened our muscles. We also imitated the feelings and stance of our parents, all unconsciously. Only at thirty-seven did I discover I had so compressed my chest that I couldn't hold a normal volume of air in my lungs. At forty-two I discovered that I was arching my back and thrusting my head forward when I tried

to sit straight. When this became painful, I began taking lessons from a person trained in the Alexander Method, and after eight months I was beginning to stand straighter. The Alexander rest position is one of the most gentle and effective means of helping your back to straighten.

Alexander Rest Position

1. Lie on a carpet, mat, or other firm surface. A bed is not firm enough.

2. Be sure you will not be interruped for ten minutes.

3. Lie on your back with your knees raised and feet firmly planted on the floor. Your feet should be about as far apart as your shoulders.

4. Rest your hands on your hip bones. You should feel your shoulders on the floor.

5. Test this position. You may find that you need a small pillow, or two or three paperback books, under your head to make your spine straight. Your head should not be thrown back, nor forced forward.

6. When you have adjusted your head and feel that your spine is straight, and you are very comfortable, you are ready to listen to your own breathing. Breathe in through your nose and out through your mouth. Make the sound "hah" or "ah" as you exhale, but without voicing. It should sound like the wind

through pine branches. Listen to your breathing and feel your back move as you breathe.

7. At the end of ten minutes put your hand under the small of your back, and your shoulders. See how much closer you are to the floor or the surface you are lying on. Feel your body as you stand up and move around.

◇ ◇ ◇

13 ❧ AUTOGENIC TRAINING

Although autogenic training can hardly be introduced, much less taught, in a few pages, it is a method that a few SAGE participants have sworn by and used to such advantage in relaxing that you, the reader, deserve at least a passing acquaintance with it. The SAGE staff and eight members of the first core group encountered autogenic training amidst the hurly-burly of a professional meeting on the California coast. A Montreal psychiatrist, who seemed unusually fastidious, formal, and European in that setting, talked about a self-training method that was widely used in Europe to cure psychosomatic diseases. He was Dr. Wolfgang Luthe, the translator of six scholarly books on autogenic training and author of considerable research.

Autogenic means "self-generated." The method evolved out of the work of Johannes Schulz, a German neurologist who observed that patients showed beneficial side effects of hyponosis, characteristic of relaxation, such as heavy limbs and warm hands and feet. These same indicators of relaxation could be induced in people by the power of suggestion with very positive effects. However it seemed important to place control over the suggestion in the hands of the patient, and this is the key to autogenic training. Luthe worked with Schulz and saw that this method helped people who suffered from diabetes, hypertension, colitis, migraine, and a multitude of seemingly unrelated symptoms.

The carefully chosen phrases of autogenic training seem to allow the trainee to release old tensions and traumas and enter a state of homeostasis and regeneration. No doctor could ever bring this about by attempting to program a patient's nervous system, for each person has a different history of traumas and needs a different order of release. Most patients would never even be conscious of the needs of their own nervous systems. Within their bodies and brains is a history of disturbing memories or blocked energies to be released. The key to healing is allowing each person's nervous system to dictate what needs to be released and in what order.

Initially all of us wondered: How could a person be cured of colitis or diabetes by repeating a few phrases each day? It seemed all the more amazing when we heard rumored stories about Luthe's own use of the method as a young medico in World War II. At one point, with a hospital full of wounded soldiers about to be captured, he had stolen a train, loaded the men aboard, and driven it himself 1,000 miles out of the invasion area. It was freezing cold and there were no medical supplies aboard, but the men pulled through on autogenic training.

There are many stories like this one, about the power of the method. However it is like the power of meditation and depends upon the trainee's ability to give the phrases full attention and to continue systematically over months. The phrases allow a person to make deep contact with his or her body. They were selected empirically, by watching hundreds and hundreds of patients. Presumably they en-

courage the brain to send messages to the body that allow
it to heal. The phrases encourage heaviness and warmth in
the limbs, regular heart rate and respiration, abdominal
warmth, and a cool forehead. Anyone wanting to understand the basis of the method and its range of applications
should consult the seven volumes edited by Wolfgang
Luthe on *Autogenic Therapy* and *Autogenic Training* (New
York: Grune and Stratton, 1964–1973). For those wishing to
practice the method with others there are teachers who
have been trained by members of the International Committee on Autogenic Training. (You can make inquiries of
ICAT by writing to the Medical Centre, 5300 Cote des
Neiges, Montreal 249, P.Q., Canada.)

Once a person has mastered the basic exercises over a
period of many months, the next step might be a series of
meditative exercises involving colors, objects, relations,
and concepts. Since the method was used mainly in medical situations, special exercises were developed for particular pathologies, along with affirmations that would help
people with specific problems, such as insomnia or smoking.

Later a verbal process was developed to enable the
trainee to understand some of the material discharged by
his or her nervous system. It was called neutralization. A
person might be doing an initial exercise, encouraging
heaviness in his arms. He could begin to feel a tightness,
even some pain in the chest. Now he should turn to his
tape recorder and talk aggressively for thirty to fifty minutes without stopping. Another person doing the same
heaviness exercise might feel a tightness like an incipient
headache at the temples. That person could prevent a headache by crying for a few minutes, since crying is a necessary release for the nervous system.

Autogenic training can offer impressive benefits, but it
must be done systematically, with full attention. It does not
take long. It simply requires concentration and a kind of
passive volition. There is no way to make an effort since

that produces tension. You cannot *try* to feel something: you can only allow it to happen.

Warning: If you have diabetes, colitis, hypertension, or some other symptom for which you are taking medication and are under medical supervision, consult your doctor before you do these exercises. Ask your physician to read the relevant sections of the Luthe volumes on autogenic therapy and advise you accordingly. Sometimes autogenic exercises produce such a normalizing change that the medication can become harmful.

Posture and Preparation

Remove all constricting shoes, tight clothing, jewelry, watches, spectacles, contact lenses, hearing aids, and so on. Be sure that you will not be interrupted for at least ten minutes.

You can do the exercises lying in bed or sitting in an armchair. In bed, lie on your back with your legs spread a little so they are not touching. Your arms should be lying at your sides, but not touching. Experiment until you make yourself comfortable. You may need a pillow under your knees so that your spine is straight. Feel the small of your back with your hand. If there is a space between you and the surface you are lying on, you need a pillow under your knees. Increase the size of the pillows until there is no hollow space between your back and the mattress. Similarly you want your head to be straight, neither thrown back nor forward. Experiment with pillows until you are thoroughly comfortable.

Do the exercises sitting in an easy chair only if the chair allows you to sit back with your head supported, your arms comfortably on the arms of the chair, and your feet firmly planted on the floor with your knees at a wider angle than a right angle. It is unusual to

find a chair so proportioned that you can sit in this way.

Have a notebook and pen ready to make a journal of all the thoughts, feelings, and sensations you experience during the session.

If you are right-handed begin with your right arm; if you are left-handed, begin with your left arm. Get relaxed before you start.

Exercise One

1. Place *all* your attention on your right arm from the shoulders down to your fingertips. If you can't feel your arm, you can rub it or touch it at first. Close your eyes and say to yourself, "My right arm is heavy." It doesn't matter whether you feel heaviness or another sensation. Pay attention to whatever you feel. Repeat sentence for thirty to sixty seconds.

2. After sixty seconds take a deep breath, clench your fists, stretch your arms overhead, and open your eyes as you exhale.

3. *Repeat this exercise three times.*

4. Write in your journal whatever you experienced.

As you are doing this exercise you need to maintain mental contact with the part of the body you are talking to. Otherwise it won't work. Be patient. Allow sensations to occur rather than trying to force them. If contact is difficult, stroke that part of the body or visualize it. Allow the phrase to flow through your mind so that you mentally say, hear, and even see it.

One man looked up with a wry smile after doing this for a minute. He was apologetic. "I didn't feel anything at all."

"Nothing?"

"Well just a little twitch in my forearm. I felt some tingling in my upper lip."

"Those are sensations."

Many people feel small twitches or tingling at first. You may even experience throbbing, the sensation that your leg is twice its usual size, or a brief pain in a part of the body that has suffered an accident, surgery, or illness as far back as infancy. These sensations may recur briefly. Then they tend to disappear. However if a pain or sensation persists for many sessions over many days you should consult your physician. It is possible that you might experience nausea, and, if so, it is important that you allow yourself to vomit. This, too, is just a discharge of stored energy.

As your body unloads tensions in the form of twitches or pains, your mind will also release thoughts, feelings, and visions. This is not bad. Your mind is simply getting rid of this old material. Don't struggle against these thoughts or feelings: Write them in your journal, or talk them into a tape recorder until you no longer need to.

We have interjected the phrase "I am at peace" into the exercise for some people. The standard way of doing autogenic training does not include that. If you decide to use the phrase, be consistent and keep it after each statement to yourself.

"My right arm is heavy. I am at peace."

Practice Exercise One with this phrase three times for thirty to sixty seconds in the manner and posture described. Then write in your journal.

Do three practice sessions a day. After four or five days you will master the exercise. Your arm will become heavy

the moment you think the words, "My right arm is heavy."
Now you are ready to go on.

The instructions remain the same as you continue. However you will accumulate new messages to additional parts of your body.

Exercise One (continued)

5. "My left arm is heavy. I am at peace."

6. "Both arms are heavy. I am at peace."

7. You will now be doing both arms in sequence and begin on your legs: "My right arm is heavy. My left arm is heavy. Both arms are heavy. My right leg is heavy. I am at peace."

As you cite different parts of your body, move all your attention to that part of your body. Pay attention to your legs from the hips to the tips of the toes. Do not move until you have allowed yourself to make deep contact and your leg becomes heavy the moment you say the phrase to yourself.

8. "My left leg is heavy. I am at peace."

9. "My arms and legs are heavy. I am at peace."

10. At some point in this exercise you may want to add heaviness to the neck and shoulders. For people with chronically tight necks and shoulders it can be extremely handy to be able to relax rapidly. After you have finished speaking to your arms and legs, add the phrase:

"My neck and shoulders are heavy. I am at peace."

This is a phrase that you may want to practice in a sitting position, allowing your neck and shoulders to droop. You can do this before and after driving a car or after any activity that causes you tension.

Exercise Two

After you make your arms and legs heavy, you may begin to feel some warmth in them. This is the next step in training.

1. "My right arm is warm."
2. "My left arm is warm."
3. "Both arms are warm."
4. "My right leg is warm."
5. "My left leg is warm."
6. "My arms and legs are warm."
7. "My neck and shoulders are warm."

Exercise Three

Repeat: "Heartbeat calm and regular." (Do not add words to make it a sentence. Say it this way.)

Exercise Four

Pay attention to your breathing without changing it or altering it. Say to yourself, "It breathes me."

Exercise Five

"My solar plexus is warm." (This is your abdomen, below your rib cage.)

Exercise Six

"My forehead is cool."

These exercises are cumulative. As you master each one, you abbreviate it. You can feel the effect immediately as you say, "My arms and legs are heavy and warm. Heartbeat calm and regular. It breathes me. My solar plexus is warm. My forehead is cool. I am at peace."

There is a rule of thumb in following these exercises: Do not do one that involves your symptom area. For example if you have just suffered a severe trauma to your right arm, do not begin with the heaviness exercise for that arm. Come back to it last, after you have mastered the other exercises. Similarly if you have cardiac symptoms, do not do the exercise for heart-rate regularity until you have mastered all the others. If you have an ulcer, do not warm your solar plexus until you have mastered cooling your forehead. By avoiding the symptom area until you have mastered all of the exercises, you allow your system to attain a depth of relaxation and healing in which you are not likely to exacerbate your symptoms.

At the end of this section are a series of phrases that have been used in dealing with specific symptoms. They are worthless until you have mastered the six basic exercises. You need to allow yourself time for this. The buildup of tension by which we acquire symptoms is long and slow, and it is by a similarly gradual process that they can be removed, a process of allowing rather than coercion. Again we must stress that you see a doctor about long-standing symptoms and check with him or her about any prescribed treatment while doing autogenic training.

It is important not to move too fast. If you don't feel heaviness or warmth at first, pay attention to the sensations you do feel. Each person has a different nervous system and a different history. You need a process that is entirely yours, very individual. You may need to linger on a particular phrase for reasons that only your body and brain could know. The important thing for you to do is pay full attention when you are doing the exercises. If you let your mind wander you will not be making contact with your body.

It is helpful to write in a journal after each three-minute session. The training is not very long, but the repetition several times a day is important. You will move more rapidly if you do it three times a day. Again it is important to focus. The focus resembles the attention you give to a mantra or repeated word or sentence in meditation. You cannot meditate by effort. You simply allow your attention to follow your direction. Be patient. Not much will happen at first. Yet the most infinitesimal sensations are signs of progress. Nothing is too subtle or small for this process. If anything you are healing yourself by a moment-to-moment attention in which you allow your deep, wise, and concealed nervous system to unravel the damages and tensions of the past.

ORGAN-SPECIFIC PHRASES

The following are a few phrases for specific conditions:

Hay fever, bronchial asthma: "My eyes are cool." "My eyelids are cool and numb."

Hay fever, vasomotor rhinitis, bronchial asthma: "My nose is cool."

Extreme tenseness of face, swelling of mucous membranes: "My jaw is heavy." "My mouth and larynx are cool."

Coughing: "My throat is cool, my chest is warm."

Disorders of sleep: "Warmth makes me sleepy. It sleeps me." "Waking does not matter. It sleeps me."

Chronic constipation: "My lower abdomen is warm."

Back pain: "My back is heavy and warm."

14 ⚜ MASSAGE FOR HEALTH AND WHOLENESS

Hand and foot massage became a kind of ritual at SAGE. Sometimes we would massage each other's hands before we worked with clay or paints. Sometimes we massaged our own hands just to relax and get ready for further massage.

Hand Massage

1. Sit comfortably and remove all jewelry. Use a little hand cream, lotion, or oil. Rub this into your hands. Then look at the backs of your hands and your fingers and nails. Look at the palms.

2. With one hand squeeze each finger of the other hand as if you were squeezing a tube of toothpaste. Start at the base of the finger. Massage around the base of each finger.

3. Pull each finger firmly.

4. Massage the back of your hand and the palm.

5. Close your eyes, lean back, and feel the massaged

hand. Compare it with the hand that has not yet been massaged.

6. Massage your other hand.

7. Flop your hands at the wrist, shaking them as if they were wet. Your hands should now feel alive and ready to massage your feet.

FOOT MASSAGE

Foot massage became an important ritual for one SAGE group. Initially everyone was skeptical. Most people stop walking around barefoot at an early age, and so they stop the natural stimulation of the underside of the foot. This is a stimulation that so-called primitive people get daily from walking barefoot. Actually the stimulation doesn't stop with the foot but goes to every part of the body and the internal organs. In *The Massage Book* (New York: Random House/Bookworks, 1972), George Downing says that if any part of your body deserves your best attention it is your feet. When you massage your feet you stimulate all the rest of the body as well. The diagrams we have reproduced from *The Massage Book* show the bottoms of the feet as "zonal." Therapists say they can feel the correspondence between each area and the glands or organs of the body.

A Shiatsu teacher instructed the first SAGE group in foot massage, and we sat with bowls of scented water and washed each other's feet.

One afternoon as we explained the foot massage for the first time to the next group, one woman was whispering to her neighbor:

"My brother was at a fair this weekend and there was a man there with a booth, charging five dollars for a foot massage. My brother said, 'Why don't you try it?' and I thought, 'Oh, how disgusting.' I can't imagine wanting to have anyone handle my feet. Ugh!" Many other people felt

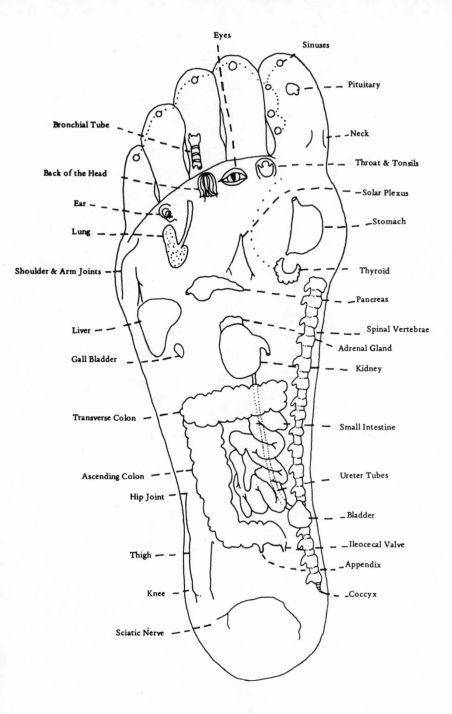

Eyes

Sinuses

Pituitary

Bronchial Tube

Neck

Throat & Tonsils

Back of the Head

Solar Plexus

Ear

Stomach

Lung

Shoulder & Arm Joints

Thyroid

Pancreas

Liver

Spinal Vertebrae

Adrenal Gland

Gall Bladder

Kidney

Transverse Colon

Small Intestine

Ascending Colon

Ureter Tubes

Hip Joint

Bladder

Ileocecal Valve

Thigh

Appendix

Knee

Coccyx

Sciatic Nerve

RIGHT FOOT

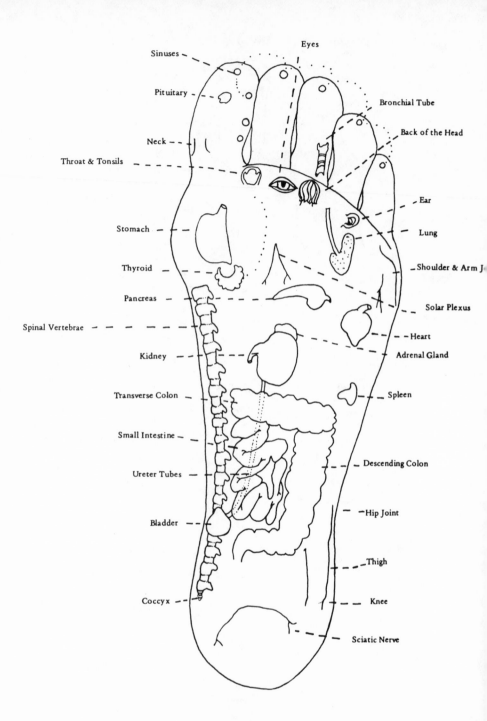

Eyes

Sinuses

Pituitary

Bronchial Tube

Back of the Head

Neck

Throat & Tonsils

Ear

Stomach

Lung

Thyroid

Shoulder & Arm J

Pancreas

Solar Plexus

Spinal Vertebrae

Heart

Kidney

Adrenal Gland

Transverse Colon

Spleen

Small Intestine

Ureter Tubes

Descending Colon

Bladder

Hip Joint

Thigh

Coccyx

Knee

Sciatic Nerve

LEFT FOOT

the same way beforehand, even if they weren't so vocal. Then we did the massage.

The same woman spoke up, "I never could have imagined I could feel so much in my feet. I mean, I never enjoyed my feet before. It's as if I never knew them!"

You may feel the same way after you massage your own feet.

Foot Massage

Sit so that you can comfortably grasp your foot and so that the sole is accessible. Begin by closing your eyes and taking a few breaths.

1. Tune your hands. Then put a little oil on them.

2. Firmly massage the soles of your feet using your thumb, or even the knuckles of your hand. If you feel soreness or pain, you know that you are stimulating a needed area. Do not press too hard on painful areas, but do not go too lightly, either. When you have stimulated the entire sole of your foot, the instep, and edge of the sole, pinch around the heel.

3. Work on the top of the foot and down between the toes. Squeeze each toe like a tube of toothpaste. Then pull your toes in a gently corkscrew rotation. Massage deeply around the base of each toe.

4. Squeeze the foot down the center and bend the toes away from your face and then toward your face.

5. Stroke your foot with both hands, one on top, the other below.

6. Close your eyes and feel that foot. Now do the same massage process on your other foot.

Walk around barefoot for a few moments and see how your feet feel. If you feel half as exhilarated and invigorated as we did, you will want to massage your own feet regularly. It is even more exquisite if you can exchange foot massage with a friend. This means that each of you have the opportunity to relax fully while you are being massaged. Many people hesitate out of delicacy, thinking that their feet may smell, or are ashamed of their bunions or arthritis. Actually the most pleasant way to exchange a foot massage is to begin with a ritual of washing your own feet, or washing each other's feet in warm water. Then rub them with scented oil or lotion. In massaging someone else's feet you can avoid any sore spots. You will still bring healthy stimulation to your friend's feet even if you massage only the soles or only portions of the feet.

Legs and Arms

The circulation of blood through your legs and arms requires good muscle tone. Squeezing down your legs and down your arms can enhance this essential circulation.

Seat yourself comfortably. If you are not wearing clothing you may want to rub some lotion or oil on your arms and legs.

1. Take both hands and begin to squeeze your right leg all the way down to the foot, as if squeezing a giant tube of toothpaste. Avoid sore spots and bruises, varicose veins, and tender places. Squeeze down your leg three times.

2. Rub the leg vigorously all the way down.

3. Slap your leg lightly all the way down.

4. Close your eyes, and feel that leg. Compare it with your unmassaged leg.

5. Repeat this entire process on your unmassaged leg.

6. Do each arm in the same way, first squeezing down from the shoulder to the hand. Then rubbing, then slapping. Make sure you give vigorous stimulation to the muscles on the inside of the arm.

7. After you have done one arm, stop and feel it, comparing it with the other arm.

8. Do the entire process for the unmassaged arm.

◇ ◇ ◇

You are now ready for your spinal massage. You may wonder how you can do that. Actually, this is one that you have known for a long time. You used to do it for yourself when you were a baby in a crib, rocking your pelvis and sliding up and down on your back. Specially trained people who practice polarity massage use a similar method.

Pelvic Rock and Spinal Massage

1. Wear clothing that is loose and will not be damaged by rubbing.

2. Lie flat on your back on a carpet or rug. Close your eyes. Take three deep breaths and imagine that your back has been dipped in black ink and you are lying on white paper. What imprint would you make on the floor? What parts of your back touch, and what parts don't even touch the floor?

3. Draw your knees up so that your feet rest flat on the floor. Your legs should be about as far apart as your shoulders—about two feet apart.

4. Now make the movements of a baby rocking himself in his crib. Begin by tilting your pelvis up, pressing the small of your back into the floor, and then tilting your pelvis down, allowing the small of your back to arch away from the floor. Repeat this until you find yourself in a rocking motion by pushing against your heels. Soon you will be jiggling yourself like an infant in the crib. You will feel your entire spine move. You will feel your head and neck move.

5. Instead of making large movements with your pelvis, push with your heels until you jiggle in a com-

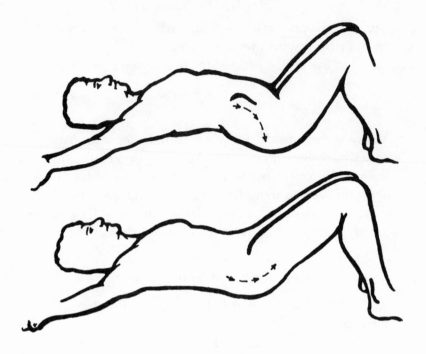

fortable rhythm, "sliding" your spine up and down.
You will know that you have found the right movement by a pleasurable feeling in your back. Continue
this movement for one minute.

This is a safe massage unless you have severe spinal problems, in which case don't do it.

1. Lie still, feeling the warmth and pleasant sensations in your body. Is there any area of your body that
feels tense? While you are lying there, imagine that
you can send your warm breath to those places.

2. Lie flat, with your legs stretched out, and feel the
places where your back touches the floor. Is any part
of you touching that was not touching before? What
imprint would you make if you were dipped in ink
now?

3. Look in the mirror and see how you are standing.
See how alive and relaxed you look.

◇ ◇ ◇

In our SAGE groups foot massage, hand massage, back massage, and body massage caused people to feel a mellow sense of enjoyment, a pleasure in physical well-being. It also left them with tenderness and closeness to the people who massaged them. To give a massage is to discover how interesting, strong, different, beautiful, and pliable your friends' heads, necks, and bodies are. It is also pleasurable to be able to soothe a person who feels irritable and tense, making them feel good and removing pains and aches. Often people who received massages would leave their grouchy, depressed moods behind and would come away looking dreamy and content.

A favorite massage to give another person is one that can be done with clothing. It is a massage for the upper back, the neck, and face. It may put your partner into a dream state or even into sleep.

Hedonistic Massage of Head, Neck, Upper Back

Be sure that you have plenty of uninterrupted time. Pick a comfortable way to sit. Your partner should lie on his or her back, head in your lap, on a towel or pillow. You can sit behind your partner with your legs spread, or you can kneel. However you sit, be sure that you make all your massaging motions with your entire back and not with your shoulders. If you overuse your shoulders, you will get tired quickly.

1. Tune your hands.

2. Tell your partner not to try to help you but to relax and pay close attention to the circular motions of your hands.

3. Reach down under your partner's back, below the shoulder blades. Make firm, slow, circular motions toward the spine with your fingers. Make circular motions up the back to the neck several times. It will feel as if you are gently scooping the back muscles toward the spine from both sides. Continue the circular motions up the spine and then up the neck to the base of

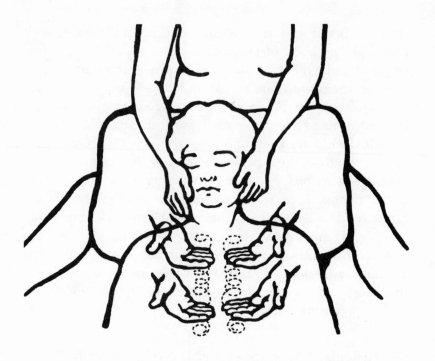

the skull. When you have done this three or four times
the hard muscle tissues should begin to feel soft and
pliable.

4. Lift your partner's head just off the pillow or
towel, in both of your hands. If the neck is relaxed,
the head will lift easily and will move easily. If the
neck is tense, the head will feel rigid and heavy, and
you should not try to turn the head. Just replace it on
the pillow or towel. If the neck and shoulders are relaxed, however, you can grasp the head gently and
feel the base of the skull with your fingertips. Very
slowly and very gently pull the head toward you,
stretching the neck ever so slightly.

Always make head movements very slowly! When a
person allows you to take his or her head in your
hands it is like trusting you with his or her life. To
move the head gently and soothe the neck requires
trust between the partners. Once the relaxation and
trust is there, the motion is extremely pleasurable.

5. Now you can give your partner a face massage just as you did it for yourself in Chapter 6. Be firm but very slow and gentle. Make circular motions with your fingertips, around the eyes, down the nose, along the cheekbones, over the gums, and down the rims of the ears to the lobes. If you ever feel that you are out of sensitive touch with your partner, stop and tune your hands again. Then feel your partner's face without touching. Finally try massaging.

6. Place the heels of your hands in the middle of your partner's forehead, with your thumbs side by side. Lift your thumbs so that you don't touch your partner's nose. Now lean so that you press with your weight on your hands. You are leaning on your partner's face, and you must put all of your concentration in your hands. Slowly, slowly, with the muscles of your back, begin to release the weight, keeping your hands on your partner's face. Lift your hands off your partner's face so slowly that your partner will never feel the separation. Keep your hands an inch over your partner's face, maintaining the contact between your fields. Feel the contact and the fields. After thirty or fifty seconds slowly begin to lift your hands higher and part them.

This massage is best done with total concentration on the contact with your partner, and your partner's eyes should be closed. You may decide that it helps your concentration to close your eyes at times, too. If you can concentrate, without tensing your shoulders, you will also feel relaxed and refreshed.

◇ ◇ ◇

Often the person doing the massage comes away relaxed, feeling a tenderness and mergence with the person he or she has massaged. Concentration on feeling soothes the mind and washes away the distinctions and petty differences created by words and concepts. Touching is nourishment. To touch is far more than to smooth and massage the body physically. It is the kind of nourishment that mothers give their infants, that lovers give each other, and that most adults give to cats and dogs—but not to each other. If it were possible to give a massage or be massaged each day, it would revitalize a sense of human connection that is all but abandoned after maturity. A massage a day would keep isolation away.

If you cannot think of anyone who would accept or give you a massage, see if a hand massage isn't possible. Teach a friend the face massage. Teach friends to tune their hands.

It takes practice to give a delectable massage. I can remember being the guinea pig for our first group's initial massages. One man had hands that felt like leather. It felt as if an elephant were walking on my face. But he loved the idea and began taking lessons. Within a month we were all asking for his face and shoulder massages. He became so skilled and so fond of massage, that he became a licensed masseur at the age of sixty-eight. Other people in the group who had never dreamed of massage as a way of communicating began to give each other long, loving massages instead of luncheons.

15 ❧ EXERCISES FOR VITALITY AND FLEXIBILITY

SAGE participants have been almost unanimous about the important changes in vitality, strength, and limberness they felt as a result of exercising. One retired business-woman began her core group with the statement that she could not exercise because of her bad back. After three months she said,

"When I first started doing yoga exercise I didn't believe I could do it. For years I had such a bad back I couldn't lift anything and couldn't move. When I first leaned forward I thought, 'Oh, I can't do this,' but I could! I had no pain at all. It was like a miracle. I can't believe what it has done for me. I never could do head rotations. Because of one of the exercises I lost a terrible knot in my neck. I've gone to specialists for two years and they couldn't help me. I can turn my head and do everything, I can't get over it."

A great deal of our pain is from tension combined with *lack* of exercise, not *from* exercise. One man with arthritis of the wrists and ankles had been advised against all exercise. He returned to his doctor after practicing yoga and other exercises judiciously for several months. His physician was dumbfounded at the changes. "I can do so much now that I couldn't accomplish before. I wish I'd known about all this ten years ago."

The people who experienced dramatic changes were the ones who had sufficient motivation to exercise daily and thoughtfully. Often the people who obtained the most benefits were people who had suffered enough distress that they were eager to try something that might help. Whatever transformation occurred was in direct proportion to how carefully, and extensively, they did the exercises.

A variety of the exercises we have used at SAGE are offered in this chapter. Some are for stretching and limbering muscles and are arranged in order of difficulty, with easier ones first. Others are designed to make the heart and lungs work harder and become more efficient. Others increase strength or endurance. Some encourage awareness.

When you learn exercises from a book, it is especially important to pay attention to your feelings at each instant. You must also remember that your wrist is connected to your arm, your arm is connected to your shoulder, which is connected to your neck, which holds your head. When you move your wrist, you affect the totality of yourself. All of the exercises need to be done in the same manner: relaxed, with leisure, and with full attention. There is absolutely no point in doing the exercises rapidly with your mind on something else. You need to relax deeply before you start. Then you cannot hurt yourself. When someone says, "I hurt my back doing yoga," it means that person could not possibly have paid close attention at the time. We learned to move thoughtlessly in school, where our calisthenic instructors generally didn't know that the careless repetition of a movement can harm the body.

At SAGE people did not injure themselves. They followed rules that are largely common sense. They did not compete. They did not emulate the instructor. They did not try to prove how well they were doing by overdoing. They did not let anyone else tell them what their limits were. They paid attention, instant by instant, to what they were feeling in their bodies. And they began each exercise relaxed.

Hopefully you will get to know your body so well that you will begin to invent the exercise routines you need. As SAGE participants exercised for several years, some of them began to know just what exercises they needed at any one time. It was no longer a matter of just repeating the same exercises at the same hour each day.

Initially Ken analyzed the needs of each person in the core group and selected the yoga postures and exercises that answered their individual requirements. He also picked exercises for the group as a whole, to enhance self-discovery, make movement enjoyable, and increase strength, vitality, and limberness. Exercise seemed like good preventive medicine to us. Becoming a helpless burden is high on the list of what none of us wants. Said one man in his late seventies, "I think I fear that more than dying. And that's the thing about this program of exercise. I don't think it'll happen if a person takes care of his body." He had been part of a three-man subgroup that met frequently with Ken to practice yoga and give each other feedback, as well as to shoot the breeze. By watching each other and telling each other what they were doing—like tensing unnecessary muscles—they could help improve the exercises and benefits. "You clench your jaw when you move your legs," one man observed of another.

Vitality and strength exercises have been demonstrated to be exceedingly powerful in rejuvenating people aged fifty to eighty-seven. One most impressive study was done in the 1960s by Dr. Herbert DeVries, a physiologist at the University of Southern California, who compared people on a carefully designed exercise program of jogging, calisthenics, stretching, and water exercise—with people the same age who were inactive. If you sit, you get heavier and less energetic. If you exercise, you relieve your nervous tension, gain energy, and lose weight. Exercise itself, without change in diet, would increase metabolism and reduce weight. When DeVries tested the metabolic rates of his fifty- to eighty-seven-year-old exercisers, he found they had risen 7 to 28 percent. Such a person would incorporate food twenty-five times faster than before, thus losing about a pound a month. Some exercises, such as walking and jogging, help to condition the heart, blood vessels, and lungs. An exercise regimen should be based on an evaluation of your fitness to start with. There is an excellent physical fitness test and exercise regimen in DeVries' book, *Vigor Regained* (Englewood Cliffs, N.J.: Prentice-Hall, 1974).

If you have doubts about your health, or have refrained from exercise for a long time, consult your physician. You might ask for a step or a treadmill test to show how your heart responds to vigorous exercise.

Most joint stiffness begins in the muscles and connective tissues—the ligaments, tendons, and fascia that seem to shorten and harden with aging and lack of exercise. When a muscle contracts painfully, it may begin to contract the connective tissue. This begins a vicious cycle often producing muscle spasm. Lower back pain is often the result of this cycle, not trauma. When areas of muscle are chronically tense, the pressure on small blood vessels in the muscle tissue causes a restriction in blood flow known as *ischemia*. Ischemia, or blood starvation, always results in muscle pain, which in turn brings about a splinting reaction in which the muscle contracts more, reducing blood more, causing more pain. Gradual exercise can reverse this agonizing process.

Gradual is our key word. No exercises should ever be forced. They should be done slowly, with close attention to how your body feels. Never overdo! Do not rush. It is a good rule of thumb not to do isometrics or other exercises that involve straining and holding your breath. Moreover if you feel slightly ill, or have a cold, don't push yourself to exercise.

Yoga and stretching exercises are a means of self-healing and self-discovery, and their effects on many SAGE people have been dramatic. People immediately respond to another person's grace and gracefulness. That is what we saw in SAGE people as they practiced yoga and stretching. Unlike all the exercises we did in high school and college, yoga depends upon steady, quiet attention to the sensations of breathing and of the body. The word "yoga" means *union*, and hatha-yoga is a means of practicing mind-body-spirit connections that lead to self-knowledge and enlightenment. Hatha ("ha" and "tha" mean *sun* and *moon*) means a uniting of opposite energies, like yin and yang.

The postures of yoga are called *asanas*. It is said they came from wise hermits who lived in the jungles of India ten thousand years ago, watching the ways animals and other creatures moved and rested. If you open a yoga book you will notice that the postures are called "the cobra," "the fish," "the locust," and so on. The basic premise of yoga is that you must know your body in order to be healthy and grow. Yogis say that all diseases are caused by an imbalance in life-style, so that a person does not use his energies and emotions correctly. In the West we assume that much of our functioning is automatic and therefore beyond our control: And we call a part of our nervous system that regulates breathing and heart rate the autonomic nervous system, as if we could not control it. Yogis have taught us that we *can* control it. People in SAGE have not only changed the volume of their breathing, but have learned to warm their hands simply by concentration. Others can reduce their pulse rate. Yogis have pointed out that most of us accept premature aging, due not to our length of time on earth, but to stress and tension, lack of exercise, and incomplete elimination, along with negative attitudes.

After practicing yoga people have noticed that their weight becomes redistributed. They no longer look disproportionately heavy over the stomach and through the ribs.

Posture is also improved, with changes in the spinal column. We stand and sit on our spines, the body's axis. The spine is composed of vertebrae, bones that are separated by cushions or discs. This column of vertebrae supports the entire weight of the body. In fact we resemble clothes on a clothes pole. It is a supple pole that enables us to move in all directions. Each vertebra has a hole in it through which runs the spinal cord, carrying all the nerves from the brain to the various parts of the body. These nerves control all the functions of the body except those of the head and a few special organs. Clearly the erectness of the spinal column is essential to health and functioning.

When a person habitually bends his vertebral column by hunching or slouching, he moves his center of gravity forward. It no longer falls between the tips of his feet but is extended further forward and he is no longer in balance. In order to maintain balance he adjusts by moving the muscles, known as *paravertebral* muscles, around the spine. When these muscles get strained, backaches occur. Some people feel that backaches are inevitable with age, but that is not true. Most of us do not stand erect, therefore we don't maintain the equilibrium of our muscles. Indeed many of us have such habitual bad posture and such tension that we are always compensating with paravertebral muscles. After fifty or sixty years of imbalance and muscle strain, along with lack of exercise and general muscle tone, it is not surprising that disc problems occur.

By age thirty most people can't touch the floor with their fingertips while keeping their knees straight. As people become older their backs stiffen because the ligaments become tight. Since the spinal column is continuous, if a person restricts movement in any one place, the smooth flow of the entire body is affected. Ligaments and tendons tend to shorten over time because of our bad posture and poor balance—and we don't know it. Bad posture exaggerates the curves of the vertebral column; people who sit a lot throw their heads and necks forward, causing the spine to compensate by bending back. This is a common cause of headaches as well as neck and shoulder pain.

Because we are largely unaware of our posture and the use of our bodies, we are surprised and unhappy when pains arise. We act as if a pain attacked us, instead of realizing that we brought it on. What happens in yoga is that each position brings the vertebra of the spine into action, stretching and twisting the spine in different ways, eventually correcting the habitual bad posture and straightening the back. Calisthenic exercises often induce people to try to touch their toes, but when this is done rapidly, the exercise is a source of back problems. Two members of our group, one of them sixty-eight and the other seventy-six, had complained that they couldn't touch their toes for years. After a number of sessions of yoga stretching it was perfectly easy for them to very slowly bend down and touch the floor with their fingertips.

The joints, too, suffer from unintentional misuse. All the bones in the body are connected to each other by joints. Some of them, such as the hips, work like a ball joint. Others, such as the knees, are hinges and cannot rotate. Joints get a tremendous wear and tear because they are subjected to constant work. Besides being mechanically moved, some of these joints are constantly pressed by body weight. Think about the lower limbs that support and move an individual throughout a lifetime and the moving weight borne by the knees or the hips. Lack of physical exercise and toxins, especially originating from heavy meat proteins, lead these joints to degenerate. This is called *osteoarthritis*. Progressively the cartilages which cover the end of the bone begin to be destroyed, and when they gradually disappear, the extremities of the bones are no longer protected by these surfaces. They fuse together. When osteoarthritis destroys the articulation of the knee or hip, a person may find himself in a wheelchair or facing surgery to replace the joint with an artificial one.

Calcium deposits begin to form around these joints early

in life. In fact anybody who turns his head will begin to hear little creaks. People who start doing yoga asanas may hear cracking sounds. Sometimes these are the calcium deposits in the joints breaking up.

Circulation is also affected by the way we live which is why heart disease is a major killer in the United States today. Among the various coronary diseases the primary killer is hardening of the arteries. This can lead to high blood pressure, which means that the heart overworks. It also may mean a rupture causing a hemorrhage, or the pipe may clog up completely, causing the death of the tissues normally supplied by the artery. When this occurs in the brain, it is called a stroke; if it occurs in the heart, it is called a heart attack. These days one needn't be old or middle-aged to have heart problems. Young men of thirty or even twenty are turning up with heart disease.

The circulatory system is benefited by the asanas not only because they generally stimulate circulation, but because they also twist and stretch the blood vessels, making them more elastic. This maintains an even pressure between heartbeats and steady bloodflow. The veins return blood to the heart by means of valves, and when the valve is defective the veins swell, meaning varicose veins. Certain postures, like the shoulder stand and the plow, have a special effect on the valves, and during these asanas the blood flows back to the heart without effort. When you do a shoulder stand, you relieve tension on the abdominal muscles and the organs, and allow the leg veins to drain down instead of up, and help the stomach and reproductive organs to go back into their proper placement. During these reverse postures, the capillary beds in the legs can be drained and thoroughly cleanse the tissues. They are not postures for people already suffering from high blood pressure.

People on the SAGE staff had studied in unusual programs and so our exercises were garnered from various sources, from Tibetan Kum Nye, the Arica program, the work of Moshe Feldenkrais, Olympic gymnastic warm-ups, Tai Chi Chuan and other martial arts, as well as from our imaginations. Like yoga many of these postures or movements were directed simultaneously at greater physical flexibility and strength, greater awareness and transformation. Because people so often asked for help with their balance, we did some introductory Tai Chi Chuan exercises, movements practiced with dreamlike slowness. Chinese people of all ages have been doing Tai Chi Chuan for centuries, a method of self-defense based on yielding rather than combating or resisting. The movements are effortless and resemble the flowing and accepting philosophy of Taoism, a guide for life expounded by Lao Tze around 600 B.C.

You will probably notice that one day is not like another. One day you may do an exercise easily. You feel limber. It goes smoothly and it is pleasant to keep your attention on your body. At another time that day, or on the next day, you expect it to feel the same but it doesn't. It is never the same. What you have felt, what you ate, how you sat or slept, and what you have been thinking have all changed you in the meantime. It may be easier for you; sometimes it will be harder.

You have to take each time separately, just as if you had no expectations at all. As you proceed with yoga exercises, you will discover many curious things about your body. You may find that the right and left sides are not identical. You may find that you are stronger or more limber in the upper part of your body, or in your lower torso and legs. You are likely to discover that there are areas where you feel a lot—and areas that you can't feel, no-man's land, gaps. You may want to massage these gap areas and talk to them. When you are resting after an exercise, compare the areas that you have been stretching with the rest of your body. See how much of your body you can feel. Part of being alive and integrated is having some conscious contact with all of your body. Also the more sensitive you become to yourself the more you will be able to heal yourself. You will begin to feel a new aliveness and integration about your body, which will influence your feelings and thoughts about life.

The exercises are presented in roughly the order that we have done them in SAGE groups.

Preparing for Exercise

1. Make some time when nobody will disturb you, when you will not have to answer the door or phone. Do not wear jewelry, glasses, or shoes. Wear soft, loose clothing.

2. It helps not to eat before exercising, and to have fresh air in the room.

3. Turn off radios and television. You will need your full attention.

4. Begin each session by lying down with your knees bent and your back as flat as possible on the floor. Breathe deeply five times.

5. Decide which exercises you will repeat each day. Test them until your grouping suits your needs. Then stay with the regimen for a while until you can feel the benefits and add to them.

6. Practice slowly.

7. Constantly ask yourself, "How does this feel?"

8. If you feel resistance, pay attention to it. As you practice you will recognize here and there a muscle stretch that is mildly uncomfortable. For instance when you bend over keeping your legs straight you will notice the discomfort of stretching your hamstring muscles which have been contracted. This is different from the severe pain of spasmodic muscles. This stretching sensation is resistance, and it stops the moment you stop the exercise. By "breaking into" this spot, directing your attention and warmth there, you can feel the discomfort begin to soften and disappear.

9. Do not try to emulate the illustrations, or to

outdo yourself or anyone else. As you explore your own limits you are healing yourself, and your limits will change.

10. Never push yourself. Never continue if you feel pain or fatigue.

11. Pay acute attention. Set your limits at that delicate edge, the boundary of resistance. Do not push from discomfort over the boundary into pain.

12. Try to balance your exercises to the extent your body permits: both sides, your upper as well as lower limbs, and your opposing muscle groups.

13. You are the only expert on yourself. By breathing and centering before you start each new exercise, you will begin to feel what your body needs at that particular moment.

14. Enjoy.

Sitting in a Chair and Rising

Position. Stand with the back of your legs very close to the seat of a stable chair, almost touching it.

Preexercise Instruction. Close your eyes before you start. Check how your body feels. Take three deep breaths with full attention and allow yourself to relax.

Instruction

1. Feel where the chair is and bend forward, bending your knees. Lower your buttocks into the seat of the chair, keeping your head forward and bending from the hips.

2. As you sit on the seat, straighten up, letting your head follow the movement of your pelvis.

3. To rise up from sitting, bend your body at the hips and bend your head forward toward your knees. Place your hands on your legs or on the arms of the chair and feel your weight shift from your buttocks to your feet. Rock back and forth so that you feel the shift in weight.

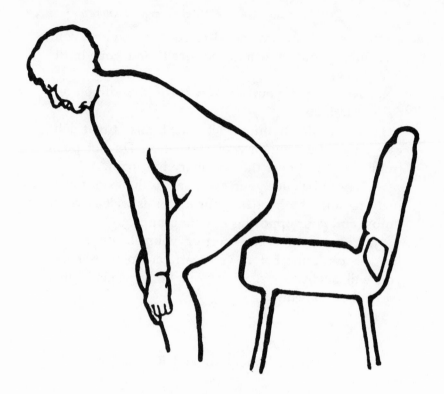

4. Begin to straighten your knees and bring your head up. Feel your body standing.

◇ ◇ ◇

This exercise, derived from the Alexander Method (see the bibliography), is an exaggerated way to sit and stand, but with practice it can make the motion very easy and smooth.

Getting up off the Floor
(if you were there in the first place)

Position. Lie on your back on the floor.

Preexercise Instruction. Close your eyes. Check your body. Take three deep breaths with full attention, allowing yourself to relax.

Instruction

1. Get up in the way you usually do when you finish exercising. Watch exactly what motions you made to get up. Did you strain your neck? Did you hold your breath? Did you tense your lower back or your jaw muscles? Did it feel good?

2. Lie down again. Then slowly, without holding your breath, roll over on your side, curl your legs, and move onto your hands and knees.

3. You are going to use your head as a weight to help you get up, without straining your neck as many people do. Start by bringing one foot forward and planting it firmly on the floor with your knee bent. Your hands will rest on the floor on either side of your foot.

4. Straighten your back leg slightly, leaving your weight resting on your forward foot. Your hips are up, your head down.

5. As you straighten your back leg, give yourself a push upward and lift your whole back.

6. Slowly bring your weight into your center of gravity as you straighten both knees, sliding the back leg toward your front leg as you unbend and come to standing.

7. If you are heavy or have particular problems, it is best to do this next to a sofa or chair that is solid enough to hold onto, or to begin with some help from a friend.

8. Watch your weight placement and your breathing each time. As you practice this, you will begin to feel weightless and effortless.

The Slow Bend

To limber the spine, and as an antidote for fatigue or depression, brings blood into the head. It also removes

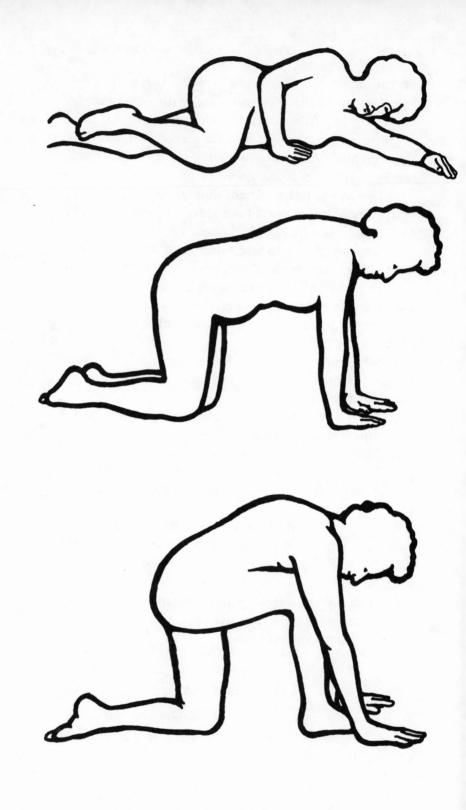

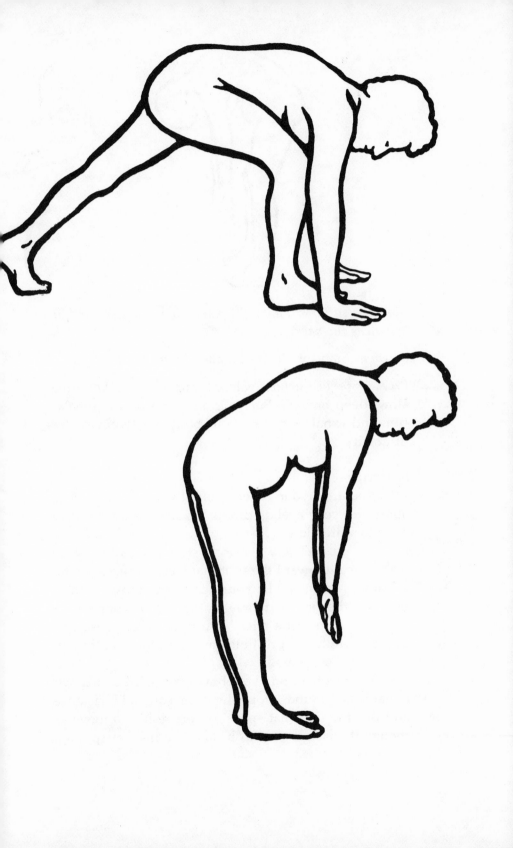

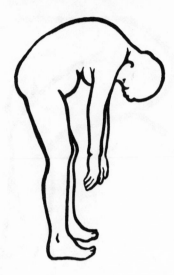

shoulder stiffness and tight hamstring muscles, and it lengthens the back.

Position. Stand with feet parallel, knees slightly bent.

Preexercise Instruction. Close your eyes. Take three slow, deep breaths. Put your attention on the inhalation and exhalation. Feel your body. Feel your center of gravity.

Instruction

1. Keeping your knees slightly bent and legs apart—let your eyelids droop and allow your head to drop forward slowly.

2. If you feel any tension, stop and direct your warm breath toward the spot that feels tense. Once the tension melts away, let your head hang down farther, bending the first vertebrae at the top of your spine. Wherever you feel a crick, or a tight spot, pause and direct warmth and breath toward the spot, focusing on it until it disappears.

3. Very slowly, one vertebra at a time, bend down toward the ground. Stop whenever you feel resistance and breathe into that spot. You are going to move as though the weight of your head and arms were pulling

you down. Bend slowly, allowing your arms to dangle. Allow the weight of your head and arms to slowly pull you toward the ground: Never force.

4. When you have bent as far down as you comfortably can, hang there for a few breaths and then slowly begin the upward journey, returning to upright in the same gradual, sensuous manner that you descended. You can imagine that each spinal vertebra is a saucer. As you slowly rise, you stack one saucer on top of another, creating the spinal column. Your head should come upright last of all.

5. After you have practiced this, you can begin to do it with your legs straight, stretching your hamstrings along the backs of your legs. This will allow you to stand with a straighter spine.

6. Next allow yourself to arch back, very gently, just a little, to compensate for the forward stretch of spinal muscles. Then return to an upright position. In all exercises, especially those that stretch, it is essential to balance so that opposing pairs of muscles are stretched. It is better not to work one muscle group without stretching its complementary muscles, since every body movement is governed by opposing muscles.

7. When you come back to an upright position, stand with your eyes closed and feel your spine.

◇ ◇ ◇

This exercise can begin to gradually make you feel as limber as a snake. A good many people have found that after several months of doing this exercise, they surprised themselves touching their toes in a way that they had not done for thirty or forty years.

Feet, Ankles and Legs

Position. Sit on the floor or on a chair.

Preexercise Instruction. Sit with your eyes closed, paying attention to your breathing and to the feeling of your feet, your toes, ankles, and calves. Take three deep, relaxing breaths with total attention.

Instruction

1. Sit on the floor with your legs stretched straight out in front of you.

2. Flex your feet so that your toes move back toward your face. This is not as easy as it sounds. You will feel a stretch along the back of your legs and the top of your foot. Hold your toes toward your face for a count of three.

3. Relax.

4. Curl your toes under and arch your feet.

5. Relax.

◇ ◇ ◇

These exercises will stretch the hamstring muscles which, in turn, will help you stand with a straighter spine, not to mention waking up your feet and ankles.

1. Sit on a chair.

2. Rotate your feet slowly, really working the ankles. Feel them as you turn them three times in one direction, then in the reverse direction three times.

3. "Play the piano" with your toes or "type a note" with your toes.

4. Stand up and feel your feet on the ground. Feel your connection to the ground.

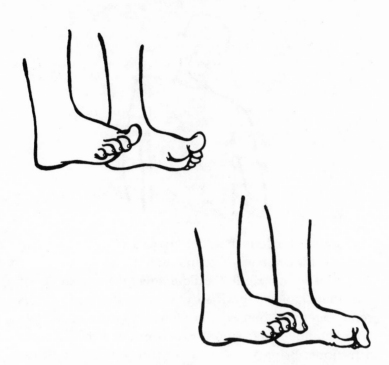

5. Take a few jogging steps, a few springy hops in place.

6. Feel how many sensations you can detect in your feet. Are they warm? Do they tingle? Close your eyes and feel your feet and your feeling of standing solidly on the ground.

Shoulder Rolls

To enliven and limber shoulder muscles.

Position. Stand with feet apart, comfortably balanced.

Preexercise Instruction. Breathe into your abdomen.

Instruction

1. Raise your right shoulder toward your right ear (not bending your head), and let it down again, the arm loose and relaxed. Do this three times.

2. Compare your right shoulder with your left.

3. Raise the left shoulder toward the left ear and allow it to drop back. Do this three times.

4. Raise your right shoulder toward your right ear and then move it back so that your shoulder blades come together, then down around and forward. Rotate your shoulder three times, backward, and then change directions. Bring your shoulder forward, down, back, and around up toward your right ear.

5. Stand with your eyes closed a moment, comparing your right and left shoulders. Does one seem larger or smaller; more alive or more relaxed?

6. Now move your left shoulder toward your left ear, moving the shoulder back, bringing your shoulder blades together, then down, and front and up toward your left ear again. Move the shoulder three times in this backward rotation. Then reverse and make the movement forward.

7. Make three slow backward rotations with both shoulders and three slow forward rotations with both shoulders.

8. Feel your back and shoulders.

Hip Rotations

To limber and ease the pelvic region, stretching muscles of the lower back, abdomen, and sides of the ribs.

Position. Stand with feet slightly apart and parallel.

Preexercise Instruction. Close your eyes. Take three deep breaths, placing your attention on the inhalation and exhalation. Feel your entire body. Feel your center of gravity. Do this thoroughly before you start.

Instruction

1. Place your hands on your hips and bend your knees. Begin to make exaggerated circles with your hips. Begin by leading with your right hip. Bring it as far to the right as you comfortably can, then as far forward, to the left, and back. Make five huge circles to the right.

2. Lead with your left hip and make five circles to the left.

3. When you have made large slow circles, you may feel like making a few smaller, faster circles in each direction.

4. Stand in place with your eyes closed and feel what sensations are taking place in your hips and pelvic region.

5. Hold your shoulders and head still as you make large hip rotations to the right and then the left.

6. Walk across the room and see whether you can feel a freer swinging of your hips.

7. Sit down in a chair for a moment and see whether the process of sitting feels any different.

◇ ◇ ◇

One woman in her mid-seventies commented about this exercise. She said its effects crept up on her after a few weeks; she was having pleasurable sexual feelings that she hadn't experienced in years.

Head and Neck Rotations

To limber and loosen the tight muscles of the neck and help relieve tension.

Position. Stand with your feet slightly apart.

Preexercise Instruction. Close your eyes and take three deep breaths. Allow your shoulders to drop, relaxing, and scan your sensations throughout your body. Feel your center of gravity.

Instruction

1. Turn your head and find a spot directly behind you.

2. Close your eyes and check to see that you are relaxed. Be sure your eyes are relaxed and your jaw is not clenched. It should be loose, the mouth a little open.

3. Begin to roll your head from side to side very slowly. Now slow down.

4. Allow your head to move slowly toward your right shoulder—take twenty to thirty seconds. Then come back to upright.

5. Move your head slowly toward the left shoulder—take twenty to thirty seconds.

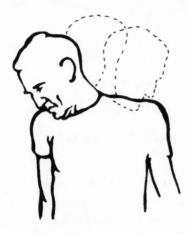

6. Allow your head and face to slowly hang forward. Begin to move around to the right infinitesimally slowly and gently.

7. Whenever you feel resistance, *stop* and breathe into the tense portion of your neck until the tension melts. It should take you a minute to rotate your head once back to the center.

8. Now rotate in the opposite direction, paying close attention to the little spots of resistance or discomfort. Stop at each one, sending your breath and attention warmly to the spot that seems tense.

9. Feel the breathing in your abdomen as you move your head.

10. Watch your breathing as you feel resistance. Never do head rolls rapidly. You can move a little faster after you have done head rolls very slowly and have loosened up all the tight spots. (It will seem easier if you first do the neck massage given in Chapter 6.)

11. When you are finished with the exercise, stop, and turn your head as you did in the beginning. Do you remember the spot that you found behind you? Can you turn to see that more easily now? Can you turn beyond the place you started today?

Side Bends

To stretch and firm the muscles of your sides.

Position. Stand with feet parallel, about as far apart as the shoulders.

Preexercise Instruction. Close your eyes. Take three very slow breaths deeply into your abdomen. Place your full attention on the inhalation and exhalation. Feel your body. Feel your center of gravity.

Instruction

1. Stretch out both arms at shoulder height.
2. Now bend to the left, like a tree bending in the wind. Allow your right arm to bend and cup your head. Feel the stretch slowly along the right side, but do not pull too far. Breathe into the stretched side.
3. Slowly come back up to center, with arms outstretched like wings, at shoulder height.
4. Feel the difference between your left and your right sides.
5. Now bend to the right, with the left arm slowly cupping your head. Stretch to the left side—breathing into it—and when you are ready, very gradually come up and return to center.
6. Close your eyes and feel your left side. Feel both sides. If this is easy, you may want to repeat it three times, keeping both arms straight and stretched. Later as you practice you may want to do it 6 times each side.

◇ ◇ ◇

Most of us have done bends rapidly in school. These stretches were adapted from yoga. They should be done slowly, with attention and relaxation.

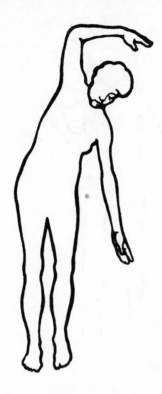

Waist Bend

To tone the upper abdominal muscles and slim the waist.

Position. Stand with your feet slightly apart.

Preexercise Instruction. Close your eyes. Take three very deep breaths, paying close attention to your inhalation and exhalation. Check your body so that you know how each part feels. Check your center of gravity.

Instruction

1. Stand with your arms outstretched at shoulder level, or with elbows bent and your hands on your waist. Make sure that your feet are firmly planted.

2. Twist side to side from the waist—*not moving your hips.*

3. Follow the motion of your arms (or of your elbows) with your eyes.

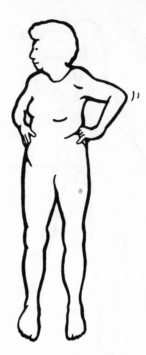

4. As you twist from right to left and back, allow your eyes to be soft and receptive. The world will seem to move. You are relaxing your eyes and exercising them, too, when this happens.

5. Twist, in a swinging way, to the right and then to the left. Keep your hips facing forward. Just swivel your waist. Do it ten times in each direction.

6. If you find yourself tensing your neck, allow it to relax. Let your shoulders drop. If your back is stiff you may want to do the slow bend before you do this. You may also want to massage your neck or do some very slow head rolls first.

7. After you have swung back and forth, stand and see what sensations you feel in your head, in your arms, in your back and legs. Does your waist feel different?

8. When you have become expert at this exercise and need variety, do it while moving your eyes in the opposite direction to your swing. If you move right, let your eyes turn left, and when you start back to the left, your eyes should turn to the right.

9. This will feel different afterward. What is the difference for you?

◇ ◇ ◇

Everyone seems to love doing this exercise. Nobody knows quite where it came from. Like a good recipe it has been around for a long time, passed along from friend to friend. It is reputed to be a great slimmer of the waist if you slowly work up to doing it thirty or so times a day.

It is important to do it with awareness.

Limbering the Hands and Wrists

Position. Stand or sit.

Preexercise Instruction. Close your eyes. Take three long, slow, deep breaths, with your attention on the inhalation and exhalation. Feel all the parts of your body. Feel your center of gravity. Feel your hands.

Instruction
1. Shake your hands as if they were mops.
2. Move the fingers as if they were typing or playing piano.
3. Make fists, then let your hands burst open with the fingers straight.
4. Clap for one minute.
5. Rub your hands together and, when they are warm, alternate making tight fists and opening your hands as wide as possible.
6. For the wrists: Rotate your hands around in the same direction three times. Then reverse the direction and rotate your hands in the opposite direction three times.
7. Move the heel of your hand toward the inside of your arm, bending at the wrist. You should feel this in the heel of your hand and the inside of the arm at the wrist.

Do this for both hands.

8. Straighten both hands as if you were pushing a large object. Hold them back toward the shoulders. You should feel this in the back of the wrist and heel of the hand.

Windmill

To improve circulation in the arms and the rest of the body. To increase shoulder rotation.

Position. Standing with your arms at your sides, feet apart.

Preexercise Instruction. Close your eyes and take three deep breaths, relaxing. Check your body for tension, for subtle sensations. Feel your shoulders and arms. Feel your center of gravity.

Instruction

1. Make five large circles forward with your left arm. Make five large circles forward with your right arm.

2. Make five circles backward with your left arm. Make five circles backward with your right arm.

3. Make five circles forward with both arms. Then make five circles backward with both arms.

4. Hug yourself.

5. Carve a large, interesting space around you by moving your arms slowly and stretching as far as is comfortable in all directions.

6. Stretch your arms up.

7. Shake your arms as if you were a rag doll.

8. Stand with your eyes closed, feeling your arms and shoulders, and breathe deeply.

Circulation depends on the motion of our bodies, as well as on the action of our hearts. The body really has five pumps. The heart is one. The muscles of the arms

and legs are four more. And motions of the abdomen also act to pump the blood.

If you feel stale or sluggish, one easy way to increase circulation is to stand, raise your hands up high, and hold them there for twenty seconds or longer. Feel the old blood returning. Now slowly lower your arms and hands and feel the tingling, feel the warmth and excited circulation of new blood pumping in.

Knee Bends and Rotations

To strengthen the upper thigh muscles and inner thigh muscles and protect the knees.

Position. Stand against a wall with the knees parallel.

Preexercise Instruction. Close your eyes and take three deep breaths. Check your body: Are you tense any-

where? Your buttocks, your hips, your knees? Breathe into your areas of tension. Check your center of gravity.

Instruction

1. Slide your back down the wall very slowly, until you come to a position that would be like sitting on a high stool.

2. Stay for a few moments, keeping the knees parallel and breathing into your legs.

3. Very slowly slide back up to standing.

4. Build up strength slowly. Gradually repeat the "sitting" rest for longer periods, standing between each repetition.

5. Move your legs and feel the sensations in your thighs and knees.

6. Stand away from the wall with slightly bent knees and bend over. Place your hands on your upper thighs.

7. Begin to make slow circles with your knees. Circle left to right, and then rest for a few moments. Then reverse and circle right to left.

8. Be very sensitive to your knees. If you feel un-comfortable in any way, stop.

9. See how walking around feels after this exercise.

This is a wonderful exercise for gradually strengthening the thighs and knees. Do it very slowly and thoughtfully. One man who overdid this exercise said he was laid up for three weeks. "I know it wasn't necessary. I was in a hurry to get results. I repeated it ten times the first time I did it."

Abdominal Massage
(known as *Uddiyama*)

To massage the intestines and other abdominal organs.

Position. Stand with feet about two feet apart and knees bent.

Time. To be done on an *empty* stomach, preferably first thing in the morning.

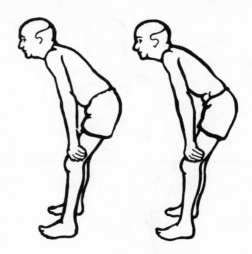

Preexercise Instruction. Close your eyes. Take three deep breaths and follow the course of the breath with your undivided attention. Check your body for tension. Relax by breathing into tense places. Feel your center of gravity.

Instruction

1. Bend forward keeping your knees bent and place your hands on your legs just above the knees.

2. Take a breath and exhale it completely through your mouth. It is important that there is no air in your body.

3. When you have completely exhaled, pull your abdomen inward and upward as if to make the navel touch the spine.

4. Release your abdomen, outward, and then pull it in again.

5. Do this slowly. You may be able to pull your abdomen in anywhere from one to five times per exhalation.

6. Relax and allow air to come in. You should be almost gasping for air. If you have air to exhale, you did the movement wrong, you did not completely exhale at the beginning.

◇ ◇ ◇

Do this exercise every day if you are concerned about constipation or flabby muscles. It improves circulation to the abdomen, helping digestion and metabolism. It is said that this simple exercise is particularly beneficial after fifty.

Picking Cherries
(or grapes)

To help you breathe deeply and energize your entire body. It increases the output of heart and lungs and limberness in the spinal column.

Position. Stand with feet apart and knees slightly bent.

Preexercise Instruction. Close your eyes and follow your breath for several deep breaths. Feel your body, your heartbeat, your center of gravity.

Instruction
1. Flex your knees slightly to avoid locking your knees.
2. Bend as far down as you comfortably can, allowing your arms to sweep toward the ground. As you bend, exhale all the air in your lungs.
3. Stretch upward, inhaling. Holding the breath for as long as you can stretch each arm to its utmost, as if you were picking cherries from a branch just a little too high to reach. Stretch your ribs and feel the muscles of your sides stretch as you reach. Take small breaths if you need to.
4. When you cannot hold your breathe any longer, or feel you have exerted yourself stretching, bend down again, exhaling all the air in your lungs. If you feel a slight dizziness you should go slowly. The dizziness may mean that you have not been breathing deeply enough in your recent life and need to increase your capacity. However do it gradually over months. If you

have any questions about this exercise—for your particular condition—ask your physician.

◇ ◇ ◇

SAGE participants have appreciated and practiced this exercise particularly. It is a favorite for giving a sense of vigor and refreshment and is especially pleasant to practice to rhythmic music. It flexes the toes, strengthens the calves, elongates the spine, stretches the sides, opens the chest, and increases the blood flow into the shoulders.

One sensuous woman who hated to exercise observed:

"The main thing I notice is the surge of energy. I could very easily crawl back into bed and stay there most of the day, but once I've done the exercise I'm up and going."

Push-Aways

To make your arms, shoulders, and back stronger and more supple.

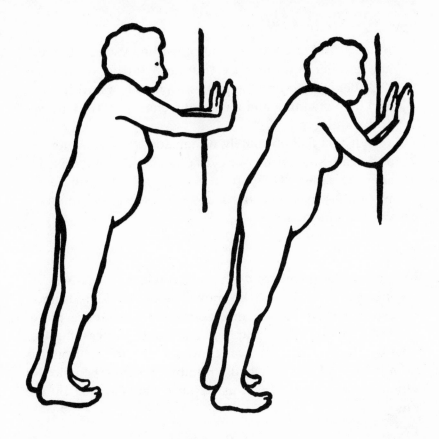

Position. Stand with feet slightly apart and face a wall that is just beyond your reach when your arm is straight out in front of you.

Preexercise Instruction. Close your eyes, feeling your breath relaxing your body. Take three very deep breaths.

Instruction

1. Unlike the pushup of calisthenic classes, this exercise is to be done consciously, slowly, and with full attention.

2. Exhale, leaning toward the wall or door, keeping your back as straight as possible, bending at the elbows. Your body will incline.

3. Try to bring your face close to the wall. As you

inhale, straighten your arms, pushing away. As you get stronger you can place your arms further down.

4. Begin by doing the push-aways only a few times, and then standing and feeling the energy in your arms and shoulders.

5. If you feel absolutely no tension, do a few more, and again stop with your eyes closed and arms relaxed at your sides. Do you feel tingling? Do you feel warmth? What sensations do you have after coming up from an incline?

One of the members of the first SAGE group, a woman in her early seventies who moved with considered grace, urged the group to try this exercise by Lawrence Morehouse (see the bibliography), a former trainer of astronauts. She said that she was feeling a lot stronger from his exercises, and soon she had a number of converts, who did them almost every day. Push-aways were favored by the men.

Back Stretching

To limber and strengthen the back and shoulder.

Position. Find a dresser, book shelf, or other piece of furniture where you can rest your hands on the top surface at shoulder level or a little below. Stand with your back to this piece of furniture, feet apart, about a foot or a foot and a half away.

Preexercise instruction. Close your eyes and relax with two deep breaths.

Instruction
1. Clasp your hands behind your back.
2. Bend forward and raise your hands so that they rest behind you on the top surface of a piece of furniture, such as a book shelf or dresser. Exhale.

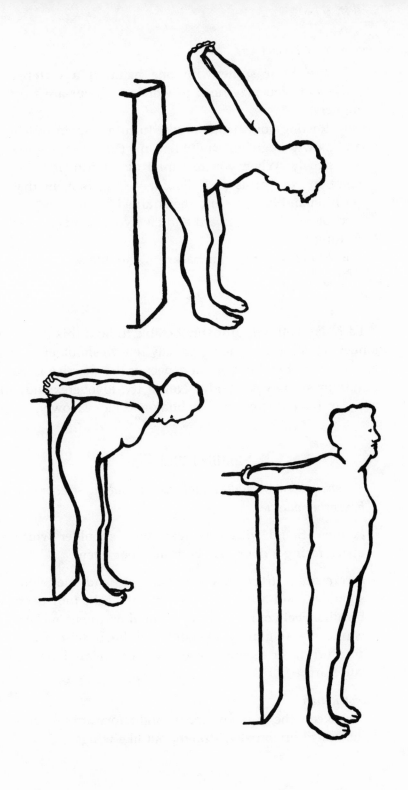

3. Feel your spine with one hand. If a vertebra sticks out, you may need to work with your arms up higher.

4. Resting your hands on the furniture again inhale and slowly begin to straighten up. Do it very gently and slowly. When you feel mild discomfort or resistance in your arms and shoulders stop. Stay in that position and breathe into the strained areas.

5. Slowly bend forward and take your hands off the furniture.

6. Stand, feeling your back and shoulders.

Each day you will probably be able to hold this position longer. This exercise may gradually relieve shoulder pains. However the most important aspect of the exercise is your mindfulness of your body. Never try to overextend, or exert, or force. Listen to your body and move slowly.

Modified Push–ups

To strengthen shoulders and calves and to stretch the hamstring muscles.

Position. Stand with your feet about shoulder width apart, facing a doorway, with the door open.

Preexercise Instruction. Close your eyes and relax your shoulders and arms with each breath. Take four deep breaths. Feel your feet firmly planted on the floor. Feel your center of gravity. Do not begin the exercise if you are hurting or feeling tense. Get very relaxed before you start.

Instruction

1. Keep the feet pointed straight forward. Extend the arms horizontally, straight out like wings.

2. Slowly lean forward, holding the doorframe, while allowing your upper body and head to enter the doorway. Your weight will rest on your forearms.

3. Keep the arms straight and make fists, keeping the backs of the hands pointing upward. Keep the knees and body straight.

4. Hold briefly at first, then five to ten seconds, and gradually work up to a minute. You can obtain more and more stretch as you place your feet farther from the doorway and lean further and further, all the way down to the coffee-table level.

5. Stop and stand, feeling your body. Where do you feel warmth or tingling?

◇ ◇ ◇

This exercise was derived from the DeVries book mentioned earlier, *Vigor Regained.* It is like a yoga exercise, an exercise in self-exploration. Some members of SAGE swear by this posture and say it has done wonders in helping them regain suppleness and strength. It is not like the push-ups we learned in gym classes, where speed and quantity were the signs of excellence. The more attention that you put on your feelings, and the more slowly you do the exercise, the more you will benefit from it. It will help prevent soreness after jogging or shoulder pains resulting from unused joints.

DeVries has said:

> One of the common complaints after unaccustomed brisk walking or jogging is a persistent soreness in the muscles of the calf. This exercise will prevent that soreness. It improves the suppleness of your lower leg muscles and the elasticity of the connective tissue around the ankle joint.
>
> Further, as we grow older, we use the arms and shoulder joints less and less throughout the full range of motion. Many of us develop ill-defined aches and pains in the shoulder as a result, and shrug them off as being "bursitis." The author has found that for many such individuals the pain can be relieved by this exercise and the following one.
>
> However if the shoulder problem has been identified as bursitis by a physician, then the physician should be consulted before using exercises for this purpose.

Centering

An excellent exercise to improve balance and calm the mind.

Position. Stand with feet parallel and about as far apart as your shoulders.

Preexercise Instruction. Do not wear shoes unless you need them for correction of some defect. Close your eyes and feel your body breathing. Be aware of yourself relaxing and let all your distracting thoughts leave with each exhalation.

Instruction

1. Bend your knees. Clasp your hands so that they touch your abdomen below the navel.

2. About two inches below the navel is your center of gravity. Stand with eyes closed, imagining that you have a weight there. Feel the weight.

3. Feel the weight while gently swinging your arms and swiveling from side to side.

4. Shift your weight from foot to foot, keeping yourself low. Make it a sliding motion, so that you slide over one leg, then the other. If you lose your feeling of a center of gravity in your abdomen, close your eyes again and concentrate on that center in your belly.

5. Now walk slowly, shifting your center of gravity between your legs, sliding. Your knees should be very bent. Now take a step or two sideways, like a crab. Keep your knees bent and your attention on the center of gravity in your abdomen.

6. Stand, eyes closed, and feel yourself breathing into that center.

◇ ◇ ◇

This exercise evolved out of Tai Chi. It will help anyone who has problems with balance.

Walking

An exercise for mind, body, and spirit.

Position. Standing.

Preexercise Instruction. Close your eyes and take three breaths deep into your abdomen. Feel your feet on the floor. Feel your spine, your weight on your feet, your joints. Feel your center of gravity.

Instruction

1. Walk around the room and notice how your back and hips and shoulders work as you walk. Notice your feet. Where do you first feel pressure, on the heel or the ball? Do you move forward on the inside or the outside of your feet? Watch, as you walk, how you breathe and what you do with your eyes, your chin, your neck and head.

2. Walk on your heels. Stand and feel your feet.

3. Walk on your toes. Stand still and feel your feet again.

4. Walk on the outside of your feet. Standing, how do your feet feel?

5. Walk on the inside edges of your feet. Was this different in feeling?

6. Roll back and forward on your feet, feeling your arch, your heels. What muscles tighten as you move? What keeps you from falling over?

7. Walk around the room with your toes pulled up from the floor.

8. Walk around the room with your toes gripping, trying to hold on. Stand, eyes closed, feeling your feet on the floor. Walking barefoot is good for your feet. How does it feel?

9. Stand with your feet together, as if you had a lead weight in your belly, like a child's clown toy. Rock forward and back, feeling that weight, that center of gravity.

10. Look down at a spot about three feet ahead of you on the floor. Walk very slowly across the room (or lawn if you are outdoors). Walk so slowly that it takes you a half hour to cross the room. Feel each tiny motion. If you do this slow walk for twenty or thirty minutes, you will find that it has the effect of meditation. Do not think about other things or talk to yourself. Just notice all the sensations in your body as you make

the slow, slow movement of shifting your weight and beginning to lift your foot and put it down.

Balancing

To calm the mind and emotions.

Position. Stand with feet parallel, about as far apart as your shoulders.

Preexercise Instruction. Close your eyes. Feel your center of gravity, below your navel. Feel your entire body as you breathe deeply. Take three thoughtful breaths.

Instruction

1. Stand next to a wall in case you need to touch it or lean against it at first.

2. Pick a spot on the carpet or ahead of you to focus your eyes on.

3. Stand on one foot for as long as you can. Then stand on the other foot for as long as you can.

4. There are many styles of balancing: You can stand like a stork, with one foot against the other

thigh, or at the groin. You can stand with one leg extended, ballet style, behind you. You can stand with your arms extended or your hands together over your head.

5. Remember to breathe deeply as you stand on one foot.

6. Afterward walk very slowly across the room. See if you can feel how you manage to stay upright without falling over. Feel the shifting of your weight from one foot to the other.

Many people at SAGE were pleasantly surprised to discover how much more pleasurable walking and other activities became when their balance improved.

Dry Swimming

For balance and grace and to calm your mind.

Position. Stand with your feet apart at about shoulder width. Your feet should be parallel.

Preexercise Instruction. With your arms hanging relaxed at your sides close your eyes. Take three deep breaths and feel your center of gravity. Begin to imagine that you are in a miraculous fluid, like liquid amber. You can breathe easily, but you will be moving as if under water.

Instruction

1. Bend your knees. As you begin to slowly move, pay attention to your center of gravity. Slowly allow yourself to move your hands, letting them float in this viscous fluid. Dry swimming comes from Tai Chi. The feeling of Tai Chi resembles swimming slowly in the air, staying very relaxed, very centered, mind quiet, attending to the feeling of the movements.

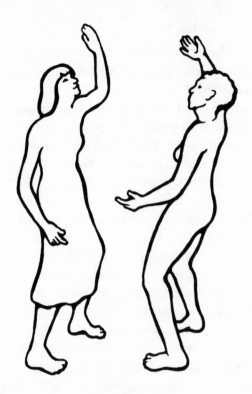

2. Slowly allow yourself to float in your translucent fluid. Make several movements slowly. Repeat each movement until it feels relaxed and very delicious. You may feel strangely silent and as if time were stretching out, even stopping.

3. Breathe into your center of gravity. Rest before going on to the next movement.

4. Bend your knees more deeply. Exaggerate, almost as if you were sitting on air, and pay attention to your center of gravity and breathing. Breathe into that center.

5. Allow your arms to begin floating up in front of you, leaving your wrists limp so that your hands dangle. Imagine there are invisible strings pulling the arms up from the wrists; let them rise, as if they were floating up to shoulder height, very slowly.

6. Slowly, slowly, let your dangling hands float up until they are straight, palms parallel with the floor.

7. Next bend your elbows, slowly pulling your hands toward your shoulders and keeping your arms close to your sides.

8. Now let your *hands* slowly turn upward so that they are parallel to your body palms forward.

9. Finally let your hands and arms float very slowly down to your sides, as slowly as you can, as if they had to float down through very thick invisible liquid. When your arms are at your sides, let them curve a little, as if the liquid pushed them just slightly away from your body.

10. Breathe and feel your center. You may feel a little tired the first few times you practice this, but you may also notice that when you finish you have an indefinable lovely sensation, as if you had been floating through time. You may notice afterward that you have a sense of greater invulnerability. If you retain your sense of center as you walk during the day, you will be harder to push over, harder to knock down. You will be gaining greater balance and inner security.

Hah!
(an exercise from the Tibetan tradition)

To transform mood, energy, and awareness.

Position. Standing.

Preexercise Instruction. Close your eyes. Take three deep breaths and sense your mood. Are you depressed or happy, angry, or sluggish? Are you tired or energized? Do you feel aggressive or passive?

Instruction

1. Stand in readiness. You will want to think the exercise through before you do it. Imagine doing it all the way through.

2. What you are going to do (first in your imagination) is to slowly draw your elbows close to your

sides, with your hands drooping. You will be drawing yourself in, before springing forward.

3. As you draw your arms in, take a deep breath.

4. When you exhale you will step forward on either foot (but choose which foot before you start), plunging your arms out straight at shoulder height. Your arms will be straight, wrists cocked, and hands palm up as if you were pushing a truck. Your weight must be balanced so that your back foot is flat on the floor. You will push the air out of your belly, explosively shouting the loud HAH! of a Samurai.

5. Then freeze. Pay close attention to what has happened in your mind, your body.

6. Slowly move back to a comfortable standing position and stay, with eyes closed, inspecting your feelings, your mind, your sensations.

7. Do this exercise three times. Each time spend a little while simply feeling what happened. Sometimes when we have done it, people have said, "All my thoughts stopped as if they were cut by a knife." "I felt my mood change. I was sour when I came in here. I feel energetic now." "I feel that time stopped." "I feel I am not thinking, I am in the present tense now."

◇ ◇ ◇

If you begin this exercise in a bad mood, you may discover that it actually helps you to transmute your feelings. If you feel soggy, you may find that it helps you to become energized. It is important to do the exercise intently and crisply. Let the shout be loud and full and sharp. It should scare prowlers away. It should be bold and express all of your power.

When you have done it three times, you can do it a fourth time and close your eyes a few seconds after you shout. What image do you see with your closed eyes? There is no right or wrong thing to see. You can also stop at the end of the HAH! and use your eyes like a camera. After a few seconds close your eyes and see what kind of detail you see in the images before your eyes.

Abdominal Strengthening

To strengthen abdominal muscles.

Position. Lie on your back, knees bent, your feet on the floor.

Preexercise Instruction. Close your eyes. Take three deep breaths and feel your back as you inhale and exhale.

Instruction

1. Flatten lower back to the floor, tilting the pelvis, then relax. Do not press on soles of feet.

2. Continue in slow rhythm, breathing out as you press the back down and breathing in as you relax the muscles.

3. If you have trouble mastering this, do a very slight lift of the head to aid in the abdominal contraction.

In the early days of the SAGE experiment, Helen MacElwain, a retired professor of kinesics and physical education at Mills College, showed us this benign way to shore up our vanity and strengthen stomach muscles. Some people in the group had been trying to do modified sit-ups. Helen cautioned that these were extremely hard on the back and provided this substitute.

It requires exactly the same attitude as any yoga exercise—an attitude of listening carefully to your feelings and sensations. These may not be the exercises that fill you with hedonistic delight, but surely they should be done slowly, aware, and with *no pain*. At the first sign of pain, stop.

◇ ◇ ◇

Toni Montez showed many SAGE groups how to strengthen abdominal muscles by uncurling from a sitting position, and curling back into one. For people with unused muscles, this method may be the best way to start, without danger of straining their necks.

Position. Sit on the floor with knees bent and feet parallel on the floor.

Preexercise instruction same as above.

Instruction
1. Bend your head and round your shoulders.
2. Slowly lower your back down to a lying position, using your hands if you need the support at first.
3. Cross your arms across your chest so that your right hand holds your left shoulder and your left hand holds your right shoulder.
4. Slowly curl your head forward.
5. Continue the upward curling if you feel strong enough, so that your shoulder blades begin to lift off the floor.

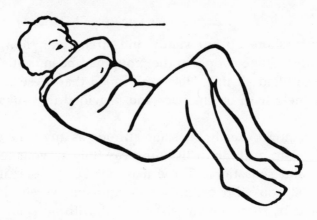

6. Do not strain.

7. If you feel strong, continue to curl toward your knees and hold that upward tilted position for a few seconds.

8. Uncurl very slowly and rest.

◇ ◇ ◇

Now, lying with eyes closed, feel your abdominal area. See if you can feel more of the complex organ system and muscles of your lower torso. Perhaps you can feel movement in your intestines. Breathe deeply, relaxing as deeply as possible, becoming very quiet. How does your abdomen feel now?

Bicycle

An old stand-by to trim the thighs and buttocks, strengthen the abdominal muscles, and raise the pulse rate.

Position. Lie on your back with your knees bent.

Preexercise Instruction. Close your eyes; feel your mood and your energy. Do you feel exhilarated or sluggish? Take three deep breaths and pay close attention to the way the inhalation enters your nose and how far out into the air you exhale.

Instruction
1. Draw your knees up.
2. Tilt your pelvis toward your face, drawing your knees up toward your chest. This raises your buttocks.
3. Resting on your elbows, place your hands under your hips to hold your buttocks up.
4. Now pretend you are slowly pedaling a bicycle. When it feels comfortable, you can pedal faster. Do this for a short time, as long as it feels good.
5. *Slowly* lower yourself so that you are lying in the starting position.
6. Rest for several minutes, feeling your body, your images, your breathing.

◇ ◇ ◇

Do you feel exhilarated? Is there any new feeling in your legs, your buttocks, your abdomen? How is your breathing?

With successive practice you can increase the amount of time that you bicycle. You can close your eyes and imagine yourself pedaling down a beautiful country road on a

sunny day. You can see the fields, the trees, hear the birds and insects. You can smell the new-mown hay and take a country vacation in your favorite place.

The Curling Leaf or Pose of a Child

A restful position to increase circulation to the head and decrease fatigue. A rest.

Position. Kneel on hands and knees.

Preexercise Instruction. Close your eyes, taking deep breaths into the abdomen. Feel your abdomen expand and let all distracting thoughts go out with your exhalation. Relax your whole body.

Instruction

1. Very slowly, as if in a dream, lower your head to the floor and gently allow your hands to slide back beside your body so that they rest with palms up.

2. Rest your head on the floor and relax your chest and your knees.

3. Sometimes people need a pillow under their knees or hands. Put a pillow under you if it hurts.

4. Some people feel tightness in the buttocks and this discomfort can be alleviated by placing a pillow under the buttocks.

5. Stay in the position so long as it feels restful.

◇ ◇ ◇

This is a restful position, one to do any time you need a spurt of energy. As you rest in this position you may even feel a little like a child, relaxed, trustful, and comfortable. If there is any place in your body that feels slight resistance or pain, breathe into it. You should do this position only so far as you can without pain.

The Bellows

Good for legs, thighs, and spine, abdominal area discomfort, and constipation.

Position. Lie on the floor with your legs outstretched.

Preexercise Instruction. Close your eyes and check how your body feels. Take three slow deep breaths with all your attention.

Instruction

1. Slowly and sensuously bring your right leg into a bent position, with your foot flat on the ground, leaving your left leg outstretched.

2. Slowly grasp your right leg behind the knee. Draw that leg up toward your chest very slowly as you inhale.

3. Wherever you begin to feel resistance, stop. Stay there. Breathe and mentally place warmth in the places that feel resistant. Stay there until you feel the resistance melt. You may feel some tension in your right thigh and in the outstretched left leg. You may feel some tension in your buttocks, or in your lower back. Whatever you accomplish will be done by your attention to these places of tension. Begin by holding for a count of six breaths if you can.

4. Let go of your leg and let it straighten out. Feel

your legs. Do they both feel the same? Does one leg feel longer, heavier, warmer, or softer? What is the difference? Rest for six breaths.

5. Draw your left leg up to your chest, gently, in the same way. Again breathe warmth and attention into the spots that feel tense or resistant until they begin to melt.

6. Allow your left leg to rest outstretched and feel your body. Rest for at least a count of six breaths.

7. Bring both legs up, clasping them behind the knees and drawing them toward your chest. See if you can keep your shoulders on the floor, but do not force them. Again breathe into resistant spots for about six breaths.

8. Let go of your legs, slowly slide down into an outstretched position, and notice how they feel. Do the feet want to turn out? Feel your spine: Are there any new sensations?

Don't be embarrassed if you let off some gas while doing this posture. Its name—bellows—comes from the fact that it relieves wind.

Chiropractic Roll

To limber the back and shoulders.

Position. Lie on the floor on your back, arms stretched out as straight as possible from your shoulders so that you form a T shape on the floor.

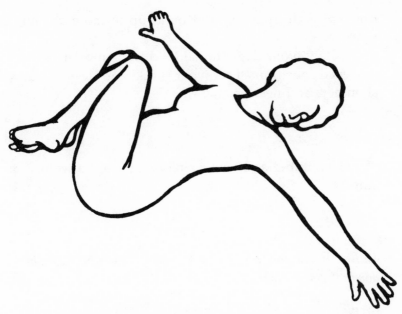

Preexercise Instruction. Close your eyes and check how your body feels. Take three slow, deep breaths with all your attention. Allow yourself to relax.

Instruction

1. Bring both knees up so that your feet are flat on the floor.

2. Allow both knees to move toward your right and let your head turn toward the left. You will feel your left hip rise off the floor and your lower back will twist a little. Allow your knees to go only as far as gravity takes them, only so far as it is comfortable. Try to keep your shoulders on the floor.

3. Bring your knees up toward the center again. Roll the small of your back into the floor as you come back toward the center.

4. Allow your knees to fall gently toward the left while your head turns right. Feel your right hip come up. Does this side feel like the other side?

5. Alternate for as many times as it feels smooth, easy, and pleasurable, first one side, then the other. Don't overdo. Perhaps you can do as many as five

times in each direction and build up to more as you practice.

6. Allow your legs to slide down into an outstretched position. Feel your back and legs, your shoulders and neck.

◇ ◇ ◇

"I feel as limber as a snake afterward," said a woman at SAGE.

The Cat

To limber the pelvic area, back, lower back, and ease abdominal discomforts.

Position. Kneel on your hands and knees.

Preexercise Instruction. Close your eyes. Take three deep breaths. Imagine that your breath is penetrating any tense spot in your body and relaxing it. Do this until you feel relaxed all over your body.

Instruction

1. Close your eyes. Imagine that you are a magnificent, silky cat, with a long, plumed tail. Feel the sensuality and limberness of the cat.

2. Keep your arms straight and check to see that your hands are under your shoulders, shoulder-width apart. See that your knees are apart and directly under your hips.

3. Exhale, and as you do so, round your back, dropping your tail down. Drop your head way down.

4. Inhale. As you do so, arch your back, stomach toward the floor, moving your tail up, and your head up slightly, but not way up. Wag your tail.

5. Repeat this slowly five times. Each time imagine yourself to be an elegant cat, stretching.

6. Lie down on your back and breathe deeply. How does your spine feel? How does your pelvis feel?

◇ ◇ ◇

You may notice, if you have lower back discomfort or abdominal discomfort, that you begin to feel better after doing this exercise. It was a favorite at SAGE, especially among cat lovers who described the elegance of their fur and particularly of their tails.

Head to Knee 1

To stretch the backs of the legs.

Position. Sit on the floor with your legs straight out in front of you.

Preexercise Instruction. Close your eyes, relax your shoulders, and pay attention to your breath. Feel your spine and your legs, breathing into any tense places.

Instruction

1. Look at your feet and curl them toward your face, feeling the stretch in the legs. Don't let your legs turn out. Keep your toes up.

2. Now bend your knee out and bring your right foot up toward the left groin. If your foot will not reach, allow it to rest comfortably anywhere against the left leg.

3. Stretch your arms above your head, taking a deep breath. As you exhale, lean toward your foot in a relaxed manner, clasping your outstretched leg wherever you can.

4. Do not force. You want to feel a slight resistance—in your back and in the back of your straight leg—but not pain. When you have found a place that stretches you so that you feel a moderate resistance, close your eyes and breathe five times into the places that feel resistant.

5. Now inhale again, and on the inhalation come back up straight with arms overhead, sitting.

6. Relax your arms and feel your body.

7. Now, sitting, think how it will feel to do the same thing on the other side. Imagine doing it with your eyes closed.

8. When you have fully imagined the movement, place your left foot against your right groin or thigh or knee. Then raise your arms overhead, inhale deeply, and on the exhalation bend over your outstretched leg and clasp where you can without forcing.

9. Again breathe five times into the places that feel resistant.

10. While bending let your head, your neck, your shoulders relax.

11. Again inhale, and on the inhalation raise your arms straight up, then relax and lower them. Straighten both legs.

12. Feel your left leg and your entire body.

Head to Knee 2

To stretch spine, back muscles, help reduce abdominal fat, and constipation.

Position. Sit on the floor with legs outstretched, shoulders relaxed.

Preexercise Instructions. Close your eyes and take three deep breaths. Feel your seat on the floor. Relax any tight places.

Instruction

1. Do not do this exercise if you have liver or spleen ailments or a hernia.

2. Keep your toes pointed directly up. Flex them toward your face for several moments.

3. It is important to keep the backs of your knees

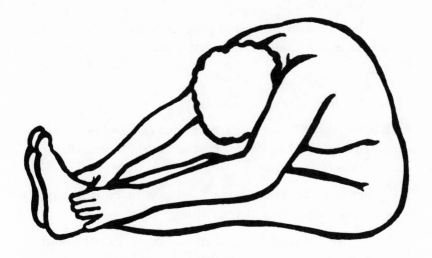

on the floor as much as you can while you move your upper body.

4. Inhale and reach up toward the ceiling.

5. As you exhale, relax, bending forward over your legs.

6. Let your head slowly fall forward and feel your body as you bend. Wherever you feel resistance, direct your warm breath. There is an edge of discomfort that tells you you are stretching your muscles, but it is not pain. Go to that edge and take six deep breaths. Do not go beyond that edge. Do not force yourself to bend farther than you can.

7. As you hold the position, breathing warmth into each area of resistance, you will feel the tension begin to dissolve.

8. As you practice this over a period of time, you will be able to move farther down on your legs and hold the position longer.

9. When you return to sitting, feel your back and your legs. Walk around, feeling your legs. Are they longer, stronger, more springy?

10. Repeat the exercise if you are ready.

◇ ◇ ◇

This balances for the Cobra pose. It stretches the spine to its fullest length and the hamstring muscles of the back of the legs.

Cobra

To strengthen stomach and back muscles, realign spine, tighten chin, help digestion, expand the chest, and stimulate the adrenal glands.

Position. Lie on your stomach with your chin resting on a towel and arms at your sides.

Preexercise Instruction. Close your eyes, breathe and imagine your spine as a chain, limp and limber.

Instruction

1. Stretch your arms out overhead, with the palms of your hands down on the floor.

2. Bring your forehead to the floor. Bring your legs and feet together and tighten your buttocks.

3. Inhale. As you exhale bring your arms up, your head up, and your chest off the floor. Keep your buttocks tight. Then slowly relax and return to the floor.

4. Relax and turn your head to one side, lying on the floor.

5. Stretch your arms out to the sides so that your body forms a cross. Bring your forehead to the floor, your legs and feet together, and tighten your buttocks.

6. Inhale. As you exhale, bring your arms, head, shoulders, and chest off the floor, keeping your buttocks tight. Hold. Then relax and return to the floor.

7. Relax, turning your head in the opposite direction from the first time.

8. Bring both arms alongside your torso with your palms on the floor. Again place your forehead on the floor, legs and feet together, and tighten your buttocks. Inhale. As you exhale, lift your head, arms, and upper torso, stretching your hands back toward your heels. Hold and then relax, returning to the floor.

9. Extend your legs, keeping your feet together. Point your toes. Bring your palms to the floor alongside your ribs. Rest your forehead on the floor and relax your elbows along your body.

10. Visualize yourself as a snake. Elongate the upper part of your body as much as you can before you come up. Inhale. As you exhale, push with your arms and let your upper body come up off the floor. Keep your elbows bent! Keep your pubic area on the floor and your shoulders down.

11. Breathe, holding the pose for a few breaths and return to the floor to relax. Repeat when you are fully relaxed.

12. Lie on your stomach feeling all the sensations and energy from the posture.

This yoga posture is a wonderful imitation of a snake, but it is not for everyone and must be done with care and full attention. Above all never force. Listen to your sensations, and do not imitate anyone else. You might imagine that you are a very warm liquid-feeling snake that has been lying in the sun. The slightest sign of pain means you have forced yourself beyond where your muscles will take you. Then this posture should be balanced by one in which you bend in the opposite direction, such as the slow bend to the floor, or head to knee.

The Bow

To stretch the lower trunk, the hip flexors, and muscles on the front of the thighs. May relieve pain from a posterior slipped disc and help posture.

Position. Lie on your stomach.

Preexercise Instruction. Close your eyes, feeling your spine. Breathe deeply three times, paying attention to the inhalation and exhalation. Relax as if you were a limp piece of cloth.

Instruction
1. Look at the position in the diagram and decide whether you will need a high pillow and a tie or belt to help you, or whether you should avoid this one.
2. Kneel on the middle of the cushion. Place the belt around your ankles.
3. Lie on your abdomen. Your knees will be raised by the cushions.
4. Reach back and grasp the belt, at first with one hand, then the other. Hold it in both hands.
5. Hold firmly onto the belt while pressing back with your lower legs, so that you arch your back slightly.
6. Tighten your buttocks so that you don't overarch your lower back. Hold this for a few seconds at first and gradually work up to fifteen seconds and a minute. Breathe in a relaxed and natural way.
7. As you feel easier with the position, you can proceed to the second step, doing without the pillows under your knees. Just use the belt. Again gradually work up to holding the position for a minute before you go on.
8. Finally do the posture without pillows or belt, if you wish.

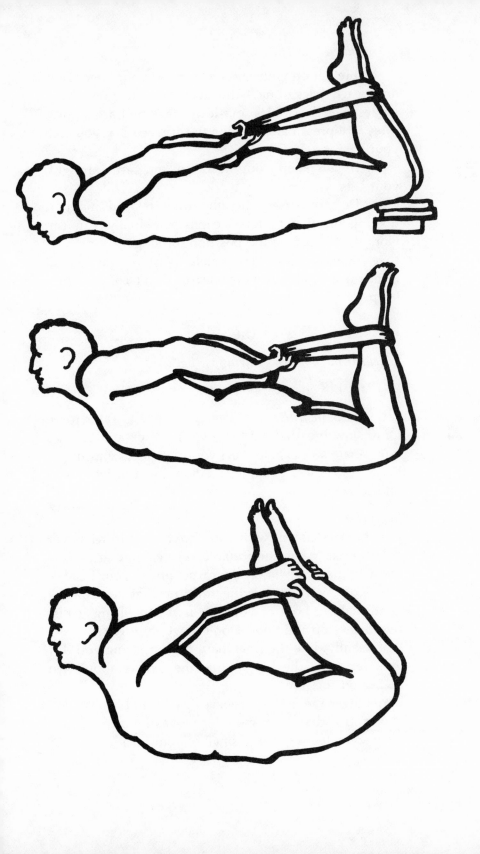

9. Lie flat on your abdomen. Bend your knees fully and reach back, one hand at a time, to grasp your ankles. Let the ankles and lower legs pull arms back. They will press back, pulling the arms so that you arch your back.

10. If you keep your head up and arms straight, your legs will do all the work.

11. Do not strain. Breathe in a relaxed manner, holding for five to ten seconds. Gradually you can work up to holding the position for longer.

12. Release *very, very slowly*. Part of the benefit comes from the way you release. Don't collapse in a heap.

The Locust

Excellent for limbering the upper back.

Position. Lie on your stomach.

Preexercise Instruction. Close your eyes. Take three long, slow breaths and feel your rib cage and back as you inhale and exhale. Feel your shoulders and upper back, your lower back, legs. Allow them to feel warm and relaxed.

Instruction

1. Lie face down, with your face turned in whatever direction is most comfortable. Bring your arms forward so that they lie on the carpet above your head.

2. Now without moving imagine that someone is gently taking hold of your left foot and lifting it just two inches off the floor. Don't move, but feel it.

3. Gently, like the imaginary person lifting you, lift your leg from the hip so that the foot is about two inches off the floor.

4. Lower the leg and repeat this several times. You may notice that your shoulder moves a little. Do you have some feeling in the small of your back?

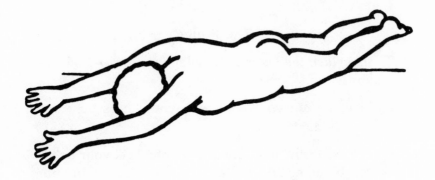

5. Now imagine someone lifting your other leg from the ankle. Get the feeling very vividly before you actually lift your leg from the hip.

6. Lift your leg and lower it several times.

7. Lift one leg, and hold it for a few breaths, then lift the other leg and hold it for a few breaths. Lower both.

8. Lie still for five minutes and feel your neck, shoulders, your back, and your legs.

The locust posture was difficult at first for some SAGE people. Imagining the posture first can help. A therapist called Moshe Feldenkrais, who was able to perform "miracle" cures on people with severe scoliosis, or near paralysis, maintained that movement takes place not so much in the muscles as in the nervous system. It is what you are "thinking" about that matters. If you ask dancers or musicians how they learn some new role or new music, they will often tell you that they quietly read through the music or choreography, sitting very still and imagining themselves performing. They may memorize the song or part of it before they actually move. Imagining a movement, by "feeling" it through very thoroughly beforehand, will make it much easier to execute.

The Bridge

To strengthen the lower back and prevent lower-back discomforts.

Position. Lie on your back with your knees bent and feet on the floor.

Preexercise Instruction. Breathe deeply. Feel your pelvis as you breathe. Breathe into any tense places in your body until you feel relaxed. This is an exercise to be done only if you can, and with a sensual attitude.

Instruction

   1. Feel the imprint of your back on the floor. Feel the solidarity of your feet flat on the floor.

   2. Move your arms beside you and turn the palms down. By tilting your pelvis raise your buttocks from the floor.

   3. Slowly round your back and bring it off the floor one vertebra at a time, until you are resting on your shoulders.

   4. Breathe deeply and imagine the breath going down your spine and out through your genitals. Allow the pelvis to relax. Hold the position for as long as you are comfortable.

   5. Slowly lower your buttocks and lie first with your knees bent, feeling your spine and pelvis. Then slowly and silkily allow your legs to straighten out by letting gravity pull them to the floor. They will slide down. You don't have to make an effort to straighten them. All you need to do is let them relax until they are almost like jelly.

   6. Lie straight on your back and feel your spine and your hips and your legs. Feel your upper back and shoulders. Has something changed?

◇ ◇ ◇

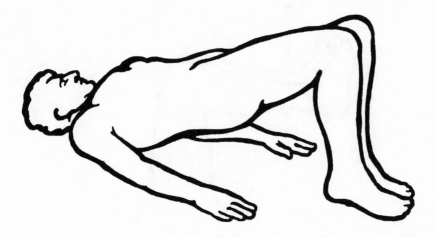

This yoga exercise became the favorite of one man in the group. He said that it really made him feel a sense of accomplishment and pleasure. He would do it every morning. "I do it to a count of twenty now. When I started I could hardly hold it to a count of three."

Half–Shoulder Stand

To stretch the back muscles, strengthen the abdominal and foremuscles of the neck. May enhance thyroid and parathyroid activity, thus enhancing glandular activity in the entire body.

Position. Lie on your back with your buttocks against a wall and legs up.

Preexercise Instruction. Close your eyes and breathe deeply five times, paying attention to the sensation of the inhalation and exhalation. Allow your entire body to relax into the floor.

Instruction
   1. Press your shoulder blades toward each other to expand your chest. Lengthen the back of your neck.
   2. Bend your knees to bring the soles of the feet

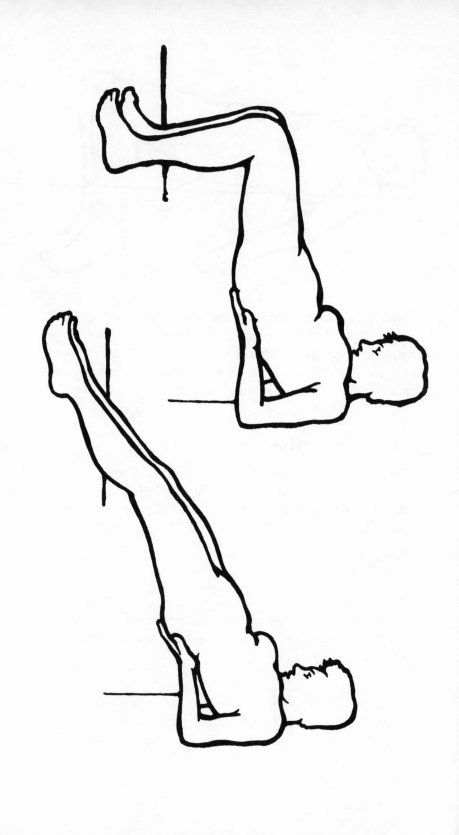

against the wall. Anyone with high blood pressure should go no farther.

3. Push your feet against the wall, bringing your buttocks off the floor, and stretch your hips toward the ceiling. Move your elbows under you as close together as possible and support your back with your hands.

4. Push with your toes and bring your hips up higher, over your shoulders. Straighten the front of your body as much as possible.

5. Keep your feet against the wall. Push your shoulders into the floor and bring your shoulder blades toward each other to take pressure off the back of your neck. If you feel any compression on the back of your neck, slowly and gently go back to the starting position; the back of the neck should be relaxed and weight should be on your shoulders.

6. Slowly come down from this position, supporting your back as much as is necessary. Let your back become round and come down one vertebra at a time. You may find it comfortable to stretch your arms overhead on the floor and let your knees come gently toward your body.

7. Gently clasp your knees from behind and pull them toward your ribs to relieve any discomfort.

8. Stretch out on your back. How does it feel? Do you feel any warmth or lightness in the upper back or shoulders? Are you energized? Rested?

This posture, used often by Toni Montez with her yoga classes and SAGE groups, is far easier than the traditional shoulder stand. In this form even people who are moderately stiff could begin to feel the benefits without neck strain or arching their backs. If you are very stiff in the shoulders or neck, do it very gradually. This is a way of facilitating blood flow back to the heart and thereby bringing new life to the entire body.

This posture will help eliminate the stiffness of poor posture and redistribute abdominal fat.

Making Faces

For face and neck muscles, flexibility, tone, and circulation.

Position. Sitting or standing.

Preexercise Instruction. Close your eyes, imagining your face. Take three deep breaths, relaxing, and imagine your face when you were a child. Feel your jaws, your eyes, your cheeks, your nose, and your forehead relaxing.

Instruction

1. You may enjoy doing this one in front of a mirror, or with a friend. Close your eyes tight, wrinkle your nose, and blow your cheeks out like a blowfish.

2. Stick your tongue out as far as you can and pop your eyes.

3. Make the face of a pouty little boy.

4. Wriggle your ears like a rabbit and chew like a rabbit.

5. Squint and frown hard! Frighten yourself in the mirror.

6. Make the ugliest face you can.

7. Purse your lips and squeeze your nose down primly. Make the face you would have if you just ate a lemon.

8. Make a bubble of air in your cheeks and rotate it around.

9. Emotions: Be very angry, very sad, sleepy, yawn. Be delighted, aggressive, sullen, defiant, humble.

10. Mimic: a lion sunning himself in the grass, a dog protecting a bone. Be coy, be seductive, be authoritative, be crazy, be a lady guarding her suitcase

at a station. Be suspicious, be defiant. Be a monkey.
Be a rat.

11. Move every part of your face.

12. Make yourself laugh.

13. When you have made faces for five minutes,
close your eyes and feel your face and head. You may
want to massage your ears, your neck, your scalp. See
if there is any part of your face that doesn't tingle.

14. Look in the mirror and see the vitality in your
face.

The following exercises will specifically refresh your
eyes:

15. Squeeze your eyes tightly closed and allow the
cheek muscles to press lids closer. *Slowly* release the
squeeze, keeping your eyes closed.

16. Raise your eyebrows as high as you can. *Slowly*
relax.

17. Close your eyes and place your thumb and
index finger on the inside corners of your eyes. Gently
squeeze the corners of your eyelids toward your
fingers. *Slowly* release the squeeze. There may be tears
if you have been doing the exercise correctly.

18. Open your mouth slightly, raising your eyebrows and closing your eyes. Raise your eyebrows up,
stretching your upper eyelids downward as much as
you can. Breathe deeply five times. Slowly release the
stretch and open your eyes.

19. Raise your eyebrows as high as you can. Keep
them raised while you lower your upper eyelids. Now
concentrate on the muscle that opens your eyes and
open your upper lids all the way to show the whites
above your eyes.

20. Look at something. Do the colors seem brighter?
Look at your eyes in the mirror.

◇ ◇ ◇

The flexibility and freshness of a child's face is partly due to its mobility. All of the muscles are exercised because a child makes funny faces, and expresses all of his or her emotions visibly. As we get older we restrain ourselves—and need to do this deliberately.

Palming

To relax the eyes and the mind.

Position. Sit in a chair, elbows on a table.

Preexercise Instruction. Breathe deeply, relaxing your body. Feel your eyes. Close them, tightening the lids, and relax them.

Instruction

1. Rub your hands together until they are warm.
2. Cover each eye with the palm of your hand, being certain that the palm is cupped so that your hand does not press against your nose.
3. Take twelve deep breaths, allowing your inhalation to bring energy into your hand so that your palms bathe your eyes. Breathe as though you breathed through your palms.
4. Suspend thinking.
5. See what you see behind your closed eyelids.
6. Each time you do this you can extend the time so that you are soon palming for ten minutes.
7. Slowly remove your hands and look around. Do colors seem brighter? Are objects sharper?

This important method for refreshing your eyes was evolved by a brilliant ophthalmologist, William H. Bates, after forty years of research on defective vision. He found he could help people normalize their vision by relaxation.

The exercise, first introduced to Bates' patients in the

1920s, arose from a profound understanding of the relationship between the eyes and the mind. Dr. Bates originally told people to allow the entire visual field in their closed eyes to become totally black—not gray, not speckled—all black. Bates understood meditation states and knew that a real rest for the eyes—which are an outcropping of the brain—would be a quietude of body and mind, a stopping of thoughts. He also seemed to have known that the palms are energy centers. The hands are used in healing.

Many of our eye problems arise because of the way we use our mind's eyes. For instance, we read a dull book and our mind wanders. We have images in the back of our head. This places the eye muscles, which focus the lens, in a funny conflict. Where should they focus—on the page or toward the rearview image? A good many of our eye problems come from not placing our attention where our eyes are. We talk on the telephone and look out the window. We drive, and while looking at traffic and the road, we fantasize or make lists of things to do. Our attention rarely is where our eyes are. No wonder our eye muscles get confused after a lifetime of mixed messages.

We also strain our eyes by "grabbing." We make an effort, strain, squint, and attempt to grasp what we see, instead of allowing the visual image to enter. We do not "trust" our eyes to convey the visual message to us: We think we must actively seek out the sight.

We also fail to rest our eyes as we work or read, by not blinking enough and not changing our angle of vision. We should stop frequently, looking around, moving our eyes and our heads. The quiet we bring by palming is a means of revitalizing our eyes.

Sunning

To give our eyes the natural light they need.

Position. Sit in the sunlight or indirect light under a tree that partly permits the sunlight through.

Preexercise Instruction. Close your eyes, and breathe deeply.

Instruction

1. Turn your head so that sunlight goes from one part of your eyes to another.

2. If you move your head from left to right, and right to left in an arc, the sun will light every point of your eyes.

3. Do this slowly twelve times, breathing deeply each time.

◇ ◇ ◇

Light is like food to your brain, but it needs all the wave lengths of natural light, not the smaller diet available in artificial light or light filtered through glass windows. If you cannot sit outside, open a window and sit in a window. If it is cold, wear a coat and lift your face to the sun. As you do this you may begin to feel how strongly we are linked to the cosmos beyond our social world. Our beings drink light: for good eyesight we need sunlight. Our body hormones are calibrated by light; and even when we are unaware of light coming through our closed lids, a nonseeing part of our optical organism is taking light deep into the brain to the pineal and pituitary glands.

An excellent book for improving vision is *Help Yourself to Better Sight,* by Margaret Corbett, a pupil of Bates's (see the bibliography).

Exercising the Voice

To strengthen the voice, chest, and throat

Position. Sitting or standing comfortably.

Preexercise Instruction. Close your eyes. Breathe deeply and sigh as you exhale. Listen to your voice sighing. Feel the vibration in your chest as you sigh.

Instruction

1. Stand up and shake your arms and shoulders re-laxedly. Shake your head and torso and knees and feet. As you shake, let your voice shake out, too. Sing, or chant, or say Hah, hah, hah . . . for a minute or two.

2. Now to get rid of self-consciousness there is only one way to exorcise the demon. Take a deep, deep breath and make a primitive sound, a shout, a *growl*, a *howl*, a *scream*—the worst shriek or hoot you can think of. Vanquish self-consciousness; so long as you feel it you are a prisoner.

3. Make deep growling sounds. Deep breaths, sounds coming from the abdomen. Make high pitched screeching sounds. So long as you do not force your voice from your throat, but allow it to come from the deep breaths you take into the lower abdomen, you will not fatigue rapidly.

4. Stamp your foot like a small child, and shout NO!

5. Fling your arms out to the sides and exhale a big Hallelujah!

6. After each sound you make, stop for a rest with your eyes closed. Listen to the resonance in yourself. How does it feel? How did your voice sound to you? What kinds of feelings arise in your chest, your throat, your head? Are you sad, excited, exuberant, angry, neutral?

7. Sit, preferably on a hard chair, holding yourself straight, with your feet planted on the floor.

8. The vibration rate of sounds can be felt in the body, and some sounds may come from the chest, or vibrate in the heart, others in the lower back, others in the head. The most awesome way of allowing sound to vibrate through you is by chanting. Unlike singing you can maintain one tone until you tire of it and move on to another. As you chant more and more sound will fill the air and your ears. You will begin to

hear a voice you never heard before—your own full, vibrant voice. Chant by breathing from the belly. You can chant doing housework, or driving, or in a group. If you are sitting still, close your eyes, relax deeply, and repeat the sound many times. All the vowels make a good chant: ay—ee—eye—oh—you

9. You can also chant:

Om (feeling it on top of your head)

Ah (feeling it in your throat)

Hum (feeling it in your center of the chest)

◇ ◇ ◇

Our voices need exercise just as much as the rest of us. Any part of ourselves that we do not use begins to stagnate. Our voices get shaky, or cracked and clouded, from lack of use. However if you have not been singing, shouting, or expressing yourself vocally for a long while, you must proceed gradually, taking as tender care of your voice as you do of your spine. It is extremely important to get very relaxed. Most of us create tension by tightening the muscles of our throats. Most of the time we are tense and self-conscious when we try to sing and think we must perform, be in tune. But our voices need to sing even if we cannot be on pitch.

16 ❧ COMMUNICATION: PARTICIPATIVE LISTENING

Most of us think there are special people we should turn to when we are troubled: We often call them therapists. Although therapists have special training, we can perform many of the same services for each other if we can learn to listen. Listening is not easy. It may be one of the highest arts on earth, and it is a skill that can change our lives.

When SAGE became a large organization, suddenly, and we disagreed about how to run it, we got a year of continuous help from an expert in communications skills. His teaching was so effective that we tried it in core groups. Older participants began to say, "I wish I'd learned this when I was younger, it would have changed my whole life." They began to be able to deal with their families in a new way and to help each other out of lifelong habits. Most older people do not get feedback (which is unlike criticism or judgment) on how they affect people when they drone on and on, or make endless repetitions. The result is that they become isolated. Poor communication habits lead to misunderstanding and emotionalism. For instance think of the well-intentioned person who wants to help and loads you down with so much opinion and advice that you become irritated instead of grateful. That person needs to learn some communications skills to be helpful in a way that you will appreciate. The repeater, too, is repeating his or her message, usually because of not *feeling* heard and understood. This person needs active listening. However real, active listening does not come naturally to most of us. It is something we need to learn and practice like a new way of walking. Still if we could listen empathetically, with understanding, we could help each other instead of relying on experts, and we could resolve our conflicts instead of going to wars.

One of the reasons that listening requires skill is that most of us are not clear in the way we communicate with each other. We are taught to be unclear. For instance when I grew up I was taught to say nice things even if I felt anger. I was taught to be polite. I was also taught to respond to the content, when spoken to, and deal with it rationally. Obediently I learned to focus on the content and ignore the feelings that seemed to underlie the message. For instance I would argue furiously with my mother over some political issue about which neither of us had much information. Did we care so much? I doubt it. We weren't able to confront our real feelings, and so we argued about external issues. What if we had really listened to each other?

We might have noticed that there were two kinds of messages going on simultaneously. One was content. "The real-estate developers are ruining this place. They are terrible." The other message was emotion. "I feel helpless and angry." But this last message was not stated. I might argue that the real estate developers were human, but this would not change my mother's opinions. Moreover by arguing I prevented my mother from really telling me how she felt. Today I realize that I was cheating us of a real relationship in which we could rely on each other. How often do you

hear people saying things that have two meanings, a statement of content and another message of some emotional
tone? How do you respond?

Have you ever heard someone growl angrily, "I'm not
angry!"

What happens to you when you hear such a message?
Which message do you really believe?

We have all learned how to give each other double messages, but if we are to communicate, we must begin to
simplify. We need to listen for double messages and we
need to decipher both meanings. We must also watch ourselves. See if you can catch yourself the next time you smile
and say something very sweet when you are really an-
noyed. Catch your contradictory messages.

Another way to clarify communication is to distinguish
between feeling and thought. Stop for a moment, decide
whether you are feeling or thinking, and then say which it
is.

Another way of making yourself clear and becoming better understood is to speak deliberately in the first person as
much as you can. Speak for yourself. When I was in college
I learned that I would gain some authority, scientific cre-
dence, and avoid embarrassment if I *never* spoke for myself. I said, "It is believed . . ." rather than "I believe . . ." When I was being obnoxious, I said, "one." It
was the same commanding "one" that you meet in eti-
quette books if you read them: "One does not wear gloves
to the table." If I needed authority, I spoke as if God were
on my side, in the plural, "we." When my back was up
against the wall, and I was being myself, I spoke for you,
instead of me. If I enjoyed a cup of tea, I said, "*You* always
feel better after a cup of tea." In writing this book I have
had to try to sort these voices out. Sometimes I speak for
myself. Sometimes I speak for SAGE and my colleagues.
Sometimes I am addressing you directly.

TRY SPENDING A WHOLE DAY SPEAKING ONLY
FOR YOURSELF IN THE FIRST PERSON. AND TRY DIS-

CRIMINATING BETWEEN THOUGHT AND FEELING SO THAT YOU CAN TELL YOUR LISTENER WHICH YOU ARE CONVEYING.

In conversation and during communication exercises it is helpful to give feedback, telling your partner or partners exactly how you are reacting. The following format will make it easier.

1. State the behavior you are responding to.
2. State your feelings as fully as you can.
3. State the effects.

FOR EXAMPLE: "When you wag your finger at me that way, I think I'm being admonished, and I feel angry and I withdraw." Otherwise the other person probably won't know that you are angry and won't understand how he or she affected you. At first it may take a great deal of mental effort and introspection to be able to discover how you are feeling and what triggers you. It is by sharing that connection that you will improve your communication and your personal relationships.

If this is new for you, it may improve your communication with people who are close to you in a most exciting way. You are on an adventure of attaining greater depth and contact and better understanding in the long run.

Why all the emphasis on feeling? Most of my conversation revolves around something I have feelings about. Even at work logistics, facts, are only a fraction of our talk, and decision-making is easy when everyone agrees. But we cannot make the simplest decision when we have discordant feelings, regardless of the facts. Certainly I do not want to talk for very long about a subject on which I have no feeling; it is empty and boring. It is like discussing the weather endlessly or amenities. When I do talk, especially when I want to convey something personal that concerns me, I want my listener to hear my full message and not cut me off. If my message is heavy I want my listener to let me

express my feelings freely, perhaps even to allow me to cry.
I don't want to feel inhibited, embarrassed, judged, or put
aside. How close I feel, and how open I become with a person, depends a great deal on how they listen to me.

Not being listened to, which is probably a common experience, can have negative effects that reverberate
through a whole lifetime. I can remember the period in the
late 1960s when I was getting divorced and felt somewhat
desolate, although my marriage had been as good as dissolved already. I didn't expect anyone to solve my life
problems or change my feelings. I just wanted somebody
to understand and let me express my feelings. One close
friend said, "Oh, it's not so bad. You'll have a new lover in
a month." I felt shut-up and belittled. Now I was angry as
well as desolate.

My father heard the facts, matter-of-factly, and acted as if
that was all there was to be said about it. I felt unfinished,
unable to express my feelings. Another person close to me
said, "Well, you never really were happy together. You
were too different." The reasons didn't matter: I still hurt.
One relative wondered why I had waited so long to get
divorced, and another friend tried to kid me out of my bad
mood. I felt then as if my feelings were quite unimportant
to them, or else so uncomfortable that they had to be kid-
ded away. Every one of these people cared about me, and I
presume they were trying to help me. Yet the result was
that I felt terribly alone. It was a familiar feeling. I look
back and I realize that I rarely felt free to tell my feelings to
people who were the closest to me, and I doubt that many
of them told me what they really wanted to say. The result
was a kind of isolation, which occurred even within the
family. None of us knew how to listen to each other in a
way that was even slightly helpful. We were more eager to
give out, sympathize, judge, suggest, and fix things up
than to hear the speaker through and really listen.

At SAGE in the winter of 1977 in the third and fourth
core groups we began working on active listening. We

used guidelines adapted from *Leadership Effectiveness Training*, by Thomas Gordon. They state very simply and briefly the do's and don'ts of effective listening. This is the kind of listening that conveys to the speaker that he is being heard and understood. A modified version of Thomas Gordon's guidelines follows. Read them over and discuss them with friends. When someone comes to you with a problem, or a troubling feeling, try to recall these guidelines. Listening is a skill. It wasn't taught at home or in school for most of us. It doesn't come naturally. It is the foundation for all relationships, for leadership, and for clear communication. Most of us are more expert at the don'ts than the do's.

As you will see from the following list of don'ts, listening means putting your own problems and opinions aside for a while. You need to be purely receptive. This doesn't mean you agree with the person speaking. It doesn't mean that you have the same feelings. It emphatically doesn't mean that you are obliged to solve his or her problems. In fact if you listen with all your heart and attention, and if you do not impose yourself on the speaker, you will help the person solve his or her problems. Often people need to be encouraged to articulate their feelings and conflicts, and then they see for themselves how to handle them. Empathic listening is the most helpful gift you can give to anyone. It goes far beyond sympathy or any amount of actual help. It says to them that you accept them as they are. You aren't trying to change them. You aren't trying to make them feel something else. You are allowing them to be themselves.

Do not consent to listen to someone if you cannot do this. If you are pressured, or cannot put your own problems and distractions aside, say "not now." In order to hear someone you must be totally available. You need to give the person all of your attention.

THE DON'TS

1. *Ordering, Directing, Commanding:* telling the other person to do something, such as, "Stop talking and start doing the dishes." Such a response tells other people that their feelings and needs are not important, and they must comply with you. Usually such messages produce fear and resentment, and the other person may fight back, resist, or test your will.

2. *Warning, Admonishing, Threatening:* telling other people what consequences will ensue if they do something that you don't think is right. "If you get divorced at this age, you'll have to raise your children alone." Often a person will respond to this kind of admonishment by saying, "I don't care. I still feel this way."

3. *Moralizing, Preaching, Obliging:* telling other people what they should or ought to do. "You shouldn't act this way," is the kind of guilt-producing statement that presses on the other person an external power, authority, or obligation. It may make the other person feel that you do not trust his or her judgment or values.

4. *Advising, Giving Suggestions or Solutions:* telling other people how to solve their problems. "Why don't you try this . . . ?" Although you may feel you are being helpful, this may make the other person feel inferior and wonder why he or she didn't think of that solution. I have had this happen months later, discovering that my suggestions were excellent but they didn't allow the other person the dignity of working out his problem, and the result was resentment.

5. *Persuading with Logic, Arguing, Instructing, Lecturing:* trying to influence the other person with facts, counterarguments, logic, information, or your own opinions. Even if you have information that you think the other person lacks, this kind of persuasion may

make him or her feel inadequate and defensive and resentful. People hate to be shown that they are wrong and will often defend their positions to the bitter end. You may know that, "The facts show that marijuana use produces early aging," but the other person may view this as a harangue and may simply discount you or assume an "I don't care" attitude.

6. *Judging, Criticizing, Disagreeing, Blaming, Making Negative Judgments or Evaluations.* These messages more than any others make people feel inadequate, inferior, stupid, unworthy, and bad. Self-concepts are shaped by judgments and evaluations. "It's your fault; you're so stubborn." "It never would have happened if you weren't so timid." Evaluation quickly influences people to keep their feelings to themselves. They know that it isn't safe to talk about anything that means anything to them. Even if they feel the evaluation is correct, they may become angry and full of hatred, for negative evaluation is destructive.

7. *Praising, Agreeing, Evaluation, Positively Approving, Offering a Positive Evaluation or Judgment.* If you judge a person positively, that person knows that you can just as easily have a negative evaluation, so, contrary to popular belief, praise is not always beneficial. It may not fit the person's self-image. If approval and praise are given often, the absence will be interpreted as disapproval. Praise is often felt to be manipulative, a way of getting the other person to do what you want him or her to do. Praise given to one person may be interpreted as negative evaluation by others who didn't receive the praise, as if they weren't so good by comparison.

8. *Name-calling, Ridiculing, Shaming:* making the other people feel foolish, stereotyping, or categorizing them. Such messages have a devastating effect on the other person's self-image. They make him feel unloved and unworthy.

9. *Interpreting, Analyzing, Diagnosing:* telling people

what their motives are, or analyzing why they do or say something communicates that you have them "figured out." Even if the analysis is accurate, the person may feel exposed. If the analysis is wrong, as it most often is, the other person will become angry at being unjustly accused. By implying, "I can see through you," you cut off further messages, and the other person will feel put down and refrain from sharing his or her feelings.

10. *Reassuring, Sympathizing, Consoling, Supporting:* trying to make other people feel better, talking them out of their feelings, trying to make their feelings go away, denying the strength of their feelings. Most of us feel that this is a helpful way to behave, but reassuring a people who are distressed may only convince them that you don't understand them. We often console or reassure people because we are uncomfortable with the other person's strong feelings, and people often think or say, "You're just saying that to make me feel better." Sympathizing often stops further communication because the person senses that you'd like him or her to stop feeling as he or she does.

11. *Probing, Questioning, Interrogating:* trying to find reasons, motives, causes, searching for more information to help you solve the problem. Asking questions can convey that you lack trust or are suspicious or doubtful. Also some questions are transparent attempts to get another person off the limb. People don't usually talk because they want you to solve their problems for them, but as a way of finding their own solutions. Children are particularly vulnerable, for adults almost always end up telling them what to do. Moreover when you question people, as they relate a problem, your questions limit their freedom to talk about what they want. This is why courtroom interrogation is so uncomfortable: You are supposed to answer only the questions asked.

12. *Withdrawing, Distracting, Humoring:* trying to get

the other people away from the problem, withdrawing from the problem yourself, distracting them, kidding them out of their feelings, pushing the problem aside. Such behavior can indicate to other people that you are not interested in them, that you don't respect their feelings, or that you reject them outright. When a person is intent or serious in his or her need to talk about something, kidding can make them feel rejected and hurt, belittled.

Putting people off or diverting their feelings and attention may seem to succeed for the moment, but a person's feelings do not always go away. Children, too, may seem to be diverted, yet the feelings crop up later. Postponed problems are not solved, and if listeners brush them aside, they soon learn to take their important feelings and problems elsewhere.

All of these twelve response types communicate nonacceptance to the speaker. They are common, almost habitual with most people. How many of them do you do?

There are alternative ways of responding.

DO'S

13. *Silence, Passive Listening:* listening without verbally responding. Silence can be a powerful message of acceptance. Sometimes all the other person needs is to be heard. Passive listening communicates acceptance to the other person if the listener gives undivided attention, setting aside all other tasks and concentrating on his or her words. The only drawback to listening silently is that the person doesn't know whether he or she has been understood. Look at the speaker's eyes as he or she talks.

14. *Simple Acknowledgment:* noncommital responses. These expressions, such as "Oh," or "I see," let people know that you are tuned in to them and offer no content, judgment, or evaluation. They simply let him proceed.

15. *Door-openers:* verbal responses that invite the speaker to say more. "Tell me about it," or "I'd like to hear more about that," encourage the speaker to continue. They leave your feelings out of the communication, but indicate that you are willing to continue listening.

16. *Active Listening:* Messages that convey empathic understanding of the speaker's communication. Active listening is the process of decoding a person's words and feeding them back, as in a paraphrase, for verification that you have understood. You do not inject your own feelings, evaluation, logic, advice, analysis, or questions. You feed back or paraphrase only what the speaker's message said to you. This will help the person express feelings freely, and may even allow a catharsis of troublesome feelings. The speaker can be less afraid of feelings when you accept them. A person who really feels that you hear him or her will feel warm and close to you. After being heard through, thinking out a problem aloud, the other person will be more willing to listen to your ideas and thoughts.

By listening acceptingly, emphatically, we can help each other powerfully. This is the basis of a therapeutic relationship, and it is fundamental to good communication in all human relationships. Listening with understanding is a powerful tool. It is enhanced if you, the listener, keep eye contact with the speaker and indicate acceptance without approval or disapproval.

Here is an example of active listening taken from a SAGE group.

C: I have a teenage grandson who used to do all kinds of adventuresome things. Now he is living with us. He used to be full of life, but now he just lies around. He gets up from the table without a word, takes his dishes into the kitchen, and goes into his room.

S: I sense that you are anxious about your grandson. He is behaving differently than he used to.

C: I am very anxious. He is so changed. He seems depressed. I don't know what to do.

S: I sense that you feel disturbed and uncertain what to do.

C: That is exactly what I feel—deep disturbance. Actually I feel better just talking about it. I had to say it to someone.

Notice that the listener did not ask questions about the grandson and did not offer any advice. She paid close attention to the speaker's content, and especially to the emotional level of the conversation. The speaker felt better because her emotions were understood. Although it might have appeared that she was seeking advice about her grandson, she actually needed to tell somebody that she was worried. People often talk about situations, or outside things, and what they really want from you, the listener, is permission to have their feelings heard.

This is the kind of listening that you will want to do in the following exercises. It is the kind of listening you may want to practice with your friends and relatives. It is an exercise in observing yourself, in watching how much you impose yourself on another person, even when you are trying to be helpful and open. All of us do that. In doing these exercises I began to see that I had made an entire career out of advising and suggesting, putting myself in a teacher role. It made me rather uncomfortable to witness how much I did this to the people around me, and I began to understand better why they responded as they did to me.

Exercises in applying these guidelines are helpful because they can allow us to practice and to evaluate our listening ability. The following score sheet is one way of checking how you did. You may want to copy it, or adapt it for your exercises with others.

OBSERVATION FORM

Don'ts
Directed, warned, moralized,
  judged, gave suggestions or
  solutions, persuaded with logic
  or argued, disagreed, approved,
  reassured, praised, ridiculed,
  interpreted, questioned,
  supported, consoled, withdrew,
  distracted, humored _____

Dos
Kept eye contact with speaker _____
Indicated acceptance without
  approval or disapproval _____
Did silent passive listening _____
Made simple acknowledgments _____
Made door-openings _____
Made active-listening response
  to feelings _____
Responded to feelings
  acceptingly, in depth _____

Many growth programs have used special structured verbal exercises to deepen self-understanding and communication. I first experienced them in Berkeley as a member of SAT—Seekers After Truth. It was a revelation to me as I sat in different small groups and listened to us all talk about the role of fear in our lives, or how we expressed our vanity. I was impressed with how differently we could respond to the same situations, what numerous alternatives there were. I found myself deeply moved by the honesty of people and appreciative of the diverse ways we experience difficulty in life according to who we are and the particular idiosyncracies of our egos. In SAGE, too, I have been moved by the fact that each of us seems to get stuck in the labyrinth of our own characters. Only when I listen to others do I realize there are many ways to react other than the habitual responses I usually make.

These exercises may allow you to deepen a friendship that is already well established. They can help you come into deeper contact with someone you know or someone you have just met.

IT IS VERY IMPORTANT NOT TO LET THE EXERCISES BECOME SOCIAL CONVERSATION; SAVE YOUR SO-CIALIZING UNTIL THE EXERCISES HAVE BEEN DONE.

The topics are not randomly chosen. Some of them arose out of the particular interests and needs of SAGE groups. Others have been used by spiritual groups and growth workshops.

It is important to maintain the structure even though it may seem a little artificial at first. If you are alone, choose one or two friends with whom you would like to deepen your relationship and share your life. Work together for two to four hours each week. Don't confuse work sessions with social occasions. You can visit with each other after the exercises. Oddly enough if you follow the instructions it will free you to probe the questions more deeply. If you listen with total attention and no judgments, you will have one of the most rewarding experiences of your life—hearing your partner or partners at their deepest level, really hearing them fully. When you speak you will have the experience of being fully heard.

NOTE: All these exercises can be done with two, three, or four people. The results with three or four people will be different from those with *dyads,* or a pair.

Exercises in Listening and Being Heard

Instructions

Read these instructions before you start until they are familiar to you.

1. When you and your partner(s) meet for a session, say hello, but postpone social conversation until later. Find a place to sit where you can face each other comfortably. Sit so that you can see each other's eyes. Start by closing your eyes and taking five deep breaths, relaxing and feeling your entire body.

2. Decide who will speak first and who will listen. The speaker will monologue for ten minutes, then rest for a minute or two in silence. Then the other partner(s) will speak for ten minutes.

3. *Listener(s)*: Sit in a calm, receptive, meditative state of mind. Just listen. Do not react. You don't need to think, judge, or comment. Don't even smile, or nod, or grunt. Sit openly, without criticism, listening to your partner. Try to listen as if your partner were yourself. It may help if you imagine putting all your concerns into a box for safekeeping until the speaker has finished.

4. *Speaker:* Don't try to interact or persuade your partner, just speak. Feel your own feelings and allow yourself to speak, realizing that you are really being heard. Be totally immersed in yourself.

5. Between monologues take more deep breaths.

6. When both or all partners have spoken, take a half hour or an hour to discuss your observations. Be as honest as you know how. Describe your feelings as you spoke or listened. Your feelings tell a great deal and may help your partners understand themselves.

What did this exercise mean to you?

Did you gain any new insights into yourself, or your partner(s)?

How do you feel now?

Were you hiding feelings during the exercise?

How about your feeling toward your partner(s)?

Topics

1. How do I postpone satisfaction in my life?

FOR EXAMPLE: Do I think things will be better,

more pleasant, deeper in the future? Am I waiting for some outside event to occur? Am I
always preparing for the future, taking care of
family, preparing entertainment? Do I forget to
stop and experience what is happening now?

2. How could each moment of my life become satisfying?

FOR EXAMPLE: If I stopped worrying about the
future . . . If I stopped thinking and had a quiet
mind . . . If I weren't so timid, and I asked for
what I wanted . . . If I weren't so polite, and I
dared . . .

3. What is it I say I want that, in my heart, I know I
don't want?

FOR EXAMPLE: To be responsible, kind, and take
care of everyone . . . To hold up my marriage
. . . To be a model grandparent . . . To have a
new home, to live to one hundred, to be young
again.

4. What are the things about myself that I hide from
myself and others?

FOR EXAMPLE: My nasty temper, critical nature,
sexual taste, my lack of compassion, my impatience, my despair, my sense of insecurity, my
sense of superiority, my sloppiness, my fear of
being disliked. We hide the things we think
others will hate or reprimand and when we hide
we are alone. Sharing the things we hide shows
us that they are not so unusual and we do not
have to be ashamed and hidden.

5. What is my self-image? Is there a difference between the image I present to the world and what I
feel is my real self?

FOR EXAMPLE: I act like a secure, forceful, agreeable person, but really I am uncertain, and I am
blustering. I seem gregarious, but really I like to
be alone, and I am shy. I act more insecure than

I am, so that people will pity me, or give me leeway. Again living up to a self-image is imprisoning. It makes me unfree and therefore less close to others.

6. What is the cause of my suffering? Will I give it up?

   FOR EXAMPLE: Most lovers would rather suffer than give up the lover who does not care for them. That is a form of culturally approved suffering. So are many illnesses. How many of us have crucified ourselves to win praise from an uncaring parent, or have moaned about our symptoms without taking care of our own health? How many of us have suffered indigestion, but never changed to a sensible diet?

7. What am I trying to avoid in life?

   FOR EXAMPLE: Am I distorting my life in order to avoid pain? Do I avoid my own feelings, or knowing them avoid expressing them? Do I avoid the feelings of others? Am I trying to avoid death? Am I trying to avoid being known, being open?

8. How have I been deaf to my own inner self, and my own inner needs?

   FOR EXAMPLE: Have I concentrated on my family, or business, and failed to notice my own need for solitude, for intimacy? Have I needed more warmth in relationships but gone on with surface friendships? Have I needed more assurance and never asked for help? Have I needed more freedom?

9. How has cynicism helped me deal with frustration?

   FOR EXAMPLE: Did I act as if nothing ever would turn out right, anyway? Did I pretend that I didn't care? Did I hide my feelings of disappointment or rage or depression by acting cynical? Did I maintain an image with other people by acting cynical and cool?

10. What lies do I tell myself to keep my life comfortable?

    FOR EXAMPLE: It's got to get better. My wishes will come true. My family will be okay. My finances are sufficient. Somebody will take care of me when I need it . . . I have planned the future well. I have a kindly heart. I am capable of important things.

11. Discuss love: Is love a fundamental condition of being in the universe?

    FOR EXAMPLE: Why do we get angry at people we love; what makes us clutch? Why do our needs get called love? What is the difference between needing and loving someone?

12. What is the role that fear has played in my life?

    FOR EXAMPLE: It kept me from extending myself in school, and therefore I didn't get feedback and learn. It kept me from trying sports, held back my physical development. It kept me from switching jobs when I wanted to. It kept me from pursuing the person I really loved. It kept me from leaving my family and becoming . . . It kept me from speaking my mind, or marrying, or being myself.

13. What am I doing on this earth? Is there a purpose to my life?

    FOR EXAMPLE: I thought of myself as a mother, but now I think I'm here to be a model for others. I think I am here to know God. I am here to lead others to God. I'm here to have a good time, and I have no purpose. I feel that my life on this earth is a preparation for something more to come . . .

14. What emotional attachments are most difficult for me to give up?

FOR EXAMPLE: Is it praise, kind words, winning, being loved, pride, dignity, generosity?

15. Consider one person very close to you and discuss with your partner what you know about his or her suffering.

FOR EXAMPLE: We tend to be aware of our own problems and suffering, but have little consciousness even of those closest to us. We hardly even spend time communicating with them, or trying to understand.

16. Prepare before you meet: List the ten people who were the most influential in your life psychologically. List the ten people who were most influential on you spiritually. Tell your partner about them and their similarities and differences.

FOR EXAMPLE: My mother, brother, and teacher were psychologically influential. They were combative, creative people. My first meditation teacher was also very egotistical, unlike the other people, ministers, and lamas who have influenced my spiritual life.

17. List the five people you have loved the most in your life. List the five people you have disliked or hated most.

Discuss these people—their similarities and differences with your partner. Discuss why you loved one group, and why you think you disliked the others.

18. Write a list of all the things you are attached to: those that give you pleasure and those you avoid which give you pain.

Share these with your partner. Then describe what your typical day would be like if you were not governed by any of the things on your list.

19. Do I still trap myself? How?

FOR EXAMPLE: Do I agree to social obligations I don't want? Do I care about appearances and keep up an image? Am I afraid of letting my emotions out, and therefore containing my real feelings?

20. What unfinished business remains in my life?

Other Possible Topics

How has vanity affected your life?

How has secretiveness affected your life?

How important is it to be "right"?

What is it you want in your life? What you would have to do to get it?

What were your biggest errors?

What has jealousy done in your life?

How do you stay in the past rather than the present?

Our body postures describe who we are and how we feel. Tell the other person what his or her body posture and facial expression makes you feel, and what it tells you.

What is compassion?

What dreams do you have for the future?

What has been the role of dreams or visions in your life?

Is there an absolute truth?

Describe your feelings, sensations, and thoughts to your partner, as they happen. Do not describe something you felt before the exercise began, or anything past or future. Stay in the present for ten minutes. You may only say, "I am wondering what your facial expression means." "I am uneasy and find it hard to know what I'm feeling." Stay with your feelings and you will be able to keep talking.

Are you the person you thought you would become?

How would you describe your relationships with the opposite sex?

What have been your best achievements?

How would you like to die? Where? With whom?

What lies beyond death?

Repeated Question Exercise

Sometimes we only dig out our deeper answers when we must answer the same question repeatedly. This technique is immensely helpful when dealing with topics that we think we know all about.

Instructions

1. *Speaker:* When you have decided who will speak first, you, the speaker, should allow yourself to become totally immersed in your own feelings and thoughts, knowing that your partner is listening with complete attention.

2. *Questioner:* Remain in a meditative, quiet state of mind. Do not react with nods, grunts, or other gestures. Just ask your question. Listen to the answer. When the speaker has finished, say "Thank you," and repeat the question in a firm, gentle voice.

3. Keep a piece of paper beside you, and at the end of each answer jot down a key word or phrase that will allow your partner to recapture his or her answers later.

4. Stop. Questioner call the time. You can set fifteen minutes for your partner or wait until your partner has answered the question many times. There will come a change in the answers: It may be laughter, a strong feeling, a sudden loss of interest, or the expression of insight. This change tells you that the exercise has accomplished its work and it is time to switch roles.

5. Switch roles.

6. When both of you have answered the questions, give the key words and phrases you listed to your partner to help you discuss the exercise.

Questions to Be Repeated: Choose One Per Session

1. What is it that keeps you stuck doing things the same way, feeling the same feelings?

I am scared to try something new. I am lazy. I care too much about what others think.

2. Who are you?

A grandmother, a fifty-six-year-old woman, a dancer, a fragile person.

3. What are you feeling now?

Jitters, anxiety, wish for you to like me, relief.

4. What are you avoiding in your life?

Pain, my family's pressure.

5. How have you used sickness in your life?

To avoid school, to get attention, to stop my husband from leaving me, to get a rest, to have time alone, to stop a routine I disliked, to get back at my daughter.

6. What conditions do you put on love?

The person has to love me back. I can't love a fool. They need to be decent and law abiding. They need to be kind and appreciate me. I will only love someone weaker than me.

7. What are you expecting?

8. How have you solved problems in your life?

By manipulating people, by methodically working things out alone, with my family, by logic, by intuition, effort.

9. What is your acquired personality and what is really you?

I am logical, considerate, competent, but underneath I'm illogical and not very responsible, and I'm lazy.

10. What would you do if you were going to die next week?

Get my favorite people around me. Say goodbye, enjoy them.

11. How do you feel toward me? Tell me something you don't like about me.

I like you. I am anxious because of this question. I wish you wouldn't stare at me. I am irritated. I want to like you. I am afraid of you. I think you will criticize me, put me down.

(One person was so upset to hear that somebody could think of something that he didn't like about her, she dwelled on it for a week.)

12. What would it take for you to love me?

You'd have to accept me fully, as I am. You'd have to love me. You'd have to be less judging. You'd have to be more open with me. I'd have to trust you. You'd have to be gentle with me. You'd have to share your feelings more.

13. What qualities do you think your ideal man or woman would have?

14. What qualities do you think are the qualities of a woman?

15. What makes you happy?

16. What do you feel about your body?

17. What would you ask to be forgiven in this life?

18. If you were to look upon your life as something you chose, and your family as the family you chose—a belief that people have who believe in reincarnation—what lessons did you come to work out in this life? Why did you choose your parents?

FOR EXAMPLE: I chose a strong, combative mother. I needed to work out what it means to be feminine and yet survive.

(In one group some people insisted they could make no sense of this. They gathered to discuss why it made no sense.)

19. What are your loveliest qualities?

20. What are my qualities as you see me?

Many of the questions in the previous exercises can be repeated for this exercise.

◇ ◇ ◇

Whether or not we are aware of it, each of us is constantly barraged with questions, from inside and out. The simple act of stating these questions aloud and hearing ourselves answer is nurturing. It gives us the chance to acknowledge that we do have the answers within us, that we have more than one answer to each question. In fact we have many, and sometimes the answers are contradictory. When we listen to others answering the same questions, we expand the range of our possibilities. After all their answers include feelings and possibilities we never thought of, and contradictions different from our own. As a SAGE participant commented, "Listening to other people in the dyads, and in the group, I begin realizing that there are all kinds of ways to experience the same thing—ways to see things. I guess I was always stuck in seeing things just my own way. Besides that I've made such wonderful friendships. I wouldn't give up this experience for anything."

These conversations drew people together in ways that the participants said they had never anticipated. They found they were developing deep friendships and camaraderie with people they didn't know, that they felt closer than they felt with old friends. These exercises could become a way for old friends to become closer and more open. This kind of shared discussion and group conversation give us the opportunity to experience the immense range of possibilities that are always open to us so long as we can listen to each other.

17 ❦ ART, LIFELINES, CMT, AND MUSIC

At SAGE many people have talked about the fact that they had to put aside or leave undeveloped the part of themselves that was expressive or creative. A great many people, indeed, lived out their lives without ever discovering the artistic aspect of themselves. They were delighted to discover that this source of pleasure and imagination was still there to be enjoyed, once they set aside some of the judgments of their critical minds.

Play seems to be our preparation for whatever we are about to create in ourselves. Sometimes it is easier to get rid of our baggage of seriousness by working without words—using art media or music. We used hundreds of variations on these art and music exercises at SAGE, and hopefully the methods outlined in this chapter will inspire you to invent your own. All of these can be done alone, or with one other person, or a small group. However, as you will probably discover, a group leader can enhance the power of the exercises, especially through encouraging the group to share feelings and experiences.

LIFELINES

Lifelines were popular among SAGE groups and were invented by Eugenia as a way of getting people to introduce themselves and their lives to the other members of their group. Some groups brought very elaborate constructions, using art, photographs, poetry, and dance. As we shared them we began to understand each other at a surprisingly profound level. Most of us have experienced complex rhythms of change and growth in our lives, but it is difficult to paraphrase what has happened in words, because we can only state one thing at a time. Lifelines allow us to make many simultaneous events graphic. It is startling to "see" your life, and to let someone else know you this way.

Materials. Work with a long piece of paper such as butcher paper. If you have nothing larger than typing paper or note paper, staple the sheets together or glue them end-to-end. You need three different colored pens, crayons, or magic markers. You will probably add other things requiring scissors and paste.

Instructions

1. Mark out your paper so that you have space for each five-year segment.

2. Think about your life in five-year spans. Draw the ups and downs of your life in three colors. One represents your spiritual life, your feelings about the universe, about God, and your deep participation in the cosmos. This should represent your deepest self and may not be related to a formal church or formal religion. These feelings may represent how you feel as you walk in the woods, take care of a sick neighbor, child, or animal, your feelings about nature, your own inner silence.

Another color should represent your psychological life: your emotions, your periods of elation or depression, feeling loved or abandoned, happiness, or anger and fear, joy, sympathy, or grief. Although all of these feelings occur daily, most of us have experienced a time in our lives when one or another feeling tone seemed to prevail. For example one SAGE woman looked back at her life and noticed that she was most insecure and frustrated from about eleven to seventeen, depressed at twenty-five, and happy and excited at thirty-five, despairing at forty-five, and happy again at sixty-three.

The third color represents physical health. Perhaps you had periods when you were exceptionally healthy, or a period of illness. Even children have serious illnesses. Often health fluctuates in some relationship to psychological ups and downs, but the pattern is hard to discern.

Spend some time relaxing and thinking about each five-year period in your life, how you felt, what your spiritual life was like, and how you would judge your physical health. When you have thought about it, take your crayons or pens and draw a line for each of the three aspects of your life, connecting the peaks and bottoms during each five-year period. You will end up with three continuous lines of three colors.

3. When you have thought about the events and feelings of each five-year period, fill in the story of your life in whatever way you wish. One woman placed photographs of her entire life on her chart, showing major events. Another drew pictures of the moves she had made from one city to another, and pictures of herself at various stages of her life. Another SAGE participant, a man, wrote poems about the four major stages of his life; another made a collage, with newspaper clippings and magazine pictures that showed his life, although they were not actually about him.

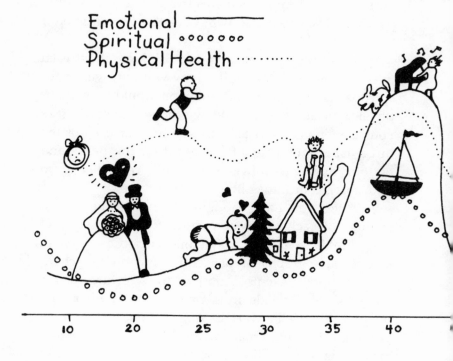

Emotional ——————
Spiritual ∘∘∘∘∘∘∘
Physical Health ···········

10   20   25   30   35   40

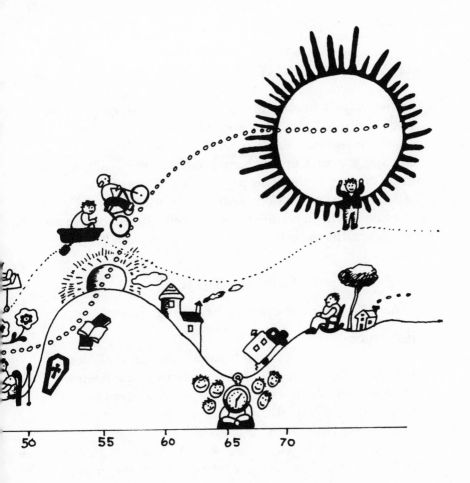

50   55   60   65   70

4. When you have completed your story, share it. Whoever shares your lifeline with you will become much closer to you. As one woman commented after a sharing of lifelines at SAGE, "You know I've heard that woman say things about herself for seven months now. This is the first time I think I understand. I really understand how courageous she is. Her life has been very alone. I just never understood that before—not really."

◇ ◇ ◇

ART AS COMMUNICATION

Another way of becoming acquainted—not so comprehensive as lifelines—is to draw something or form a shape and then share feelings about it with a group. Virginia Goldstein and David Cunningham brought their skills in art and art therapy to SAGE as part of the process of discovery. They began each session with a relaxation exercise and sometimes with movements or fantasy. The following are examples of the experiences they created at SAGE.

Sketching a Treasure

Materials. You need drawing paper and crayons.

Instruction

1. Lie down comfortably and take several deep breaths, relaxing deeply. Move away from the feelings of this room, to a warm, sunny place, a meadow. In your mind's eye look around and see what kind of a place it is. How are you dressed? You have a lot of energy, and you get up and walk to a stream that is bubbling and clear. You see something on the ground that you really admire. You pick it up and walk back to the meadow. Now let the meadow fade, and when

you are ready, allow the feelings of this room to return. Slowly open your eyes and sit up.

2. Sketch your treasure.

3. Share your drawing with the group.

◇ ◇ ◇

This is what some of the SAGE participants said:

"I picked up a smooth rock with speckles. It was yellowish water in the stream and I knew the rock wouldn't be as pretty when I took it out of the water. It felt good in my hand, smooth.

"I took my rock and scratched a face on it."

"I found a place in the mountains like in my childhood, with wild Aruncuas. I picked a big bunch and they are in my drawing."

"In my background in a tenement with immigrant families there was never time or the facilities to develop my imagination. I'm just beginning to do that. I couldn't see the country. I drew a fire hydrant in Brooklyn. In the summer we would open the hydrants and play in the water."

Draw a Tree

Materials. Paper; two or three colors of either paint, crayon, or pens.

Instruction

1. Begin by lying down and taking six deep breaths, paying attention to the way the air comes in your nose and brings energy into your whole body. Feel the exhaled air leaving your body, taking away wastes. Let your arms and legs grow heavy and your back and shoulders relax. Relax your jaw, letting your mouth open, your eyes relax.

2. Recall some places in nature that you particularly love. Allow yourself to be there, wherever it is. And

now imagine that you are the seed of a tree, warm and dark within the earth. You are beginning to grow. Feel yourself growing roots, sprouting, and sending a tiny shoot above the ground. Feel the moist warm soil around you and the sun and air above. Feel your roots growing deeper and your sprout rising toward the sun. Grow more quickly, until you imagine yourself a full-sized tree. Feel the wind in your branches and leaves. Feel the rain, the air, the sun.

3. When you have felt what it must be like to be that tree, very slowly begin to feel your body and open your eyes, coming back to this room.

4. Take two colors and draw that tree. It doesn't have to be realistic. Simply draw what it feels like to be that tree.

5. When this is done in a group, wait until everyone has had ten minutes to draw, and then encourage people to react to each drawing. Start by focusing on a drawing and asking, "Whose tree is that? Where does it come from?"

"That's mine. It started as a kind of pine. I wanted it to be graceful but it wasn't, so I put fruit on it."

"It's graceful, just like you."

"Thank you. I like your tree. It has all different kinds of flowers and fruit and birds."

"It was supposed to be the mating of a sun fairy and moon fairy."

"You talk like the writer of children's books."

"I am. I illustrate them."

◇ ◇ ◇

That was the first time she had said anything about herself in the group as a whole, and as each person described his or her tree, there came more self-descriptions and extensions of themselves. The trees allowed the members of this highly individualistic group to share themselves indirectly without discomfort, and to go more deeply into their feelings than they had before. At this particular session we had drawn the trees on butcher paper that had been taped around the room, and had used thick pastels. It created a forest of different personalities that we could see in a glance.

Fantasizing in Clay

Materials. Modeling clay, water, towels, hand lotion, a large work table.

Instruction

1. If this is done in a group, everyone choose a partner. Sit opposite each other with a bowl of warm water between you. Wash your hands. Dry them. Partners massage each other's hands with hand lotion. (If you are doing this alone, massage your own hands with lotion.) When being massaged close your eyes and relax deeply, feeling the massage. When massaging explore your partner's hands gently. Do not talk.

2. Take a large lump of clay to work with, and sit wherever it is comfortable around a table.

3. Close your eyes. Concentrate on the feeling of the clay between your hands as you work it, keeping your eyes closed. Allow your fingers to explore, poke, caress, and mold it any way they want, but don't look. Press, stretch, and pat and punch. Take ten minutes. When you have done as much as you want, open your eyes, but don't judge the clay. Just finish it.

4. In a group ask each person to place his or her finished clay in the middle of the table. The sharing is most important. "Since your clay sculpture represents a feeling you had, you will want to talk about it as a part of yourself. When you look at someone else's clay, *you* see it, and so you will want to describe their sculpture as a part of yourself, too."

Here is an example. "I see this clay. I am a seashell with the sand around me. I feel washed by the sea and clogged by mud." Once again this technique comes from gestalt therapy as developed by Fritz Perls. Since all perceptions reside with the perceiver, he saw that the habit of talking about things "out there" denied one's experience within.

"That looks like a big, fierce Chow dog."

"Try phrasing it as if you are what you see."

"I am a big fierce Chow dog. Actually I'm not fierce, I'm sad. One of my ears is lopped off."

"I am a frog."

"I am an old dog with no place to go," said another.

Finally the sculptor spoke. "I am a dog, big and loving. And I am lonely. I didn't mean to make a dog. I just found my hands doing it. I just moved to an apartment where they won't let me have a pet, and I guess I must be missing a pet."

Each shape evoked different reactions. A hemispheric concave shape got this response:

"I am an amphitheater, and someone inside is sorrowful."

"I am a wave underwater."

"I am a casserole."

"I am an embrace—love."

"I'm male, female . . . a ship."

"I am a baby in the cradle, in the womb," said the creator.

This clay experience is extremely powerful, for we actually experience the inner images of other people and can respond with our own images and feelings.

5. At the end of the session take the shapes and roll them back into the clay they came from. People are often reluctant to destroy theirs, for they mean something personal, but they would surely clutter our space if we kept them. They are, after all, material representations of our experience. If we were to materialize all of our life experiences and hang onto them, the uni-

verse would swiftly become an enormous junk pile. The destruction of the clay images gave a completion to the session that many of our experiences do not have. By destroying our images we were freed to go on to another good experience without looking back.

CMT

One liberating art process now available was developed by Dr. Wolfgang Luthe, pioneer in autogenic training. While searching for additional ways to free people from psychosomatic and emotional binds, he began experimenting with art. His knowledge of meditation, philosophy, and autogenic training helped him evolve what he called *Creativity Mobilization Technique*. His book by that title was published in 1976 by Grune & Stratton and contains the theory, instructions, and case histories. After reading this book Virginia and I decided to try it on ourselves. We set up easels in the basement of Virginia's home, papered the walls to protect them, bought the poster paints and brushes prescribed, and prepared to work for six to eight weeks.

CMT is a process of painting without controlling, without intending to produce an artistic painting, to please anyone, or achieve anything. Luthe's idea is that the motor movements of painting with a brush, and cutting out all thought, help us to rebalance the use of our brains. In most of our schooling and social life we overuse the left hemisphere, it is thought, the hemisphere that dominates rationality, language, and control. We underuse the right hemisphere which is believed to be more intuitive and spatial. Although the following brief description of the procedure offers an introduction, anyone seriously interested in CMT will wish to get a copy of Luthe's book and read about it in detail.

As I experienced it, the rules were very demanding. It

hardly felt like painting. It was more like a disinhibiting process with colors. I remember that spring I would show up at Virginia's door early in the morning, often half asleep, with a bundle of old newspapers. For the first two weeks, roughly, we used only primary colors, raw, harsh, poster colors. According to the instructions we were to make as big a mess as possible on the paper—no thought, just mess painting. It was a stage of freeing feelings. We grunted, yelled, hurled paint at the paper and made some ugly-looking messes. Unsatisfactory as the result may have seemed, there was something in the process that brought about a release and change of feeling. We wrote our feelings and dreams and thoughts in a log before we began and then after finishing. The change in mood was often dramatic. The process became addictive. I began to dream about color. After a while I wanted to paint all the time.

Time. You need about two and a half hours a day, four days a week, for eight to twelve weeks.

Space. You need space for a table that will hold paints and an opened newspaper. You need space for drying fifteen sheets of newspaper. (You could lay out newspaper in another room, as a floor protector, and dry the paintings there.) Or you might hang up clothesline and hang your paintings in rows if space is limited.

You should have a window, for light and fresh air. A space about ten by ten feet is just sufficient.

Materials. Poster paint. You need the following colors: black, white, green, red (real red, not orange or pink), blue (ultramarine), yellow, dark purple (not violet), and brown. You can buy powdered gouache or tempera and mix it yourself, or you can buy it in bottles. You may also need some laundry starch to thicken the paint if it is thin.

Pint jars or cans with necks 2 to 3 inches wide, such as pint mason jars.

Eight paint brushes, one inch wide. (Get inexpensive brushes for painting walls, not art brushes. If possible buy natural pig bristle instead of nylon, and cut the brushes to three-quarters of an inch.)

A bucket of water.

Old clothes that can be covered with paint.

Fifteen newspaper sheets a day (gather up three hundred before you start). Do not use half sheets. You will paint on them fully opened.

A notebook in which to keep a journal.

Sticks or spatulas for mixing paint.

After the first few weeks you will want to get more brushes, jars, and colors since you will probably want to mix many more colors as you go. At first you will work with only the eight primary colors.

A table. It must be large enough to hold an opened newspaper, as many as twenty jars of paint, and some water. You may not want to work at a table, in which case you can buy a four foot by eight foot panel of wallboard at a lumber store and use it as an easel. Lean it against the wall and set a small table of paints near it. Get push pins to tack your newspaper to the cellutex. If you cannot get "soft" wallboard use an old door. (Pushpins are better than tacks because tacks are harder to locate when they are encrusted with paint.)

Plastic sheets. You will want to cover the floor, walls, and ceiling around the area where you are painting. You can use butcher paper, or old plastic tarpaulin, or sheeting of plastic. Cover enough area so that you will feel free to splash, even throw paint.

Instruction

Once you are dressed for painting and have already poured your eight colors into jars or cans and placed a brush in each one, and arranged your newspapers so that you have fifteen sheets ready to start, be sure that nobody will interrupt you. Turn off radios and television, stereos. Lock out your animals. They should not be in the room. Take the phone off the hook, or don't answer it.

1. Sit down, quietly, and date a page in your journal. Write down what you are thinking, feeling—dreams you recall from this morning, whatever comes to mind. How do you feel now?

2. Get water in a large container for washing brushes.

3. Mix your paints so that they are creamy in consistency and spread well. Do not get them watery, or too thick. You can use clothes starch to thicken watery paint.

4. Tack down your newspaper so that it will not move as you paint.

5. Start painting. Take two minutes per painting. You may want to set a clock where you can see it until you get used to the timing. You are ready to paint. Your paper is ordinary newspaper.

You are not doing art. You are messing.

Anything goes. So long as you *don't* control it or think about it. You might think of yourself as about four years old. You are going to make the biggest mess you know how, on the paper, and on yourself, too. You have only two minutes to cover 90 percent of the page. Do not create a painting: Just grab brushes and paint without thinking. Let your gut feelings guide your hand. Abandon your aesthetic preferences. Abandon your fastidiousness. Indulge in pure messiness, on the paper, and around you; you can liberate yourself from the petty rules that bind your own creativity. Your paintings *should* look dirty! You *should* get dirty! Do not guide your brush. *Anything* goes!

6. When you have covered 70 to 90 percent of the page, place it to dry and go on immediately to the next

mess painting. Don't stop at the edge of the paper as you paint. Go beyond the edges, paint on the table, on the easel. Let the paint fly onto the walls, the plastic will protect them.

7. Do not stop to look at what you have just done. Do not judge it or care what it looks like. Make a MESS! Paint fifteen or as many as you can without undue fatigue.

8. When you are finished, sit down and write your notes in your journal. Write about the session as fully as you can, about your feelings, images, and your feelings now that you are done.

9. Clean your brushes, cover the paint, and look over the painting you have done. Let it speak to you nonverbally. Don't judge it. It's supposed to be messy. What do the particular messes say to you about your feelings when you did them? Do you feel something when you look at them? Select two that interest you and put them up where you can look at them in your home, until the next session, when you will replace them.

None of us love being messy or producing messes, and yet we did love it as young children. Somewhere we were taught to be neat and clean at the expense of everything else: Cleanliness is a form of bondage. We may say that the rule is to make a mess, and still a little voice inside urges us to make neat margins, to paint a design, something nice. Fight that urge. Instead be outrageously dirty. Splash your paint. Throw your paint at your paper. Use your hands. Get it all over you and the paper. This is the hardest step in getting free.

The next step is to allow yourself to make noises while painting. Howl, scream, curse, cry, laugh, sing, hum, and whistle. Do whatever comes out. Don't *try* to make sounds. Just don't stop the sounds that want to come out.

If your room is not soundproofed or away from other people, explain to them that this is a process and arrange it so that you will not feel embarrassed.

At first, while you are painting, you may have thoughts or questions. "Why am I doing this? What value does it have?" There are no good answers: You need to go along with the process just as you went along with life, itself. At first you may be concerned with your paints, your paper, the costs, the time it takes to clean up. Or you may feel your paintings look terrible. After you have painted a few times, the mechanics will fade away.

◇ ◇ ◇

You will be painting and have thoughts about other things. The trick is to let them drift through your mind like clouds. You may feel angry, and shout, throw paint, and growl, or rage. The important thing is not to stop yourself. If you find yourself crying, don't think "It's ten minutes, I've cried enough!" Don't arbitrarily stop yourself. Your nervous system knows how much you need to cry, it knows what your conscious mind does not know.

Sometimes you may feel the opposite of intensity. One orthopedic surgeon commented that he looked forward to each session and that surprised him, since he found a certain boredom each time. You follow your arm, and your arm may want to make repetitive motions. This is inevitable and important to the process. Don't interrupt it. Later, when you look over the work of many sessions, you will see repeated themes or designs.

If after a number of sessions you find yourself stuck, repeating the same thing over and over, or unable to move, you might try to use your nondominant hand. For right-handed people that means using the left hand. Left-handed people will use the right hand.

It is important to leave yourself enough time after a session so that you are able to follow through on any impulse you feel: to take a walk, rearrange your room, sit and think, whatever comes to mind. The sessions are not over, in their effect, when you have cleaned up your paints.

At the end of each session you will probably want to experiment. Use your fingers, your hands, try spattering, folding the paper, stepping on it, and throwing paint at it. By the end of two weeks you will find yourself needing to mix more colors. If you have made real messes during your first two weeks, you can then begin to allow yourself more colors. If you have had trouble getting messy, stay with that. It is the foundation for liberation. Once you mix more colors, you can create any palette you like, so long as you mix them before you start painting.

At this stage I found myself eager to paint, dreaming about colors. Even if I felt tormented when I arrived to paint, I felt quite excited and exhilarated when I finished. Finally I began to have fewer thoughts. I didn't come in wanting to draw a particular thing and feeling frustrated by the rules. I found myself just watching my hand and watching the color unfold. Because I am right-handed, I decided deliberately to use my left hand. After nine weeks, finally, my feeling was one of total effortlessness. My hand painted, but there was nothing in my mind—until the last when I might then finish off what had evolved. Sometimes I felt as if I'd been painting for a week, sometimes the session seemed terribly short, ten minutes.

It is very important to unleash feelings. If you feel like crying, if your eyes itch, your chest feels tight, let the tears flow. They will finally leave you released if you don't block them. The same for anger or aggression. Slash at the paper, throw the paint, shout.

In the early weeks of painting, people sometimes feel nervous, or get headaches, cold feet or hands, and pains in the neck and shoulders, all of which tends to disappear later on. In addition Luthe has found that people become more creative, aware, and aesthetically developed as the process continues. Their attitudes may change profoundly. For example, they may begin to see something in a messy newspaper that they formerly dismissed as trash.

Once (after two, three, or four weeks) the no-thought mess-painting becomes easy and rapid and effortless, a person may begin to see paintings evolve. They evolve without thought or intention, flowing from the hand, passively. Then it is possible to have a much larger selection of colors. It is important to continue moving fast, but now, you can rapidly select your colors, allowing your hand to select, not planning ahead. You may find that a partly complete mess painting actually is an abstract landscape, or a lovely design. When you know that you are effortlessly painting, and have no thoughts, along in the fifth or sixth week you may find that your mess paintings are becoming paintings. Do not become self-conscious. If you find that a painting is evolving and you need another minute or five minutes to finish it, you can begin to do that. On the whole continue your pace, roughly two minutes per newspaper.

I found myself quite ecstatic on some days, and on others I returned to making messes. That is the way it goes. You may make effortless no-thought messes, and even evolve some paintings, and find yourself cycling back to a time of aggression or other feelings that need release. There is no such thing as linear progress. This process has to be played out at your pace, by your nervous system. Sometimes I would arrive at a morning session gloomy and depressed. I would start out making a few messes and, getting angry, hurling paint, splashing everything, talking angrily. Then at some indefinable moment the emotion I felt was no longer labeled, no longer an emotion. It was pure excitement, an energy guiding my arm, and colors were forming on the paper. Magically something quite unexpected would arise on the paper, a left-handed painting that was not a mess. I would be tempted to try for another. The moment I intended to do a painting, it became awkward, and forced, and it lacked the flow of the thoughtless one. I had to stop thinking and preconceiving.

A woman in the first SAGE group decided that our enthusiasm was contagious. She was ready to try. Her husband lined a room in the house with plastic: This was a major step for her, since it was the guest room. She had never taken a space for herself before. At first it all seemed terribly clumsy and demanding. She was still working and had to paint early in the morning or late at night. She was tired and a little depressed. The first few weeks she looked at what she was doing and wanted to quit. Yet her diary showed that she felt more energy, and felt better after painting than before. Her paintings began to grow interesting. She was mixing new colors and noticing color around her. She was noticing the decor in the clinic where she worked. Toward the end her paintings were beginning to be interesting. Her husband had built her a frame, into which she could insert a new painting each day. Framed they looked good—to her surprise.

Other people began to ask about the process, and finally Virginia decided to start classes. She was so inspired by this experience in her life—and she had been an artist— that she spent several weeks working with Dr. Luthe in Montreal. (Note: There is now a certified course in CMT, and an International CMT Association that developed out of this work.) These instructions do not permit as detailed and systematic a process as Dr. Luthe conducts, and as Virginia is conducting with SAGE staff and participants. However if it is done without reserve, messily, and unthinking, each person's own repressed and hidden creativity will ultimately begin to emerge. Whether it finally expresses itself in gardening, crochet, ceramics, music, dance, bookbinding, or some inventive hobby such as carpentry or home decorating, the liberated creative energy begins to take form. Difficulties at first, like discharging angry feelings, or crying, speed the process of releasing that energy for a new kind of feeling and expression.

One thing that almost everyone has said as the process took hold was that they felt a new excitement, the kind of excitement they had felt at age sixteen, and it made life more dynamic and vital, more unexpected.

MUSIC

A very different process using music and sound was developed by Helen Bonny. By listening to music in a special relaxed state people experienced things that everyone had previously imagined must come from drugs, or from prolonged esoteric practice such as meditation, or from mystic revelation. Helen Bonny had observed the work of Dr. Stanislav Grof, a Czechloslovakian psychiatrist who had experimented with psychedelic drugs in Prague and learned a great deal about his own consciousness. Dr. Grof was interested in the very deep transcendent experience that could be experienced by ill people when they were carefully guided by music. He found that a great many cancer patients no longer felt pain after this experience, or fear. Many had learned about themselves so deeply that they could live out their last days, weeks, or months in a state of blessed freedom they had never known during their "healthy" lives. Helen Bonny wondered whether music alone might not have some profound emotional effects. She began to devise special programs of classical music and tried out different combinations on hundreds of people. After experimenting she began to see that certain programs of music had particular effects. For instance the Fauré Requiem and Bloch Cello Concerto elicited sadness, while other programs repeatedly evoked transcendent feelings. After reading her book with Louis Savary, *Music and Your Mind* (see the bibliography), we decided to try this at SAGE. Although it is possible to do this by yourself, it is a great help to have someone you trust sitting nearby, to guide you and assist you.

Preparation. Set aside at least two hours when you will not be interrupted. Remove all tight clothing, jewelry, shoes, eyeglasses, or contact lenses. Lie comfortably on a bed or couch, and be sure that it will be warm enough. Use a light blanket for cover.

Select the kind of music you want to hear, or allow your guide to program your session. Try out earphones. The best effect is obtained by using comfortable earphones.

Instruction

1. The role of the guide is one of reassurance and nurturing as the listener lies still. The guide can change the tape or record and assist the listener if he or she needs help getting up to use the bathroom, get a drink of water, or talk about the experience. Do any one of the guided relaxation procedures in Chapter 12 until fully relaxed.

2. Turn on the music.

3. Stop when you feel like stopping. Each person will have an individual tolerance for the experience and for lying still. My mother and I had both experienced sessions with Dr. William Soskin, a psychologist, some of them lasting almost five hours, but there were people at SAGE who became restless after half an hour.

4. Share the experience as fully as possible. Do not rush, but allow enough time for feelings to emerge and be cleared.

◇ ◇ ◇

One SAGE woman angrily wrested off the earphones in ten minutes. "I can't stand this music," she said. "I feel as if you are trying to make me sad. It's like a funeral. And I do not want to hear another tape!"

Another woman listening to the same program sat up

with an ecstatic smile, "I was wandering in some mountains, in meadows, very high up, where flowers were in
bloom. The clouds, the air, the sounds—it was an ecstasy I
can't describe. I felt very close to God."

"I never heard the music," said another person after a
long session. "I began to have images of my childhood, of
scenes with my father. I saw a peculiar image of a woman
in a window. That's when I began to cry and you held me.
I felt sad, all the sadness of my life, and the things that are
gone, and then feeling that I will be gone soon. When I
saw that woman looking out of the window, suddenly I felt
a kind of assurance that everything was all right, everything everywhere, that I need never worry any more, as if
there were a kind of love embracing me with its fluid all
around me. I felt warm and safe and happy, but I don't
remember hearing the music."

At SAGE we found that we hadn't enough staff or time
to provide each participant with a music session lasting
one to four hours. Out of necessity we tried a music session in the group, following the same procedures. We lay
on the rug and breathed. We did a relaxation exercise in
which our expanded bodies were floating. Then we put on
a record by Paul Horn, which combined his flute music
with sounds of rain, natural sounds of animals, and children. That was all we did.

After listening for twenty minutes the members of the
group began to sit up very slowly. One woman was quietly
crying. A man looked around the room with tears in his
eyes, having revisited the farm where he had lived and the
sweetheart he had loved as a boy. Many people have vivid
images, and three revisited childhood places. Afterward
we sat around, voyagers from another world. Each person's
eyes had that look of having been faraway, and the room
was charged with deep, intense emotions.

We encouraged everyone to share the experience, but left
reticent people alone, not wishing to prod them. We later
learned to be less timid, for unspent emotions leave a per-

son with a huge energy charge. If it is not resolved, expressed, transformed, or dealt with, the person continues on with an internal distraction. We had never thought of this as a serious problem, but two years later in another exercise we saw the possible consequences of leaving people alone with intense and unspent feelings. At that time we had taken the group back to childhood, and in a fantasy encouraged each person to tell his or her child self something that would have helped in living.

"I would have told myself not to be so timid, to venture out, that it was worth the risk," said one man.

"I lacked confidence. I wanted to tell myself, 'You are okay.' "

Two women sat silent, pensively looking down, and said they would rather not participate. Later one of the women slipped and fell, spraining her knee. She said she had blanked out, but the doctors' tests showed no signs of stroke or heart disease. We asked her whether she mightn't have been so preoccupied with her feelings that she became unaware of her surroundings at a moment of critical balance. She could not recall feeling immersed. Still we wondered about our own responsibility to her. When an emotion is pushed under it often loses its original form. It is hard to recapture the stimulus experience, and yet the emotional energy can interfere with attention, with functioning. We call it being absentminded. People sometimes have accidents when they are bothered by something under the surface.

The need to express feelings is part of almost all the exercises in this book, but is perhaps particularly relevant to music sessions which may seem so long, quiet, and attenuated. On that afternoon at SAGE we ended late and the group members felt rushed to leave. It was typical of the way we lead our lives. Even though several members of the group were inwardly disturbed, they were pressed to get away. In the hierarchy of importance, everything comes before our feelings, and if they are negative we push them aside. Later we may have a near-accident on the freeway, or become irritated with a child.

The best time to deal with feelings is now, while they are happening, but most of us, particularly older people, have been taught to postpone feelings and be nice, smooth, and pleasant with others. An experience such as a music session is an opportunity to learn how to follow through and express feelings on the spot.

18 ❦ FOOD AWARENESS AND NUTRITION

We are composed of what we eat and how we eat it. Yet most of us pay little attention to our bodies in this regard, for we eat what and how our culture has taught us. Some cultures seem to have developed healthy life-styles, judging from the ebullient vitality and longevity of people. Their eating habits seem to reflect almost exactly the guidelines that professionals in the field of nutrition are now telling us we must follow. People who live long, vigorous lives seem to eat almost no animal fats, but grains, fresh fruits, and vegetables. "Eat little and selectively" seems to be the mandate from the Abkhasians. Eat in a leisurely way and chew your food. This, too, seems to be their habit. These healthy old people happen to practice what most of us talk about. The guidelines can be summed up briefly:

- Undereat.
- Eat grains, nuts, fresh fruits, and vegetables.
- Undercook or eat food raw.

- Avoid meat and animal fats, salt, sugar, coffee, black tea, alcohol, and food additives.
- Eat in a leisurely way, with an attitude of peacefulness.
- Chew your food thoroughly.
- Select food by listening to your body and learn to eat so that it benefits you.

This chapter was written to help you examine your food habits. It will elaborate on some of the ideas that emerge from the confusing mass of literature at this time, but it will not discuss specific physical needs and problems. To find such detailed information you may want to consult the *Nutrition Almanac*, or other books cited in the bibliography. The main purpose of this chapter is to help you think about your food habits and how they affect you.

CHANGING EATING HABITS

Take a lenient, listening attitude toward yourself. Some of the ideas may be too new to accept all at once. You may recognize that suggestions are beneficial, but you may not be ready to make uncomfortable changes in your shopping or preparing of meals. Let yourself experiment with new ideas gently. A process of osmosis often will accomplish more than disciplined, iron-willed resolution.

At SAGE, because we did not live together, we could not work on our food habits at daily mealtimes. We invited experts on nutrition to speak and advise us, and then each of us was on his or her own. Often we felt resistance, frustration, and finally a small change leading to another small change. One person commented, "It took me a year after Bernie Rappaport (a psychiatrist involved in nutrition) talked to us. I'd feel guilty every time I put sugar on my cereal. And after about a year I found I wasn't doing it any more."

Dr. Rappaport had outlined a stringent diet and excited

us all by his own obvious health and exuberance, as well as the possibility that we could be so healthy. Then after the excitement died down, we all confessed that we had continued to eat in our habitual ways. His suggestions were too far from our food habits to emulate all at once. A year later some of us were actually using his suggestions.

To change diet sounds simple but it turns out to be almost as difficult as changing one's identity. The way we eat and what we eat is emotionally ingrained to the point of being almost sacred. We fondly refer to the way grandmother fried zucchini or mother's dark chocolate pie, remembering not only the taste but the love and care we received from our families in the dishes they prepared. It is unthinkable that those loving meals and rituals about food ("have a tiny bit more'") might be bad for us. Many of them have lasted a lifetime and supported us in times of stress. It is hard to accept that we have actually harmed ourselves by eating as our families and culture taught us.

Nobody ever told us that we should be reducing our daily calorie intake about ten calories a year, for every year past thirty. In other words if I'm sixty I should be eating 300 calories less each day than I did when I was thirty. We are active when we are young, eat with appetite, and digest well, not gaining too much weight. As we get older we reduce our physical activity, drive instead of walk, go to dinner parties, bridge parties, eat rich food, and watch television. In such circumstances becoming overweight is inevitable. There are two ways to deal with the problem. One is to increase physical exercise. The other is to begin cutting out foods, especially those with empty calories, substituting foods that are more nutritious. You might decide to omit candy and cookies, sugar and cream in coffee, rich sauces, mayonnaise, butter, soft drinks, liquor, potato chips, and the like. If you start eating celery and carrots and fruits instead, you will be truly nourishing yourself.

Part of our difficulty in exchanging empty foods for healthy ones is that we live in a rich and commercially oriented country, where food habits dangerous to health are advertised at us very cleverly from all sides. In the United States sugar is added to almost all canned and processed foods, and we are about to become the diabetes capital of the world. With our sedentary and stressed lives and our consumption of beef and animal fat we are also about to become the world's proving ground for cardiac disease. Most of us grew up thinking that steak and butter were especially good for us, that ice cream, soda pop, and potato chips were treats. Candy, cake, and sweets were given to us when we were good, as rewards. We ate instant cereals, "enriched" foods, meat, fruits and vegetables that were canned, dried, or frozen, and took only minutes to prepare. We never imagined that the foods that lasted so well on the shelves also contained some unfamiliar chemicals to help preserve them, chemicals we are now discovering to be toxic. We had evolved tasty, appealing, packaged foods, requiring almost no preparation. And by eating them well-off Americans were combining malnutrition with obesity.

This may not be news to you. It wasn't really news to me even fifteen years ago, although there weren't a lot of hard-hitting books around stating the case so clearly. Still when I made an active decision to change my eating habits it took me two years before I was comfortable without red meat, coffee, and incessant sweets. I had long had reason to change. My rich meals and hasty way of eating burdened my digestive system, and I was plagued with gas pains and constipation, along with a feeling of fatigue and inertia after a big dinner. After a dinner party I'd drink alcohol to subdue my stomach ache, and the next morning I still felt traces of undigested food, and thought I just needed some coffee. Like many women I enjoyed cooking tasty, elaborate meals that others ate with relish. At mealtime I basically paid little attention to the act of eating, the nuances of taste, the feeling of the food in my body. I was too busy serving and socializing.

One day a friend took me to a feast in an expensive

Chinese restaurant. Suddenly, for no reason I knew, I stopped talking, sat quietly, and actually tasted the food. I had always loved the Chinese food at that place, I thought. That moment was a revelation. The strong flavoring and bitterness of an artificial taste enhancer, MSG, were fighting on the roof of my mouth. Just a moment's attention told me that the food was too strongly spiced, too oily and harsh for me. Why did I believe I loved it? As a child I had refused foods that felt bad to me. But as a well-trained adult, with years of practicing inattention or divided attention, almost anything became acceptable. Once I felt the discrepancy between my real needs and tastes and those that were purely social, I began wanting to eat in a way that neither my family nor any restaurant would offer. It was inconvenient to ask for salad at breakfast, for instance, and I began growing skeptical of everything, not just commercial advertising but vitamin products, health faddists, nutritionists, everyone. As I read, I felt as if I had been surrounded by enemies. Here we could afford to be the best-fed, healthiest people on earth, yet most of our food was being grown on overused land, with synthetic fertilizers, then picked unripe, stored in refrigerators after being sprayed with insecticides and fungicides, often developed out of war gases, and finally treated with preservatives. Animals were being injected with hormones. And much of our food was so processed that its vitamin and food value were almost nil. Moreover I had been reading writers like Adele Davis, Henry Bieler, Paavo Airola, and Roger Williams, to name a few, who felt that many of our health problems are linked to improper eating.

Like many people at SAGE, I was frustrated by the difficulty in changing my own habits of overeating, cooking food so long that it lost all vitamin value, and eating too rapidly. In one SAGE group, inspired by a speaker on nutrition and chiropractic, we all tried to remember to chew each bit of food thirty times. Slowing down by chewing thoroughly meant for me that I ate less, until I forgot and began gulping like a dog again. I actually tasted what I ate, and there were many things I had been eating that I no longer liked the taste of. One simple change had enormous ramifications.

I also knew that I was helping my digestion, for part of our digestive system is in our mouths, in the saliva enzymes that break down food molecules. The enzymes in saliva work on carbohydrates. However the only way to benefit from them is to chew thoroughly, and not to dilute the digestive enzymes by drinking liquids with the meal.

Because there are different enzymes in different parts of the digestive tract, some writers suggest eating only one kind of food at a time and beginning a meal with protein. Unmetabolized food, such as protein, causes gas and elimination problems. We inhibit our digestive enzymes in many ways, by smoking, drinking alcohol, and taking depressant drugs such as barbiturates. These all depress the activity of our liver, which produces many of the enzymes we rely on to detoxify substances that could otherwise poison us. Without knowing much more one can understand why food rich in animal fats, white sugar, and refined flour and poor in roughage and vitamins, eaten when agitated or fatigued, and swallowed with a lot of liquids or alcohol is a recipe for indigestion and constipation. Indeed if you eat rich food and do not exercise you can expect constipation within about forty-eight hours. The antidotes to constipation are equally simple: raw vegetable salads, raw fruit, new potatoes, bran added to cereals, and exercise (see Chapter 15).

BASIC PRINCIPLES

You may have sighed as you read that, wondering why anyone would bother to write something that everyone already knows. Perhaps the reason for repeating is obvious, that health is a whole process, and knowing that we ought to do something does not make it easy to accomplish.

Sometimes a new bit of information about it, or a new perspective can help. Look at the most obvious food rule of all. We all know it, but how many of us practice it?

Eat less, especially after thirty.

In the 1920s Clive McCay at Cornell University experimented with underfeeding rats as a way of extending their life-spans. He gave one group of young rats a balanced laboratory diet. The other group was fed a balanced diet with vitamins and minerals, but a drastically reduced calorie level, about a third of "normal." These underfed rats were glossy and healthy when the others were "senile," and their life-spans were about double those who were well fed. Skinny rats seem to live longer: This seems true of people, too. We do not need to look at the Hunza, or Abkhasians: We can see that in our midst. But most of us aren't skinny, and we find the excess weight hard to remove.

Freak diets don't keep weight down. There are quick diets for every taste: Some say you should eat nothing but meat and whipped cream; others prescribe milk and bananas; and while one says to be fat free, another urges you to swallow all the fat you want. It is safer to reduce slowly, not by quick diets or fasting. The first principle of dieting is to eliminate empty calories, alcohol, all sweets, refined flour, fried foods, and high cholesterol items such as beef, cooked eggs, and butter. (Potatoes, which are rich in vitamins and minerals, contain only seventy-two calories, while a slice of cake contains 200–400.)

There has been a lot of research on food content, and nutrition experts pretty much agree about the proper selection of foods. Ideally we should eat a low-fat diet, consisting mainly of raw vegetables and fruits and grains. We should drink plenty of water, but not with meals.

Many people at SAGE who were unmoved by the rules of good diet became excited by a book, *Live Longer Now*, by Drs. Leonard, Hofer, and Pritikin (see the bibliography). This outlined a diet and exercise program that had resuscitated hundreds of people with severe cardiac disease. Two people in their early seventies promptly tried it and reported that their blood pressure was down ten points in one case, and twenty points in the other. One of them, a retired psychiatrist, also used information from Roger Williams (see the bibliography) and Linus Pauling to eliminate his cataracts. With these examples of improved health from nutrition, SAGE participants began to develop real interest in their own diets.

Cooking should be minimal. If we must cook food, vegetables should be quickly steamed or lightly sauteed, preferably in a cold-pressed oil. The minute you start to boil, steam, fry, or heat them, most vegetables lose 80 percent of their vitamins. This means that dehydrated, preserved, and canned foods have little vitamin content. Frozen foods are better, but still have less vitamins than fresh. No foods should be cooked twice, or deep fried. Choice of vegetables and proper eating can make a major contribution toward health. For example I knew a Dutch family that survived near starvation in World War II by eating potatoes. Potatoes are rich in vitamins and minerals, which lie just beneath the skin. If you prefer to boil potatoes and do not eat the skin, boil them in their skins. Then peel them and eat the yellow layer just beneath the skin.

The body requires several major elements: protein, or food with nitrogen in it; carbohydrates; some fat; and vitamins and minerals. *Most of the elements the body requires are found in vegetables, nuts, peas, beans, grains, eaten in the right combinations, with occasional milk or eggs.* Vegetables and fruits supply such organic minerals as iron, potassium, lime, and soda which act as blood purifiers, producers of electromagnetic energy, and eliminators. Most of our vitamins come from vegetables, especially eaten raw. If need be these can be juiced or put into a blender. The best source of trace minerals is seaweed, which is delicious dried and is sold in Japanese or Korean food stores. However you can buy kelp or dulse tablets.

Lecithin is another necessity. It is found in natural oils in raw egg. The more fats you eat the more lecithin you need, for it appears to break down fat and cholesterol. It is a source of the important B vitamins, choline and inositol, which seem to be lacking in many people with coronary disease. Eggs have natural lecithin, but high temperatures destroy it. So one way to add lecithin to your diet is to make eggnogs with orange juice (and vanilla), raw eggs, and other fruits. Ironically when you cook an egg it leaves you with cholesterol, whereas if you eat it raw the yolks will give you lecithin that breaks down cholesterol. Many older people have been advised not to eat eggs, because we almost always cook them. But yolks could be eaten raw in salad dressings in combination with lemon, garlic, and herbs. Otherwise lecithin can be purchased from health food stores in liquid, capsule, or granular form. Everyone needs some in their daily diet, according to many nutritionists.

A general rule after age thirty is to: *Reduce intake of meat, butter, and whole milk, particularly of animal fats.*

Twenty percent of our weight is protein, and we need protein renewal each day. However there is a more efficient way of ingesting protein than by eating meat. In fact we waste grain feeding it to cattle, since we can get whole proteins by mixing the proper grains together. Most people do not realize that you obtain protein from a vegetable diet, but this is how the poor people of Mexico and India have survived for centuries on rice and beans. If you eat rice and lentils or rice and red beans together they make a full protein. If you eat a tablespoonful of peanut butter and sunflower seeds you have the equivalent of steak.

Proteins are built out of amino acids. There are eight of these that we cannot supply in our bodies; these are called the essential amino acids. The human body has an amino-acid pattern that must be filled out completely to make human protein. Therefore we must eat amino acids in a certain proportion in order to synthesize the proteins in our bodies. If just one amino acid is missing from the pattern, all the others are of less use for making protein. This means we get full protein if we combine things. For instance wheat contains sulfur amino acids but lacks lysine. Beans have lysine but not sulfur, and the two can be combined to make a whole.

There are food combinations, far less expensive than meats and processed foods, which offer a better protein and richer array of vitamins and minerals. Two excellent books explain how to combine foods to obtain all the essential amino acids, *Recipes for a Small Planet* by Ellen Burkman Ewell, and *Diet for a Small Planet* by Frances Moore Lappé (see the bibliography).

We need to ask how many calories we will consume to obtain one gram of usable protein. Most seafoods are very low in calories yet high in protein, five to ten calories per gram. For each gram of usable protein you get ten calories from lean lamb, fourteen from lean steak, fifteen from hamburger, eighteen from lean pork. Rib lamb chops give thirty-two calories with every gram of protein. It may surprise you to know that you don't get many more calories by eating beans. For each gram of usable protein soybeans only give twenty calories, mung beans twenty-five, or garbanzo beans forty. From cottage cheese you only get seven calories; from buttermilk only twelve. Because of fat content nuts and seeds are higher in calories per gram of protein, forty for sunflower seeds or peanuts.

According to *Diet for a Small Planet* we need about .28 grams of *usable* protein per pound of body weight per day. You can calculate your exact daily need for protein by multiplying your body weight by .28. If you weight 128 pounds, then you need 35.8 grams per day.

FOOD ABUSE

We all know about drug abuse, and the fact that overstressed people often get addicted to drugs that diminish their sense of pain. Is the same thing true of our overuse of foods that are "bad" for us, such as sugar, salt, coffee, tea, and refined flours? The answer seems to be yes.

Let us look at sugar, which is one of the most abused foods in our country at present. Many people eat sweets when they are hungry, instead of eating more nourishing food. Others eat them when they feel upset and angry. This is a time when they grab foods rather automatically. If you watch what foods they reach for, these are mostly sugars, to give them a little burst of energy. In part because of the rate at which our population has eaten refined sugar, diabetes is widespread, and many people suffer from a complaint known as hypoglycemia. What this means is an inability to maintain blood-sugar (glucose) levels. When blood sugar is low, people very often feel depressed or a little bit irritable. Usually they will get restless and go searching for candy or ice creams or other carbohydrates. This quickly raises blood sugar levels, triggering production of insulin which in turn lowers blood-sugar levels, creating a harmful cycle conducive to addiction.

Since we don't eat around the clock, blood sugar has to be supplied from storage. Most of our cells synthesize glycogen, which is a basic substance converted into glucose, but only the liver stores glycogen. We need this blood sugar, this glucose, at all times. Between meals the glycogen is supplied by the liver, converted into glucose, and transformed into usable energy required by the brain. But the harmful cycle described above depletes the level of glycogen in the liver. The cure for this condition is small, frequent, high-protein meals and a drastic reduction in sugar and other refined carbohydrates. Removal of refined sugars from the diet restores the body to equilibrium.

We create this sugar craving by eating a diet of refined, depleted foods. As Adelle Davis has pointed out in *Let's Eat Right to Keep Fit*, lack of adrenal activity, which feels like exhaustion or irritation, can come from deficiencies such as pantothenic acid, which is found in yeast, whole grains, and green vegetables. (It is destroyed by cooking.) This commonly follows illness, stress, drugs, or emotional upset. Loss of pantothenic acid can result in low blood sugar, which means dizziness, exhaustion, and nervousness. A diet of refined foods also lacks sufficient potassium, which makes people feel listless, get gas pains, constipation, and even irregular pulse. It is amazing that millions of Americans suffer these symptoms, for potassium exists in so many fruits and vegetables. However when soaked or boiled the potassium is thrown away. Salty foods exaggerate the symptoms. They allow the potassium level to drop and the blood sugar to drop so that whenever blood sugar is low, the diet must emphasize cutting down sodium as well as building up potassium intake.

Salt, like coffee and tea, becomes such a needed stimulant that we behave like addicts. A person may seem a little happier and more alert after eating a bag of potato chips or salting his food heavily. The salt acts like a stimulant. It raises blood pressure and water retention, and a person who eats a lot of salt may feel a little depressed if he or she stops suddenly. The salt has been whipping the endocrine glands beyond their own normal output, and the body has become depleted.

Coffee and tea do the same things. We feel tired or sluggish and make ourselves feel alert and cheerful by whipping our adrenal glands into action. Our heart rate increases. We feel energetic. We do it because it feels good at the moment, but we are overtaxing our bodies and depleting our overall energy. A radical change in diet would occur if people were to stop and meditate before preparing food, asking what their bodies really want. A person who eats with attention will taste the toxic additives in processed foods, and feel the depression when the sugar, salt, coffee, or tea jag has worn off.

But most people feel separate from their bodies and do not consult them. Obviously nobody knows your body the way your body does, so you may want to try an experiment. For one day promise your body that you will stop, quiet yourself, and listen to what it wants before you eat or drink anything. There are relaxation exercises in this book, and in this chapter, that can help you do that.

You can also review the elements of a balanced diet, consulting Adelle Davis, Roger Williams, Paavo Airola, Carleton Fredericks, and others (see the bibliography), to understand how you must amplify your diet to deal with stress or illness. Hippocrates once said, "Food shall be thy remedy," and modern doctors are rediscovering the medicinal properties of ordinary foods and vegetables.

THE BALANCED DIET

You undoubtedly remember a time when a meal of fried chicken or beef, mashed potatoes with gravy, well-cooked green beans or corn, and iceberg lettuce was considered balanced. I look back a little nostalgically sometimes at those days of innocence, for surely that meal does not seem ideal to me now. Today's version would more likely be broiled fish, baked or boiled potato, and a salad of raw green beans, spinach, lettuce, and cabbage. Back in the old days a lemon meringue pie would have been dessert. Today it is likely to be fruit. Both meals contained some of the basic elements we need: protein, fat, carbohydrates, vitamins and minerals, roughage, and water. However as we are beginning to learn, the selection and preparation of those elements can be more or less nutritious. Dr. Bieler felt that very rare beef or lamb, raw milk, and raw or lightly cooked egg yolks were the most easily digested proteins. He also suggested that raw fruits and vegetables, peanuts, avocados, and legumes were a basic storehouse for nutrients. Some nutritionists elect brown rice as the most useful carbohydrate, others vote for the white boiled potato, with cereals and the sugars of fruits and vegetables coming next. Roughage is essential because of the anatomy of our intestines. The least irritating forms are leaves and stalks and stems of vegetables, the most efficient being skins of nuts, such as almonds, and bran.

To eat truly nutritiously and economically is a matter that takes some consideration. A balanced diet for you must consider your weight and activity, your geographical location, your age, and special quirks of digestion. This chapter can offer you some provocative information, some guidelines, but you need to make your own personal assessments. You can decide how many calories you need by evaluating your daily activity and exercise: Do you burn up the calories you eat each day? This chapter will give you a start in assessing whether your food is really nourishing for you. You can do this by listing the foods you eat and seeing how many of them are processed, canned, dried, frozen, or precooked. How fresh are your vegetables and fruits?

You can consult the *Nutrition Almanac* chart of the composition of foods to assess the nutrients in your diet, and there are many helpful books suggested in the bibliography. The discussion of vitamins and minerals that follows is necessarily very abbreviated, but it will indicate the vital role of these elements in our health, a function that is virtually demolished by processing and heavy cooking.

VITAMINS

Each vitamin is like a catalyst controlling the body's use of minerals. If the trace minerals aren't there, there isn't much for the vitamin to do. Some vitamins are coenzymes, which means they work with another vitamin. For example vitamin D and vitamin A work together.

Vitamin A can be dissolved in oils but not in water, and it is stored in the fat in the kidney and liver and used with vitamin D. Lack of vitamin A will show up in a very dry or scaly skin, in kidney stones, poor digestion, trouble seeing at night, and lowered resistance to infection. Some foods that are high in vitamin A are: fish liver oil, beef liver, broccoli, carrots, apricots, parsley, spinach, sweet potato, tomato, turnip leaves, and watercress.

Vitamin B₁ is soluble in water, not in oil. Boiling and pasteurization partly destroy it. Vitamin B is particularly needed when carbohydrates are in the diet. It has a stimulating effect on the appetite and also helps digestion. Lack of it may show up in a slow heart beat and poor appetite, nervousness, and gastrointestinal disorders. There is a lot of vitamin B_1 in: dried food yeast, wheat germ, dried beans, peas, oatmeal, egg yolks, and asparagus.

Vitamin B₂ is stored readily in the body and is necessary to good skin and vision. It is soluble in water. Deficiency can be seen in lack of stamina, loss of hair, ulcerations of the tongue, and cataracts. B_2 is found in: liver, dried food yeast, wheat germ, milk, almonds, avocado, turnip greens, kale, egg yolks, and beet tops.

There are other B vitamins with important functions. Quite a few experts recommend brewer's yeast and wheat germ as a source of B vitamins, but B_{12} is found mainly in animal products. Yeast is a vegetable composed of tiny cells about the size of red corpuscles and held together loosely like grapes. It is partly destroyed by cooking. Many people take yeast powder, mixed in juice such as tomato juice, as a food supplement

Vitamin C is soluble in water. It can be steam cooked but ordinary cooking methods and pasteurization cause it to vanish. Dried fruits, for example, don't contain vitamin C unless they are dried in a vacuum. Vitamin C is essential for adrenal-gland functioning and very important in increasing resistance to infection and bacteria. It keeps the blood vessels in healthy condition. Deficiency can show up in physical weakness, rapid heart, respiration, tendency to disease, headaches, and defective teeth. Vitamin C is found in: rose hips, oranges, broccoli, cauliflower, strawberries, grapefruit, tomatoes, spinach, turnip greens, green peppers, cabbage, and asparagus.

Vitamin D is soluble only in fats and oils. It is stored in the skin, and is converted to vitamin D$_2$ by sunlight—ultraviolet radiation from the sun. This vitamin controls the calcium content of the blood and is essential for good muscle tone. It also regulates the metabolism of phosphorus. Lack of vitamin D may result in soft, fragile bones, and in muscle cramps and twitching. Vitamin D is not found in fruits and vegetables or cereals, but can be found in fish liver oils or irradiated vitamin D milk or can be absorbed from sunshine.

Vitamin E is another essential. It is dissolved only in oils and not affected by cooking or drying, but sunshine destroys it. It is stored in our fat and muscles and is continually being used up so that it must be renewed regularly. Lack of vitamin E may produce loss of hair and many other symptoms. Large doses of vitamin E seem to promote longevity of the cells and is particularly advantageous as a person gets older. It is found in: wheat germ oil, corn oil, peanut oil, eggs, and wheat germ.

MINERALS

Calcium is needed for bones and teeth; it aids in blood clotting and also helps in the regulation of our heart muscle, since it is an important element in the working of the nervous system. About 90 percent of our calcium is in our bones, but according to some experts, we replace all our body calcium every six years; so we need an adequate supply daily. We can get it from milk and milk products, salmon, sardines, egg yolks, figs, turnip greens, watercress, blackstrap molasses, and kale.

We also need *phosphorus* in every cell. This maintains the slight alkaline property of the blood. Along with calcium, the phosphates that are formed help the bones, skin, and teeth. Lecithins, which are phosphorus compounds, are widely distributed in the body, found in the gray tissue of the brain. About 90 percent of the phosphorus is in the skeleton. Good sources of phosphorus are: dried food yeast, wheat germ, milk, dried peas and beans, pecans, brown rice, rye flour, soybeans, walnuts, peanuts, and sardines.

Iron builds red corpuscles and plays an important part in carrying the oxygen of the blood to all the tissues of the body. Iron deficiency results in anemia. There are many good sources of iron: liver, egg yolks, blackstrap molasses, wheat germ, dried beans and peas, spinach, lima beans, raisins, peaches, apricots, parsley, and prunes.

Iodine is essential to thyroid gland function. Kelp, dulse, and various seafoods are good sources. Dulse is probably the best.

Potassium is also essential. Junk food diets as well as the use of diuretics can lead to potassium deficiency. Potassium is found in all fruits and vegetables.

Sodium is most important in forming the digestive juices, the saliva, bile, and pancreatic juices, but it is generally excessive rather than deficient in our diets. It is better to take in natural sodium than to use table salt. It is found in small amounts in almost all foods, and in heavy quantities in most processed foods such as soup, processed meat, and margarine.

Magnesium is essential, too, for strong bones, and for building the tissues of the lung. It is lost in cooking and processing. Magnesium is found in: milk, nuts, whole grains, green vegetables, and brown rice.

Sulfur, too, must be replenished. It is a constituent of the hemoglobin in the blood and helps keep up body resistance, stimulate the bile secretion, and is important to the skin and hair. It is found in egg yolks, fish, lean meat, cabbage, dried beans, and brussels sprouts.

Chlorine is something we very rarely think about as a body requirement. It helps clean the blood, reduce fat, and keep the joints supple. It is also used in the digestive juices, particularly gastric juice. Most fruits and vegetables are sources of chlorine.

There are, in addition, copper, zinc, cadmium, and other

elements that the body uses in trace amounts, very tiny amounts. These also come from the foods in a balanced diet.

As you go down these lists, you will notice that there are certain foods that are rich in most of the vitamins and minerals that you need. Among them are dried food yeast, eggs, wheat germ, carrots, cabbage, spinach, turnip greens, and broccoli. To simplify preparations it may be worthwhile to go through and pick out the foods that contain what you need to eat every day. Build around these.

A diet without processed foods, but which includes fresh fruit and salad every day, nuts and grains, a little raw milk or yogurt is a balanced one. Occasionally it will include some rare lean meat, eggs, or fish. This diet replenishes the body's main needs: protein, or food with nitrogen, some carbohydrates, a little fat, vitamins and minerals, and roughage.

EATING FOR BENEFIT: HOW WE EAT

In the late 1960s a number of research studies on animals and people indicated that the best time to eat our heaviest meal is early in the day. Adelle Davis used to say that we should eat breakfast like a king, eat lunch like a prince, and dinner like a pauper. In much of the world people eat their heavy meals at midday. Our metabolism changes with our activity and time of day. You can metabolize the same meal far more efficiently at breakfast or lunch than you can in the evening. Exercise certainly enhances the more rapid metabolism of food. It is ironic that we pick evening for our heaviest, richest, most social meals.

I have begun listening to some of the wise older people at SAGE, who complain that they don't like being invited out for heavy meals. When I visit them, I notice they serve me a lot, but they themselves eat frugally. "I just don't sleep well after a big meal," was a typical comment. They must be listening to their bodies. Certainly they know something about an important aspect of eating that younger people, especially busy people, tend to forget—the importance of our attitude, our state of mind and body when we eat. They like quiet and a peaceful atmosphere.

Surely what you are thinking conditions your body. If you are angry or upset, your chemistry is different than if you are serene and happy. You might imagine that your emotions are like the herbs you mix with foods, influencing the quality of the food you prepare. The way you serve it also influences how people around you will eat. If you relax before you prepare food, and serve it in serving bowls, then everyone can decide what foods and how much he or she wants.

Before sitting down to a meal it is important to be quiet. You may want to pause and relax, clear your head of the day's tensions. The ceremony of grace allows you to take that pause. For people of many religions, eating is a sacred act. You may even want to acknowledge where your food came from, vegetables grown in the light of the sun, a part of the universe, and animals who have given their lives so that your body can be nourished. You may want to take a moment for silent appreciation of the way in which the energies of the universe are replenishing you.

This pause before eating can allow you to see whether you are hungry, or whether you are simply sitting down because the family or your guests are eating. You might look at the food, if you are hungry, and see exactly what food and what kind of food your body wants. When you eat it, how do you feel: disappointed, indifferent, irritated? We are so well trained not to taste and feel food and not to pay attention to the act of eating that it may seem difficult at first. An exercise that helped quite a few of us at SAGE is the following:

Aware Eating

1. Lie down and loosen your clothing and begin to relax. Pay attention to the way your heels feel, how heavy they are. Move your attention slowly up your

legs, buttocks, back and shoulders, and along your arms, allowing a wave of relaxation to move up to your neck and head, and relax your eyes, jaws, cheeks, and forehead.

2. When you feel pleasant and calm and relaxed, sit up. Set a watch or clock in front of you and take *one small piece of food:* one raisin or a grape or a half-inch piece of carrot, or one tablespoon of cereal; whatever you have that you would ordinarily consider to be a *small* bite of food.

3. *Take ten minutes to eat this piece of food.* Focus your attention on the way your hand and arm feel as you prepare to take the morsel from a plate. Do it slowly, slow motion. Feel how you anticipate bringing it up to your mouth. Do you start to salivate as your hand touches the food, or as it lifts toward your mouth? Watch your hand and the food. Feel the inside of your mouth as you watch. Feel your tongue, your lips, the roof of your mouth. As you approach your lips, how do they open? How does the food feel between your teeth? How does it taste? What happens as you slowly begin to chew? When you swallow, try to feel the food as far as you can.

◇ ◇ ◇

This exaggerated, slow-motion exercise may tell you something that you never realized before. It is a way of bringing your attention back to the actual process of eating, and the way it feels. You once knew this as an infant, before you were taught to hurry up.

There are many sensations involved in eating. Most people are not aware of them because they are too busy with other thoughts or with conversation. It is good to eat silently and pay attention. Feel the food in your throat. Are you chewing fast? Is your mind wandering? The food is going to remain in your stomach between two and four hours, so that whatever messages you get from your stomach in that time will tell you how the food you ate is getting along with you. If you feel discomfort, think over the foods you've just eaten and ask yourself what might cause the complaint. Between meals notice your energy level. If you have a great burst of energy soon after eating, and then a great decrease in energy a couple of hours later, so that you are hankering for something sweet, you may need more protein. You may not feel the same burst of energy that you do from sugar; the energy is built up more slowly, but by adding protein and decreasing sugar you can get a much more even supply of blood sugar.

You may also have noticed that it is not good for your body to receive very cold or very hot substances, so if you are going to eat something iced, let it melt in your mouth. Don't swallow cold drinks rapidly, and don't eat very hot soups for you are scalding your stomach. It is because we do not pay attention to our body sensations that we gain weight. Don Gerrard, in *One Bowl*, (see the bibliography) offers an entirely different way of regulating weight by eating attentively.

> I am able to lose weight at any time without going hungry, without placing restrictions on the kind of food I eat. I do not have to think about calories. I can eat any food I really want, but I automatically control my weight while eating in a nourishing and satisfying way.
>
> I call eating with my head "social eating." My attention at those times is focused outside myself. I don't hear what my body feels about the food. On the other hand whole body eating begins when I first feel hungry and ends only when digestion is complete. The more you eat food you can use, the more you eat food that your body likes and you like, the more harmoniously and completely your body can use them, leaving less to be stored as fat. The more you are aware of the

signals of hunger and hunger ceasing, the less you will tend to overeat.

The principles of this book are best absorbed by reading it, but they can be outlined. The first one is: Choose a bowl that you would like to eat from, just one bowl that really pleases you. Consider this bowl a symbol of your right to eat and renew life. Eat all your food from this bowl. It may mean that you will eat only one or two foods at a time. The most important thing in developing your body sensitivity is to eat alone. If you live with other people, and somebody else prepares food for you, just take your bowl of food and eat it somewhere else, with all your attention on the eating and the food. Do not listen to the radio, or read, or talk. After three or four days of eating alone, you will find that it brings you a quiet and unusual pleasure. It is necessary to eat alone for a while because most of our eating habits are social. We all eat a lot of food because we are with other people. Eat when you are hungry, and as often as you are hungry, but stop the moment hunger ceases. This is usually before you feel full. Eat only one food at each meal, occasionally two. When you get hungry, pick out exactly the food you want to eat at that moment. Abandon all foods that you can feel are disruptive to you.

Learn to follow the signals of your body. For example where in your body do you feel hungriest: the mouth, the throat? Look and smell the food before you put it in your bowl. Does it seem to be exactly the food that you want to eat right now? If not, put it aside, and find the food that is more satisfying.

This is a subtle endeavor. As Don Gerrard says, "Generally speaking the sensations you are seeking in your body are more subtle than those commonly recognized as a digestive upset." He suggests focusing on what happens to a bite of food and seeing whether you feel sensations of emptiness, weight moving from one place to another, pressure changing, an internal area changing temperature, a vibratory movement or pulsation, a continuous gurgling sound. "They are merely those little feelings that seem always to be going on inside your body," he says. "Pay attention to them. Consider them messages."

Another way of assessing your eating habits and how they affect you is to stop eating for a day or two and give your body a rest. There are many extreme and faddish theories about fasting, but many people have found that they function better if they rest their bodies from the business of digesting. Upton Sinclair used to fast, drink water, and rest one day each week. Some people recommend taking just liquids and an enema of warm water to clean out the lower part of the intestine. After a day of fasting you will find it easier not to eat compulsively, or socially, but to honor your real body needs.

If you now survey your own food habits, you may find as I have that you have been abusing food, using it to compensate for bad moods and fill emotional emptiness. You may find you have been eating too rapidly, or eating foods that distress your body. In all likelihood nobody ever taught you that your body can tell you as much about food as books can.

EPILOGUE:
GROUND RULES

The principal rule of the SAGE program, the rule of this book, indeed the rule of personal growth is simply: *pay attention*. Your body will give you more pleasure and will improve more from short periods of full concentration than from ceaselessly repeated movements with your mind "out the window." Similarly you can read all the books on personal growth and understand all the concepts—yet they will do you no real benefit until you start using them. It is a little like expecting to lose weight because you buy all the latest books on diet. If you don't read them, and then don't practice them, they will not do you much good from the shelf.

In our early groups we deliberately deemphasized the intellectual rationale we may have had for choosing the procedures we did. This was an unspoken ground rule, to avoid endless "head tripping," but it sometimes backfired. One intellectual and precise doctor used to ask for explanations and literature about our methods. "I need to understand what I'm doing," he would insist, sometimes curtly.

Later, after an exercise, when asked what he felt, he might reply, "You know, that exercise reminds me of the Jungian concepts of the animus. . ." Raised on the East Coast, and educated at Radcliffe College, I too had felt a need for concepts to validate my experience, to make me at ease with feelings and above all to give me a sense of meaning, a sense that there was a rational structure in my work. It took me a while at SAGE to know that my leaps were not usually made through intellectual understanding, or through just repeating exercises. They seemed to come through experiences that deeply permeated me on several levels, body-feeling-mind-spirit. When these are dramatic and occur in a church they are called conversion. At SAGE and in most of life these experiences might be flashes, or undramatic discoveries of a new flexibility or new dimension of feeling that built from one practice session to the next.

We wanted SAGE to be organic. It was an unspoken ground rule. Our ground rules evolved from our experiences, our personalities, and also our ideals. They can be listed very succinctly. We wanted to teach in teams and rotate leadership. We wanted an equal relationship with participants. We did not want to lay out a curriculum, or to emphasize credentials or methods. Instead we wanted to be honest about our own feelings, giving all of us permission to be human, and we tried to answer the needs of group members.

At the start we stated that we did not want a teacher-student relationship. We did not want an "us and them" situation, nor were we an eminent faculty pouring wisdom on the unwashed. Nonetheless we sometimes acted exactly that way without knowing it. Our participants did not want to hurt our feelings, and often we did not hear them, so sometimes it took a year to get feedback from the very people we had been unwittingly condescending to.

To have an equal relationship with our participants meant establishing an honest human bond, and perhaps that was the most important and most natural and most rewarding ground rule.

We began as an experiment and did not know in advance exactly what we were going to do, so we refused to lay out a curriculum. We did not want to emphasize our credentials, either, perhaps in false humility. It was our hope to avoid "professionalism," titles, degrees, and authority roles. We set out to offer experience—not a list of validated techniques.

Little did we know how irritating lack of curriculum was from the other side. Curious participants thought we were deliberately mystifying them. One woman prodded, "*Surely* you must know what you are going to do next! What is sensory awareness? Why did you ask us to pay attention to our breaths?" She was adamant about wanting to know what we planned and what the methods were called. She nipped at us like a terrier. "You *could* tell us about your background, and what your degree is in. You could list the methods you are going to use."

We had only the roughest notion of what we would do. We thought we'd begin by teaching deep relaxation, then centering and limbering exercises. As people relaxed we would introduce exercises to increase their awareness of their senses, sight, touch, smell, and hearing. Gradually we would move into yoga and massage. Hopefully the relaxation would deepen into meditation and members would learn to massage each other and exchange feelings and thoughts openly. Originally we expected to cover the entire smorgasbord of possibilities from modern body therapies, the human potentials movement, from martial arts, spiritual disciplines, and the fine arts. We hoped to create, in one place, all the experiences that younger people had spent years and thousands of dollars to find in workshops, ashrams, growth centers, courses, and therapy. Most older people cannot afford the money or energy for this kind of search, and since the methods were available to us, we wanted to offer them all.

Simultaneously we knew that our techniques were unimportant next to the need to participate in increasingly deep human interchanges. We were usually ready to forget our methods and deal with participants directly in whatever way they needed. But we didn't always succeed.

"You know," said one plump woman after learning to get up and down onto the floor a la Feldenkrais for almost an hour, "I've been waiting all afternoon for someone to ask me how I'm feeling after my surgery. . . ."

Our initial rule with ourselves had been to use our pooled skills to *respond to the needs of group members* rather than assume we could anticipate their needs and design a rigorous program based on our assumptions. We wanted to avoid the pigeonhole of the highly trained person who can offer only the techniques he happens to know—whether these are massage, bioenergetics, or dance—while the participant might urgently need posture work or autogenic training.

We wanted the flexibility to listen and offer whatever people needed—and if we lacked the skills, to find them outside our staff. This became harder as SAGE grew larger.

Another important rule—that we did not invariably follow—was to be square with the group about our own feelings at the moment. I floundered with this rule: I was always trying to anticipate what would be "good for the group" instead of just acting directly out of my feelings. Exposing myself was counter to everything I'd ever learned about leadership. Still when Eugenia wept in the group it gave everyone permission to cry when they felt like it. Being human and honest was powerful.

Our unspoken but most important rule was: We all have permission to be human. This is a fundamental of relaxation. Most of our tension occurs in the muscles we use to hold back or suppress emotions that are "unwanted," such as anger, fear, sadness, even love. These muscle tensions are quite unconscious. Most of us don't realize that we have tight jaw muscles from holding back things we shouldn't say. When this tension becomes extreme, it can take the form of a psychosomatic illness—temporal mandibular joint disease. Many of us suffer from stiff necks, from backaches, and headaches, or indigestion—yet we rarely associate these symptoms with tension, and particularly emotional tension. If we had exercised our privileges as human beings all our lives, we would have had fewer symptoms and a less stable way of behaving—moving easily from the expression of anger, to joy, to grief, to apprehension or silliness.

We wanted to be available for the reality of feeling—indeed we wanted to remove all dichotomies between body, mind, spirit, emotions, and environment. If a person wanted to be held while he cried one moment, he might laugh the next and ask for a book or a meditation exercise.

We could also expect any change to change the whole. For example several people noticed that breathing relaxation seemed to give them more energy. "I haven't had this much energy in the last twenty years," said one person. Since lack of energy was a major complaint, a slight increase meant enriching life in many ways, more social activity, more physical exercise, and more pleasure.

Yet who would say that the energy came solely from breathing exercises? When we were doing so many things at once it was hard to believe that change stemmed from a particular technique.

We were so excited about the changes we saw that we had a hard time living up to our own rule: *"Have no goals. Only invest yourself in the process."*

We did not want participants to compete or perform. We did not expect them to accomplish a certain goal in an exercise. Nonetheless we were pleased when they reported how much they had grown. No goals—but please a little change. We exulted like a bunch of hens in the kitchen after a session.

We would sit around the kitchen table sharing our excitement. Of course the process is full of pitfalls, for it keeps on changing, and insomnia might strike again in two nights after an emotional crisis. The process had not cured anybody of anything. Still the slightest improvements were cause to celebrate. These people were in their late sixties and seventies. Everyone had told us that such improvements couldn't happen this way. But we knew that if these people could change themselves, so could we!

One ground rule was: We will use our group time to share joint and present experience, not to discuss or try to solve anyone's personal problems.

We knew of therapy groups in which older people shared problems. Often they spent their precious time together entirely focused on their complaints and negative feelings. We felt that we could create alternative ways of being, that we could all share in our group sessions. We then focused our discussions on that experience. It was simple, and it was positive.

By sharing our experiences we began to know each other well, even though there were many things we didn't know about each other's lives and problems. We didn't need to acquire that information in the usual fashion. Slowly it seeped into the group.

Within three months of the first session, the participants had begun drawing sustenance from the group and each other. They were able to share some of their deep worries and fears about illness, dying, and their families. They had become a kind of family. They were looking, talking, feeling, and thinking differently. Moreover they had something they considered exciting to look forward to. Having begun to experience some positive inner changes it was no longer the same tired old world, or the same old life.

From the beginning we decided that there would be no casualties—although everyone told us that older people would develop problems from the physical exercises and we would run the risk of being sued. We felt they could take responsibility for themselves. *Our* responsibility was not to protect them from exercise, or water everything down, and ask five physicians to approve each move. Our responsibility was to be very clear with each person that exercises were for individual benefit. If a person had a condition that he or she thought might prohibit a certain movement, our advice was: Don't do it!

In group exercises people were reminded, "Listen inwardly to your own body. Do not emulate the teacher. Do not compete to do it better than your neighbor. Do not try and perform. The purpose is self-development—for each of you to move in a way that benefits you."

There were no casualties. We found that anyone who takes responsibility for himself, and who does exercises in this thoughtful way would not hurt himself. It requires strict attention to what one is doing. If one's mind wanders, a person is likely to push, strain, or make errors.

Looking back at the first three months of our experiment I can see that we lived from hour to hour and day to day. We were excited and quite "hooked" by the process, for it affirmed our sense of the miraculous. Very soon after we started we began seeing personalities change and symptoms diminish. To the outside world there was probably little to observe. To us, close as we were, each day brought us a sense of being in on the secrets of living.

The changes were having important consequences in people's lives. One man struggled with a sense of loss after his retirement and began making friends within the group. He had been so busy that he had never had time for deep friendships outside his work. In addition he was beginning to use relaxation and breathing exercises to mitigate the pain of severe arthritis. This allowed him to continue working on a house he was then rebuilding.

"I'll be up on the roof," he said, "and the neighbors must think I'm nuts. I'll get tired, so first I bend way over forward and then bend back. And then I breathe. They must wonder what I'm doing up there."

A woman who had suffered from long periods of depression began to talk about her feelings. She was very angry.

As she began to articulate her anger to people in the group, her feelings of misery and depression began receding. She was allowing herself to say that she was really angry at her husband for not being the companion she wanted, and for being cold to her needs.

All of us were excited by a sense of mutual discovery. I found myself thinking that if a woman could begin to change her relationship to her husband at seventy-four, surely I could begin to change mine at forty-four. We shared a sense of hope. I could see an arthritic person beginning to do yoga and moving as sinuously as a snake. If he could do that with his arthritis, after doctors told him he'd never exercise again, I might be able to limber my stiff upper back and perhaps learn how to sit in lotus position. The experience was synergistic. If a member of the group found new skills or improved in some way, we all saw new possibilities for our own lives.

There is another important statement that should not be left out: our commitment. Those of us who began SAGE were so convinced that it would work that we gave it all our energy. To each of us, for our own reasons, the work was so rewarding that we were willing to give up almost everything else in our lives. It seemed that we had been gathered together for a purpose, and in accomplishing the purposes of SAGE, each of us was fulfilling some extremely compelling life change and growth. That may account for some of our success. It accounted for a great deal of our satisfaction.

BIBLIOGRAPHY

TRANSITION AND AGING

Bangott, Lillian R. and Richard A. Kalish. *A Time to Enjoy: The Pleasures of Aging.* Englewood Cliffs, New Jersey: Prentice-Hall, 1979.

Benel, Sula. *Abkhasians, the Long Living People of the Caucasus.* New York: Holt, Rinehart & Winston, 1974.

Birren, James, Robert N. Butler, Greenhouse, Sokoloff, and Yarrow. *Human Aging.* Washington, D.C.: DHEW Publication No. (ADM) 77-122-1971.

Birren, James, and Diana Woodruff, eds. *Aging.* New York: D. Van Nostrand, 1975.

Butler, Robert N. *Why Survive? Being Old in America.* New York: Harper & Row, 1975.

—— and Myrna Lewis. *Aging and Mental Health.* St. Louis: Mosby, 1977.

Carp, Frances M., ed. *Retirement.* Behavioral Publications, Inc. 1972. Dist. by David White Co., 14 Vanderventer Ave., Port Washington, N.Y. 11050.

Comfort, Alex. *A Good Age.* New York: Crown, 1976.

Cowgill, Donald O., and Lowell Holmes, M.P. *Aging and Modernization.* New York: Appleton Century Crofts, 1972.

Curtin, Sharon. *Nobody Ever Died of Old Age.* Boston: Atlantic Monthly Press, 1972.

de Beauvoir, Simone. *The Coming of Age.* New York: G. P. Putnam's Sons, 1972.

Eisdorfer, Carl, and M. P. Lawton. *The Psychology of Adult Development and Aging.* Washington, D.C.: American Psychological Association, 1973.

Ellison, Jerome. *Life's Second Half, The Pleasures of Aging.* Old Greenwich, Conn.: Devin Adair, 1978.

Harris, Louis, et al. *The Myth and Reality of Aging in America: A Study for the National Council on the Aging.* National Council on the Aging Inc., Washington, D.C. 1976.

Hess, B. B. *Growing Old in America.* New Brunswick, N.J.: Transaction Books, 1976.

Lawton, George. *Aging Successfully.* New York: Columbia University Press, 1946.

Rosenfeld, Albert. *ProLongevity.* New York: Alfred Knopf, 1976.

Sheehy, Gail. *Passages.* New York: E. P. Dutton & Co., 1976.

Silverston, Barbara, and Helen Kandel Hyman. *You and Your Aging Parent.* New York: Pantheon, 1976.

Simmons, Leo W. *The Role of the Aged in Primitive Society.* New Haven, Conn.: Yale University Press, 1945.

Tibbitts, Clark. *Handbook of Social Gerontology.* Chicago University Press, 1960.

Woodruff, Diana. *Can You Live to Be One Hundred?* New York: Chatham Square Press, 1977.

BODY-MIND UNITY FOR HEALTH

Barlow, Wilfred. *The Alexander Technique.* New York: Alfred Knopf, 1974.

Brooks, Charles. *Sensory Awareness: The Study of Living as Experience.* New York: Viking Press, 1974.

Brown, Barbara. *New Mind, New Body—Bio-Feedback: New Directions for the Mind.* New York: Harper & Row, 1974.

Dychtwald, Kenneth. *Bodymind.* New York: Pantheon, 1977.

Dunn, Halbert L. *High Level Wellness.* R. W. Beatty, Arlington, Va. 1961.

Feldenkrais, Moshe. *The Case of Nora.* New York: Harper & Row, 1977.

———. *Awareness Through Movement.* New York: Harper & Row, 1972.

Friedman, Mayer, Ray H. Rosenman. *Type A Behavior and Your Heart.* New York: Knopf, 1974.

Geba, Bruno, *Vitality Training for Older Adults.* New York: Random House/Bookworks, 1974.

Jencks, Beata. *Your Body.* Chicago: Nelson Hall, 1977.

Keleman, Stanley. *Your Body Speaks Its Mind.* New York: Simon & Schuster, 1975.

Leadbeater, C. W. *The Chakras.* Wheaton, Ill.: Theosophical Publishing House, 1972.

Lowen, Alexander. *Depression and the Body.* New York: Coward, McCann, 1972.

———. *Bioenergetics.* New York: Coward, McCann, 1975.

——— and Leslie Lowen. *The Way to Vibrant Health.* New York: Harper Coliphon, 1977.

Pelletier, Kenneth R. *Mind as Healer, Mind as Slayer.* New York: Delacorte Lawrence, 1977.

Reich, Wilhelm. *Character Analysis.* New York: Farrar, Straus & Giroux, 1949.

Schutz, William. *Joy, Expanding Human Awareness.* New York: Grove Press, 1968.

Selye, Hans. *The Stress of Life.* New York: McGraw-Hill, 1956.

———. *Stress Without Distress.* New York: Lippincott, 1974.

Todd, Mabel E. *The Thinking Body: A Study of Balancing Forces of Dynamic Man.* Dance Horizons, 1801 E. 26th St., Brooklyn, N.Y. 11229, 1968.

Watson, David L., and Roland Tharp. *Self-Directed Behavior*. Monterey, CA: Brooks/Cole Publishing, 1977.

RELAXATION

Benson, Herbert. *The Relaxation Response*. New York: Avon, 1975.

Bernstein, Douglas A., Thomas D. Borkovec. *Progressive Relaxation Training: A Manual for the Helping Professions*. Champagne, Ill.: Research Press, 1973.

Jacobson, Edmund. *You Must Relax*. New York: McGraw-Hill, 1962.

———. *Progressive Relaxation*. Chicago: University of Chicago Press, 1974.

Luthe, Wolfgang. *Autogenic Training*. New York: Grune & Stratton, 1965.

———. *Autogenic Therapy*. Vols I–VI. New York: Grune & Stratton, 1969–73.

White, John, James Fadiman, eds. *Relax: How You Can Feel Better*. New York: Dell, 1976.

EXERCISE

Bristow, Robert. *Aches and Pains: How the Older Person Can Find Relief Using Heat, Massage, and Exercise*. New York: Pantheon, 1974.

Cooper, Kenneth H. *Aerobics*. New York: M. Evans, 1968.

Cooper, Kenneth H. *The New Aerobics*. New York: Bantam Books, 1970.

Cooper, Mildred, Kenneth Cooper. *Aerobics for Women*. New York: Bantam Books, 1973.

Craig, M. *Miss Craig's Face Saving Exercises*. New York: Random House, 1970.

Delza, Sophia. *T'ai Chi Ch'uan: An Ancient Chinese Way of Exercise to Achieve Health and Tranquility*. New York: Cornerstone Library, 1972.

deVries, Herbert A. *Vigor Regained*. Englewood Cliffs, N.J.: Prentice-Hall, 1974.

Feng, G. *Tai Chi*. New York: Collier, 1970.

Gore, Irene. *Add Years to Your Life and Life to Your Years*. Briarcliff Manor, N.Y.: Stein & Day, 1975.

Huang, Al Chun-liang. *Embrace Tiger, Return to Mountain: The Essence of Tai Chi*. Moab, Utah: Real People Press, 1973.

Higdon, Hal. *Fitness After Forty*. Mountain View, CA: World Publications, 1977.

Konofsky, Nicholas. *The Joy of Feeling Fit*. New York: E. P. Dutton, 1971.

Leonard, Jon N., J. L. Hofer, and N. Pritikin. *Live Longer Now—The First 100 Years*. New York: Grosset & Dunlap, 1974.

Morehouse, Laurence E., and Leonard Gross. *Total Fitness—In Thirty Minutes a Week*. New York: Simon & Schuster, 1975.

Proxmire, William. *You Can Do It: Senator William Proxmire's Exercise, Diet and Relaxation Plan*. New York: Simon & Schuster, 1973.

Rosenberg, Magda. *Sixty-Plus, Fit Again: Exercises for Older Men and Women*. New York: J. B. Lippincott, 1977.

Sheehan, George. *Dr. Sheehan on Running*. Mountain View, CA: World Publications, 1975.

Smith, David. *The East West Exercise Book*. New York: McGraw Hill, 1976.

YOGA

Brena, S. F. *Pain and Religion*. Springfield, Ill.: Charles C. Thomas, 1972.

———. *Yoga and Medicine*. New York: Julian Press, 1972.

Christianson, Alic, David Rankin. *Easy Does It—Yoga Over Sixty*. The Light On Yoga Society, 1978.

Hewitt, James. *The Complete Yoga Book*. New York: Schocken Books, 1978.

Iyengar, R. K. S. *Light On Yoga*. New York: Schocken Books, 1972.

Marga, Ananda. *Teaching Asanas, The Ananda Marga Manual for Teachers*. Los Altos, CA: Amrit Publications, 1973.

Phelan, Nancy, Micheal Volin. *Yoga over Forty*. New York: Harper & Row, 1965.

Rama, Swami, Rudolph Ballantine and Swami Ajaya. *Yoga and Psychotherapy*. Honesdale, PA: Himalayan International Institute, 1976.

Satchidananda, S. *Integral Hatha Yoga*. New York: Holt, Rinehart & Winston, 1970.

Vishnudevenanda, S. *The Complete Illustrated Book of Yoga*. New York: Julian Press, 1960.

MASSAGE

Carter, Mildred. *Helping Yourself with Foot Reflexology*. Englewood Cliffs, NJ: Parker Publishing Co., 1969.

Downing, George. *The Massage Book*. New York: Random House/Bookworks, 1972.

———. *Massage and Meditation*. New York: Random House/Bookworks, 1974.

DeLangre, Jacques. *The First Book of Do–In*. Hollywood, CA: Happiness Press, 1971.

———. *The Second Book of Do–In*. Hollywood, CA: Happiness Press, 1976.

COMMUNICATION SKILLS AND THERAPY

Bateson, Gregory. *Communication and Social Psychiatry*. New York: Norton, 1950.

Beecher, Willard, Marguerite Beecher. *Beyond Success and Failure*. New York: Pocket Books, 1971.

Berne, Eric. *Games People Play*. New York: Grove Press, 1969.

Gordon, Thomas. *Leadership Effectiveness Training*. New York: Wyden Books, 1977.

Laing, R. D. *The Divided Self*. New York: Penguin Books, 1970.

————. *Knots*. New York: Pantheon Books, 1970.

Perls, Frederick. *Gestalt Therapy*. New York: Verbatim, Bantam Books, 1971.

Prather, Hugh. *Notes to Myself*. Moab, Utah: Real People Press, 1970.

————. *Notes on Love and Courage*. New York: Doubleday, 1977.

Putney, Snel, J. Gail. *The Adjusted American: Normal Neuroses in the Individual and Society*. New York: Harper & Row, 1972.

Rogers, Carl. *On Personal Power*. New York: Delacorte, 1977.

————. *On Encounter Groups*. New York: Harper & Row, 1970.

————, and Barry Stevens. *Person to Person: The Problems of Being Human*. Moab, Utah: Real People Press, 1967.

————. *On Becoming a Person*. New York: Houghton Mifflin, 1961.

VISION AND VISUALIZATION

Bates, W. H. *The Bates Method for Better Eyesight Without Glasses*. New York: Pyramid, 1940 and 1971.

Corbett, Margaret D. *Help Yourself to Better Sight*. Hollywood, CA: Wilshire Book Co., 1974.

Huxley, Aldous. *The Art of Seeing*. Montana Books, 1716 N. 45th St., Seattle, WA 98103, 1975.

Jackson, Jim. *Seeing Yourself See*. New York: E. P. Dutton, 1975.

Samuels, Mike, Nancy Samuels. *Seeing With the Mind's Eye*. New York: Random House/Bookworks, 1975.

SLEEP AND DREAMS

Faraday, Ann. *Dream Power*. New York: Coward, McCann, 1972.

————. *The Dream Game*. New York: Harper & Row, 1974.

Garfield, Patricia. *Creative Dreaming*. New York: Simon and Schuster, 1975.

Jung, Carl. *Memories, Dreams, Reflections*. Recorded and edited by Aniela Jaffee. New York: Pantheon, 1963.

Luce, G., J. Segal. *Sleep*. New York: Coward, McCann, 1966.

————. *Insomnia*. New York: Doubleday, 1968.

EXPANDING THE MIND

Assagioli, Roberto. *Psychosynthesis*. New York: Viking Press, 1971.

Bateson, Gregory. *Steps to an Ecology of Mind*. New York: Ballantine Books, 1972.

Campbell, Joseph. *The Mythic Image*. Princeton, NJ: Princeton University Press, 1974.

————. *Myths to Live By*. New York: Bantam Books, 1973.

————. *Hero with a Thousand Faces*. Princeton, NJ: Princeton University Press, 1968.

Erickson, Milton H. *Advanced Techniques of Hypnosis and Therapy*. Jay Haley, ed. New York: Grune & Stratton, 1967.

Ferguson, Marilyn. *The Brain Revolution: The Frontiers of Mind Research*. New York: Taplinger, 1973.

Green, Elmer, Alyce Green. *Beyond Biofeedback*. New York: Delacorte Press/Lawrence, 1978.

Haley, Jay. *Strategies of Psychotherapy*. New York: Grune & Stratton, 1963.

————. *Uncommon Therapy*. New York: Norton, 1973.

LeShan, Lawrence. *Alternate Realities*. New York: Ballantine, 1976.

Maslow, Abraham. *Toward a Psychology of Being*. New York: Van Nostrand Reinhold, 1968.

————. *The Farther Reaches of Human Nature*. New York: Viking Press, 1971.

May, Rollo. *Love and Will*. New York: Dell, 1974.

Mishlove, Jeffrey. *The Roots of Consciousness*. New York: Random House/Bookworks, 1975.

Monroe, Robert. *Journeys Out of the Body*. New York: Doubleday, 1972.

Neumann, E. *The Origins and History of Consciousness.* Princeton, NJ: Princeton University Press, 1959.

Ornstein, Robert. *The Psychology of Consciousness.* New York: Viking Press, 1973.

———. *The Nature of Human Consciousness.* New York: Viking Press, 1974.

Penfield, Wilder. *The Mystery of the Mind: A Critical Study of Consciousness and the Human Brain.* Princeton, NJ: Princeton University Press, 1975.

Progoff, Ira. *At a Journal Workshop: The Basic Text and Guide for Using the Intensive Journal.* Dialogue House, 1975.

———. *The Cloud of Unknowing.* New York: Julian Press, 1967.

———. *The Well and the Cathedral.* Dialogue House, 1976.

Roberts, Jane. *Seth Speaks.* Englewood Cliffs, NJ: Prentice-Hall, 1972.

———. *The Nature of Personal Reality.* Englewood Cliffs, NJ: Prentice-Hall, 1974.

Smith, Adam. *Powers of Mind.* New York: Random House, 1975.

Tart, Charles, ed. *Altered States of Consciousness.* New York: John Wiley and Sons, 1969.

Watts, Alan. *Psychotherapy East and West.* New York: Mentor, 1963.

———. *The Book on the Taboo against Knowing Who You Are.* New York: Pantheon, 1966.

White, John, ed. *Frontiers of Consciousness.* New York: Julian Press, 1974.

———. *The Highest State of Consciousness.* New York: Doubleday, 1972.

Whitmont, Edward. *The Symbolic Quest.* Princeton, NJ: Princeton University Press, 1977.

DEATH AND DYING

Dickinson, Peter A. *The Fires of Autumn.* New York: Drake Publishers, 1974.

Evans-Wentz, W. Y. *The Tibetan Book of the Dead*. New York: Oxford University Press, 1957.

Garfield, Charles. *The Psychosocial Care of the Dying Patient*. New York: McGraw-Hill, 1978.

Grof, Stanislav, Joan Halifax. *The Human Encounter with Death*. New York: E. P. Dutton, 1977.

Keleman, Stanley. *Living Your Dying*. New York: Random House/Bookworks, 1974.

Kubler-Ross, Elizabeth. *On Death and Dying*. New York: Macmillan, 1968.

————. *Death the Final Stage of Growth*. New York: Prentice-Hall, 1975.

Mannes, Myra. *Last Rights*. New York: William Morrow, 1974.

Moody, Raymond. *Life after Life*. New York: Bantam Books, 1977.

Morris, Sarah. *Grief and How to Live with It*. New York: Grosset & Dunlap, 1972.

Pincus, Lily. *Death and the Family*. New York: Pantheon, 1974.

Peterson, James A. *Widows and Widowed: A Creative Approach to Being Alone*. New York: Association Press, 1977.

Weisman, Avery D. *On Dying and Denying*. New York: Human Sciences Press, 1972.

Winter, Arthur, ed. *The Moment of Death*. A Symposium. Springfield, Ill.: Charles C. Thomas, 1969.

HEALTH AND SELF-HEALING

Bernhard, Yetta. *How to Be Somebody*. Millbrae, CA: Celestial Arts, 1975.

Carlson, Rick J. *The End of Medicine*. New York: John Wiley & Sons, 1975.

Geba, Bruno. *Breathe Away Your Tension*. New York: Random House/Bookworks, 1973.

————. *Vitality Training for Older Adults*. New York: Random House/Bookworks, 1972.

Huxley, Laura. *You are Not the Target*. New York: Farrar, Straus, & Giroux, 1963.

Illich, Ivan. *Medical Nemesis, The Expropriation of Health*. New York: Pantheon, 1976.

Krippner, Stanley, Alberto Villoldo. *The Realms of Healing*. Millbrae, CA: Celestial Arts, 1976.

LeShan, Lawrence. *You Can Fight for Your Life*. New York: M. Evans & Co., 1977.

Levin, Arthur. *Talk Back to Your Doctor*. New York: Doubleday, 1975.

McGuire, Thomas. *The Tooth Trip*. New York: Random House/Bookworks, 1973.

Muramoto, Naboru. *Healing Ourselves*. New York: Avon Books, 1973.

Nocerino, N. Pringle, K. Sehnert. *Health Activation for Senior Citizens*. Arlington, Va.: Health Activation Network, 1977.

Pelletier, Kenneth. *Mind as Healer, Mind as Slayer*. New York: Delacorte, 1977.

Popenoe, Chris. *Wellness*. New York: Yes, Inc./Random House, 1977.

Oyle, Irving. *The Healing Mind*. Millbrae, CA: Celestial Arts, 1974.

Samuels, Mike, Hal Bennett. *The Well Body Book*. New York: Random House/Bookworks, 1973.

Sehnert, Keith H., and Howard Eisenberg. *How to be Your Own Best Doctor—Sometimes*. New York: Grosset & Dunlap, 1976.

Shealy, Norman. *Ninety Days to Self-Health*. New York: Dial, 1977.

Simonton, O. Carl, Stephanie Matthews, James Creighton. *Getting Well Again*. Los Angeles: J. P. Tarcher, Inc., 1978.

Ulene, Art. *Feeling Fine*. Los Angeles: J. P. Tarcher, Inc., 1977.

NUTRITION AND FOOD AWARENESS

Airola, Paavo. *How To Get Well*. Phoenix: Health Plus, 1974.

———. *Are You Confused?* Phoenix: Health Plus, 1977.

Ballantine, Rudolph. *Diet and Nutrition. A Holistic Approach*. Honesdale, PA: Himalayan Institute, 1978.

Bieler, Henry. *Food is Your Best Medicine*. New York: Vintage Press, 1965.

Brodsky. *From Eden to Aquarius*. New York: Bantam Books, 1973.

Davis, Adelle. *Let's Eat Right to Keep Fit*. New York: Harcourt Brace & World, 1954.

———. *Let's Get Well*. New York: Harcourt Brace & World, 1965.

Dufty, William. *Sugar Blues*. New York: Warner Books, 1975.

Ewald, Ellen Buchman. *Recipes for a Small Planet*. New York: Ballantine, 1973.

Fredericks, Carlton. *Carlton Fredericks' High Fiber Way to Total Health*. New York: Pocket Books, 1976.

Gerrard, Don. *One Bowl*. New York: Random House/Bookworks, 1974.

Jacobson, Michael F. *Nutrition Scoreboard*. New York: Avon, 1975.

Kirschmann, John D., ed. *Nutrition Almanac*. New York: McGraw-Hill, 1973.

Lappé, Frances Moore. *Diet for a Small Planet*. New York: Ballantine Books, 1975.

McCay, Clive, L. A. Maynard, et al. "Retarded Growth, Life Span, Ultimate Body Size, and Age Chances in the Albino Rat after Feeding Diets Restricted in Calories." *Journal of Nutrition*, Vol. 18, 1939.

Rodin, Judith. "The Puzzle of Obesity." *Human Nature*, February, 1978.

Stone, Irwin. *The Healing Factor—Vitamin C Against Disease*. New York: Grosset & Dunlap, 1972.

Williams, Roger. *The Wonderful World Within You*. New York: Bantam Books, 1977.

————. *Nutrition Against Disease*. New York: Bantam Books, 1971.

SEX

Butler, Robert N., Myrna I. Lewis. *Sex After Sixty*. New York: Harper & Row, 1976.

Comfort, Alex. *The Joy of Sex*. New York: Crown Publishers, 1972.

Goldberg, Herb. *The Hazards of Being Male*. New York: Signet, 1976.

Kaplan, Helen Singer. *The New Sex Therapies*. New York: Quadrangle, 1974.

Masters, William H., Virginia E. Johnson. *Human Sexual Response*. Boston: Little Brown & Co., 1966.

Montagu, Ashley. *Touching: The Human Significance of the Skin*. New York: Columbia University Press, 1971.

Peterson, James A. *Love in the Later Years*. New York: Association Press, 1975.

Rosenberg, Jack. *Total Orgasm*. New York: Random House/Bookworks, 1973.

Rush, Anne Kent. *Getting Clear: Body Work for Women*. New York: Random House/Bookworks, 1973.

Zibergeld, Bernie. *Male Sexuality*. Boston: Little Brown & Co., 1978.

ART AND MUSIC

Arguelles, Jose, Miriam Arguelles. *Mandala*. Boulder, Colo.: Shambhala, 1972.

Bonny, Helen, Louis Savary. *Music and Your Mind*. New York: Harper & Row, 1973.

Halprin, Lawrence. *The RSVP Cycles*. New York: Braziller, 1970.

Keyes, Margaret F. *The Inward Journey: Art as Therapy for You*. Millbrae, CA: Celestial Arts, 1974.

Leedy, Jack J. *Poetry the Healer*. New York: Lippincott, 1973.

Luthe, Wolfgang. *The Creativity Mobilization Technique*. New York: Grune & Stratton, 1976.

McKim, R. H. *Experiences in Visual Thinking*. Monterey, CA: Brooks/Cole, 1975.

Nicolaides, Kimon. *The Natural Way to Draw*. New York: Houghton Mifflin, 1941.

Rhyne, Janie. *The Gestalt Art Experience*. Monterey, CA: Brooks/Cole, 1973.

PHILOSOPHY AND MEDITATION

Brunton, Paul. *The Secret Path*. New York: E. P. Dutton, 1953.

Bucke, R. M. *Cosmic Consciousness*. New York: E. P. Dutton, 1969.

Capra, Fritjof. *The Tao of Physics*. Boulder, Colo.: Shambhala, 1975.

Carrington, Patricia. *Freedom in Meditation*. New York: Doubleday, 1977.

Castenada, Carlos. *The Teachings of Don Juan*. New York: Ballantine Books, 1968.

———. *A Separate Reality*. New York: Simon & Schuster, 1971.

———. *Journey to Ixtlan*. New York: Simon & Schuster, 1972.

———. *Tales of Power*. New York: Simon & Schuster, 1976.

De Chardin, Teilhard. *The Phenomenon of Man*. New York: Harper & Row, 1959.

De Ropp, R. S. *The Master Game*. New York: Dell, 1968.

Foundation for Inner Peace. *A Course in Miracles*. New York: Foundation for Inner Peace, 1975.

Goleman, Daniel. *The Varieties of Meditative Experience*. New York: E. P. Dutton, 1977.

Govinda, Anagarika, Lama. *The Way of the White Clouds.* Boulder, Colo.: Shambhala, 1970.

———. *Foundations of Tibetan Mysticism.* New York: Samuel Weiser, 1960.

———. *Creative Meditation and Multi-Dimensional Consciousness.* Wheaton, Ill.: Theosophical Publishing House, 1976.

Harding, Douglas. *On Having No Head, A Contribution to Zen in the West.* New York: Harper & Row, 1972.

Humphries, Christmas. *Concentration and Meditation.* New York: Penguin, 1968.

Huxley, Aldous. *The Perennial Philosophy.* New York: Arno, 1945.

James, William. *The Varieties of Religious Experience.* New York: Modern Library, 1936.

Johnston, William. *Silent Music: The Science of Meditation, Consciousness, Healing, and Intimacy.* New York: Harper & Row, 1974.

Jung, Carl, G. *Modern Man in Search of His Soul.* New York: Harcourt Brace, 1935.

Lao Tzu. *Tao Te Ching.* Translated by D. C. Lau. New York: Penguin Books, 1965.

———. *The Way of Life According to Lao Tzu.* Translated by Bynner, Witter. New York: Putnam, 1962.

LeShan, Lawrence. *The Medium, the Mystic, and the Physicist.* New York: Ballantine Books, 1973.

———. *How to Meditate.* New York: Bantam Books, 1975.

Merton, Thomas. *The Silent Life.* New York: Farrar, Straus & Giroux, 1957.

Needleman, Jacob. *The New Religions.* New York: Doubleday, 1975.

Pearce, Joseph Chilton. *The Crack in the Cosmic Egg.* New York: Julian, 1971.

———. *Exploring the Crack in the Cosmic Egg.* New York: Julian Press, 1976.

Rajneesh, Bhagwan Shree. *Just Like That, Talks on Sufi Stories.* Rajneesh Foundation (dist. Motilal), New Delhi, India, 1975.

————. *The Way of Tao.* Motilal Banarsidass, 1978.

————. *Meditation: The Art of Ecstasy.* New York: Harper & Row, 1978.

Rudrananda, Swami. *Spiritual Cannibalism.* New York: Links Books, 1973.

Schwarz, Jack. *Voluntary Control.* New York: E. P. Dutton, 1978.

————. *The Path of Action.* New York: E. P. Dutton, 1977.

Shah, Idries. *The Sufis.* New York: Doubleday, 1964.

————. *Caravan of Dreams.* New York: Penguin Books, 1968.

Shattuck, E. H. *An Experiment in Mindfulness.* Samuel Weiser, 1972.

Smith, Huston. *The Religions of Man.* New York: Harper & Row, 1958.

————. *Forgotten Truths.* New York: Harper & Row, 1976.

Suzuki, Shunryu. *Zen Mind, Beginner's Mind.* New York: John Weatherill, 1970.

————. *Time, Space, and Knowledge.* Emeryville, CA: Dharma Press, 1978.

————. *Kum Nye.* Emeryville, CA: Dharma Press, 1978.

————, ed. *Reflections of Mind.* Emeryville, CA: Dharma Press, 1975.

Thich Nhat Hanh. *The Miracle of Mindfulness.* Boston: Beacon Press, 1976.

Trungpa, Chogyam. *Meditation in Action.* Boulder, Colo.: Shambhala, 1970.

————. *Cutting Through Spiritual Materialism.* Boulder, Colo.: Shambhala, 1973.

————. *The Myth of Freedom and the Way of Meditation.* Boulder, Colo.: Shambhala, 1976.

Tulku, Tarthang. *Gesture of Balance.* Emeryville, CA: Dharma Press, 1976.

Watts, Alan. *Psychotherapy East and West.* New York: Mentor, 1963.

————. *The Spirit of Zen.* New York: Grove Press, 1958.

Yogananda, Paramahansa. *Autobiography of a Yogi.* Los Angeles: Self-Realization Fellowship, 1969.

ARTICLES AND BOOKS ABOUT SAGE

Ansley, Helen G. "A New Life at 76," *Modern Maturity*, October, 1976.

Beyers, Charlotte K. "The Holistic Medicine Show," *San Francisco Magazine*, July, 1976.

Dychtwald, Kenneth. "SAGE and NAHG: Creating a New Image of Aging," *Yoga Journal*, January, 1976.

Dychtwald, Ken. "The SAGE Project: A New Image of Aging," *Journal of Humanistic Psychology*, April, 1978.

Ellie & Margaret & Mac & Alice & a Few Others. "Talking about SAGE," *Noetic News*, Spring 1976.

Elwell, C. C. H. "The SAGE Spirit," *Human Behavior*, March, 1976.

Fields, Suzanne. "The Greening of Old Age: SAGE Can Be a Spice of Life," *Innovations*, Spring 1977.

Houston, Jean. *"The Elderly Are Not Obsolete," The New York Times*, 25 May 1975.

Kendall, Adelaide. "SAGE," *The Holistic Health Handbook*, Berkeley, 1978.

Laughingbird. "SAGE," *The New Age Journal*, January, 1975.

———. "The SAGE Project: New Life in Old Age," *Berkeley Monthly*, 2 December 1976.

Luce, Gay. "On Learning from the Old," *Quest*, March, 1978.

McDonald, Worden. "An Old Guy Who Feels Good." *California Living*, 28 November 1976.

———. *An Old Guy Who Feels Good*. Berkeley: Springs Press, 1978.

Preuss, Karen. *Life Time, A New Image of Aging*. Santa Cruz, CA: Unity Press, 1978.

POSTSCRIPT

In this book I have described SAGE as a small, intuitive group that in three years grew into a substantial and nationally known organization.

You can become an active part of our network, obtain information about ongoing programs, training, workshop courses, and join in the adventure of fulfilling our mutual vision.

You can also help SAGE, for it is a nonprofit organization that depends on grants and individual contributions to continue its work.

To become a member of SAGE, write

SAGE
Claremont Office Park
41 Tunnel Road
Berkeley, California 94705

INDEX

GAY GAER LUCE, Ph.D.

a psychologist and science writer, founded the SAGE program in 1974. She has taught biofeedback and relaxation techniques and Kum Nye, breathing, massage, and exercises developed by Rinpoche Tarthang Tulku. She has written many articles, both popular and scholarly, on health, psychology, biological rhythms, and drug therapy. Her books include *Sleep* and *Insomnia* (both with Dr. Julius Segal) and *Body Time*.